Part of Nature, Part of Us

As part of nature he is part of us.
His rarities are ours: may they be fit,
And reconcile us to ourselves in those
True reconcilings, dark, pacific words.

—*Wallace Stevens*

Part of Nature,
Part of Us
Modern American Poets

Helen Vendler

Harvard University Press
Cambridge, Massachusetts
and London, England
1980

Copyright © 1980 by the President and Fellows of Harvard College
All rights reserved
Printed in the United States of America

Library of Congress Cataloging in Publication Data

Vendler, Helen Hennessy.
    Part of nature, part of us.

    1. American poetry—20th century—History and criticism—Collected
works. I. Title.
PS323.5.V4   811'.5'09   79–20308
ISBN 0–674–65475–7

Pages 375–376 constitute an extension of the copyright page

For David

Son, and my friend, I had not called you so
To me, or been the same to you, if show,
Profit, or chance had made us; but I know
What, by that name, we each to other owe,
Freedom and truth; with love from those begot.

— *Ben Jonson*

Contents

Foreword

This collection includes both book reviews and essays on modern American poets. I had written essays for some years, before, by a lucky chance, I began reviewing: *The Massachusetts Review* annually commissioned someone to consider the year's work in poetry, and in 1966, when I was teaching at Smith, I was asked to take it on. It seemed to me then a windfall, and seems no less to me now, as books arrive in the mail carrying the one form of writing that is to me the most immediate, natural, and accessible. It took some time for me to discover that poetry—especially modern poetry—did not seem accessible or natural to many readers; this gulf in understanding prompted the substance and tone of most of my reviews. I see now that these shorter pieces urge the simplicity, naturalness, and accessibility of the poems they consider, to the neglect, perhaps, of the difficulty, peculiarity, and density of those same poems; but in that emphasis lies the difference between reviewing and the writing of criticism. A book about a poet can be the work of ten years, an essay the work of ten months; but a review is often the work of ten days. Anyone would rather write the book or essay, becoming in the process Stevens' "man who has had time to think enough" (or at least to think as well as he can). In the review, written to a deadline, the poet waits on the scant leisure of the writer. It is a system mortally unfair, and most unfair to the most original, as we know from the history of mistaken opinion. On the other hand, reviews are written out of the freshness of first impressions, and they carry more of the gratitude or surprise of a first encounter, preserving the literary moment and the personal one at once.

The ten years during which these reviews and essays were written were very rich ones. Through publication of books like the facsimile *Waste Land*, Holly Stevens' *Souvenirs and Prophecies*, or e.e. cummings' *Collected Poems*, readers of my generation could look back on our first great modern poetic texts, and judge them from a new distance; in the continuing work of Ammons, Berryman, Bishop, Ginsberg, Lowell, Merrill, Nemerov, Rich, Warren, and others, we could watch the writers of our twenties and thirties enlarge, change, and become the interpreters of our whole cast of mind and feeling; lately we have seen poets of a subsequent cluster—Bidart, Glück, Peck, Simic, Dave Smith, Charles Wright—appear in print, convincing us that American poetry remains in good hands.

I have named in these lists only poets I have written about, and not all of those. There are omissions in these essays, some by chance, some by design. No one's sensibility is adequate to all writers: it will be seen that I am happiest writing about Stevens and Lowell. I regret that the occasion has never arisen for me to write about Ashbery or Snyder; they should be in this book because they have a place in my affections. In some short pieces not included here I have noticed other forms of poetic excellence, especially translations by Bishop and Bly.

There are various perspectives—regional, historical, ideological—from which to describe the depth and genuineness of modern poetry in America. My own preference is to focus on poets one by one, to find in each the idiosyncratic voice wonderfully different from any other. A poem by Ammons does not sound like a poem by Merrill, and neither sounds like a poem by Lowell. It is given to only a handful of people in each century, in any language, to invent a written voice that sounds like no one else's. All other poets of the century become part of a common music, but the voices of genius live vividly in their oddness and their intensity. Still, if they had nothing in common with us—if they were not, as Stevens says, part of nature and part of us, their rarities would not be ours, and we could not hear them speak. To write about them is to try to explain, first to oneself and then to others, what common note they strike and how they make it new. Strangely enough, it is often easier to see eccentricities of surface, vagaries of structure, or originality of sentiment than to perceive, within the unfamiliar, the powerful appeal made to our own experience.

At times my gratitude to the poets has been reluctant. To anyone brought up on Shakespeare, Keats, and Tennyson, the accommodation to the modern—in spite of the links which outnumber the discontinuities—must be sometimes a painful pleasure. Every commentator knows the simple obstinate resistance occasioned by a new style, and knows too that the best expositors of it will be the poets themselves, who, when they write criticism, create a prose so pressing in its self-justification that it lasts, with their poems, forever.

When I was in school I read, besides anthologies, books about poets to find new poets and new poems and to reassure myself that there were people in the world who, to paraphrase Auden, "exchanged messages" about poetry. I did not care, or even notice, who had written those books, but I was glad they existed. In agreeing to collect these pieces, I remembered my younger self in the library; it is for her counterparts today that this volume is intended.

H.V.

Part of Nature, Part of Us

Wallace Stevens

The False and True Sublime

The preeminent question life asked of Stevens was whether the sublime was livable. "Poetry is not a literary activity; it is a vital activity," Stevens wrote to Richard Eberhart, and the question poetry raised for Stevens was whether he could write well, without irony, of his life, whether in it he could find any sublimity or any human grandeur. Stevens' sense of the world became one of extreme relativity, and an almost killing skepticism arose in him about his own statements, even those most deeply felt. There is a withering irony in his earliest manifesto, "The Comedian as the Letter C," which could have presaged for him a perpetual self-diminishment in a long self-deprecating career. In his American environment—pragmatical, inventive, derisive—there seemed no room for a poetic sublime, either in experience or in language. How, he asked in "The American Sublime," was General Jackson to pose for his statue; how is an American sublime possible? How can General Jackson avoid seeming ridiculous? Is there a democratic hero? And what can be the response of the audience? Life demands some nobility; one cannot "go barefoot / Blinking and blank."

> But how does one feel?
> One grows used to the weather,
> The landscape and that;
> And the sublime comes down
> To the spirit itself,
>
> The spirit and space,
> The empty spirit
> In vacant space.

"Wallace Stevens: The False and True Sublime" first appeared in the *Southern Review*, Summer 1971.

1

Like so many other poems in Stevens' early volumes, "The American Sublime" is feeling more than it can say and must await the long late poetry of Stevens' old age to find its proper expansion. Nevertheless, it sounds the note of one of Stevens' persistent subjects. To propose an American sublime, for Stevens, was to liberate an old notion: the sublime had so long evoked vastness and grandeur of conception, nobility of diction and a vehemence of passion, a sizable awe and a posture of ecstatic reverence, that a brief remark defining it as "the empty spirit in vacant space" was the boldest of manifestos. Stevens' proposal of a denuded sublime frightened even himself, and instead of pursuing it, he ended "The American Sublime" with a hopeless set of questions: "What wine does one drink? What bread does one eat?" The received sources of the sublime—philosophic or religious genius, visionary power, revolutionary fervor, humanistic enthusiasm—seemed, by and large, absent in Stevens' postwar America. If he were to find a theory of poetry and a theory of life, wine to drink and bread to eat, it would be a long search, ending not in sacramental transformation, but in rock and ice, the primitive ascetic forms of bread and water which precede even the epicurean natural forms of bread and wine.

The search for the twentieth-century sublime is not peculiar to Stevens, but in him it avoids the ideological or political or religious forms that it takes in Eliot or Auden or Crane, and so can be seen purely as a poetic search creating its own images of quest and finding, refusing to borrow the vocabulary of an institution or a movement or a historical myth to shore up its own creation. The theory of poetry that evolves from Stevens' search is a difficult and finally mysterious one, but it resulted in the very great poems of Stevens' last years, and in the sublimity they define. The way to that desolate sublime is an exemplary way in the modern world, and therefore in charting Stevens' path I do not object, though objections could be made, to his insistence on the necessity of the sublime; whether or not it is necessary to everyone, it was clearly necessary to him, and any poetry which concerned itself only with the malady (or charms) of the quotidian remained for him, to the end of his life, a lesser poetry. "The things that we build or grow or do are so little when compared to the things that we suggest or believe or desire," he writes in his *Letters*, and the true function of poetry, for him, was a reaching to those long projections of suggestion, belief, and desire that stretch to the grand, the sublime, and the unnamable.

There were, in brief, two quarrels in Stevens' mind, both of them visible from the beginning. One quarrel was between the sublime and the not-sublime; the other was between two forms of the sublime—the received and the new. The first quarrel cannot detain us long here, but it deserves a brief mention. On the whole, the aesthetic of *Harmonium* combines those enemies of the sublime, Imagism and Impressionism, the first appearing in Stevens' poems of a single scene, as the firecat bristles, the blackbirds hover, black takes domination, and six significant landscapes emerge; the second, Impressionism, gives rise to Stevens' insistence on gesture, on undulation and motion, his wish to capture the shifting scene moment by moment, whether in "Sea Surface Full of Clouds" or in "The Ordinary Women." But these poems, though they may certainly be read as visual, gestural, and momentary, are disturbingly allegorical as well. Perhaps our feeling that the sequential order of stanzas in "Sea Surface Full of Clouds" is important and cannot be rearranged at will convinces us that a "meaning" beyond the visual is intended. Or perhaps the question put in each stanza of the poem disturbs its pictorial consistency: "To be blue," as Stevens was to say later in "The Ultimate Poem is Abstract," "there must be no questions." On the other hand, it is perhaps only the necessary linear form of poetry which prompts us to interpret poems more allegorically than we normally do the visual arts and forces us to see a poem as a problem secreting its own resolutions. When we in fact come to the attribution of "meaning" to even the simplest poems in *Harmonium*, we find that the meanings are generally ironic, often playful, and rarely demanding, whether in terms of the heroic, the tragic, or the sublime. These dimensions, historically so allied to Romanticism, seem to Stevens, as he says in "Sailing after Lunch," "wholly the vapidest fake." He would rather "say the light wind worries the sail, / . . . say the water is swift today." And yet, coexisting with the impressionist or phenomenological wish to "expunge all people and be a pupil / Of the gorgeous wheel" (a wish later making Stevens a passive subject to the Sleight-of-Hand Man's manipulations of the universe), we find certain poems of uneasy sublimity in Stevens' "early" period.

The sublimity of these poems (notably "Sunday Morning" and "To the One of Fictive Music") is uneasy because it seems to require the suppression of the gestural Stevens we find in the other verse. For this "grand style" Stevens puts on the robes of Wordsworth and Keats and seeks a false sublime in the Paterian deification of private emotion, whether of pleasure or of pain:

Divinity must live within herself,
Passions of rain, or moods in falling snow,
Grievings in loneliness, or unsubdued
Elations when the forest blooms.

This is at once too catholic and too facile. If divinity lies within every mood, then it is scarcely distinguishable from the quotidian. Besides, there is in the passage a leveling tone which colors all passions, elated or sorrowful, with one hue of mournful nostalgia. The stiffening and masculine factor necessary to the sublime is simply absent (as it is not in Stevens' models). To insert some such stiffening, Stevens falls back, in "Le Monocle de Mon Oncle," on irony, which confuses the tone of that very interesting poem almost to the end. As the poem closes, however, something odd happens—the poem finds a middle ground of tone which is neither grand nor satiric, but may be called evaluative:

> . . . I pursued
> And still pursue, the origin and course
> Of love, but until now I never knew
> That fluttering things have so distinct a shade.

This neutral and sober tone has neither the fierce loathing of "The Emperor of Ice-Cream," as it savagely affixes a ruthless beam, nor the rhapsodic cadence found in the ode "To the One of Fictive Music." It seems to me a new tone in *Harmonium,* cognitive rather than descriptive, satiric, or rhapsodic, with none of the defensiveness elsewhere pervading *Harmonium* and showing up in Stevens' pronouncements, however whimsical or charming, against rationalists, roosters, and so on.

Stevens is tempted by the false sublime not only of moods in the mind but of beauties in the flesh:

> Beauty is momentary in the mind;
> The fitful tracing of a portal;
> But in the flesh it is immortal.

That is the plangent fleshly sublime, yearning toward the female image; when it yearns toward the male image it is tinged with envy, as Stevens' divine ingenue watches

> . . . the cool night and its fantastic stars,
> Prime paramour and belted paragon,

Well-booted, rugged, arrogantly male,
Patron and imager of the gold Don John
Who will embrace her before summer comes.

Stevens' queasiness about his artificially sublime, fleshly creations
forces him to surround his Susanna with red-eyed elders and simpering Byzantines, and induces a sadistic overtone in his Don John.
Neither creation is unforced; each is a false route. The sexual body
cannot, for Stevens, be the source of value, however much he wishes
it were. Later, when he has given up on the sexual body, he tries
(prompted by the Second World War) to find a source of the sublime in the larger-than-life heroic body: his hero

. . . walks with a defter
And lither stride. His arms are heavy
And his breast is greatness. All his speeches
Are prodigies in longer phrases.

Susanna, Don John, and the hero are all external to Stevens himself, and it may perhaps be true to say that each poet's sublime can
only be found with the compass of his own qualities. Even the
Yeatsian mask turns out at last to be only the face of the poet unmasked. In these poems Stevens seems to be deliberately seeking
what Yeats would have called a false mask. In a true mask-seeking,
the sensual man would seek the ascetic mask, because the ascetic
would be the embodiment of his own self-loathing, a true contemplative peer of his active deeds: the converse would be equally
true, as the ascetic would seek the sensual to embody his own repressed desires. But what are we to make of the ascetic who is such,
not out of an Augustinian repudiation, but purely and only out of
natural temperament? It will be false in him to seek images of the
sublime in the sensual which bears no natural affinity, even by
contrast, to his own spirit.

There is another quality that these fleshly sublimities—Susanna,
Don John, and the hero—have in common. All of them are described
in the comparative or superlative degree. Susanna is immortal, while
beauty in the mind is momentary; Don John is the prime paramour;
the hero walks with a defter and lither stride than others, and speaks
in longer phrases. These are, in short, all extrapolations upward
from the level norm into the visionary ether, and Stevens wishes
over and over that he could find such analogous but transfigured
forms:

True transfigurers fetched out of the human mountain,
True genii for the diminished spheres,
Gigantic embryos of populations,
Blue friends in shadows, rich conspirators,
Confiders and comforters and lofty kin.

The list could be prolonged almost indefinitely, if we were to add Stevens' Muses, his "impossible possible philosophers' man," and so on. But Stevens is no Kubla Khan who can decree a celestial sublime at wish. When he himself realizes his impotence, intermittently throughout his career, he swerves to the other extreme and proposes a theory of poetry nearest to the one espoused by the Imagists, that a poem may consist only of an achieved gesture, that of a man skating, a woman combing her hair:

The poem of the mind in the act of finding
What will suffice . . .
                    It must
Be the finding of a satisfaction, and may
Be of a man skating, a woman dancing, a woman
      Combing. The poem of the act of the mind.

The gestures are shrewdly chosen—none of them is a gesture accomplishable by a beast, they are all human, and distinctively human, actions—but, nevertheless, a poetry of gesture alone, just as much as a poetry of celestial extrapolation alone, veers dangerously away from the centrally human. Stevens oscillates between the desultory and the grandiose, alternately seeking the trivial and the Platonic, but finding his sublime, for the moment, only at the disappointingly unreal extreme of the Platonic, "tranquillizing with this jewel / The torments of confusion."

And yet, all these false sublimes, with their attendant false effort toward the grand style, nevertheless represent, even while being falsifications, a true path for Stevens. It was the sublime he needed, or nothing. The doubts we voice about these way stations are matched by his own suspicions: "To say more than human things with human voice, / That cannot be." Blackmur's description of Stevens' aim—to make superb statements discreetly so that their beauty would show before their force—is more a description of Stevens' achievement than of his desire. To say grand things grandly —and in this he was, of course, in competition with his romantic forbears—was in fact what, again and again, he tried to do. The attempt in style is a reflection of the attempt in life to live without feeling oneself antlike or absurd or petty or negligible. At times, Stevens seemed all of these to himself:

> Now it is September and the web is woven,
> The web is woven and you have to wear it,
> The final dwarf of you, waiting to be worn.

He speaks in another poem, "The Latest Freed Man," of having the ant of the self changed to an ox, by the simple force of the shining sun. We may assume, since the transformation was notable enough to deserve a poem, that usually he felt antlike rather than oxlike. The constant self-deprecation in his titles and in the names he assumed in his poems represents the obverse to the persistent aspiration toward the sublime; and running through all the poems, though most explicit in "Mrs. Alfred Uruguay," is the real dilemma of whether one reaches the sublime by fleeing the real or by seeking it.

The problem leads to Stevens' remarkable alternations of style, and to a consequent puzzle for anthologists. There is the terse and ironic Stevens, the elegiac and philosophical Stevens, the aspirational and incantatory Stevens, the playful Stevens, the Stevens of the news of the day, the Stevens of pure description. Though Stevens, in many poems, among them some of his most successful, skirted the problem of grandeur and nobility, nevertheless it troubled him and continued to recur throughout his life.

Where then did Stevens finally find a nobility in life and a corresponding possibility of grandeur in language? We can isolate certain poems which we feel to be genuine and unforced expressions of the self he most truly found himself to be, but it is difficult to find a phrase which resumes the sense and the effect of these poems. The best phrase, I think, characteristic of them all, occurs in Stevens' "Reply to Papini": the poem at its truest, he says, is "the heroic effort to live expressed as victory." Like many of Stevens' aphorisms about poetry, this one separates into a remark about thought and a remark about style, the poetry of the idea and the poetry of the words. Such a poem, we conclude, is always tragic, concerned as it is with an effort perpetually renewed against overwhelming odds and therefore perpetually failing (as "Esthétique du Mal" tells us), but such a poem is also always sublime, because the effort, a failure in its end, is nevertheless a victory in style. The peculiar sadness existing even in Stevens' most affirmative poems of this nature, notably in "To an Old Philosopher in Rome," arises from Stevens' conviction that "a fantastic effort has failed." Nevertheless, there subsists "a total grandeur at the end," and so, in the poem about Santayana, we have the parallel of the dilapidated with the perfect, of the trivial with the grand, of the domestic with the celestial. These parallels, Stevens says, become one, but at first the sublime seems a version of the old false self we already know, an evolution from the ordinary, an extrapolation from the norm:

> How easily the blown banners change to wings . . .
> Things dark on the horizons of perception,
> Become accompaniments of fortune . . .
>
> . . . The newsboys' muttering
> Becomes another murmuring . . .

However, this simple extrapolation, complicating itself into "a confusion . . . a portent . . . a moving transparence," reverses its direction and descends from the sublime to the ordinary:

> Speak . . .
> So that we feel, in this illumined large,
> The veritable small.

These confusions of direction are recapitulated in Santayana's perplexed impatience:

> Impatient for the grandeur that you need
> In so much misery; and yet finding it
> Only in misery, the afflatus of ruin.

Stevens finds the sublime not by extrapolating beyond the limited real, but by seeking out that real and finding grandeur not even in its undamaged form but rather, in a paradox familiar in English poetry at least since the Renaissance, in a ruin:

> . . . the naked majesty, if you like,
> Of bird-nest arches and of rain-stained vaults.

These are remarks, under the veil of metaphor, about human suffering. Though we cannot seek it for ourselves, yet we repudiate the blankness of a happy people in a happy world. The sublime, for Stevens as for other tragic poets, is necessarily contingent upon suffering. His lady of fictive music had never suffered, and even his woman in "Sunday Morning" seems untouched by any "moods" she has experienced or any "grievings" she has undergone, so reflective and ripe is her tone. His heroes, with their brutal strength, were Goliaths who had never known a David; his soldiers, if they died, died absolutely and with wounds red as roses. It was late in Stevens' life, if we can judge from the poems, before he found the imaginative equivalent for his conviction of tragic sublimity and of its accompanying effort.

Stevens inherited the conception of the nobility of effort from his Romantic predecessors: but whereas in Wordsworth the effort and expectation and desire are directed toward "something evermore about to be" (the effort in itself a plenitude), and in Shelley the effort is foredoomed to that collapse whence Hope will create "from its own wreck the things its contemplates," in Stevens the extra-solipsistic flight is always viewed after the fact. We look back, tragically and comically and ironically, to the extravagant and doomed efforts of men to live nobly and to create lastingly:

> The sun, in clownish yellow, but not a clown,
> Brings the day to perfection and then fails. He dwells
> In a consummate prime, yet still desires
> A further consummation. For the lunar month
> He makes the tenderest research, intent
> On a transmutation which, when seen, appears
> To be askew. And space is filled with his
> Rejected years.

The clownish sun, in these efforts and failures, is one with man. And still, in spite of all dismaying outcomes, "The yellow grassman's mind is still immense, / Still promises perfections cast away." This charming parable presents our awkward attempts at sublimity in a comic version; but in a leaner time, Stevens feels that the sun's deployment in the sky, the poet's in the tower, are enterprises untenable in this world, that to live with fictive creations of the achieved sublime is no longer possible:

> He turned from the tower to the house,
> From the spun sky and the high and deadly view,
> To the novels on the table,
> The geraniums on the sill.

He adds, and we must add, that "being up high had helped him when up high," but "the height was not quite proper, the position was wrong."

It is true, as Harold Bloom has remarked, that there exists at least one great poem of the later years, "Puella Parvula," affirming a vast triumphal sublimity of the imagination:

> ... over the wind, over the legends of its roaring, ...
> Over all these the mighty imagination triumphs
> Like a trumpet ...
>
> The *summarium in excelsis* begins.

But this effortless ease, as the verse rises to its glory, brackets a desperate vocative:

> Keep quiet in the heart, O wild bitch. O mind
> Gone wild, be what he tells you to be: *Puella*.
> Write *pax* across the window pane. And then
>
> Be still.

Such fragile and fragmentary sublimities are not the sublime, even though their terms be sonorous. And so I should like to propose that it is not in attempting to bring days to perfection (the comic version), nor in attempting to quiet the wild bitch in the heart (the strenuous version), but rather in the incorporation of the imperfect and the tragic that Stevens discovers the sublime.

Not all versions of sublimity need affirm the destitution of the dying Santayana, aureoled though it be. There is a sublimity of inception as well as a sublimity of dissolution; they both share the same poverty, they both manifest the same riches. It is true that the poem on Santayana may, with some effort, be thought of as a poem of inception, since Santayana is about to become his works:

> ... He stops upon this threshold,
> As if the design of all his words takes form
> And frame from thinking and is realized.

And yet the poem is remembered as a poem about an old man and a death; the verses cast a long backward shadow, not a forward one.

The truest sublimity in Stevens appears, I think, in two forms. One form, best seen in the poem on Santayana, embodies "the heroic effort to live expressed as victory." The poems of this sort are at once elegiac and celebratory, effort and yet mastery at once. The second form of sublimity is also embodied by Stevens in an aphoristic phrase, this one from" A Discovery of Thought:" "the effort to be born / Surviving being born." This is, strictly speaking, an un-imaginable state of affairs, suggesting both a memory of the birth-struggle and a persistent continuation, all through adult life, of the liberating effort toward birth. Both of these "definitions" of sub-limity include the notion of effort and are therefore sublimities of process rather than of achievement. It is not the triumph of the trumpeting imagination, but the scrawny cry of its emergent birth that represents Stevens' utmost sublime. It is a sublime of denuded language, a sublime of indicative effort, as the pale sunshine and scrawny cry of March testify to the wish to transform winter into spring:

> At the earliest ending of winter,
> In March, a scrawny cry from outside
> Seemed like a sound in his mind.
>
> He knew that he heard it,
> A bird's cry, at daylight or before,
> In the early March wind.
>
> The sun was rising at six,
> No longer a battered panache above snow . . .
> It would have been outside.
>
> It was not from the vast ventriloquism
> Of sleep's faded papier-mâché . . .
> The sun was coming from outside.
>
> That scrawny cry—it was
> A chorister whose c preceded the choir.
> It was part of the colossal sun,
>
> Surrounded by its choral rings,
> Still far away. It was like
> A new knowledge of reality.

In this transparently beautiful poem, Stevens claims all that can be claimed for any sublime experience—that it confers "a new knowledge of reality." If it were to be objected that the conven-tional sublime is still present here in the invoked presence of the colossal sun, whether far away or not, we have at least Stevens' re-mark in a late letter: "Robins and doves are both early risers and are connoisseurs of daylight before the actual presence of the sun coarsens it." We may believe that Stevens' fastidiousness, more acute than ever in his old age, saw something overblown and coarse in the fulsome creations he had previously sponsored—the brute

11

hero, the bejeweled Muse, the sprawling Portent, the pontifex-Serpent. The absolute, finally, disappoints the connoisseur, who sees it as insufficiently nuancé, too heavy and final.

Stevens had said prophetically in "Owl's Clover" that "memory's lord is lord of prophecy"—that prophetic or sublime utterance must incorporate the past in its vision of the future, must embody the failures, rejections, wildnesses, rebellions, and despairs of the writer if, from his winter, he is to invoke spring. So, in "Not Ideas about the Thing but the Thing Itself," the sublime arises out of the "debris of life and mind" represented by the exhaustion of winter, the March wind, the battered panache of the winter sun, and sleep's faded papier-mâché. But indeed "memory's lord is lord of prophecy," since without the memory of other scrawny cries in other winters, the sleeper would not be able to recognize that faint cry as the harbinger of spring. Since, as Wittgenstein said in a Stevens-like moment, forms of words are forms of life, we are being asked to judge, through the medium of a poem such as this, whether we as well do not find hints and faint transfigurings more satisfying than full choral radiance, however we acknowledge the aesthetic claims of perfection. The question is familiar to us from Wordsworth, who set the budding rose above the rose full-blown. But in Wordsworth this prizing of inception over fulfillment is linked to a pathos of youth fled away and revolutionary hope deceived. Endurance, not inception, is the Wordsworthian essence of old age. Stevens' inceptions are precisely sublime and not pathetic because they coexist with the stoic vision instead of preceding it.

We may ask, in that case, what reality we can predicate of the colossal sun, which belongs neither to the poetry of inception nor to the poetry of stoicism. If we are to locate the true sublime of Stevens' last years in the scrawny cry and the pale gleam, what name are we to give to the choir and to the colossal sun? I would call the "choral rings"—those flawless synesthetic combinations of sunlight and sound—the perfect, not the sublime. The human sublime, since "the imperfect is our paradise," lies in "flawed words and stubborn sounds," as Stevens tells us in "The Poems of Our Climate." I take "Not Ideas about the Thing" as a submerged autobiography, a justification of Stevens' own sparse poetry. Earlier, he had hoped that "some harmonious skeptic soon in a skeptical music" would create a new mode of desire, and yet he had acknowledged that the nightingale was a bird he would never hear. If the nightingale represented the only sublime, then he, and all modern writers, would be denied that realm most proper to poets. "We shall die in the wilderness," said Arnold. But for Stevens, both the elegiac sublime of ruins—the "profound poetry of the poor and of the dead"—and the celebratory sublime of inception—"A chorister whose c preceded the choir"—were possible to the modern poet, who ceded nightingales and choral rings to his predecessors and his descendants. What is important to Stevens is that the inceptive should be seen as a form of the perfect, and therefore as a genuine part of the sublime. The planet on the table bears, after all, a recognizable, if in some way absurd, resemblance to the planet in space: Stevens' poems bear

> Some affluence, if only half-perceived,
> In the poverty of their words,
> Of the planet of which they were part.

It seems wonderfully significant that at this point in his old age Stevens could stop mocking himself with ironic names like Dr. Homburg or Professor Eucalyptus or Canon Aspirin, and call himself, simply, truly, and without irony, Ariel.

In the several late poems of inception printed in *Opus Posthumous*, Stevens' final sublime receives unquestionable definition, especially in "The Dove in Spring," "The Course of a Particular," "A Discovery of Thought," "The Desire to Make Love in a Pagoda," and "July Mountain." These are the poems of "an always incipient cosmos," of "the few things / For which a fresh name always occurred," of a "bubbling before the sun / . . . too far / For daylight and too near for sleep," of "the first inch of night . . . / The morning's prescience." In "A Discovery of Thought," the most vivid parable of this sublimity, we see "the cricket of summer forming itself out of ice":

> . . . An antipodal, far-fetched creature, worthy of birth,
> The true tone of the metal of winter in what it says:
> The accent of deviation in the living thing
> That is its life preserved, the effort to be born
> Surviving being born, the event of life.

In the presence of such severe writing, which is nevertheless so gravely devout, we can only assent to the proposition that such a sublime is "worthy of birth." Poetically, the theory ratifies itself.

But since my concern here is with the theory rather than with its incarnations, I must close with Stevens' last theoretical statement

on the sublime. It occurs in a poem not the equal of his greatest, but for the purposes of exposition one of his clearest texts—
the 1954 Columbia Phi Beta Kappa poem, "The Sail of Ulysses."
The poem exists to praise the human particulars from which
abstractions, systems, and largenesses spring, and upon which they
repose.

> The living man in the present place,
> Always, the particular thought
> Among Plantagenet abstractions,
> Always and always, the difficult inch,
> On which the vast arches of space
> Repose, always, the credible thought
> From which the incredible systems spring,
> The little confine soon unconfined
> In stellar largenesses—these
> Are the manifestations of a law
> That bends the particulars to the abstract,
> Makes them a pack on a giant's back,
> A majestic mother's flocking brood,
> As if abstractions were, themselves,
> Particulars of a relative sublime.

To write the poetry of the difficult inch is to know the mile, to hear
the brood is to see the mother, to name need is to know solace. And
thus, the poem continues, the sibyl of the self is not an "englistered
woman, seated / In colorings harmonious . . . / On the seat of hali-
dom," like Stevens' "One of Fictive Music." On the contrary, the interior paramour is now poor:

> It is the sibyl of the self,
> The self as sibyl, whose diamond,
> Whose chiefest embracing of all wealth
> Is poverty, whose jewel found
> At the exactest central of the earth
> Is need.

We cannot doubt that the diamond at the central of the earth is
what poetry means by the sublime; and yet "The sibyl's shape / Is a
blind thing fumbling for its form . . . / A child asleep in its own life."
Stevens recognizes his previous—and delusory—perfect sublime as
an inhuman thing:

14

> The englistered woman is now seen
> In an isolation, separate
> From the human in humanity,
> A part of the inhuman more . . .

For a poet who began with rapturous praise of the inhuman more (and who never quite forsook it, since what else is the *summarium in excelsis?*), this admission represents a slow lifetime's acquaintance with the human less. It was, it is true, a partial, solitary, remote, and inching acquaintance with the human on the part of a man "vitally deprived," a man who was never able to write the section of *Notes Toward a Supreme Fiction* to be called "It Must Be Human," a man who wondered in his last months whether he had lived a skeleton's life. Better a skeleton's life than a deity's, we could answer, the skeleton being at least a part of the human less. By this descent from the inhuman more, whether out of age, exhaustion, experience, or wisdom, Stevens was able to relax his forced apotheoses, to cease asking for a guaranteed and unflawed sublime. He found, instead, in his last poems, a special state in which effort—the heroic effort to live, to utter the scrawny cry—survives the achievement. One possesses at last both states at once: "the effort to be born / Surviving being born." Even in this fantasy, or dream, Stevens refuses to let effort be forgotten in achievement; effort, undone by fate and successful only in fantasy, is finally the quintessential definition of life as of art, and the product, the poem, in order to be sublime, must remind us always of the effortful process that gave it birth.

Souvenirs and Prophecies

Although Wallace Stevens was born in 1897, he was not really famous until the 1954 publication of his *Collected Poems;* his "impersonal reticence," as his daughter names it, kept him very much out of sight. Eliot, Frost, and Williams are still better known and better represented in the anthologies; Stevens' place in the modern

This review of *Souvenirs and Prophecies: The Young Wallace Stevens* by Holly Stevens appeared in the *New York Times Book Review*, January 30, 1977.

movement has not yet been canonically fixed. There is no major biography. The *Collected Poems* was incomplete. After Stevens' death, Samuel French Morse edited *Opus Posthumous*, which included poetry and prose, both early and late, omitted from the earlier collection; Robert Buttel published some of the juvenilia in his book, *The Making of Harmonium;* and Stevens' daughter Holly published the letters (with some journal entries interspersed)— in the mutilated form in which she had inherited them. Now Holly Stevens has decided to publish the complete juvenilia and the complete journals, thereby completing the Stevens canon, and her father's papers have passed into the collection of the Huntington Library. There is a certain sadness in seeing Stevens finally complete and library-owned; he has now become his admirers.

The journal reprinted in full in *Souvenirs and Prophecies* was begun in the fall of 1898, when Stevens was a nineteen-year-old sophomore at Harvard. The previous January, Stevens had published his first poem, prophetically named "Autumn." This collection carries us from these beginnings through 1914, when Stevens was thirty-five; at thirty-six, he would publish his first major poem, "Sunday Morning." "Ordinary annotation," says Holly Stevens of the unpublished material, "seemed insufficient; what did seem essential was to interweave the available material (even though that made necessary the repetition of a good deal that has been previously published) and some of my own speculations, to provide a background for what my father has described . . . [as] 'a man's sense of the world.' "

Eventually there will be a scholarly edition of the early poems and the journal, but for now it is more useful, I think, to have what Holly Stevens has given—a relatively complete portrait of the artist as a young man (even at the cost of reprinting texts we have already seen in part), so that the journal fragments and first poems can be placed in the context of Stevens' character and life, and can be related—by Holly Stevens' glances forward—to the later work.

In the light of Stevens' drift toward discursiveness in the later work, it is significant that he inscribes on the first page of his 1899 notebook Keats's remark that "to philosophise I dare not yet." Nothing is more strongly visible in this collection than the coexistence in Stevens of the visual and the ruminative. In 1900 he makes a list, every member of which is entitled "Thought for Sonnet"— and yet several of these "thoughts" are expressed in entirely visual ways: "Birds flying up from dark ground at evening: Clover, deep grass, oats, etc. to Circle & plunge beneath the golden clouds, in &

about them, with golden spray on their wings like dew. Produce an imaginative flutter of color."

If this is a "thought" to the young poet—comparable to other, more conventional "thoughts" in the list ("Is there no song of Love to outquench the thought of Death"), then there were remarkably fluid boundaries between seeing and thinking in Stevens, and we can read the visual observations in these letters, poems, and journals as in part a record of thoughts.

The young man who appears in this book seems unusual chiefly in his eight years of solitude once he leaves home and Harvard. He works briefly for a newspaper in New York, then spends a year in New York Law School, clerks in a law office for two years, is admitted to the bar, then works at various business jobs till, shortly before his thirtieth birthday, he marries Elsie Kachel. The solitude is somewhat alleviated in the five years before marriage by his occasional visits to Elsie, but for the most part he spends the years from twenty-two to thirty—those years in which young artists characteristically join groups of their peers—utterly alone. (His work apparently did not interest him, nor did his companions at work.) He sees some Harvard classmates when they pass through New York, and he goes once on a six-week trip to British Columbia with the lawyer for whom he had clerked. But his usual life in these years consists of weekdays at work, evenings at home alone in a small New York apartment, and long solitary walks, sometimes for thirty or forty miles, on Saturday afternoon or Sunday. He writes in 1904: "Here am I . . . at the age of twenty-five, without a cent to my name, in a huge town, knowing a half-dozen men & no women."

And, a week later: "I'm in the Black Hole again, without knowing any of my neighbors. The very animal in me cries out for a lair. I want to see somebody, hear somebody speak to me, look at somebody, speak to somebody in turn. I want companions. I want more than my work, than the nods of acquaintances, than this little room."

It is not surprising that the following summer he falls in love.

The marriage was a strange match: on the one hand, Stevens, an exquisitely educated young man, reading French and English poetry and following French avant-garde art; on the other hand, Elsie, who after dropping out of high school during her first year, went to work selling sheet music by playing the pieces on a piano in a department store. Holly Stevens says briefly about her mother: "All her life, at least during the time I knew her, she suffered from a persecution complex." After their marriage, the Stevenses lived a reclusive life in New York, seeing few, if any, people. Elsie spent the summers at home in Pennsylvania with her family. Stevens, says his daughter, resembled his own father, who (in Stevens' words) "spent the greater part of his life . . . at his office; he wanted quiet and, in that quiet, to create a life of his own."

Stevens' life might have been different had his father not been so insistent that he earn his keep. In Stevens' first fall at Harvard his father wrote him:

"Our young folks would of course all prefer to be born like English noblemen with entailed estates, income guaranteed, and in choosing a profession they would simply say—'How shall I amuse myself'—but young America understands that the question is— *'Starting with nothing, how shall I sustain myself and perhaps a wife and family—and send my boys to College and live comfortably in my old age?'* Young fellows must all come to that question for unless they inherit money, marry money, find money, steal money or somebody presents it to them, they must *earn* it and earning it save it up for the time of need."

In later life, when Stevens could have afforded trips to Europe, he never left America: by then it was too late. He never created a life in society for himself, or a network of friends; his friendships were epistolary, not personal. He refused to give the Charles Eliot Norton lectures at Harvard in his old age, because he knew that if he took a year off from his insurance office, the Hartford Accident & Indemnity Company where he was a vice president, he would not be able to return; he left the office only to die. Poetry and work remained in uneasy coexistence from the earliest years of manhood recorded in this collection down to the last years of his working life.

The poems printed here are slight, and Holly Stevens confesses that even with all the materials in view, she cannot explain "the great leap from the juvenile verses to 'Sunday Morning.'" The Orientalism and "decadence" of the early verses are wholly conventional: if we hear of a lady "that winked her sandal fan / long ago in gray Japan," we can only be astonished at Stevens' eventual originality in the disposition of such materials. Holly Stevens' connections between the negligible early verse and the later poetry will be of help to readers still piecing together Stevens' world. One of the most touching of these juxtapositions places a 1908 poem against one written in 1953. In 1908, Stevens, as Caliban, watches the moon as his double Ariel, haunting him with its "wild, starry tune"; by 1953, Stevens has attained the voice that earlier seemed out of reach, and can say, speaking of himself in the third person, "Ariel was glad he had written his poems."

The chief connections to the mature poetry appear here in the journal and letters. It is hard to know whether to laugh or to cry at the mixture of self-knowledge and priggishness: "The feeling of piety is very dear to me. I would sacrifice a great deal to be a Saint Augustine, but modernity is so Chicagoan, so plain, so unmeditative . . . At the same time, [a moral life] is an inhuman life to lead. It is a form of narrowness so far as companionship is concerned. One *must* make concessions to others; but there is never a necessity of smutching inner purity."

Of course the path from this innocence to some version of experience is a predictable one; the various byways it takes provide one of the interests in this book. More than ten years later, Stevens writes of his dying mother, "She was, of course, disappointed, as we all are." His disappointments are chronicled here: "Somehow what I do seems to increase in its artificiality. Those cynical years when I was about twelve subdued natural and easy flow of feelings . . . For instance I have been here at Wily's almost a month, yet never noticed the pathos of their condition. The memory of one day's visit brought tears to [a friend's] eyes. I am too cold for that."

"I wonder," asks a late poem, "have I lived a skeleton's life?" The idealizing letters to Elsie attempt an intimacy that seems not to have lasted in the marriage. (Mrs. Stevens was angry that Stevens published poems originally addressed to her; she did not read his later work.) What does last in the poems, and is striking in the journals, is the rapport with the weather and the landscape: "The day of the sun is like the day of a king. It is a promenade in the morning, a sitting on the throne at noon, a pageant in the evening."

Sentences like the one about the sun, written in Stevens' twenties, have all the authority of the late poetry and prose. His imaginative life was already structuring itself in fantasy. "Sometimes, just before I go to sleep, I fancy myself on a green mountain—southward, I think. It's simply green, the grass—no trees, just an enormous, continental ridge."

The fantasy was variable: "I'm going to come down from the green mountain tonight and imagine a warm sea booming on a tropical coast." The green mountain and the tropical sea, like the kingly sun, are constants of his imagination.

As a young man, he already liked aphorisms: after mentioning Leopardi's *Pensieri,* Pascal's *Pensées,* and Rochefoucauld's *Maximes,* he comments, "I should like to have a library of such things," and, as his daughter tells us, he did. His taste in painting reveals his innate sense of his own world: a painting that he liked showed "a step or two of road, a roadside house of white, a few trees" at dawn; the painter, he said, had caught "the abandoned air of the world at that hour, that is, abandoned of humans." We recall "The Auroras of Autumn" and its deserted cabin on the beach. He feels, in March, "a revulsion against old things—habits, people, places—everything: the feeling the sun must have, nowadays, when it shines on nothing but mud and bare trees and the general world, rusty with winter . . . Earth and the body and the spirit seem to change together, and so *I* feel muddy and bare and rusty." Perhaps the truest thing that can be said about Stevens' poetry is that in it we see a poet who is capable of being at once the sun and the earth it shines on—as here he identifies himself first with the sun's revulsion and then with the earth's muddiness. Stevens' turnings in inner and outer weather are already clear in his later journal entries, even mutilated as they were by his wife or himself. It is a pity that the most personal parts of the letters and journals are gone. What remains gives us not, as the blurb would have it, "a charming self-portrait . . . of an especially engaging youth," but rather the solitary evolution of an unworldly, reclusive, puritanical, hardworking American young man, who wrote poetry almost in secret, and thought he was a Caliban occasionally visited by an Ariel-muse. It is a more peculiar story than the blurb, and more interesting.

Stevens and Keats's "To Autumn"

Throughout his long life as a poet, Stevens returned again and again to Keats's ode "To Autumn." The history of those returns provides a classic example of how literary materials can be reworked by a modern artist. We are accustomed to this process in modern art, especially in painting and sculpture. Gombrich has pointed out how artists reproduce, not what they see, but some amalgam of that and an antecedent pictorial schema already in their minds. For Stevens, Keats's ode offered an irresistible antecedent model; Stevens hovered over the ode repeatedly in his musings. He became, to my way of thinking, the best reader of the ode, the most subtle interpreter of its rich meanings. Our understanding of latent significance in the older poem broadens when the ode is seen refracted through Stevens' lines. At the same time we may perceive, in Stevens' departures from the ode, implicit critiques of its stance.

A modern work of art may comment on an older one in several different ways. Stevens defined poetry as an art embracing two different "poetries"—the poetry of the idea and the poetry of the words. My own work on Stevens has hitherto been chiefly a commentary on the poetry of the words, but here I turn to the poetry of the idea. Stevens helpfully remarked that the idea of God was a poetic idea; it seems from his poetry that he considered the idea of a seasonal cycle a poetic idea as well, since it embodied the natural counterpart to the poetic "exhilarations of changes," the motive for metaphor:

> You like it under the trees in autumn,
> Because everything is half dead . . .
>
> In the same way, you were happy in spring,
> With half colors of quarter-things.

The seasonal idea, though immemorially present in lyric, seems to have been mediated to Stevens through Keats, no doubt through the sonnet on the human seasons as well as through the odes. In commenting on a received aesthetic form, an artist can take various paths. He may make certain implicit "meanings" explicit; he may extrapolate certain possibilities to greater lengths; he may choose a detail, center on it, and turn it into an entire composition; he may alter the perspective from which the form is viewed; or he may view the phenomenon at a different moment in time. We are familiar with these strategies in painting, in the expansion and critique of classical forms practiced by all subsequent schools, but most noticeably for us, perhaps, in the dramatic and radical experimentation with classic forms in our own century. Stevens is modern as Cézanne is modern; he keeps the inherited shapes, is classic in his own disposition of materials, is rarely bizarre, and stays within the central tradition of Western art. Stevens' "copies" never forget their great originals; but we may see, in following

Stevens' experiments with the materials of the autumn ode, how a modern originality gradually declares itself, while deliberately recalling, even into old age, the earlier master's prototype.

The presence of Keats's ode within a great many of Stevens' poems is self-evident. The single most derivative moment in Stevens is the end of *Sunday Morning;* in *Credences of Summer* and *The Auroras of Autumn* Stevens composed two "panels" to the autumn ode; and there are lesser appearances of fragments of the ode throughout Stevens' work. Anyone familiar with the poem will recognize in Stevens' verse the replication of Keats's fruits, autumnal female presence, cottage (transmuted to an American cabin), cornfields (changed to American hayfields), wind, muted or unmelodious birds, stubble plains (reduced to bare stalks or thin grass), clouds, and bees. Our recognition of such echoes is usually intermittent; but to read through Stevens' poetry with the ode "To Autumn" in mind is to be suffused by the lights that Stevens saw presiding over the trash can at the end of the world, that resting place of tradition:

> ... Above that urn two lights
> Commingle, not like the commingling of sun and moon
> At dawn, nor of summer-light and winter-light
> In an autumn afternoon, but two immense
> Reflections, whirling apart and wide away.

The end of "Sunday Morning" is a rewritten version of the close of Keats's "To Autumn"; such risk-taking in a young poet argues a deep engagement with the earlier poem. The resemblances are obvious and have been often remarked. Both poets use successive clauses of animal presence (gnats, lambs, crickets, redbreast, and swallows in Keats; deer, quail, and pigeons in Stevens); both poems close with birds in the sky (gathering swallows in Keats, flocks of pigeons in Stevens) and with the sense of sound (including a whistling bird in each); Keats's soft-dying day becomes Stevens' evening. Stevens' stance, unlike that of Keats, is the homiletic and doctrinal one inherited from religious poetry and so dear to American poets. However, Stevens, as a modern poet, offers no single doctrine but rather a choice among truths: we live either (1) in chaos, or (2) in a system of mutual dependency, or (3) in a condition of solitude, which may itself be seen as (3a) lonely ("unsponsored") or (3b) liberated ("free"), but which is in any case inescapable. The passage allowing doctrinal choices is followed by the passage on deer, quail, berries, and pigeons (those wilderness forms replacing

Keats's domestic ones), in which the doctrinal options are alluded to but, in the end, left undecided. The quail utter "spontaneous" cries, and their adjective hearkens back phonemically to our "unsponsored" state; the pigeons fly in an "isolation" etymologically resembling our "island" solitude; the "chaos" of the sun recalls orthographically the "casual" flocks of pigeons. In the end, as the pigeons inscribe their transient motions in the air, their calligraphy is read (by the poet seeking significance) as elusively ambiguous, and doctrinal choice dissolves in mystery. But although metaphysical certainty remains unattainable, the truth of existence is clear. The final motion, whether or not definable as one of chaos, dependency, solitude, freedom, or un-sponsoredness, is "downward to darkness." In such an ending, *be* is finale of *seem*, and death is the only certainty uninvaded by metaphysical doubt. While Keats rests in the polyphony of the creatures in their autumnal choir, Stevens (though his adoption of Keats's principal trope, enumeration, shows him as not insensible to the plenitude around him in the scene) makes his landscape depend for its significance on what it can explicitly suggest about metaphysical truth.

With the example of Keats's beautiful implicit meanings before us, we may tend to recoil from what seems crudity in Stevens, as he speckles the visible scene with invisible queries: chaos? dependency? solitude? unsponsored-ness? freedom? isolation? casualness? ambiguity? The coercion of cadence forces the innocent landscape to enact a Stevensian entropy:

> And,
> in the isolation of the sky,
> at evening,
> casual flocks of pigeons make
> Ambiguous undulations as they sink,
> downward to darkness,
> on extended wings.

Stevens' final clause is, of course, imitated from Keats's passage on the gnats among the river sallows,

>   aloft   lives
> borne   or   as the light wind   or
>   sinking   dies.

Keats's imitation of randomness is changed by Stevens into an imitation of decline. But Keats, after writing about the gnats, went on to forbid himself such naive stylistic equivalences:

And full-grown lambs loud bleat from hilly bourn;
Hedge-crickets sing; and now with treble soft
The red-breast whistles from a garden-croft;
And gathering swallows twitter in the skies.

These clauses are the source for Stevens' earlier ones (such as "Deer walk upon our mountains"), but Stevens has reversed Keats's rhetorical order. Keats writes a long clause about the gnats, then follows it with shorter ones dwindling to "hedge-crickets sing," then broadens out to end his poem. Stevens writes short clauses followed by a final long one. The result is a gain in climactic force and explicit pathos, but a loss in stoicism and discretion of statement. Keats's pathos (at its most plangent in the small gnats who mourn in a wailful choir, helpless in the light wind; less insistent but still audible in the bleating lambs; but largely absent in the whistle and twitter of the closing lines) reaches us with steadily diminishing force, in inverse relation to Keats's recognition of the independent worth of autumnal music, without reference to any dying fall. Stevens' pathos, on the other hand, is at its most evident in the closing lines. In short, Stevens has adopted Keats's manner—the population of animals, the types of clause, the diction, even the sunset landscape—without embracing Keats's essential stylistic argument against nostalgia. Nor has he imitated Keats's reticent diction and chaste rhetoric; instead, he writes with an increasing opulence of rhetorical music, and imposes explicit metaphysical dimensions on the landscape.

The imitation, however inferior to its source, argues that Keats's ode had penetrated Stevens' consciousness and imagination and was already provoking him to see the world in its light, even if he found the world insufficient without attendant metaphysics. Keats's ode continued to provide Stevens with material to the very end of his life. In the "Adagia," Stevens asks the question which the ode, among other works, must have prompted: "How has the human spirit ever survived the terrific literature with which it has had to contend?"

If, on the total evidence of Stevens' poetry, we ask how he read "To Autumn," we can isolate, for the moment neglecting the chronology of the Collected Poems, elements of his understanding of the ode. He thought, at first, that Keats was being evasive in the stasis of the first stanza, that he was avoiding the most repellent detail of natural process—death. (Stevens was, in taking this severe

view, misinterpreting Keats, whose subject was not natural processes, but human intervention in natural process—harvest, rather
than death.) In "Le Monocle de Mon Oncle" and "Sunday Morning" Stevens, insisting that everything "comes rotting back to
ground" and that "this luscious and impeccable fruit of life / Falls,
it appears, of its own weight to earth," writes what seem taunts
directed at the changeless ripeness of Keats's first stanza:

> Is there no change of death in paradise?
> Does ripe fruit never fall? Or do the boughs
> Hang always heavy in that perfect sky?

Allowing the fruit to follow its natural trajectory, Stevens lets
Autumn not only "swell the gourd" but strain it beyond its own
capacity to swell until it becomes distorted in shape and its skin
becomes streaked and rayed:

> It comes, it blooms, it bears its fruit and dies . . .
> Two golden gourds distended on our vines,
> Into the autumn weather, splashed with frost,
> Distorted by hale fatness, turned grotesque.
> We hang like warty squashes, streaked and rayed,
> The laughing sky will see the two of us
> Washed into rinds by rotting winter rains.

In spite of this "realist" critique of Keats's benign autumn,
Stevens' poetry here is still Keatsian: no new style of language has
been invented to support the new harshness of position. And the
unfairness of the critique is of a piece with the "realist" position.
Stevens comes much closer to the true Keatsian stance in a later
poem, "On the Road Home," where plenitude is seen to stem not so
much from any group of items in the landscape as from the refusal
of doctrine in favor of perception, of measuring the world not by
thought but by eye:

> It was when I said,
> "There is no such thing as the truth,"
> That the grapes seemed fatter . . .
>
> It was at that time, that the silence was largest
> And longest, the night was roundest,
> The fragrance of the autumn warmest,
> Closest and strongest.

Whatever the objections that could be urged against the final for-mulation here, it is, in its near-tautology and solemn playfulness, recognizably Stevensian and not Keatsian in language. Even when metaphysically in agreement with Keats, the later Stevens speaks in his own voice.

When Stevens writes, in "The Rock," his final retraction of the "realist" view expressed in "Le Monocle," he alludes to his own dictum from the early poem ("It comes, it blooms, it bears its fruit and dies") but he quietly corrects himself by omitting the death. The leaves which cover the rock, standing for the poem as icon, "bud and bloom and bear their fruit without change." This is not written in agreement with Keats, who allowed his fruit to change, if not through death at least through harvest, winnowing, and cider-making. But neither is it written to correct him. It is written to give credence to the plenty of the world as it is preserved not on the earth but in the mind, always Stevens' chosen territory. The leaves

> . . . bloom as a man loves, as he lives in love.
> They bear their fruit so that the year is known,
>
> As if its understanding was brown skin,
> And honey in its pulp, the final found,
> The plenty of the year and of the world.

Here, precisely because he is speaking of internal, not external fruition, Stevens is able to leave the fruit on the tree, the honey in the hive, without irritably reaching out to force them to fall and rot, or to be harvested.

No other source in poetry was so rich for Stevens as Keats's second stanza. Keats's goddess of autumn, nearer to us than pagan goddesses because, unlike them, she labors in the fields and is herself threshed by the winnowing wind, varies in her manifesta-tions from careless girl to burdened gleaner to patient watcher— erotic in her abandon to the fume of poppies, intimate of light in her bosom friendship with the maturing sun, worn by her vigil over the last oozings. She reappears in innumerable guises in Stevens' work, but is more often than not maternal: "The mother's face, / The purpose of the poem, fills the room" ("*The* Auroras of Au-tumn"). It is probable that her maternal nature was suggested by Keats's ode (which itself borrows from Shakespeare's image of "the teeming autumn, big with rich increase, / Bearing the wanton burden of the prime, / Like widow'd wombs after their lord's de-cease"). Keats's season is an earth-goddess whose union with the sun makes her bear fruit; the sun, his part in procreation done, departs from the poem as the harvest begins, and the season gradually ages from the careless figure on the granary floor to the watcher over the last drops of the crushed apples. Finally, when she becomes herself the "soft-dying day," she is mourned by creatures deliberately infantine, as even full-grown sheep are represented as bleating lambs: these creatures are filial forms, children grieving for the death of the mother. Stevens, I believe, recognized these implications and brought them into explicitness.

The most beautiful modern commentary on Keats's invention of a humanized goddess of the ripe fields is Stevens' poem "The Woman in Sunshine":

> It is only that this warmth and movement are like
> The warmth and movement of a woman.
>
> It is not that there is any image in the air
> Nor the beginning nor end of a form:
>
> It is empty. But a woman in threadless gold
> Burns us with brushings of her dress
>
> And a dissociated abundance of being,
> More definite for what she is—
>
> Because she is disembodied,
> Bearing the odors of the summer fields,
>
> Confessing the taciturn and yet indifferent,
> Invisibly clear, the only love.

The "poetry of the idea" here comes from Keats, the "poetry of the words" from Stevens. The iconic "image," surrounded by words like "empty," "dissociated," "disembodied," "taciturn," "indifferent," and 'invisibly clear," is wholly Stevensian, as is the rhetoric of "it is only," "it is not," and "it is empty." Stevens has taken a detail from his source—Keats's form of an autumn goddess—and has enlarged it to fill a new and more modern space. This goddess assumes various forms in Stevens, most of them beneficent. When Stevens is depressed, "mother nature" (as she is named along with a matching invention, "father nature," in "Lulu Morose") turns either actively malevolent (curdling the kind cow's milk with lightning in "Lulu Morose") or, worse, devouring but indifferent (as in "Madame La Fleurie," where mother and father nature are conflated into one androgynous mother who feeds on her son, "a bearded queen, wicked in her dead light"). But such "corrections" of Keats's goddess are infrequent in Stevens. Rather, Stevens tends to expand Keats's figure until she becomes one of "the pure perfections of parental space, / . . . the beings of the mind / In the light-bound space of the mind." Though he acknowledges fully the fictive nature of the goddess, Stevens can move insensibly into speaking of her as if she were real, as if she were in fact all there is of reality. In this, he learned from Keats's fully formed and fully imagined relation to the autumn goddess, whom Keats begins by celebrating in tones of worship and ends by consoling in the accents of intimacy: "Think not of them, thou hast thy music too."

Keats's third stanza gave Stevens his crickets, his bare spaces, and all his autumn refrains of thinning music. But, more centrally, it invited him to participate in its debate on the value of a diminished music, and in its speculation on the relation of that music to the ampler choirs of spring. Stevens recognized, I think, that Keats's ode is spoken by one whose poetic impetus arises from a recoil at the stubble plains; the method of the ode is to adopt a reparatory fantasy whereby the barren plains are "repopulated" with fruit, flowers, wheat, and a providential goddess. But Keats subsides, at the end, into the barrenness which had first stimulated his compensatory imagination, and he leaves in the fields nothing but his poem—that autumnal thin music—where there had briefly been an imagined feast for sight and touch.

Nostalgia, so gently put aside by Keats when his goddess sighs for the songs of spring, is more vindictively suppressed by Stevens in one of the more astonishing poetic descendants of the ode. "Think not of them," says Keats to that part of himself which has looked longingly backward to the nightingales' spring songs. Stevens begins his corresponding late passage in "Puella Parvula" by telling us that "every thread of summer is at last unwoven." It is the "season of memory, / When the leaves fall like things mournful of the past." But over the dissolving wind, "the mighty imagination triumphs," saying to inner nostalgia not Keats's kind words but rather,

> Keep quiet in the heart, O wild bitch. O mind
> Gone wild, be what he tells you to be: *Puella.*
> Write *pax* across the window pane. And then
>
> Be still. The *summarium in excelsis* begins.

The taming of mind to the season is common to Keats and Stevens, but Stevens' regret, the regret of the man who rarely had the satisfactions of summer, is more bitter. What is left from romance is "the rotted rose," and the later poet must squeeze "the reddest fragrance from the stump / Of summer." The violence of the modern supervenes on the Romantic sunset.

These, as Stevens would say, are only instances. For Stevens' grandest meditation on "To Autumn" we must look to two of his long poems. "Credences of Summer" centers on the moment when "the hay, / Baked through long days, is piled in mows," the moment before the stubble plains. "The Auroras of Autumn" centers on the approach of "boreal night" after "the season changes." The light wind of Keats's soft-dying day modulates into a fiercer form: "A cold wind chills the beach." The stubble plains, at the end of "The Auroras," are metaphorically ignited to form the flares of the aurora borealis, "the lights / Like a blaze of summer straw, in winter's nick." In between "Credences" and "Auroras," radiating back to the one and forward to the other, stands Keats's ode.

The boldness of "Credences of Summer" lies in its suggestion that the perception of Keats's bees—that "warm days will never cease"— is no self-deception to be patronized, however wistfully, by the poet, but rather one of the authentic human states of being:

> . . . Fill the foliage with arrested peace,
> Joy of such permanence, right ignorance
> Of change still possible . . .
> > The utmost must be good and is
> And is our fortune and honey hived in the trees.

And yet Stevens knows that the song of "summer in the common fields" is sung by singers not themselves partaking of that summer, just as Keats's ode of summer fruition and repose is sung by one gazing at the shorn stubble fields. Stevens' singers are "far in the woods":

> Far in the woods they sang their unreal songs,
> Secure. It was difficult to sing in face
> Of the object. The singers had to avert themselves
> Or else avert the object. Deep in the woods
> They sang of summer in the common fields.
>
> They sang desiring an object that was near,
> In face of which desire no longer moved,
> Nor made of itself that which it could not find.

In spite of this admission that singers sing out of desire rather than out of satisfaction, Stevens' poem begins, as Keats's does, with the benevolent fiction that the singers are in the midst of the landscape they celebrate:

> Young broods
> Are in the grass, the roses are heavy with a weight
> Of fragrance and the mind lays by its trouble.

This is the moment of the marriage of earth and sky, the time of conspiracy between the sky-god, the sun, and the earth-goddess, the queen, to produce the young broods: this is "green's apogee / And happiest folk-land, mostly marriage hymns."

Keats had begun his ode with the symbolic marriage of earth and air, but had sketched it with the lightest of suggestions: in Stevens the family constellation appears and reappears, as he draws Keats out to iconic completion:

> These fathers standing round,
> These mothers touching, speaking, being near,
> These lovers waiting in the soft dry grass.

The queen is "the charitable majesty of her whole kin," and "the bristling soldier" is "a filial form and one / Of the land's children, easily born." Like the earthly paradise where flowers and fruits coexist, this paradise contains harmoniously all stages of human existence—the young broods, lovers, fathers and mothers, and an old man—but its chief emblem is "the youth, the vital son, the heroic power," the filial form whom age cannot touch. Yet, after the admission that "a mind exists, aware of division," the heroic attempt to maintain the privileged moment falters, and Stevens' more grotesque version of stubble fields makes its appearance, with a presiding form resembling Keats's redbreast. There is even a recollection of Keats's river sallows:

> Fly low, cock bright, and stop on a bean pole, Let
> Your brown breast redden, while you wait for warmth.
> With one eye watch the willow, motionless.
> The gardener's cat is dead, the gardener gone
> And last year's garden grows salacious weeds.

Keats's twice-repeated "soft" appears in this canto: "Soft, civil bird," and "not / So soft." For the agricultural laborer-goddess and

her creatures Stevens substitutes the gardener and his cat, deriving
the gardener perhaps from Keats's "gardener Fancy" in the "Ode
to Psyche." Stevens' way of solving the encroachments of decay on
his scene of happiness is to attribute to his singers, although they
are only the creations of "an inhuman author," a will of their own,
as though the author is himself mastered by the rise of desire in
the hearts of his characters:

> . . . The characters speak because they want
> To speak, the fat, the roseate characters,
> Free, for a moment, from malice and sudden cry,
> Complete in a completed scene, speaking
> Their parts as in a youthful happiness.

These characters who speak of their own free will resemble
Keats's creatures, who, in spite of the season's sadness, sing their
own music. It is clear from Stevens' ending that "malice and sudden
cry" are likely to be the ordinary states of the characters of the
inhuman author, and that the miraculous lifting for a moment of
their usual oppressive state enables, not youthful happiness, but a
state resembling it. Seen in this way, "Credences of Summer" becomes, like "To Autumn," a backward-glancing poem, as its author,
for a moment liberated from misery, looks for the perfect metaphor
for the feeling he experiences in that moment and decides that youthful hapiness (after spring's infuriations are over, after one's mortify-
ing adolescent foolish selves are slaughtered) is the vehicle he needs.
It is only in retrospect that we see the hovering of a divided mental
state at the end of the second stanza:

> This is the last day of a certain year
> Beyond which there is nothing left of time.
> It comes to this and the imagination's life.

"This"—the perfect day—staves off for a while the full realization
of the other—the imagination's life. But by the end of the poem, in
the meditation on the observant mind, imagination is in the ascendant and the rich day has decayed into the salacious garden. The
war in the poem between the warmth of Keatsian language and the
chill of metaphysical analysis means that Stevens has not achieved
a style which would embrace both the physical pine and the metaphysical pine. The presentation of summer cannot coexist, in tone
or diction, with the anatomy of summer; and the anatomy, skirted
and then suppressed in Keats in favor of self-forgetfulness, is al-

lowed full play by Stevens. If the bees are given credence, so is the undeceiving questioning of the aloof, divided mind, and Stevens' poem, unable to maintain a Keatsian harmony, divides sharply in consequence of its "mind, aware of division."

If "Credences of Summer" goes both backward from Keats and further with his questioning (thereby losing the miraculous, if precarious Keatsian balance), "The Auroras of Autumn" fastens on the question "Where are the songs of spring?" and makes a poetics of it. Keats stops in autumn to imagine spring and rebukes himself for his nostalgia, which implies a criticism of the season in which he finds himself. "Think not of them," he says of the spring songs. Stevens, in contrast, decides to think deliberately about them. What does it mean—for life, for poetry—that we cannot rest in the present, in any present? It means that the desire for change is more deep-rooted than the pleasure of any permanence, no matter how luxurious:

> Is there an imagination that sits enthroned
> As grim as it is benevolent, the just
> And the unjust, which in the midst of summer stops
>
> To imagine winter?

Every making of the mind moves to find "what must unmake it and, at last, what can." After being "fattened as on a decorous honeycomb," "we lay sticky with sleep," like Keats's bees. Stevens is Keatsian in accepting the fact of change; he is also Keatsian in his elegiac strain, substituting a Keatsian "farewell" for the even more Keatsian "adieu":

> Farewell to an idea ... A cabin stands,
> Deserted, on a beach.

Stevens is Keatsian, too, in making the goddess who presides over the dissolution of the season a maternal figure who says not farewell or adieu but (as to children) good-night, good-night:

> Farewell to an idea ... The mother's face,
> The purpose of the poem, fills the room.
>
> She gives transparence. But she has grown old.
> The necklace is a carving not a kiss.

Stevens offers a critique of Keats by leaping over Keats's set piece of sunset and twilight bird song and taking his poem beyond the

death of the mother, after sunset, into boreal night. The birds, instead of going downward to darkness or gathering into a Keatsian
flock, are set wildly flying:

> The theatre is filled with flying birds,
> Wild wedges, as of a volcano's smoke.

Across his sky Stevens displays his auroras, his earthly equivalent
to the heavenly serpent-god sloughing skins at the opening of the
poem, both symbols of change. The auroras are beautiful and intimi-
dating at once; they leave us in the state of Keats's gnats and bleating
lambs, "a shivering residue, chilled and foregone." The auroras
change "idly, the way / A season changes color to no end, / Except
the lavishing of itself in change." All natural changes are equal;
there is no entropy in nature; all events are simply songs of "the
innocent mother." The spectre of the spheres, like the inhuman
author of "Credences of Summer," contrives a balance to contrive
a whole. This new poetic wishes not only to relish everything equally
(in itself a Keatsian ideal), but to relish everything at once, to
imagine winter in summer and summer in winter, to meditate

> The full of fortune and the full of fate,
> As if he lived all lives, that he might know,
>
> In hall harridan, not hushful paradise,
> To a haggling of wind and weather, by these lights
> Like a blaze of summer straw, in winter's nick.

This finale of "The Auroras" is an implicit boast. Everything, however, is intrinsically less expressible than something. The close of
the poem is less beautiful than the vision of the aurora itself. In
this respect Stevens is Keatsian, substituting one form of landscape,
the later auroras, for another, the Romantic sunset.

An earlier poem of Stevens arises from the Keatsian injunction
that prompted "The Auroras"—"Think not of them"—and is in
fact an extended thinking-and-not-thinking; "The Snow Man"
might well be called "The Man Standing in the Stubble Plains."
Snow, like harvest, eliminates vegetation; and Stevens, like Keats,
faces the question of how to praise a world from which the summer
growth has disappeared. Keats's "light wind" blowing over the bare
fields is intensified, always, in Stevens into a "wind" of "winter"
(and Stevens relishes the phonemic echo). Oddly enough, beheld

with a mind of winter, the world does not appear bare: the boughs of the pine trees are crusted with snow, the junipers are shagged with ice, the spruces are rough in the distant glitter of the January sun. It is only with the introduction of the wind, and misery and the few remaining leaves on the deciduous trees that the world becomes "the same bare place" and the regarder and beholder—who saw such a rich world—becomes a listener who, nothing himself, "beholds / Nothing that is not there and the nothing that is." The turn from beholding to listening, borrowed from Keats's ode, coincides, as it does in Keats, with a pained turning from plenitude to absence. But Keats finds a new plenitude—of the ear—to substitute for the visual absence. Stevens, finding it impossible to sustain the plenitude perceivable by a mind of winter—that plenitude of encrustation, shagginess and rough snow-glitter—reverses Keats and finds bareness in listening. He turns, therefore, from the Keatsian trope of plenitude—enumeration—which he had employed in his listing of pines, junipers, and spruce trees, and uses instead a trope of reductiveness, becoming a modernist of minimal art: he hears, in a deadly repetition of the same few words (italics mine),

> *the sound of the wind*
> *the sound of* a few leaves
> *the sound of the* land
> full *of the same wind*
> that is blowing *in the same* bare place
> for the *listener* who *listens in the* snow
> and, *nothing* himself, beholds
> *nothing that is* not there
> and the *nothing that is.*

Another fairly early attempt at "thinking with the season" occurs in "Anatomy of Montomy," where Stevens, conceding the pathetic fallacy, urges us to have it on nature's terms, not our own. Since the earth "bore us as a part of all the things / It breeds," it follows that "our nature is her nature":

> Hence it comes,
> Since by our nature we grow old, earth grows
> The same. We parallel the mother's death.

But the earth has a wider vision than our narrow personal pathos:

She walks an autumn ampler than the wind
Cries up for us and colder than the frost
Pricks in our spirits at the summer's end,
And over the bare spaces of our skies
She sees a barer sky that does not bend.

This widening of perspective is borrowed from Keats too, though it applies Keats's technique (broadening from the cottage and its kitchen garden and orchard to the cornfields and outbuildings and finally extending to the horizon, the boundary hill and hedges, the river, and the sky) only to the bare spaces of Keats's final stanza. It seems, as we read Stevens, that each aspect of the autumn ode called out to him to be reinterpreted, reused, re-created into a poem.

Much later, in "World without Peculiarity," Stevens "rewrites" "Anatomy of Monotony," achieving at last, however briefly, the power to think with the season. What is most human is now no longer (in Stevens' hard saying) sadness, pathos, nostalgia—that projection of ourselves into and onto other things which fail, die, or wane—but rather solitary existence as a natural object. Stevens may be remembering, in his extraordinary central stanza, Whitman's line about "the justified mother of men":

What good is it that the earth is justified,
That it is complete, that it is an end,
That in itself it is enough?

It is the earth itself that is humanity . . .
He is the inhuman son and she,
She is the fateful mother, whom he does not know.

She is the day.

Though there are here no verbal echoes of Keats, this seems to me a poem that could not have been thought of except by someone who had incorporated into his imagination that sense of the independent life of nature voiced in the autumn ode.

Just as Stevens' "Woman in Sunshine" removes the mythological solidity from Keats's goddess in the fields and reminds us of what she is, a fictive construct, so "Less and Less Human, O Savage Spirit" wishes for a god both silent and quiet, "saying things," if he must, as light and color and shape "say things," a god who "will not hear us when we speak." This god, unable to say "Where are the songs of spring," is at once more earthly and more disembodied than Keats's goddess, pressing further toward the fictive and the inanimate at once.

Always in Stevens there is a new precipitate from the Keatsian solution, because mind and sense cannot coexist in equilibrium. No writer, in Stevens' view, could avoid the asking of the fatal question about the songs of spring. Stevens writes, in "The Ultimate Poem is Abstract," a second-order reflection on the inevitability of questions: Keats (or a poet like him) is treated ironically and called "the lecturer / On This Beautiful World of Ours," who "hems the planet rose and haws it rope, / And red, and right." But his hemming and hawing into roses and rosehips and red haws cannot last:

> One goes on asking questions. That, then, is one
> Of the categories. So said, this placid space
>
> Is changed. It is not so blue as we thought. To be blue,
> There must be no questions.
>   . . . It would be enough
> If we were ever, just once, at the middle, fixed
> In This Beautiful World of Ours and not as now,
>
> Helplessly at the edge, enough to be
> Complete, because at the middle, if only in sense,
> And in that enormous sense, merely enjoy.

Such a poem is a rewriting, at a second-order level, of the Keats ode; it recounts in an abstract way Keats's attempt to remain "at the middle" of the beautiful world, praising its generosity to all the senses, its plenitude of being. The invasion of Keats's enjoyment by questioning, an *event* in the ode, becomes a *topic* for Stevens. And in other poems Stevens comments on each stage of the Keatsian process—how one sees first the earth "as inamorata," but then sees her "without distance . . . and naked or in rags, / Shrunk in the poverty of being close." She has been a celestial presence among laborers, an angel surrounded by paysans, an "archaic form / . . . evoking an archaic space." But then her appurtenances fade (the moon is "a tricorn / waved in pale adieu") and "she is exhausted and a little old" ("Things of August").

Stevens' late poetry of receptivity and inception, coming after the poetry of age and exhaustion, is nothing short of astonishing. Here Stevens follows Keats's "Human Seasons" beyond the winter of gross misfeature, finding "the cricket of summer forming itself out of ice," "not autumn's prodigal returned, / But an antipodal, far-fetched creature" ("A Discovery of Thought"). As he listens to winter sounds in "A Quiet Normal Life," he hears "the crickets' chords, / Babbling each one, the uniqueness of its sound," and decides to do without the archaic forms:

> There was no fury in transcendent forms.
> But his actual candle blazed with artifice.

Stevens forgoes (in "Looking across the Fields and Watching the Birds Fly") "the masculine myths we used to make" in favor of "a transparency through which the swallow weaves, / Without any form or any sense of form," and he decides that our thinking is nothing but our preestablished harmony with the grand motions of nature:

> We think, then, as the sun shines or does not.
> We think as wind skitters on a pond in a field . . .
>
> The spirit comes from the body of the world . . .
>
> The mannerism of nature caught in a glass
> And there become a spirit's mannerism,
> A glass aswarm with things going as far as they can.

This sublime self-transformation into a modern version of an Aeolian harp immolates the mind. If we pose questions, it is because the earth poses them. There is no longer any need to say "Think not of them": everything is permitted, because everything is a natural motion.

Stevens' last tribute to the stubble plains is his transmutation of Keats's bareness into "The Plain Sense of Things." This poem presses Keats's *donnée* to its ultimate point. There is no goddess, even a dying one; there is no memorial gleam cast through rosy clouds; there is no music; there are no touching filial forms; the surrogate animal for the human is not the laden honeybee, but the inquisitive pond rat:

> After the leaves have fallen, we return
> To a plain sense of things. It is as if
> We had come to an end of the imagination,
> Inanimate in an inert savoir . . .
>
> Yet the absence of the imagination had
> Itself to be imagined. The great pond,

The plain sense of it, without reflections, leaves,
Mud, water like dirty glass, expressing silence

Of a sort, silence of a rat come out to see,
The great pond and its waste of the lilies, all this
Had to be imagined as an inevitable knowledge,
Required, as a necessity requires.

"To Autumn" represented, for Keats, a retraction of the "Ode to Psyche." In the earlier ode Keats had hoped that the imagination could be fully reparatory for an external absence; piece by piece, in "Psyche" he constructs his interior fane to compensate, warmly and luxuriously, for the earthly temple that the goddess lacks. By the time he writes "To Autumn," he has lost, not the impulse (his impulse on seeing uninhabited stubble plains is to go home and write a stanza loaded and blessed with fruit and to invent an indwelling harvest goddess), but the ability to close with "a bright torch, and a casement ope at night, / To let the warm Love in!" "The absence of fantasia" in the bare fields might have tempted Stevens earlier to a compensatory opulence of reconstruction (like his populating his cabin with four daughters with curls in "The Comedian"), but now he finds a discipline in poverty. The comedian Crispin had boasted that he would find "a new reality" at last in another detail borrowed from Keats and expanded into its own poem: an unmusical bird cry. The "wailful choir" of the autumn ode gives way, in Stevens' poetry of old age, to an imagined choir of aubade, as Stevens draws the ode forward from its sunset into the new sunrise of "Not Ideas about the Thing but the Thing Itself":

At the earliest ending of winter,
In March, a scrawny cry from outside
Seemed like a sound in his mind . . .

That scrawny cry—it was
A chorister whose c preceded the choir.
It was part of the colossal sun,

Surrounded by its choral rings,
Still far away. It was like
A new knowledge of reality.

There is no "new reality": there is only a "new knowledge of reality." The "marvellous sophomore" had boasted "Here was the veritable ding an sich, at last." But his boast was premature. Stevens did not find "the thing itself" until very late, and then in a scale

Keatsian in its humility. "Not Ideas about the Thing but the Thing Itself" is Stevens' most beautiful late reflection on his own beginnings (as the comedian as the letter "C" becomes the chorister whose "c" preceded the choir) and on Keats's ode and its minimal music. Nonetheless I close not with this last successful meditation but instead with a poem that in its own relative failure shows Stevens' stubborn ambition, even at the expense of violent dislocation of form, to have plenitude and poverty at once, to possess Keats's central divine figure opulently whole and surrounded by her filial forms, while at the same time asserting the necessary obsolescence of her form and of the literature about her. She remains, he asserts, for all her inevitable vanishing, "The Hermitage at the Centre":

> The leaves on the macadam make a noise—
> How soft the grass on which the desired
> Reclines in the temperature of heaven—
>
> Like tales that were told the day before yesterday—
> Sleek in a natural nakedness,
> She attends the tintinnabula—
>
> And the wind sways like a great thing tottering—
> Of birds called up by more than the sun,
> Birds of more wit, that substitute—
>
> Which suddenly is all dissolved and gone—
> Their intelligible twittering
> For unintelligible thought.
>
> And yet this end and this beginning are one,
> And one last look at the ducks is a look
> At lucent children round her in a ring.

Stevens' response to Keats's ode was so long-lived that the central problems of the ode—process, termination, interruption of ripeness, the human seasons, the beauty of the minimal, the function of nostalgia, the relation between sense and thought, and so on—became central to Stevens' poetry as well. His attempts to go "beyond" Keats in various ways—to take the human seasons further, into winter, into boreal apocalypse, into inception; to find new imagery of his own, while retaining Keats's crickets and bees and birds and sun and fields; to create his own archaic forms in the landscape—define in their evolution Stevens' own emerging originality. Though he retains a classical structure to his verse, his diction and rhetoric become ever less visibly Romantic, as a plain sense of things and an absence of fantasia supervene. Everywhere we hear Stevens meditating on Keats, whose fashion of beholding without comment must have seemed to Stevens prophetically modern. Stevens sensed that the poem of presentation was the poem of earth: Just to behold, just to be beheld, what is there here but weather—these are the assumptions Stevens found and grasped for himself in the most untranscendental of the great Romantic odes.

Apollo's Harsher Songs

"The words of Mercury," Armado says at the close of Love's Labor's Lost, "are harsh after the songs of Apollo." Apollo's songs, like those of Orpheus, are conventionally thought to be full "of linkèd sweetness long drawn out," but the criterion of sweetness or melodiousness has always been questioned by our greater poets. On the whole, Wallace Stevens is still considered one of the euphonious, "sweet," "aesthetic" poets, against whom the anthologies range our modern realists and ironists. There is some truth in the opposition, of course, or it would not have been made: "The Idea of Order at Key West" sounds different from "The Waste Land." I choose here to enter Stevens' work by way of an interrogation of his harsher poems, those in which a brutality of thought or diction reveals feelings obscured by playfulness or obliqueness in his more decorative poems. I do this in part because I think the role of feeling in Stevens' poems has not yet been clarified. It is popularly believed that Stevens is a poet preoccupied by the relations between the imagination and reality, and there is good reason for the popular belief, since Stevens so often phrased his own preoccupation in those unrevealing words. The formula, properly understood, is not untrue; but we must ask what causes the imagination to be so painfully at odds with reality. The cause setting the two at odds is usually, in Stevens' case, passionate feeling, and not merely epistemological query.

One poem by which to enter this topic is "Chaos in Motion and Not in Motion" (1947); the title is itself unnerving as a violation of

"Apollo's Harsher Songs" first appeared in the AWP Newsletter, May 1979.

the axiom that a thing cannot be and not be in the same way at the same time:

> Oh, that this lashing wind was something more
> Than the spirit of Ludwig Richter . . .

> The rain is pouring down. It is July.
> There is lightning and the thickest thunder.

> It is a spectacle. Scene 10 becomes 11,
> In Series X, Act IV, et cetera.

> People fall out of windows, trees tumble down,
> Summer is changed to winter, the young grow old,

> The air is full of children, statues, roofs
> And snow. The theatre is spinning round,

> Colliding with deaf-mute churches and optical trains.
> The most massive sopranos are singing songs of scales.

> And Ludwig Richter, turbulent Schlemihl,
> Has lost the whole in which he was contained,

> Knows desire without an object of desire,
> All mind and violence and nothing felt.

> He knows he has nothing more to think about,
> Like the wind that lashes everything at once.

The poem is composed of many reminiscences of former poems; it treats its subject with a mixture of comedy, irony, pathos, and brutality. I isolate Stevens' moments of brutality toward himself and his life because brutality, in Stevens (and in other poets as well), is usually a sign of extreme discomfort, misery, and self-hatred. Many of Stevens' poems—read from one angle, most of the best poems—spring from catastrophic disappointment, bitter solitude, or personal sadness. It is understandable that Stevens, a man of chilling reticence, should illustrate his suffering in its largest possible terms. That practice does not obscure the nature of the suffering, which concerns the collapse of early hopeful fantasies of love, companionship, success, and self-transformation. As self and beloved alike become, with greater or lesser velocity, the final dwarfs of themselves, and as social awareness diminishes dreams of self-transcendence, the poet sees dream, hope, love, and trust—those activities of the most august imagination—crippled, contradicted, dissolved, called into question, embittered. This history is the history of every intelligent and receptive human creature, as the illimitable claims on existence made by each one of us are checked, baffled, frustrated, and reproved—whether by our own subsequent perceptions of their impossible grandiosity, or by the accidents of fate and chance, or by our betrayal of others, or by old age and its failures of capacity. In spite of the severe impersonality of Stevens' style, in spite even of his (often transparent) personae, it is himself of whom he writes. He has been too little read as a poet of human misery.

The human problem—stated late but very baldly in "Chaos in Motion and Not in Motion"—is that its hero "Has lost the whole in which he was contained, / Knows desire without an object of desire, / All mind and violence and nothing felt." I do violence to these lines in detaching them from what precedes and follows them, but I do so for a reason. More often than not, the human pang in Stevens is secreted inconspicuously in the poem, instead of being announced in the title or in the opening lines. It is the usual, if mistaken, way of commentators to begin at the beginning and to take Stevens' metaphysical or epistemological prolegomena as the real subject of the poem, when in fact they are the late plural of the subject, whose early candor of desire reposes further down the page. And so I isolate what I take to be the psychological or human "beginning" of the poem, its point of origin in feeling, which, though it comes late in the poem, serves as the center from which the other lines radiate.

This center, which I have just quoted, tells us that the worst thing that can happen to a poet has happened to its hero: he has stopped having feelings. In Stevens' words, he is "all mind and violence and nothing felt." Since feeling—to use Wordsworthian terms—is the organizing principle of poetry (both narratively, insofar as poetry is a history of feeling, and structurally, insofar as poetry is a science or analysis of feeling), without feeling the world of the poet is a chaos. As we know, as the poet knows, the absence of feeling is itself —since the poet is still alive—a mask for feelings too powerful to make themselves felt: these manifest themselves in this poem as that paradoxical "desire without an object of desire," libido unfocused and therefore churning out in all directions—like a wind, as the last line of the poem says, "that lashes everything at once." Unfocused and chaotic libido does not provide a channel along which thought can move. Once there is an object of desire, the mind can exert all its familiar diversions—decoration, analysis, speculation, fantasy, drama, and so on. But with no beloved object, the mind is at a loss; the hero of the poem has "lost the whole in which he was contained . . . / He knows he has nothing more to think about." The landscape is the objective correlative to this state of mind: "There is lightning and the thickest thunder."

The poem, as I have so far described it, ought to be a poem of *sturm und drang,* beset by the turbulent wind of desire, surrounded by its attendant *donner und blitzen.* But the brutality of the poem is that it treats its own problem with indifferent irony. The hero is "Ludwig Richter, turbulent Schlemihl," and his sufferings are watched through a monocle:

> It is a spectacle. Scene 10 becomes 11,
> In Series X, Act IV, et cetera.

This passage is a self-quotation from "Like Decorations in a Nigger Cemetery," in which inception itself is satirized:

> An opening of portals when night ends,
> A running forward, arms stretched out as drilled.
> Act I, Scene I, at a German Staats-Oper. (XIX)

We all begin in the hope of romantic embrace: by the time "Chaos in Motion" is written we have moved on from Act I, Scene I, to the tenth series of performances in the Staats-Oper, and in that tenth series we are in the fourth act of some play, and in that fourth act we are moving from scene 10 to scene 11: in short, we are almost to Act V. And surely Series X is the last of the season. The poet has watched these operatic performances of desire too many times: like anyone middle-aged he has ceased to believe in the "running forward, arms stretched out"—but the wild thrashing of unfocused desire continues. It has preoccupied Stevens elsewhere; in "Puella Parvula":

> Keep quiet in the heart, O wild bitch. O mind
> Gone wild, be what he tells you to be. *Puella.*

In "Chaos in Motion" Stevens quotes another early poem, the triumphant "Ploughing on Sunday." There, while his docile neighbors troop off to church, the poet, violating the Sabbath, blasphemously harnesses his team to the plough and takes to the fields, full of indiscriminate joy in the sun and wind alike: in that poem, "the wind pours down," while now "the rain is pouring down." It is July, the month of credences of summer, when the plenitude of desire was felt in the past, and the mind could lay by its trouble. Now, in disbelief in the existence of any object of desire, the old seasonal myth of sun and love is abandoned, and with icy detachment Stevens enunciates all conceivable tragedies as though they could be watched with ultimate *froideur:* suicide, "people fall out of windows"; the decay of nature, "trees tumble down"; the ice age, "summer is changed to winter"; decline, "the young grow old"; violation of natural process in a chaotic upheaval of life and art, "the air is full of children, statues, roofs / And snow." The *theatrum mundi* itself collapses, its fall coincident with the collapse of its impotent institutions and its stage scenery: "The theatre is spinning round, / Colliding with deaf-mute churches and optical trains." In this Götterdämmerung, harmony itself is reduced to elemental monotony: "The most massive sopranos are singing songs of scales."

All of this is normally material for elegy, and most of it has been or will be material for elegy in Stevens:

> The last leaf that is going to fall has fallen.
>
> She is exhausted and a little old.
>
> The general was rubbish in the end.
>
> A cabin stands, deserted, on a beach.

A roof abandoned, a statue broken, a leafless tree, a fall of rain, a beloved grown old, a church of bird-nest arches and of rain-stained vaults, a theater or capitol collapsing—all can elicit lament, and do, except when Stevens is being brutal. In "Chaos in Motion" the unbearable acceleration and offhand inventory of the spectacle—"People fall out of windows, trees tumble down, / Summer is changed to winter, the young grow old"—borrows a common cinematic brutality (used in film for comic effect)—to reproduce the look of the *theatrum mundi* to the eyes of the old, who have seen the cycle too many times repeated. The old seraph in "Notes" has seen too many springs:

> The Italian girls wore jonquils in their hair
> And these the seraph saw, had seen long since,
> In the bandeaux of the mothers, would see again.

The seraph has gone though his own cycles of seraphic chasity and Saturnalian desire (when he turns to a satyr): he has desired the mothers and the daughters alike, and has turned from both in surfeit and disbelief. Even in spring, the world, to this jaded Stevens, seems "a withered scene."

Stevens' grand claim on us in his later poems is his willingness to refuse lyric emotions. The truth is, he tells us, that the old detach themselves from empathy and, with a certain weary sense of déjà vu, see their grandchildren predictably rising to adolescent erotic idolatry and entrusting themselves to Summer's warmth, only, in their turn, to encounter failure, loss, cold, age, and death. One greets this spectacle, in middle age, without the tragic emotions with which one passed through the cycle oneself. And yet there is no diminution in desire: there is only a loss of belief in a possible object adequate to desire. The tonelessness with which Stevens recounts the disastrous events around him is meant to reflect his own sense of inevitable and repetitive human fate. And yet tonelessness is the ultimate lyric risk. The reader who can penetrate irony, brutality, rapidity, and tonelessness to see behind them a catastrophic loss of feeling, a fear of unleashed libido with no conceivable object, and the despair of a mind of genius that has nothing more to think about, will read "Chaos in Motion and Not in Motion" as a poem reflecting one of the fundamental miseries of the old.

The brutality of style I have dwelt on in "Chaos in Motion" has early roots in Stevens, but when it appears in *Harmonium* it is usually preceded or followed by some softening of perception. Two cases exhibiting this softening must suffice: in "Anecdote of the Prince of Peacocks" Stevens meets his own potential madness; in "The Apostrophe to Vincentine" he meets the unaccommodated object of desire before she has been clothed in the beauty of fantasy. Each poem is distanced by being given a rhetorical title—"Anecdote of," "Apostrophe to"— so that, even though they are, unusually for Stevens, written in the first person, they scarcely share at all in the lyric convention of personal experience. The poet—here, the Prince of Peacocks, full of showiness and *superbia*—meets the Saxon-named Berserk: he meets him in the realm of poetry—sleep and moonlight. But Berserk is "sharp as the sleepless," a phrase suggesting that if the Prince of Peacocks should wake into the dread sunlight of experience, he would go mad. The impossibility of the poet's evading Berserk, even in dreams, is the purport of the colloquy between the two. When the poet asks, "Why are you red / In this milky blue? . . . / Why sun-colored, / As if awake / In the midst of sleep?" Berserk answers that he sets his traps in the midst of dreams, forcing the poet to recognize the hazards of mentality even in the kingdoms of escape. At this point in the poem the diction turns brutal:

> I knew from this
> That the blue ground
> Was full of blocks
> And blocking steel.

However, Stevens' retreat from brutality into incantation is immediate:

> I knew the dread
> Of the bushy plain
> And the beauty
> Of the moonlight
> Falling there,
> Falling
> As sleep falls
> In the innocent air.

This is an unrewarding ending to a poem which began so promisingly as an exploration of the threats—reaching even to breakdown—posed by consciousness.

"The Apostrophe to Vincentine" is a bolder poem. The female, imagined naked, is nothing more to her poet than a lean, small, white, nameless animal, dwarfed by the magnitude of the scale of earth and sky. Nevertheless, the poem allows her to preexist this reductive imagining. She is already, in the poet's mind, Heavenly Vincentine; he is already enamored. Still, he engages in the deliberate aesthetic exercise of depriving her of all interiority and humanness and exterior garments, trying to see her as a purely visual object, an isolated biological phenomenon. This peculiar exercise prefigures Stevens' later enterprises of viewing the *ding-an-sich*. But it is one thing to try to see the sun or a March morning without evasion; to see the Platonic beloved in this way is in itself deeply repellent to Stevens. Melodramatically he affixes Roman numerals to each stage of Vincentine's appearance. Number I, though reserving the final repellency—animality—for later, otherwise presents the unadorned female figure in pure visuality:

> I figured you as nude between
> Monotonous earth and dark blue sky.
> It made you seem so small and lean
> And nameless,
> Heavenly Vincentine.

In II, Vincentine is allowed warmth (that is to say, her poet is allowed to see her as flesh, not only as outline). She is given a dress
to wear, a modified green (like that worn by the spring "queen . . .
in slipper green") to contrast with the monotonous earth and dark
blue sky. She is also given hair (as a modified brunette). Peculiarly,
her other attribute besides warmth is cleanliness; one suspects the
exigencies of rhyme:

> I saw you then, as warm as flesh,
> Brunette,
> But yet not too brunette,
> As warm, as clean
> Your dress was green,
> Was whited green,
> Green Vincentine.

In III, Vincentine is allowed, so to speak, a soul, exhibited in her
independent motion; she is also placed in a society, so that her voice
can be heard and so that she can express feeling:

> Then you came walking,
> In a group
> Of human others,
> Voluble.
> Yes: you came walking,
> Vincentine.
> Yes: you came talking.

In her progressive assumption of human attributes as she approaches the poet, Vincentine changes from a tiny animal outline
in the cosmic scale to a living woman, around whom the cosmos
falls into place. She becomes in fact the heavenly or Platonic axis
on which all creation turns, rendering monotonous earth no longer
monotonous but rather a place imbued with her reality. Or so we
believe when the fourth stanza begins:

> And what I knew you felt
> Came then.
> Monotonous earth I saw become
> Illimitable spheres of you.

This transformatory rhetoric generally leaves behind the original
dwarfed state and leads to the language of apotheosis. Stevens, after

accomplishing the apotheosis of earth, refuses to remain on the level of the glorified and re-does his apotheosis twice more, each time reiterating Vincentine's original state of nude leanness, but making her, as she was not at the beginning, a "white animal," in the uneasy phrase, "that white animal, so lean":

> Monotonous earth I saw become
> Illimitable spheres of you,
> And that white animal, so lean,
> Turned Vincentine,
> Turned heavenly Vincentine,
> And that white animal, so lean,
> Turned heavenly, heavenly Vincentine.

Brutality and apotheosis end in a stalemate. We remember Vincentine at least as powerfully in her repellent incarnation as a white animal so lean as in her named and transfigured state, brunette, dressed, walking, talking, and feeling. The poem shows us a mind willing and welcoming the decor of thought and fancy, while unable to rid itself of primal reductiveness and visual disgust. The reductive diction, telling us in itself that poetry and apotheosis are *not* one, but remain in a problematic relation, marks the speaker as a man caught between the nameless lean, on the one hand, and illimitable spheres of the beloved, on the other. There is no diction equally appropriate to both.

In an altogether harsher poem from *Harmonium*, Stevens subjects his own idealizations to ridicule. "The Virgin Carrying a Lantern," an unsettling poem with a Pre-Raphaelite title, embodies Stevens' brutality in the negress who watches malevolently the more seraphic and elegiac postures of life and supposes "things false and wrong" about "the lantern of the beauty / Who walks there." The poem pretends to ally itself unequivocally in its declarations with the innocent virgin:

> There are no bears among the roses,
> Only a negress who supposes
> Things false and wrong
>
> About the lantern of the beauty
> Who walks there, as a farewell duty,
> Walks long and long.
>
> The pity that her pious egress
> Should fill the vigil of a negress
> With heat so strong!

The simpering Victorian voice, reproving the negress' suppositions as "false and wrong," expressing indignation at the negress' strong "heat" ("the pity" of it!), and endorsing the "pious egress" of the virgin, is entirely contradicted by the brutal left-hand side, so to speak, of Stevens' diptych: if the negress supposes bears, it is because she is acquainted with bears, while the virgin knows only roses; the negress is in the dark, the virgin bears a lantern; the negress, with her strong "heat," is sexual, the virgin chaste; the negress an impious spy, the virgin a pious vestal. The trouble with the virgin's universe, which would be pleasing if it contained only roses, dutiful virgins, lanterns, and pious farewells, is that it contains the negress, her vigil, her heat, and her suppositions. The negress makes the virgin ridiculous; no one engaged in a "pious egress" can ever be poetically respectable. The negress' heat has the last word. The poem may be seen as a rewriting of Blake's lamb and tiger: the virgin is what Melville would have called a radiant ninny, but there is none of Blake's admiration for his tiger embodied in Stevens' figure for the dark, for the heated, and for the bestial in himself.

These earliest examples from *Harmonium*—Berserk, the animal Vincentine, and the negress—show Stevens already aware of certain incompatibilities—between waking and dreaming, between the animal and the heavenly, between chaste piety and strong heat— against which his only defenses were a comic or ironic language, a rhetorical distance in entitling, a reduction of the lyric potential of the "I" who speaks, and, most of all, a rather tedious polar separation of imagery: the milky blue of moonlight opposed to the red of sunlight, the small animal Vincentine contrasted to the illimitable heavenly Vincentine, the pious virgin distinguished from the heated negress. Crispin thought placatingly that his life could be a voyaging "up and down between two elements," but the ranker element in "The Comedian" is described with too little of the brutality that honesty would dictate; instead, Stevens treats it with the same unchanged high rhetoric that is the vehicle for all of Crispin's experience. Crispin is not made sufficiently unhappy by the tension between his two elements: Berserk, who comes summoned by Stevens' incapacity to mediate between sun and moon, never invades "The Comedian."

If we turn our attention to the shape of Stevens' whole career, we can see three large phases in his management of this problem. (I would take "Chaos in Motion" as the harsh turning point between the second and third phases.) The first phase, represented by the poems I have instanced from *Harmonium,* resorted to certain concealments of tension, on the one hand, and to violent dislocations of sensibility, on the other. Both were attempts at accommodation, and brought Stevens to the state of misery in which he met the traditionally invulnerable Berserk, his traps, and his blocking steel.

The second phase finds Stevens attempting to exorcise these private tensions by resorting to a solution in the social order. As he tries to see depression as a social, rather than a personal, emotion, he thinks it may be ended by social cohesion rather than by interior resolution. An early example of a poem that goes very wrong— though the number of these is legion among the war poems—is "The Men That Are Falling." This poem begins wonderfully, in private loss, as the moon "burns in the mind on lost remembrances." As the poet leans on his bed, he realizes that the pull he feels to it is not the pull of sleepiness, but of desire:

> This is not sleep. This is desire.

> Ah! Yes, desire ... this leaning on his bed,
> This leaning on his elbows on his bed,

> Staring, at midnight, at the pillow that is black
> In the catastrophic room ... beyond despair,

> Like an intenser instinct. What is it he desires?

Some confrontation with the erotic lost remembrances evoked by the empty pillow where the beloved should lie is in order, but Stevens places instead an imagined head, a male one, on the pillow—"the head of one of the men that are falling," in part a double of himself, in part his opposite. A flicker of brutality is allowed to enter in the description of the iconic head, "thick-lipped from riot and rebellious cries," but the soldier is redeemed from the subhuman by the "immaculate syllables / That he spoke only by doing what he did." Stevens thinks to turn his attention here to those moral "words" of heroic action "that are life's voluble utterance," insisting that right action alone is the arena for the resolution of inner pain. But by turning the acts of soldiers into a form of utterance, he suggests that his own "immaculate syllables" spring as well from a form of death, symbolized by the absence of the inamorata on the pillow. Having died to her, he rises into syllables. The impotence he characteristically evokes in misery is "cured" in this poem by the dangerous example of the hero, always a seductive icon for Stevens. Just as he had tried in *Harmonium* for a euphony symbolized in the Infanta Marina, binding together nature, thought, and art, so in *Parts of a World* he imagines a synthesis among flying birds, marching soldiers, and rolling drums—the motions of nature, the motions of social action, and the motions of the music of war. The consequent self-effacement represents the effacement of the psychic problem of private misery, and the poet's aversion from the corresponding aesthetic problem of the relation of that misery to both art and nature. The oppositions between euphony and cacophony, harmony and eccentricity, the seraphic and the satiric, are in Stevens symbols for the discrepancy between the irresistible yearnings of desire and the irreversible misery at its failure. But the war poems turn the symbolic focus outward; as a result, they become forced.

In the notion, developed in several middle poems, of a contradictory plurality of "truths," Stevens began to solve conceptually the problem of the conflict between desire and loss. But the conceptual concession to plurality did not in itself invent a style representative of the several truths of appetite and failure. The evasions inherent in retaining an old style for new perceptions can be seen in the poem most clearly articulating the creed of plural truths, "On the Road Home":

> It was when I said,
> "There is no such thing as the truth,"
> That the grapes seemed fatter.
> The fox ran out of his hole.
>
> You ... You said,
> "There are many truths,
> But they are not parts of a truth."
> Then the tree, at night, began to change.

The two figures "said we stood alone." The man in "Anglais Mort à Florence" had stood at last "by God's help and the police," but here God and social institutions have disappeared. The narrator continues, in an argument against the Logos:

> "Words are not forms of a single word.
> In the sum of the parts, there are only the parts.
> The world must be measured by eye."

The "you" replies with a comparable indictment of idolatry:

51

"The idols have seen lots of poverty,
Snakes and gold and lice,
But not the truth."

These sentiments are all very well; they are anti-Platonic, nominalist, iconoclastic. The poem asserts that the expression of such dry sentiments enhances nature:

It was at that time that the silence was largest
And longest, the night was roundest,
The fragrance of the autumn warmest,
Closest and strongest.

The "rhyming" superlatives here suggest a Platonic extension and extrapolation of nature, as well as a Platonic coherence of the parts of nature; this extension, extrapolation, and coherence represent Stevens' unresolved wish that the sum of the parts should be more than the parts. Brutality of language ought to appear in coincidence with the absence of Platonic reassurance; in this poem the nominalist theme is not allowed its appropriate style.

It is one of Stevens' claims to greatness that he went on to invent a new style—the style of parts as parts, of words refusing to form a single word, of the many truths not part of "a" truth, the style of many of the most interesting late poems. For Stevens, one theoretical problem in inventing such a style lay in the suspicion that it would call metaphor into question. Metaphor implies analogy and resemblance, neither of which can be stable in a world of nonce effects. In *Harmonium* Stevens had decided, in "Metaphors of a Magnifico," to distinguish between fact (twenty man crossing a bridge into a village), distinctive individual experience (twenty men crossing twenty bridges into twenty villages), and collective perception (in which the twenty men become one man):

Twenty men crossing a bridge,
Into a village,
Are twenty men crossing twenty bridges,
Into twenty villages,
Or one man
Crossing a single bridge into a village.

This is old song
That will not declare itself ...

Brute fact, in the second essay at the rendering of this sight, seems to win the upper hand: "Twenty men crossing a bridge / Into a village, / Are / Twenty men crossing a bridge / Into a village." However, all speculation about the truths occurring on the far side of the copula is vanquished, finally, by the sensuous particulars of the scene, as the Magnifico ceases to be a philosopher of perception, ceases even to be a spectator, and becomes a participant:

> The boots of the men clump
> On the boards of the bridge.
> The first white wall of the village
> Rises through fruit-trees.
>
> Of what was it I was thinking?
>
> So the meaning escapes.
>
> The first white wall of the village ...
> The fruit trees ...

At one point the Magnifico's view had been as "certain as meaning," but in the sensual experience, "the meaning escapes." These separations between speculation and experience are still present in the absolute disjunction between the dispute on truth and the fat grapes of "On the Road Home."

The most strictly comparable poem in the later work to "Metaphors of a Magnifico" and "On the Road Home" is "The Motive for Metaphor," a poem in which the interpenetration of thought (with its consequent vocabulary of words, things, metaphor, expression, obscurity, motive, and so on) and sense (with *its* vocabulary of seasonal change, colors, moonlight, trees, clouds, and birds) is almost, except for the ending, complete. The partial truths, earlier so eagerly embraced as a solution for the absence of authority, now rightly take on the impoverished colors appropriate to them, instead of nostalgically imitating, in Platonic superlatives, the very consolations they were meant to forgo.

The degree of self-loathing Stevens felt in sacrificing his absolutist "Platonic" self—that which believed, with all an acolyte's sincerity, in religion, love, and art—is evident in the self-contempt at the beginning of "The Motive for Metaphor" with which he addresses his new, "partial" self:

You like it under the trees in autumn
Because everything is half dead.
The wind moves like a cripple among the leaves
And repeats words without meaning.

In the same way, you were happy in spring,
With the half colors of quarter-things,
The slightly brighter sky, the melting clouds,
The single bird, the obscure moon—

The obscure moon lighting an obscure world
Of things that would never be quite expressed,
Where you yourself were never quite yourself
And did not want nor have to be,

Desiring the exhilarations of changes:
The motive for metaphor, shrinking from
The weight of primary noon,
The ABC of being,

The ruddy temper, the hammer
Of red and blue, the hard sound—
Steel against intimation—the sharp flash,
The vital, arrogant, fatal, dominant X.

Whatever voice it is that speaks here, it speaks dismissively of the poet's love of half colors and quarter-things. He loves half dead things in autumn and quarter-things in spring, the voice says, because such things represent change: a half dead thing can die, a cripple was once healthy, a moon can wax and wane, a single bird can become a chorus, a cloud can melt, a sky can brighten. Spring and autumn are the seasons of change. But the speaking voice detests those exhilarations of changes which are the motive for metaphor. This new, self-contemptuous voice which opens "The Motive for Metaphor" sees the seductiveness of change as an evasion of the obdurate, blocking, trapping knowledge of the fatal and dominant self, the self that, under all the changes, one is. That is the self that the sharp light of noon, without any shadows, would reveal. It is at once the ABC of being and also its X, the Alpha and Omega of self, that which the Prince of Peacocks had been afraid to face— Berserk and his traps of steel. In moonlight, says the self-accuser in "The Motive for Metaphor," "you yourself were never quite yourself / And did not want nor have to be." You shrank from the weight of primary noon. But the speaker knows, now, with entire intimacy, "the hard sound— / Steel against intimation—the sharp flash, / The vital, arrogant, fatal, dominant X." That steel is both vital and fatal, ABC and X, the infant self and its later hierophant. This is a very brutal poem, in which Stevens is much unkinder to his younger self than he will be in his last poems. But it is a relief, after earlier evasions, to hear him being so harsh.

The final hammer and knife-blade, the smith's hammer and the executioner's edge, are extremely beautiful, but just slightly over-done. The speaker has not yet been wooed entirely away from his more shrouded and nuanced haunts, in spite of his sortie into a con-temptuous tone. The trouble with biding in autumn and spring after they no longer mediate adequate self-knowledge is that the words one writes about them cease to have any meaning, and the divine afflatus is crippled. Stevens—it is part of his greatness—was quick to see when he was being false and, in spite of the im-mense stubbornness of his slow nature, was willing to force himself unwillingly on to the next stage of discovery, even if it meant new desolation. "The Motive for Metaphor" finds him falling back on the natural ground of his own life and private misery, rather than looking toward the social order for a collective example of ethical escape. The misery in "The Motive for Metaphor" lies in the pain of the choices it offers: a crippled, half-dead, and meaningless life in autumn (it being now no longer possible to return to spring) or a submission to what one shrinks from: a brutal solar weight, a hard hammer, the surgical flash of the fatal X. Stevens dreads being exposed to that sun, being tempered by that hammer, finding that blocking steel against his intimations (though he no longer believes he will go mad under the trial, as he did when he was the Prince of Peacocks). With the dread there coexists a compelling attraction— the exhilaration of a new sort of self-knowledge, a change into the changelessness of a final, permanent self. Because the new phase incorporates the motive for all the previous ones, the desire for change (which is the motive for metaphor), it attracts. But the poem implies that the new self-knowledge that it implicitly recom-mends will be the last possible phase, the fatal phase, and therefore the end of poetry. This suspicion causes both the nostalgia for previ-ous seasons of happiness, no matter how evasive, which the poem candidly exhibits, and the desire for the new.

Stevens' style in "The Motive for Metaphor" is, comparatively speaking, one of apparent simplicity. But the old Platonism, the desire for harmony, is smuggled in by way of two flurries of apposi-tion, at the middle and end of the poem. Apposition is a figure which of itself implies that things can be aligned in meaningful parallels, that metaphorical equivalences are a portion of significance—that

the weight of primary noon
the ABC of being
the ruddy temper
the hammer of red and blue
the hard sound
steel against intimation
the sharp flash
the vital, arrogant, fatal, dominant X

can all be substituted, one for the other, to signify a dreadful exposure from which the earlier, more fugitive poet, shrinks. In this
parallelism Stevens betrays his nostalgia for synthesis and system:
brutality has extended to his self-perception, and to his imagery,
without yet having reached his syntax. "Chaos in Motion and Not
in Motion" extends this brutality to syntax, letting that crippled
wind fully loose, allowing it to lash everything at once, changing
the self-loathing of "The Motive for Metaphor" to self-irony, refusing soothing syntax in favor of rapid primary syntactical forms.

In his last years Stevens writes a poetry of powerful retrospective
weight in which all the attitudes exhibited and assumed over a
long life are admitted to the arena, each seen as something authentic
in its time. The worst bitternesses, when they recur, as they do
even in "The Rock," subside. Brutality appears, and recedes. In the
great and heartbreaking poem of self-evaluation, "Things of August," Stevens forgives all his selves, remembers all of them, ac-
cedes to the unintelligibility of the world, and celebrates the new
text of it he has created. He is now, as he will say in "The Rock,"
the "silent rhapsodist" of the earth. Of all the poems I could choose
to show the last stage of Stevens' harshness, I will turn to one about
sexual feeling in old age, called "The Dove in Spring":

> Brooder, brooder, deep beneath its walls—
> A small howling of the dove
> Makes something of the little there,
>
> The little and the dark, and that
> In which it is and that in which
> It is established. There the dove
>
> Makes this small howling, like a thought
> That howls in the mind or like a man
> Who keeps seeking out his identity

> In that which is and is established ... It howls
> Of the great sizes of an outer bush
> And the great misery of the doubt of it,
>
> Of stripes of silver that are strips
> Like slits across a space, a place
> And state of being large and light.
>
> There is this bubbling before the sun,
> This howling at one's ear, too far
> For daylight and too near for sleep.

The dove is Venus' bird, its absence mourned earlier in *Harmonium*, in "Depression before Spring," when, though the cock has crowed, "ki-ki-ri-ki / Brings no rou-cou, No rou-cou-cou," and "no queen comes / In slipper green." It is the "tempestuous bird," the "dove in the belly" who "builds his nest and coos" when things of the world appear promising and bright. It is the dove that rises up every spring when the Italian girls wear jonquils in their hair. Stevens is seventy-four as he writes this poem, his last word almost on the persistence of desire. What is one to make of the voice of Venus' dove at seventy-four? Hatred, irony, and comedy can appear in the literature of sexual meditation in old age; one thinks of Yeats. But Stevens' meditation is entirely respectful and serious; he does not feel absurd or reprehensible for harboring the dove; what he feels is a sadness for the dove and for himself. The dove is imprisoned behind walls, in the dark. It can no longer coo; it can only howl. A howl is its singing, and it decides to sing even an unlovely song, rather than fall silent. The dove knows that somewhere outside there is a great bush that is its natural habitat; at the same time, it doubts that any such bush exists. This doubt causes its misery: it howls of "a place and state of being large and light," but all it has of that light is what it perceives in slits through its prison bars, in stripes of silver. The dove's small howling takes place at night. It prevents sleep, without presaging a new day. Spring's infuriations, the poem tells us, are never over. They take, in old age, forms that may seem degenerate—a dove displaced from a bough to a prison, a dove that does not coo but howls, a dove that cannot any longer see the undulating silver fans of any imaginable mate—but if truth is to be told, even degenerate forms must be allowed their pathos of expression.

I do not mean to sentimentalize Stevens in insisting that his poems are meditations on emotions of love, idolatry, loss, self-loathing, and self-forgiveness. He is so chaste in self-revelation that his emotions are easily passed over. A poem like "The Dove in Spring," written in "the little and the dark," sees the sexual impulse, and all the love and idealization it gave rise to in life, as strictly parallel to the impulse to thought and the impulse to self-definition. In allowing a syntactic parallelism betwee these three impulses—the sexual, the intellectual, and the personal—Stevens is resorting not to Platonism but to memory, the memory of how his life had structured itself around three persistent shapings of identity. The grief of the ending of the poem is not the elegiac sorrow for the great bush or the large light state, but rather the grief of Tithonus, that one can neither die nor live, as one endures the last protests and affirmations of desire.

James Merrill once remarked in a *Paris Review* interview that Stevens "continues to persuade us of having had a private life, despite—or thanks to—all the bizarreness of his vocabulary and idiom." On the whole, criticism has avoided the evidences of that private life, but it is, as Merrill says, so inseparable from the incomparable style invented to express it that it is a failure of imagination to discuss the style without its subject. The lapses and failures of idealization—especially the idealization of romantic love, forced on us by nature, culture, and, above all, literature—press Stevens to an ever more stringent, and even harsh, analysis of the interrelation of emotion's flights and their eventual correction in time. It may be that the harshness or brutality which I have been describing is Stevens' defense against a Romantic sweetness, though I think not. It is rather, I feel sure, the expression of an anger that a mind so designed for adoration never found adoration and sensuality compatible; they remained locked compartments, a source of emotional confusion and bitterness. In the end, however, Stevens' unwillingness to abandon either of his two incompatible truths—the truth of desire and the truth of the failure of desire—led to a great amplitude of human vision not granted to those who live more comfortably in body and soul, and to a truth-telling ease not granted to those who have fewer difficulties to confess.

Marianne Moore

In 1921 the Egoist Press, in London, published a small volume of twenty-four poems by an American woman named Marianne Moore. She had not submitted the poems to the press. Two of her women friends, both writers—H.D. and Bryher—had taken the poems (all previously published in magazines) and seen them into type. Three years later, enlarged to fifty-four poems (with three of the original twenty-four dropped and others revised), the volume was issued in the United States, under its now famous title *Observations*. Like *Prufrock, and Other Observations* (1917) and *Harmonium* (1923), it was a book to be read whole; like them, it has become in literary history an index of the state of American art after the First World War. Pound, Eliot, and Stevens all liked *Observations*. In 1923, Eliot had written a flattering review of the 1921 *Poems*, and he was later to contribute an introduction to Moore's 1935 *Selected Poems*. Pound displayed, as he often did, the most accurate grasp of a new poet. He saw as early as 1918 that Moore's work belonged with the "utterance of clever people in despair . . . a mind cry . . . 'In the midst of this desolation, give me at least one intelligence to converse with.' "

The despair is the arresting part of *Observations*. For the first thirty years of her life, Marianne Moore had no literary society to speak of; after 1918, when she and her mother moved to New York, she lost her isolation and, with it (though this can only be conjectured), some measure of her gift for despair, dismissiveness, and denunciation. She was born, in 1887, the younger of two children; her brother, Warner, was seventeen months older. Her father had gone insane; she never knew him. After the father left the family, Mrs. Moore took the children to live in the house of her widowed father, a Presbyterian minister, in Kirkwood, Missouri, a suburb of

"On Marianne Moore" first appeared in the *New Yorker*, October 16, 1978.

59

St. Louis. He died when Marianne was seven. Mrs. Moore then moved to Carlisle, Pennsylvania, where she, Marianne, and Warner lived in an extraordinary and peculiar intimacy of shared reference, which persisted all through their later lives and produced an enormous number of family letters. Warner became a Presbyterian minister, like his grandfather; as soon as he had a parsonage, Mrs. Moore and Marianne moved in with him. When he became, shortly afterward, a Navy chaplain, traveling abroad, Mrs. Moore and Marianne moved to Greenwich Village. Later, when Warner was assigned to the Brooklyn Navy Yard, they moved to Brooklyn. Moore's verse, published in *The Egoist* and *Poetry*, had attracted attention even before she moved to New York. Within a few years after the move, she was writing for *The Dial*. Soon she began serving as its acting editor, and then, for three years, was its editor—until, following Scofield Thayer's nervous breakdown, the magazine (which he had founded with Sibley Watson) was discontinued, in 1929. After the stint with *The Dial*, Moore in effect worked only as a writer. (She had taught for four years in her twenties and was for a while during her thirties a part-time librarian in the branch library across from her house.) Her life became one without public event, lived quietly in Brooklyn, punctuated by various publications and prizes.

The *Selected Poems*, published when Moore was forty-eight, added eight new poems. Subsequent volumes show a falling off, in the judgment of many critics. The *Complete Poems*, published in 1967, is not complete (an "Author's Note" says tightly, "Omissions are not accidents") and revises several well-known poems—notably the celebrated "Poetry"—out of all recognition. The reader who wants to know Moore's work in any orderly way has to track down the juvenilia in magazines, to find the 1921 *Poems* in a rare-book room, to disentangle the early poems from the later ones in the 1924 *Observations*, to separate these from the poems added in the 1935 *Selected Poems*, and so on. The state of the prose is no more satisfactory. *Predilections* (1955) is not the *Complete Essays and Reviews* that we need. The early prose has to be found in the review pages of *Poetry* and *The Dial*. As things now stand, anthologists have tended to print the later, easier, more explicit poems, and have thereby—to my mind, at least—done Moore a disservice. (*The New Oxford Book of American Verse* offers one poem from 1921; most are from the later volumes.) As for Moore's letters, they are not yet published. Some are in private hands, some are in restricted library collections, and some, along with a mass of

Moore papers, can be read in the Rosenbach Foundation collection in Philadelphia. In short, no complete view of Moore will be easy to acquire for some years to come. A biography is scheduled to be written by Clive Driver, Moore's literary executor.

In the meantime, the poems stand, to the public eye, relatively alone. Few readers today can remember when *Observations* appeared. Most readers, unluckily, are likely to have known Moore first and last through the favorite anthology pieces—a scanty selection, insufficient to give a steady sense of her odd but instinctive rhythm ("a kind of pleasing jerky progress," as she called it) and her biting wit. The biographical fact of first importance to recall in reading Moore is that she spent her college years at Bryn Mawr as a biology major. She had failed Italian and German (though she subsequently passed them) and for a time did not have the grades necessary to take English electives. "I thought, in fact, of studying medicine," she said in an interview with Donald Hall, adding that "precision, economy of statement, logic employed to ends that are disinterested, drawing and identifying, liberate . . . the imagination." In this assertion, Moore set herself firmly against one sort of American writing—the breezy rhetoric of native oratory, the afflatus of romantic sentiment, the optimism of self-help—and just as firmly placed herself in alliance with another American attitude toward words: our pragmatic, taxonomic, realistic conviction that words are useful, practical, and exact; that they can convey the specifications for a bridge, the identifying marks of an animal, the geographical directions for an explorer, and even, in our earliest literature, the path to salvation. To write so that no single word can be misunderstood is a mark of the American pride in accuracy, punctual speech, and laconic completeness; the abstractions of metaphysical dispute are as foreign to this sort of American as are the pleasures of mystification in the service of sentiment.

Moore disliked enigmas and disliked being thought enigmatic; she wanted to be lucid without sacrificing implication. The deliberate (as it seemed) hermeticism of some modern verse repelled her. "Enigmas are not poetry" was the final line, in the truncated version printed in the second edition of *Observations* (1925), of her most famous single poem—the one called "Poetry," which begins, "I, too, dislike it." Moore's balance between lucidity and implication always remained precarious, as she herself knew. Pressed into an unwise explicitness by her horror of the Second World War, she wrote a bad poem called "In Distrust of Merits," which was monotonously anthologized because of its concurrence with popular sentiment. In commenting on it later, she said, "I do like it; it is sincere, but I wouldn't call it a poem . . . [It is] haphazard; as form, what has it? It is just a protest—disjointed, exclamatory. Emotion overpowered me. First this thought and then that." If in that instance emotion overpowered Moore so that implication was sacrificed to banality of outcry, in other instances the factual overwhelmed her so that feeling was sacrificed to baldness of transcription. The early poems visibly skirt both dangers, but are happily preserved from both by their brio and their scornful energy. They are the work of a girl who knows what she likes, and knows even more what she dislikes.

Moore must from childhood have had edge, sharpness, watchfulness, and wit. Bryn Mawr gave her the habit of scientific observation and, perhaps in conjunction with her mother, a sense of justice wronged. She remembered and later quoted a speech given by M. Carey Thomas, the president of Bryn Mawr:

> Men practically reserve for themselves stately funerals, splendid monuments, memorial statues, membership in academies, medals, titles, honorary degrees, stars, garters, ribbons, buttons and other shining baubles, so valueless in themselves and yet so infinitely desirable because they are symbols of recognition.

Not only did men form a self-perpetuating élite, not only did they ignore women, they also categorized and patronized them:

> [You] have heard men say: "There is a feminine
> temperament in direct contrast to
> ours which makes her do these things. Circumscribed by a
> heritage of blindness and native
> incompetence, she will become wise and will be forced to give
> in. Compelled by experience, she
> will turn back; water seeks its own level."

Supercilious male writers "write the sort of thing that would in their judgment interest a lady; / curious to know if we do not adore each letter of the alphabet that goes to make a word of it." The lady in this instance bites her tongue (or so we imagine, reading these lines), only to have her revenge later in immortalizing the fool who writes for "ladies."

Moore's asperity in the poems written in her twenties and early thirties shows the revengeful impatience of one not suffering fools gladly. The poems display a whole gallery of self-incriminating fools—self-important, illiterate, unimaginative, sentimental, defensive, pompous, cruel. For each of the fools, a portrait. There is the opinionated and conclusive Steam Roller: "You crush all the particles down / into close conformity, and then walk back and forth on them." There is the critic who did not understand that Hebrew poetry had its own compositional rules, and asserted that "Hebrew poety is / prose with a sort of heightened consciousness." There is the military man of "warped wit": "You use your mind / Like a millstone to grind / Chaff." There is the terrifyingly ornamented woman who speaks only to wound, her scalpels "whetted / to / brilliance by the hard majesty of . . . sophistication." There are the snobbish "high priests of caste . . . kissing the feet of the man above, / kicking the face of the man below"; the conventional poet, "the Coliseum / meet-me-alone-by-moonlight maudlin troubadour"; the humburg who thinks that *"summa diligentia"* means that "Caesar crossed the Alps on the 'top of a / *diligence'* "; the pedants of criticism, "saying it is not for us to understand art; finding it / all so difficult"; the "pedantic literalist" in whom everything once alive and erect has drooped and withered; the "embalmed" statesman who stalks about "with moribund talk, / Half limping and half ladified." The interesting thing about Moore's poems of fools or knaves is that most of them are addressed very coolly to their victims. To the lady of the scalpels, Moore, the former biologist, will say, "Why dissect destiny with instruments which / are more highly specialized than the tissues of destiny itself?" To the pedantic literalist, "You are like the meditative man / With the perfunctory heart." To the moribund politician, "We find / No / Virtue in you—alive and yet so dumb." To the Steam Roller, "As for butterflies, I can hardly conceive / of one's attending upon you." These deadly anatomies, so impossible in well-bred life, are unsparingly uttered in print: Moore tells all her fools to their faces exactly what she thinks of them, finding her own annihilating metaphor for each one. Hers is the aggression of the silent, well-brought-up girl who thinks up mute rejoinders during every parlor conversation. Because Moore showed her work to her mother, and sought her mother's approval before publishing, it seems probable that Mrs. Moore shared her daughter's astringent judgment as well as her intelligence and her gift for a sharp phrase. In a note to the *Selected Poems*, in lieu of a dedication to her mother Moore wrote, "In my immediate family there is one 'who thinks in a particular way'; and I should like to add that where there is an effect of thought or pith in these pages, the thinking and often the actual phrases are hers."

In these early years, Moore showed no inclination to mince matters or to spare the hapless. Her early reviews in *The Dial* display the same short way with fools exercised in the early poems. "Criticism," Moore was to say in 1965, "should stimulate an improved understanding of the subject discussed—'with a truce to politeness' as Montaigne says." She was severe, in the early twenties, on Vachel Lindsay, affronted as much by his improper use of tenses as by his carelessness of phrase. "To speak of 'Christ, the beggar,' is inexact," she wrote in a characteristic sentence, "since it has never been said of Christ that he begged; he did without." Reading her now, we may feel that under her penetrating glance none of us would 'scape whipping, but her moral fervor with respect to language came from her tremor at its every nuance, her princesslike apprehension of every pea-size solecism. Clumsy language was a torture to her: beautiful language was for her a physical experience. Delighted by phrases of others, she copied them down and inserted them, sometimes in quotation marks, in her poems. In the company of someone who used language crudely or unfeelingly she experienced a helpless rage:

> I can but put my weapon up, and
> Bow you out . . .
> Since in your hearing words are mute, which to my senses
> Are a shout.

That poem—suppressed after *Observations*—is called "To Be Liked by You Would Be a Calamity." It must often have seemed to Moore, to whom understatement was the figure of predilection, that most people around her were shouting, and that a brief or dry phrase from her would be "mute" to them. It may be that she gave up hope in later years of reaching a general audience with her fine ellipses; if Eliot and Stevens understood her, they were not instances easily multiplied. Eliot was more forbidding than hospitable in his 1935 introduction: "To the moderately intellectual the poems may appear to be intellectual exercises; only to those whose intellection moves more easily will they immediately appear to have emotional value." If the "moderately intellectual" were not intellectual enough to grasp her intent—and by "moderately intellectual" Eliot meant a group well educated by American standards—Moore might well have despaired of company and broadened her effects.

But the early poems, one senses, were written entirely to please herself, an odd girl in her twenties, turning from her dissections to her verses. Speaking of her early influences, in an interview with Howard Nemerov, she recalled "feeling over-solitary occasionally (say in 1912)—in reflecting no 'influences;' to not be able to be called an 'imagist.' " Her repudiation of that label is just, as is her repudiation of the label "syllabic verse": "I do not know what syllabic verse is. I find no appropriate application for it"—and yet she has so often been described as a poet deriving from Imagism who writes in syllabic verse that the discrepancy between the common view and her own begs some explanation. The prosodic knot is the easier to untie: though she sometimes counted syllables in composing her *lines*, the stanza, and not the line, was for her the poetic unit. Stanzas, she said, came to her first, unplanned: the words clustered "like chromosomes," and she fixed stanzas until the tune sounded right. She was "governed by the pull of the sentence as the pull of a fabric is governed by gravity" (and the pull of the sentence on her mind is as evident in the most commonplace letter of thanks from her— but her letters were never commonplace—as in the densest poem). The rhythm of the stanza and the rhythm of the sentence impelled the poem; the syllabic count imposed some strictness on her procedure, but even in the non-syllabic poems, written in a species of free verse, her rhythms are instantly recognizable. Whatever small formalities she employed—her internal rhymes, her "light" rhymes, her syllable counts—did not define her practice or her originality. Jean Garrigue, so far Moore's best critic, wrote, "Of *Observations* one might say: it is first and last a voice. The voice of sparkling talk and sometimes very lofty talk, glittering with authority." Moore's rightful insistence that the syllabic label did not define her can be ratified by viewing the unpleasant results of the syllabic experimentation of poets lacking her independent and bristly grace.

In his 1923 review of *Poems*, Eliot praised her rhythm without being able to define it:

> Rhythm, of course, is a highly personal matter; it is not a verse-form. It is always the real pattern in the carpet, the scheme of organization of thought, feeling, and vocabulary, the way in which everything comes together. It is very uncommon. What is certain is that Miss Moore's poems always read very well aloud. That quality is something which no system of scansion can define.

Since Eliot's truths do not make for easy textbook summary, the syllabic label, being a simple one, persists. The ready coupling of Moore's work to the Imagist movement is even more limiting. She had been brought up, she told Pound, on the minor prophets, on Blake, on Hardy; they, not the Imagists, were her true antecedents. Eliot saw that her use of images was too rapid to be called Imagism: "The second image is superposed before the first has quite faded." But, more important, the Imagist power, such as it was—and it now can be seen to have been, in itself, weak—was photographic, mimetic, perceptual. Moore's early poetry, by contrast, takes as its chief subject states of the soul, not external "reality." Geoffrey Hartman rightly remarks that many of her poems are really "poems of Spiritual Combat, and show in Miss Moore that clear identifying mark of the Puritan: an extreme reverence for created things coupled with an extreme distrust of the self." If in attempting to describe the souls of people who are oppressive like streamrollers, or modestly contractile like snails, or patient and enduring like elephants she needed metaphor, she was not in that need unusual. If Disraeli seemed to her like a chameleon, with his "parti-colored mind"; if Shaw resembled a "colossal bird . . . [with] brazen claws"; if Kenneth Burke was "a psychologist—of acute, raccoon-like curiosity"; if a conventional diplomat seemed a mummified ibis; if Molière might be thought a peacock unfurling his broad tail for spontaneous delight: surely, though these images may be drawn from a private or restricted code book, they are not the issue of an Imagist creed. They come, rather, from religious usage, as in illustrations of the deadly sins the lustful man sits on a goat and the glutton on a pig. The difference between Moore and the emblem-writers is that she has a much more lively interest than they in real pigs and peacocks; she takes, so to speak, the two sides of the emblem equally seriously.

And this is the other side of her early work, balancing her ridiculings and her repudiations: satirist that she was, she was also, by temperament, affectionate. Her affections went first of all (after her family) to people who were in some way both beautiful—conventionally or unconventionally—and strong. There is no doubt that some of the early poems on animals or objects are also, even principally, about human beings. The one on the elephant is, or ought to be taken as, a poem about Moore herself—her most personal and "lyric" poem, one that she suppressed when compiling the *Complete Poems*. That it could have been dropped on grounds of taste is inconceivable; it surely ranks among her most natural and beautiful pieces. It was called "Black Earth" in *Poems*, in *Observations*, and in *Selected Poems*. The name was changed in 1951, in the *Collected Poems*, to the more obscure "Melancthon"—a title

66

drawn from the Greek translation of the surname of the sixteenth-century German reformer Schwarzerd (meaning "Black Earth"). Moore may have intended a side-glance at the doctrine of predestination, which she took up in her own way in the poem called "The Monkey Puzzle": "But we prove, we do not explain our birth."

All possible touching things are said in "Black Earth." It belongs with another poem that was published in her first volume but suppressed in the *Complete Poems*—the poem entitled, in an arithmetical proportion, "Diligence Is to Magic as Progress Is to Flight." Flying carpets, says the poem, are the recommended means of travel in the realm of romance, and magic flights are, of course, all very well in their way; but some people progress, if oddly, by simple diligence. "With rings on her fingers, and bells on her toes, elephants to ride upon"— the song made an impression on Moore, and she made a poem about a woman who rides not on flying carpets, those "scarecrows / of aesthetic procedure," but, rather, on the laborious elephant, one of those "tough-grained animals as have outstripped man's whim to suppose / them ephemera." "Black Earth" pursues the analogy of "Diligence," but more inwardly. The elephant here speaks wonderfully for itself: "I do these / things which I do, which please / no one but myself." In spite of this leisured mastery, the elephant has not had an easy past: its skin is "cut / into checkers by rut / upon rut of unpreventable experience." The poem dwells on the need to preserve "spiritual poise" in the midst of all this scarring; the elephant has looked "at electricity and at the earth- / quake and is still here." The poem is agitated by all of Moore's central concerns: the nature of power, the nature of identity, the impassivity of selfhood, the wounds of circumstance, the failures of human perception. "I see and I hear," muses the poet-elephant, who accuses man, seen through his eyes, of self-delusion, of having eyes and seeing not, of having ears and hearing not: that "wand-like body . . . which was made / to see and not to see; to hear and not to hear; / that tree trunk without / roots, accustomed to shout / its own thoughts to itself." Moore was perfectly and inhumanly removed, at such a moment, from her fellow human beings. The removal—her superior amusement and denigration—was the source of her virgin strength.

When the local librarian suggested to Mrs. Moore that Marianne might like to work in the library, since she was so often there, Mrs. Moore said no—that if Marianne joined the staff she would probably feel she had no time to read. In the interview with Donald Hall, Moore continued the anecdote: "When I came home she told me, and I said, 'Why, certainly. Ideal. I'll tell her. Only I couldn't work more than half a day.' If I had worked all day and maybe evenings or overtime, like the mechanics, why, it would *not* have been ideal." The "ideal" has strange ways, however. Moore's intense inner life had been fed by her obsessive family relations, by her schooling at Bryn Mawr, and by her first literary engagements; but the permanent arrest of her life—with her mother, without employment, in the Brooklyn apartment—may ultimately seem a cause for regret. She was protected from vicissitude, but she was also shielded from those irregularities and abasements of life which open new, if darker, chambers of thought. Her life gave less opportunity than some for the worst dilemmas of passion or conflicting loyalties. She took a dim view, even very early, of human attempts at what we would nowadays call "communication": "The I of each is to / the I of each / a kind of fretful speech / which sets a limit on itself." Between the 1921 and 1924 volumes, she wrote her great poem "Marriage," in which she examined, satirized, envied, and dismissed—as a possibility for herself—that institution in which two "I"s attempt a real speech.

I will return to "Marriage," but I must stop for a moment longer on the 1921 *Poems*, in which we can see, besides the satiric impalings, beyond the tenderness of "Black Earth," a prompt and inquisitive lyric gift in poems of a startling independence of thought. I have in mind poems like "England" (stemming from an early two-month trip with her mother; it makes one wish she had traveled more in her first youth), "When I Buy Pictures," "Dock Rats," and "In the Days of Prismatic Color." These unsentimental poems have always at least one abyss hiding in their neat parterres, some crevasse down which the unwary reader could slip. Moore's most characteristic gesture is a throwaway remark revealing whole horizons explored and rejected. If she calls Greece "the nest of modified illusions," she is asking us to have illusions and to have—stunning word—"modified" them. It is almost the word of a seamstress. To tailor an illusion is already a cataclysmic fall from innocence, but the notion is so innocently slipped in that the careless eye skids over it. It has been said that America is barren because it has no ruins; for Moore it is deficient because it has "no proof readers, no silkworms, no digressions." What is this discontented patriotism that longs for a literate page, a natural fabric, an idiosyncratic learning, and sickens and dies for the lack of them? Can it be the same patriotism that turns on itself and insists that fineness must exist in America? ("It has never been confined to one locality.")

Moore's crevasses are for herself, not her audience; like George Herbert, whom she resembles in her self-incrimination, she might say, "My God, I mean my self." When she buys pictures, she wishes to avoid (not surprisingly, given her severity) her own besetting sins:

> Too stern an intellectual emphasis . . . detracts from one's enjoyment;
> it must not wish to disarm anything.

"Poetry" is an indirect self-reproach for her painstaking absorption in "all this fiddle." Other early poems utter suspicions about "the passion for setting people right" ("in itself an afflictive disease"); about the wish of human nature to dominate, to "stand in the middle of a thing"; about being diverted by the "mystery of construction" from "what was originally one's / object—substance at the core." Certain excuses for sins are offered: for a cat, it is natural to have "the disposition invariably to affront," since "an animal with claws wants to have to use / them." A poet with an affronting or diverting tongue may want to have to use it, too, and Moore's rebellious outspokenness about herself and others, no matter how disciplined by the angular geometry of her verse, is the chief ornament of the early volumes. It is no accident that when she wrote about the poet, in an essay bearing the name of her two polarities, "Feeling and Precision," she compared the writer to a clawed lion: "The lion's leap would be mitigated almost to harmlessness if the lion were clawless, so precision is both impact and exactitude, as with surgery."

Moore's first ethical impulse was, we might say, an Aristotelian one, interested in the taxonomy of the virtues and vices. The early poems served to set her mind in order about what was virtue, what vice— a question that was for her almost indistinguishable from what was art, what ugliness. She conceded later that Shakespeare's villains were not illiterate, but she added that rectitude "has a ring that is implicative." The long process of deciding what she liked, what she disapproved of, whom she admired, whom she found foolish or wicked, how her mind worked, what sort of literary form she should write in, occupied Moore for the classic two decades—from fifteen to thirty-five—of such human search. The poems that resulted (Observations came out when she was thirty-seven) represent one of the most individual, private, and conclusive inquiries into identity ever brought into print by an American woman. Her young eye was willing to look even at death (in "A Grave"), but she drew back from dramatizing it; her invariable diffidence of rhythm avoided grand climax. Pound wanted her to rearrange the last line of "A Grave" to gain emphasis, and she did it to please him, but she did not forbear to tell him she preferred the original phrasing. She was right, and later she changed the poem back to suit herself.

One oddity of literary history is that Moore became known, with a peculiar disregard for the brilliant character sketches in *Observations*, as an animal poet, a writer of texts to go beside a *National Geographic* photograph of an ostrich or a pangolin. (*Life,* in 1953, featured her in a story headed "*Life* Goes on a Zoo Tour with a Famous Poet: Marianne Moore Calls on Some Animals She Often Writes About.") In part, Moore was herself to blame for this absurdity: her distrust of emotions made her increasingly submissive to fact; her isolation made her more dependent on books; and the war caused her flexible ethical meditations to rigidify into moral outcries. Animals became an end in themselves, as human beings became more remote or more repellent. The disjunction between her mind and her heart is reflected in two statements made in the same interview (she was then approaching eighty): the first was that now, as always, the "forces which result in poetry" are "irrepressible emotion, joy, grief, desperation, triumph"; the second was that "every day it is borne in on us that we need rigor—better governance of the emotions." To govern the irrepressible is the paradoxical aim of all art, but her governance seems to have become an almost habitual censorship. When the pain of the irrepressible emotion and the pain of governance remain intertwined in the poems, the poetry weighs on us as it did on her. Conversely, when the emotion is a wholly innocent one—usually, in her case, a visual emotion (her religious upbringing seems not to have repressed sight and hearing)—her pure joy brings her closer than any other American poet to the Whitman of Manhattan and the sea. The exhilaration of port activity passes, transfused, unchanged, into "Dock Rats," and even Whitman could not better the description of the fishing boats and the waves in "A Grave":

> the blades of the oars
> moving together like the feet of water-spiders as if there were no
> such thing as death.
> The wrinkles progress upon themselves in a phalanx—beautiful
> under networks of foam,

and fade breathlessly while the sea rustles in and out of the seaweed.

That limpid delight appears in all her contemplations of the variety of the natural world. In her pursuit of its stranger forms, she is like the Herbert of the "outlandish proverbs" and natural curiosities:

> Most things move th'under-jaw; the Crocodile not.
> Most things sleep lying; th'Elephant leans or stands.

No one is likely to forget Moore's ostrich who digests hard iron, or that human frigate bird compared to Handel, "never . . . known to have fallen in love," or the swan "with swart blind look askance / and gondoliering legs." But the shield of the animal metaphor eventually became almost impenetrable. It was true of Moore, as of her "student" (in the poem of that name), that she was too reclusive for some things to touch her, not because she had no feeling but because she had so much.

It is not sentimental, I hope, to see her great, if confined, poem "Marriage" as her most nearly perfect union of the pain of feeling and the pain of governance. The Marvellian theme that Paradise was Paradise only when Adam was there alone is touched on in the early poem "In the Days of Prismatic Color," which, after beginning in an airy, happy, rainbow-hued atmosphere, quickly darkens into a miserable debate with itself about the value of complexity, darkness, and sophistication. By the time of "Marriage," complexity has inexorably entered, as prelapsarian radiance is intruded on by the worldly cynicism of Bacon and then by Moore's own expostulating humor:

> I wonder what Adam and Eve
> think of it by this time,
> this firegilt steel
> alive with goldenness;
> how bright it shows—
> "of circular traditions and impostures,
> committing many spoils,"
> requiring all one's criminal ingenuity
> to avoid!

When, at the age of eighty, Moore published "Marriage" in the *Complete Poems*, she added a prefatory sentence to the "Notes" to the poem, saying that it consisted of "statements that took my fancy which I tried to arrange plausibly." It was a dignified way to rebuke overbiographical readings of the poem; but nothing else she wrote contains nearly so many quotations and references. She had been squirreling away others' remarks on marriage with intense attention: more statements "took her fancy" on this subject than on any other on which she composed a poem. A "plausible arrangement," to a poet, means an arrangement that feels faithful to the emotional force that has given off the poem: in "Marriage," an unmistakable satiric comedy exists in tension with an equally unmistakable longing and admiration. The poem vacillates between thinking that marriage should be the most natural, easy, and companionable of arrangements and thinking it a dangerous enterprise: "men have power / and sometimes one is made to feel it." Both the sweetnesses and the hatreds of marriage enter the poem, which sees both the propriety of human union and its competing narcissistic destructions:

> He loves himself so much,
> he can permit himself
> no rival in that love.
> She loves herself so much,
> she cannot see herself enough.

In herself she clearly did not find that simplicity of temper, as she calls it, which sees in homely rules a natural order of things that it easily obeys. People with that simplicity repeat phrases and attitudes in marriage which Moore compares to "the statesmanship / of an archaic Daniel Webster," saying—as though marital government were blissfully easy—"Liberty and union / now and forever," as they pose for their stolid daguerreotypes: "the book on the writing-table; / the hand in the breast-pocket." If that ending seems to a reader affecting, he will like Moore.

Many of the early poems, all brilliant, remain relatively unpossessed by readers in part because of their peculiar titles, which have nothing to do with their subjects. "An Octopus" is improbably about a glacier and a mountain, "The Fish" is about a scarred cliff and the ocean that batters it—though, of course, neither is really "about" its putative topic. Intellectually speaking, "An Octopus" is about multiplicity, and how it appears from different angles of vision, and "The Fish" is about the interfaces, as we might now call them, between the ocean, its creatures, and the adjacent land. Emotionally speaking, the glacier poem—written about Mount Rainier, and full of compressed detail—may be taken as a poem about America and its nature and its unclassical art, and as a poem about a life journey; while the fish poem reproduces the sliding motions of the sea creatures, the brutal pressure of the water, and the stolid endurance of the cliff, all intermixed in what one might feel to be a transcription of conflicting motions of the nervous system transliterated into earthly symbols.

In the last major poetic effort of her life, Moore spent a decade translating the fables of La Fontaine. Perhaps a flagging of her own inner energies made such a work proper, but the constraints of sense invaded her elegant rhythms and made the translations, in spite of many felicities of phrase, finally unsatisfying as poems by Moore. When they first appeared, Howard Nemerov called them "very jittery as to the meter." Not a great deal should be claimed for them, not even for Moore's affinities with La Fontaine: he was less soulful than she, and his animals have an existence not so much biological or visual as fabular. He was not a naturalist; Moore was.

Moore's poetry has so far not been especially well served by commentary, with the exception of Jean Garrigue's brief pamphlet *Marianne Moore* (1965). The most intimate and attractive short essay on her work was done, under the title "Her Shield," by Randall Jarrell; yet even Jarrell did not quite seem to grasp that her poems are not about "nature," but about herself. His witty remark "She sent postcards to only the nicer animals" falls slightly awry, like the gibes about what Wordsworth would have done if he had grown up among scorpions instead of sheep. It is a tribute to Moore's accuracy of drawing that Jarrell should allow her metaphors the veracity of photographs. He found her early poems too oblique and mannered; now that we are perhaps more accustomed to them, they seem not the "dry glittering expanse, i.e., a desert" that he found them but, rather, descriptions of self, full of candor as well as of reticence. (Even the critiques of knaves and fools are indirections for finding her own direction out.)

Most of her commentators have been men; with the exception of Geoffrey Hartman (who did the notes on the sleeve of the Yale Series recording of Moore reading her work), they have on the whole made Moore more shrinking and squeamish than she is. They bring up Dickinson. Eliot brought up Christina Rossetti. Pound, after his early sponsorship, said in a letter, "Marianne is scarce an exuberance, rather protagonist for the rights of vitrification and petrifaxis." William Carlos Williams, who once called her "our saint," compared her work to a "brittle, highly set-off porcelain garden." Jarrell said that some of her poems "have the manners or manner of ladies who learned a little before birth not to mention money, who neither point nor touch, and who scrupulously abstain from the mixed, live vulgarity of life." Words like "tidy," "fussy," "finicking," and "ingenious" turn up. Denis Donoghue thinks her poems resemble "things like ice-skating, which are hard play." David Perkins says, "She was untouched by existential angst, and the delighted reading of her work among so many highly sophisticated writers resembles Werther's love for Charlotte." There is no doubt something in Moore that elicits this uneasiness in male commentators, no matter how strongly they extol her virtues. Perhaps her work is in fact more "feminine" than it may appear to a woman reader, to whom Moore's angle of vision may seem more congenial. Or perhaps Moore's occasional contempt for the world of male power provokes a counterattack on what may seem to some her miniature version of life.

The book-length studies of her work by male admirers have not in themselves been notable works of literary criticism. A full-length book by a sympathetic reader who is also a woman is consequently a good addition to the available criticism. Laurence Stapleton, a professor of English at Bryn Mawr, is the first critic to write at length about the formidable assemblage of Moore materials in the Rosenbach collection, and her book—*Marianne Moore*—is most interesting in its revelation of Moore's habit of incessant work, and in its description of the reading and conversation notebooks from which poems were quarried. Stapleton writes always as an advocate, and is loath to grant any falling-off in Moore's work, tranquilly defending even the later poems and the translations. (She is admirably informative about the original fables and about the virtues of Moore's solutions to problems of expressive difference between English and French.) Younger readers looking for a reader's companion for their first tackling of Moore and could do no better than to have Stapleton's book at hand. She paraphrases concisely, dissolves Gordian knots, and offers unobtrusive factual helps. She knew Moore; she has evidently spent years with the poems and feels wholly at home with them. Although her emphasis veers a little stiffly between the strictly thematic and the strictly technical, she is consistently reliable on both—though she does not, I think, find a more comprehensive ground, subsuming the two. Her argument is embodied in her subtitle, "The Poet's Advance." It is useful to have a lengthy, reasoned case made for the view that Moore got better after *Observations*. (Jarrell and others would agree; still others, like

Hugh Kenner, would dissent.) Stapleton's quotations from early drafts (especially revealing in the case of "Marriage") and from letters and family papers enrich the instructive running commentary on the poems.

The fragments of biographical fact which appear now and then equally please and horrify. We might have been happier not knowing that "on a visit to the circus or the zoo [Moore] collected [elephant hairs], seizing an opportune moment to snip some from the tail or the trunk, using a small scissors that she carried with her for this purpose." We may wince at the familiar style she affected in letters, as in one to her brother on a bracelet of elephant charms which he had sent her: "I can't make out what they are standing on . . . I gotta determine this. Well Bible [her brother] as I said to Cub, Badger [her brother] has imagination . . . This here bracelet is not "cold" . . . so I figure I am gonna wear it pretty much all the time."

Stapleton's commentary always derives from pleasure, and from a conviction of Moore's worth. If Moore could be better served by a book that discriminated more severely between her poetry and her verses, this well-stocked volume, full of hitherto unpublished fact and quotation, nonetheless cannot fail to make Moore's work much better known and more widely appreciated. Even the footnotes are full of interest. We learn from one of them that Bryher offered Moore five thousand dollars "so that she and her mother might spend some time in England," but "the offer was refused." Another note reveals that in 1943 Moore's "combined income from royalties . . . and for reading manuscripts for the Macmillan Co. totaled $310, supplemented by less than a thousand dollars from other sources." It is no wonder the Moores sometimes referred to themselves as field mice. Donald Hall, in his readable book on Moore, quotes a pen portrait by Robert McAlmon in the roman à clef *Post Adolescence* (though the character is called Martha Wullus, she is recognizably the young Marianne Moore): "A Dresden doll thing with those great contemplative Chinese eyes of hers, and that wisplike body with its thatch of carrot-colored hair, so picturesque too in her half-boyish clothes." That this young girl grew up to tell herself, "It is better to be lonely than unhappy," that she took herself in hand and decided to go her solitary way in her delicate but unconventional rhythms, is itself remarkable, since her need to steady herself into satire, security, and peace hints at undertows of fear, anger, and discouragement. Stapleton speaks of Moore's insubordination; it was a quality from which Moore profited, but of which she could scarcely entirely approve. Marguerite Young told, in a festschrift for

Moore's seventy-seventh birthday, how the poem "Nevertheless" arose: Moore, seeing in a box of strawberries a mishapen green one, almost all seeds, said, "Here's a strawberry that's had quite a struggle," and found thereby a first line. It is a pity that Moore's own struggle culminated in things like the weaker poems and the preposterous exchanges with the Ford Motor Company over the naming of the Edsel, but it may be true, as Yeats said, that "all great men are owls, scarecrows, by the time their fame has come."

T. S. Eliot

The manuscript version of *The Waste Land*, the most famous of modern poems, is at last available. It is a version bound to raise whatever dust has settled over its celebrated lines. The poem appeared, with no notes, in October 1922, in *The Criterion;* the notorious notes, by now almost canonically part of the poem, were added to fill out the manuscript for book publication in December. By the time of his death in 1965 Eliot was, principally on account of *The Waste Land,* a culture hero, attracting thousands to his lectures. His audiences were like lemmings: moving in obedience to obscure compulsions, they swarmed to hear him, filling halls to overflowing.

When I was seventeen, I caught pneumonia—and thought it no bad bargain—sitting on the floor of Harvard's unheated Memorial Hall, hearing Eliot's lecture piped through from Sanders Theatre. Hardly anyone there, I suppose, had come out of interest in poetic drama, his putative subject; we all wanted to catch a glimpse of the author of *The Waste Land,* and we tried not to feel disappointed at the stooped and courtly figure bowing left and right as he left the hall. Never did anyone look less like a *poète maudit.* But back in the twenties he was still "the fabulously beautiful and sibylline" Eliot of Conrad Aiken's description, a sibyl who arose from the pages of *The Criterion* saying, "I want to die," and then launched into the famous explanation: "April is the cruellest month."

The reception of *The Waste Land* was various enough to provide one of the most entertaining chapters in modern literary history. Encouraged by Eliot's genial notion of 1929 that "genuine poetry can communicate before it is understood," a generation of critics disburdened themselves of theories about *The Waste Land.* One of the

This review of the facsimile edition of T. S. Eliot's *The Waste Land* appeared in the *New York Times Book Review*, November 7, 1971.

few sensible remarks, as one might expect, was made by I. A. Richards, who saw in the poem Eliot's "persistent concern with sex, the problem of our generation, as religion was the problem of the last." In spite of the transparent truth of Richards' account, the symbol-hunting critics outnumbered him, and their tribe is legion even now: in a book written recently I read that Sir Henry Harcourt-Reilly (in *The Cocktail Party*) "drinks gin, juice of the tree of resurrection, and water, symbol of purification." Oh blessed juniper bush!

Eliot's first reaction to his critics was, understandably, irritation: "When I wrote a poem called 'The Waste Land' some of the more approving critics said that I had expressed 'the disillusionment of a generation,' which is nonsense. I may have expressed for them their own illusion of being disillusioned, but that did not form part of my intention."

By the time of a late broadcast on Vergil, he had mellowed: "A poet may believe that he is expressing only his private experience; his lines may be for him only a means of talking about himself without giving himself away; yet for his readers what he has written may come to be the expression both of their own secret feelings and of the exultation or despair of a generation." That formulation comes nearer the truth, and what began as a poem about sex ended up representing something more. Whoever read *The Waste Land* was stopped dead by it, for good or ill. Pound said it was "about enough to make the rest of us shut up shop," and William Carlos Williams wrote that it "wiped out our world as if an atom bomb had been dropped upon it."

In the shock of absorption, nobody bothered much to inquire out of what matrix the poem had come; like Everest, it was simply there. The notes provoked violent self-education all round; critics had to go and read everyone from Ezekiel to Jessie Weston, not to speak of the Buddha. For the young, who felt no professional obligation to look up the quotations, the poem existed in a lovely penumbra, a rainfall of hazy words in French, German, and Italian, and was felt to be the greater for it.

Who was Eliot, what was he, that all our young attend him, was a question scarcely asked. Eliot's fabled reticence made sure, later on, that it could not be asked. It is only since his death that some fragments of biography have appeared, and we still lack most of his letters. Even Valerie Eliot's introduction to this volume gives fewer biographical details than we could have wished, but we are finally in possesion of the bare bones of the history of *The Waste Land*.

Eliot had definitely left America, against his parents' wishes, to make a life in England; his disapproving father had made a will in which no property was left to Eliot outright, as it was to his brother and sisters, but only in trust, to revert to the family (and not to Eliot's wife) when Eliot should die. Vivien Eliot was becoming more and more distraught from "nerves," neuralgia, migraines, colitis, and the other afflictions which were to result in her final nervous collapse ("an invalid always cracking up, & needing doctors, & incapable of earning anything" as Pound put it). The work in Lloyds Bank, reviewing for *The Athenaeum*, teaching evening courses, and writing *The Sacred Wood* had overburdened Eliot beyond endurance.

Below and beyond all these lay those stresses, still obscure but no doubt familial (reinforced by the death of his father in 1919 and a summer-long visit from his mother and sister in 1921) which were to lead to his final adherence to the Anglican Church. A doctor, on the basis of physical symptoms (tachycardia is mentioned), prescribed a three-month "rest," but Eliot wanted something more: "He is known as a nerve man and I want rather a specialist in psychological troubles," he wrote to Julian Huxley. On November 18, 1921, Eliot went alone to Lausanne and placed himself under the care of one Dr. Roger Vittoz. No details of his treatment have been made public.

In January he returned from the sanitarium, "with a damn good poem (19 pages) in his suitcase," said Pound; "the best I have ever done," said Eliot. The poem was, it can be argued, the best he was ever to do. By March 1923 he was writing to John Quinn, "I am worn out, I cannot go on," and Richard Aldington was reporting to Pound that already, so shortly after the treatment, Eliot was "going to pieces" again. We must see *The Waste Land*, then, in the extremity of its composition, written by an American confined in Switzerland, who was having what we can only describe as some sort of nervous breakdown.

The shame at that time of having to acknowledge to the world one's own inability to go on earning one's living was immense; no male American could conceive of a greater humiliation. Switzerland seemed like a nerve-center surrounded by all of European culture, desiccated or fruitful; and in his sanitarium the disconsolate chimera that had been Tom Eliot began his long lament:

> Jerusalem Athens Alexandria
> Vienna London

Unreal..
London Bridge is falling down falling down falling down . . .
These fragments I have shored against my ruins.

Some of the "fragments" out of which the poem was composed,
it is known, had preexisted it and had been, indeed, thought of as
complete poems in themselves. Conrad Aiken mentions having heard
Eliot recite "A woman drew her long black hair out tight," and the
poems "The Death of Saint Narcissus" (previously called, according
to Aiken, "The Love Song of Saint Sebastian"), "The Death of the
Duchess," and others (reproduced now in their original forms)
contributed bits and pieces to the completed whole. On the other
hand, Eliot may have meant, by "fragments," all those lines not his
own which, inserted at strategic points in *The Waste Land*, opened
the poem to charges of being a hoax, a plagiarism, and a joke.
"Immature poets imitate; mature poets steal," Eliot had written in
1920; and his thefts were on a grand scale. They formed, in fact, a
principal of composition.

Matthew Arnold, in *The Study of Poetry*, had isolated, from the
grandest poems he knew, their grandest lines, lines which he
christened "touchstones" by which all other poems could be tried.
To read Arnold's "touchstones" is to sense *The Waste Land* in
embryo:

> And what is else not be overcome . . .
> De plusurs choses a remembrer li prist . . .
> Absent thee from felicity awhile . . .
> Καὶ σέ, γέρον, τὸ πρὶν μὲν ἀκούομεν ὄλβιον εἶναι.
> In la sua volontade è nostra pace.

Just as Eliot's rhythms rise from the songs in "Empedocles on
Etna," and just as his essays find their model in Arnold's, so *The
Waste Land* is the anguished poem Arnold should have written,
an antiphonal duet between his aridity and his touchstones.

But there is a third, and un-Arnoldian, component in *The Waste
Land*—the modern talk. How did Eliot learn it? Where did he find
the rhythms of the pub and the marital quarrel? Not even Browning,
though he hovers behind these dialogues, ever quite conceived of
anything so rapid and nervous:

> "My nerves are bad tonight. Yes, bad. Stay with me.
> "Speak to me. Why do you never speak. Speak.
> "What are you thinking of? What thinking? What?
> "I never know what you are thinking. Think."

And even more remarkable than that staccato are the cursive sleazy rhythms of Lil and the others in the pub:

When Lil's husband got demobbed, I said—
I didn't mince my words, I said to her myself,
HURRY UP PLEASE ITS TIME . . .
What you get married for if you don't want children? . . .
Goonight Bill. Goonight Lou. Goonight May. Goonight.

The editorial notes say that Eliot called this passage "pure Ellen Kellond": she was "a maid employed by the Eliots who recounted it to them."

Half the poets in England at that point probably had maids; Eliot's genius was to listen to what his maid said, write it down, and make it poetry. Arnold's notion of poetry did not allow for that sort of transcription: there were no touchstones in the kitchen. For Arnold, there were probably no touchstones in the mysterious East, either, since to qualify for insertion into the immortal list, things had to resonate through Western culture. Shantih, not to mention Datta, Dayadhvam, and Damyata, imply a fatal willingness in Eliot to take all culture as his province.

The religious ending of *The Waste Land* has been so controversial for so long that it is hard to see it anew, but it certainly bears ominous overtones of what was to come in Eliot's verse, both in the preciousness of "Ash-Wednesday" ("Eliot's monument to self-pity," as Blackmur called it) and in the religiosity of the *Four Quartets*. Is nervousness cured by ethics? Can "the heap of broken images" be put together again, like Humpty-Dumpty, by a heap of moral injunctions? Can Hieronymo's madness be ministered to by words from an Upanishad? To the Upanishads, in later days, Eliot added Krishna, St. John of the Cross, Blessed Julian of Norwich, and so on. And all manner of thing shall be well. But was it? Certainly not in the verse, which stretched feebler and feebler through the tracts of the *Quartets*, reposing on that unlikely poetic:

Desiccation of the world of sense,
Evacuation of the world of fancy,
Inoperancy of the world of spirit.

With *Burnt Norton* Eliot became the first of the modern line of poets named by Christopher Ricks "the wistful guilties." The embarrassments of the plays are beyond comment. The career tailed off more disastrously than any other in living memory, with only sporadic lines reminding a reader of what Eliot once had been.

Returning from the disheartening late work to the early poems is like turning from the "Ecclesiastical Sonnets" to "The Prelude" (though on a much smaller scale, needless to say). If Eliot is to claim a place in English poetry, it will have to be on the basis of the poems written before 1930. We may all be deceived, even in this, and future ages may discover, as Harold Bloom has mischievously prophesied, that Pound and Eliot are our Cleveland and our Cowley. The judgment of history will at least be facilitated by this new volume, which reprints not only the manuscript drafts of *The Waste Land* itself, but also the manuscripts of those previously written poems (nine of them, by my count, some still unpublished) which contributed some lines to the whole, or were proposed by Eliot to Pound as possible components of the poem.

The drafts have a curious history. In the fall of 1968, the New York Public Library announced that it owned the long-misplaced manuscript of *The Waste Land*. Eliot, in 1922, had sold it to the New York lawyer and patron of artists John Quinn for $140. Quinn's niece, in 1958, after searching for it and finding it among Quinn's papers in storage sold it, without informing Eliot, to the Berg Collection for $18,000. As Ezra Pound says in his preface, the Jamesian "mystery of the missing manuscript is now solved." Nobody who knows *The Waste Land* will be sorry to have the new material published, but it is, regrettably, pretty much all bad. Ezra Pound's service to Eliot in cutting the manuscript was everything it has been reputed to be, and the poem will remain a symbiotic triumph of his editing conjoined to Eliot's composing. The newly revealed poems and passages, by their truly awful lines, paradoxically confirm the worth of the poem as we have known it since 1922. We could scarcely have become attached to a *Waste Land* that included Eliot's repellent dirge:

> Full fathom five your Bleistein lies
> Under the flatfish and the squids.
> Graves' Disease in a dead jew's eyes!
> When the crabs have eat the lids . . .
>
> See the lips unfold unfold
> From the teeth, gold in gold.
> Lobsters hourly keep close watch
> Hark! now I hear them scratch scratch scratch

At least this "poem" mercifully remained extrinsic to the whole, except for one line. But in the original manuscript of *The Waste Land* proper, there are things almost as bad, notably a long passage in heroic couplets at the beginning of "The Fire Sermon" detailing the morning activities of one Fresca (already present in "Gerontion" which Pound vetoed as a prelude to *The Waste Land*). Fresca gets up, has coffee, "labours" on "the needful stool" (Pound saw the absurdity of the *stool's* needfulness) while reading *Clarissa*, reads and writes letters, and finally takes a bath:

> This ended, to the steaming bath she moves,
> Her tresses fanned by little flutt'ring Loves;
> Odours, confected by the cunning French,
> Disguise the good old hearty female stench.

Pound, blue-penciling out the lady's levée, wrote in a letter, "You can't parody Pope unless you can write better verse than Pope and you can't." Exit Fresca. We also lose a long initial pub-crawl in Boston (replaced by the English pub scene) and, from "What the Thunder Said," "an infant hydrocephalous" who "fiddled (with a knot tied in one string)."

From "Death by Water," Pound cut a lengthy passage on sailors who endure a blank-verse shipwreck near the Dry Salvages. In this, there are overtures of Dante, Tennyson, "The Ancient Mariner," and Homer, all voiced in lines with much talk of trysails and main gaff jaws and garboard strakes and fore cross trees. Two men come down with gleet. What is gleet? Even Webster's is too delicate to say, except that it involves an inflamed "bodily orifice" and an "abnormal discharge." Under Pound's frown, exit gleet, sailors, codfish, bears, iceberg, sirens, and shipwreck. Only Phlebas the Phoenician, remains, rising and falling with the sea-currents, a memorial, perhaps, to the Jean Verdenal who drowned in 1915 in the Dardanelles, to whose memory Eliot dedicated his first volume.

Pound's marginal snorts make lively havoc in these pages. When Eliot tergiversates with "perhaps" and "may," Pound scribbles, "Make up yr mind—you Tiresias if you know know damn well or else you dont." When Eliot turns stagey, Pound turns comic:

> London, your people is bound upon the wheel!
> Phantasmal gnomes, burrowing in brick and stone and steel!

"Palmer Cox's brownies," notes Pound dryly: exit the brownie-gnomes. So it is not for some haunting lost echoes of great poetry that this manuscript will interest anyone. It provokes, though, questions about the composition of this celebrated poem, and a new judgment about its sources in Eliot's previous work.

As far as we can see from the drafts reproduced, several early poems were quarried for what became lines of *The Waste Land*. The earliest of these pieces date from 1914, and an Emersonian fragment, derived from *The Bhagavad-Gita* crossed with the Gospels, already foreshadows Eliot's ending; it begins "I am the Resurrection and the Life," and dismally ends, four lines later, with "I am the fire, and the butter also." At least, compared with that, "Shantih shantih shantih" is a distinct improvement. The other earliest pieces are fragments which become "After the torchlight" and "A woman drew her long black hair out tight."

Then we come to "The Death of Saint Narcissus," which long had an underground reputation as a poem "suppressed" after having been set up in galleys for *Poetry*. It is pure decadent fin-de-siècle stuff, Swinburnian in content if not in cadence, a masturbatory fantasy all mixed up with religion, masochism, and narcissism. It bears thinking about as an early indication of Eliot's species of religious interest. "Come under the shadow of this grey rock," it begins, in a line which slightly changed, would become one of the most famous in *The Waste Land*. We are offered, after we come in, the esoteric sight of the mutilated body of Saint Narcissus, who, "aware of his legs smoothly passing each other," was "stifled and soothed by his own rhythm."

With logic that is odd indeed, this prompts a choice of vocation:

> Struck down by such knowledge
> He could not live men's ways, but became a dancer before God.

After thinking that he had been a tree "twisting its branches among each other," he "knew that he had been a fish":

> With slippery white belly held tight in his own fingers,
> Writhing in his own clutch, his ancient beauty
> Caught fast in the pink tips of his new beauty.

Then, he continues, he had been a young girl raped by a drunken old man:

Knowing at the end the taste of her own whiteness
The horror of her own smoothness . . .
So he became a dancer to God.

He finally, "because his flesh was in love with the burning arrows," embraced the arrows and was satisfied as "his white skin sur- rendered itself to the redness of blood." A creepy poem. It ends with Narcissus / Sebastian "green / dry, and stained / With the shadow in his mouth."

This poem is linked to another, called "Exequy," where twining Adepts of love are joined by a superior spirit:

But if, more violent, more profound,
One soul, disdainful or disdained,
Shall come, his shadowed beauty stained
The colour of the withered year,
    Self-immolating on the Mound
Just at the crisis, he shall hear
    A breathless chuckle underground.
SOVEGNA VOS AL TEMPS DE MON DOLOR.
Consiros vei la pasada folor.

Pound told Eliot not to include this in *The Waste Land*, but it is of a piece with the rest in its final disparagement of sex. Though *The Waste Land* is obsessed with sex, it hasn't a good word to say for it, a bias that justifies Randall Jarrell's fine malice in saying that Eliot would have written *The Waste Land* about the Garden of Eden.

Though Jarrell never wrote at any length about Eliot, he conjec- tured in a long aside: "Won't the future say to us in helpless aston- ishment: 'But did you actually believe that all those things about objective correlatives, classicism, the tradition, applied to *his* poetry? Surely you must have seen that he was one of the most subjective and daemonic poets who ever lived, the victim and helpless bene- ficiary of his own inexorable compulsions, obsessions. From a psy- choanalytical point of view he was far and away the most interesting poet of your century.' "

The publication of these early poems, drafts, and fragments of *The Waste Land*, however disappointing in literary terms, can but arouse new commentaries which may liberate Eliot from the strait- jacket of dreary sectarian criticism: his reputation may not be en- hanced in any degree, but it may take on a truer coloring. His solemn hagiographers, it is to be hoped, will be replaced by a genera- tion of lively and unintimidated readers, quick to see his essential genius, but just as quick to perceive its progressive extinction.

Robert Penn Warren

Robert Penn Warren proposes, in this brief sequence of poems, a new hero for our time: the naturalist-artist John James Audubon. He is a hero peculiarly acceptable to the American intellectual mind, a mind which trusts next to nothing—not its own abstract byways, not the visionary corridors of art, not the blunt highroad of social engagement. When these delusory paths, promising only more refinement, more mysticism, or more crudeness, seem yet the only entries to the actual, a man like Audubon, who blended art and science, the natural and the cerebral, the tender and the violent, without any consciousness of unease, appeals irresistibly as a model.

Audubon never distrusted, not for a moment, his extraordinary calling, and in the end he was justified in his unwavering pride. His confidence had a stunning simplicity: "Ever since a Boy I have had an astonishing desire to see Much of the World and particularly to acquire a true knowledge of the Birds of North America." An inexplicable mission, an arrest in latency: with the collector's passion unsatisfied, Audubon went on, clear of conscience in shooting birds, rapt in the discovery of species, immensely knowledgeable in ornithology, obsessive in his recording of detail, hunching and curving his specimens to fit them into his elephant folio pages, sacrificing most other rewards of life to the production of his unequaled plates, and yet observing and noting down as well, in letters and journals, the life around him.

Audubon's art is muscular and avid: his birds and his rats alike inhabit a world of beak and claw and fang, of ripped-open bellies and planted talons. Violence caught in act, at the heart of Audubon's work, is at the heart too of this collection, where Robert Penn Warren retells, with his peculiar narrative Ancient-Mariner talent, a raw

This review of Robert Penn Warren's *Audubon: A Vision* appeared in the *New York Times Book Review*, January 11, 1970.

incident of craftiness, torture, and death, purportedly witnessed by Audubon.

The incident seems considerably milder as it appears in Audubon's recollections of the prairie; Warren's version has more sex, more murder, and more poetry. Warren's narrative, like the two stories of wretched death in his *Incarnations* (1968), is horribly memorable in plot, while the language tends very often to efface itself in pure transparency. Warren can make a climax out of five unremarkable words (as Audubon lies transfixed in a cabin, threatened with murder)—"He hears the jug slosh." But there occur, here and there, clotted descriptions on which the plot depends. Audubon, in his first approach to the cabin, sees a shape:

> The face, in the air, hangs. Large,
> Raw-hewn, strong-beaked, the haired mole
> Near the nose, to the left, and the left side by firelight
> Glazed red, the right in shadow, and under the tumble and tangle
> Of dark hair on that head, and under the coarse eyebrows,
> The eyes, dark, glint as from the unspecifiable
> Darkness of a cave. It is a woman.

She and her murderous sons are finally hanged by passing travelers:

> The face,
> Eyes a-glare, jaws clenched, now glowing black with congestion
> Like a plum, had achieved,
> It seemed to him, a new dimension of beauty.

The problem of the poem lives in that face, and in the face of preying beasts:

> The dregs
> Of all nightmare are the same, and we call it
> Life. He knows that much, being a man,
> And knows that the dregs of all life are nightmare.
>
> Unless.
>
> Unless what?

Audubon's work and equanimity answer the "unless." To terror and nightmare he answers with vision by night ("In my sleep I continually dream of birds") and drawing by day. Warren's elegy for Audubon succeeds in all but one respect: we believe the life (even so intensified and interpreted), we believe the death, one of the silences of the frontier, but the immortality ("I see your lip, un-drying, gleam in the bright wind") is perhaps unearned. Never-theless, two of Warren's great questions—the nature of love and the meaning of life in time—are incarnate here in his fitting parable of the chosen hunter-artist-hero. Of love: "One name for it is knowl-edge." Of life: time is the necessary condition for the living-out of Audubon's "story of deep delight."

To our American taste, Audubon, self-taught, pragmatic, eccen-tric, solitary, attentive, and proud, seems, for better or worse, our sort. We may miss a wilder fancy, or a more human love, or a softer beauty—Audubon is no Keats—but the uncivilized American forest, with its wastes punctuated by savages and criminals, bred a different sort of Romantic. This inside of America is Robert Penn Warren's territory, and these striking vignettes of a man question-lessly happy in his environment and his birds map out for us a possible happiness, incorporating the gory and the ethereal at once.

Like some previous sequences in Warren's *Collected Poems* (1966) and later work, these poems tell us that one spurt of feeling is inadequate to any detailed subject, and yet that a single long poem, in its composure, is false to the discontinuous feelings that an event, or a person, or a vision can provoke. So Warren gives us these linked poems, so many tangential observations around the self-contained sphere of the actual and its complex of man, event, and scene.

Toward the middle of the poem, after the violence, Audubon still continues "to walk in the world," and is rewarded by a plain sim-plicity of truth:

> His life, at the end, seemed—even the anguish—simple.
> Simple, at least, in that it had to be,
> Simply, what it was, as he was,
> In the end, himself and not what
> He had known he ought to be.
> The blessedness!

This is, we might think, the indifference of the old masquerading as happiness: "When such as I cast out remorse / So great a sweet-ness flows into the breast / We are blest by everything"—we have precedent for such feelings. But Warren confirms his assertion with a stunning completion:

> To wake in some dawn and see,
> As though down a rifle barrel, lined up

Like sights, the self that was, the self that is, and there,
Far off but in range, completing that alignment, your fate.

Hold your breath, let the trigger-squeeze be slow and steady.

The quarry lifts, in the halo of gold leaves, its noble head.

The grim and the contented coincide, and neither is falsified. The enduring attraction of Audubon lies in his equable representation of both, and it is perhaps a mark of the worth of this poem that a reader should feel it adequate to its hero and to his beautiful and predatory birds.

W. H. Auden

If poetry, as Auden once defined it, is the clear expression of mixed feelings, then this new volume is not all poetry. The feelings here are often unmixed, and these conservative moments give even Auden pause:

> Can Sixty make sense to Sixteen-Plus?
> What has my camp in common with theirs,
> With buttons and beards and Be-Ins?

Auden's answer is "Much"—immediately qualified by "I hope." A crusty crankiness at modern life in Manhattan opens this collection: we live in "numbered caves in enormous jails," surrounded by the "lawless marches" of the Asphalt Lands; "mean cafés" entertain the lazy, while the stultified workers view "vulgar rubbish" and listen to "witless noise," making their "lewd fancies . . . of flesh debased."

We begin to wonder whether the Johnny Carson show and *Playboy* deserve such gravity, but luckily Auden himself wonders too, and puts his disgust down in the end to the dyspepsia of an insomniac night, but not before he has given us, with his genius for glum myth, a vision of the state to which Megalopolis is heading, a savage future where the "human remnant" will be

> stunted in stature, strangely deformed,
> numbering by fives, with no zero,
> worshipping a ju-ju *General Mo*,
> in groups ruled by grandmothers,
> hirsute witches who on winter nights

This review of W. H. Auden's *City Without Walls and Other Poems* appeared in the *New York Times Book Review*, February 22, 1970.

> fable them stories of fair-haired Elves
> whose magic made the mountain dam,
> of Dwarves, cunning in craft, who smithied
> the treasure-hoards of tin cans.

This spooky and enticing fantasy, with its surreal details by Voodoo out of Wagner-cum-George MacDonald, not only replaces the lumpish satire that precedes it, it also gives us once again Auden-the-saga-sayer, writing the Anglo-Saxon alliterative line as only he can, claiming a metric he singlehandedly revived. Even in ill-temper, Auden offers a lot.

There are five or six very handsome poems in this volume, along with some rather trifling commissioned things, some forgettable translations from *Mother Courage,* and some touching occasional poems. Nothing Auden does of his own and on his own is ever uninteresting: as the liveliest man-of-letters in the English-speaking world, he deserves only front pages; his trifles are better than others' lifework.

On the other hand, he has, like any poet, his special talents, and he has always been at his most acute in self-definition (a very partial self-definition, and critics have been at pains to point out the organs omitted from the anatomy, but still a brilliant taxonomic replica, however disemboweled, proceeds from the analysis). Here, he pronounces himself a son of Horace, one of the tribe of "The Horatians," those who in England in the past lived

> a life without cumber, as pastors adjective
> to rustic flocks, as organists in trollopish
> cathedral towns . . .

> [in] obscure nooks into which Authority
> never pokes a suspicious nose, *embusqué* havens
> for natural bachelors
> and political idiots.

However strange coming from this inhabitant not of Barchester but of the East Village, the poem is nevertheless Auden's poetic apologia, and ends as the Horatians speak their apologetic self-defense:

> . . . "As Makers go,
> compared with Pindar or any

> of the great foudroyant masters who don't ever
> amend, we are, for all our polish, of little

stature, and, as human lives,
compared with authentic martyrs

like Regulus, of no account. We can only
do what it seems to us we were made for, look at
the world with a happy eye
but from a sober perspective."

Criticism of Auden has reproached him for not being foudroyant, confessional, grand, romantic, radical, and tragic: the Nobel Prize, in this serious century, passed him by. The irreverent and dazzling undergraduate has left behind, or so it seems, the age of anxiety, and has come to Trollope, "small dinner parties, small rooms," and "a genteel sufficiency of land or lolly."

The conservatism of the old continues to be a stumbling block to the young, but Auden has at least not forgotten what being young was like. His enduring status as an outsider—the bachelor among the married, the Englishman among New Yorkers (or Austrians or Greeks), the writer among the inarticulate—gives him a certain perpetual adolescence, embattled against the grownups. And yet his own aging has landed him with those grownups, outside the vertiginous fairgrounds of youth.

In a beautiful poem he gives immortal permanence to those roller coasters and Ferris wheels that no adult would willingly ride on again, but that children see as all colorful test and adventure. In the Fun House,

Mopped and mowed at, as their train worms through a tunnel,
by ancestral spooks, caressed by clammy cobwebs,
grinning initiates emerge into daylight
as tribal heroes.

But the old, "those with their wander-years behind them," like Auden, require "caution, agenda," and keep away from the fair-grounds:

. . . to be found in coigns where, sitting
in silent synods, they play chess or cribbage,
games that call for patience, foresight, maneuver
like war, like marriage.

Conservative subjects can be chilling to poetry, and in this book they often reveal Auden's old weakness—the either-or mentality that divides and categorizes its mixed feelings into Upper and Lower, or Left and Right, or Fairground and Cribbage. The clear expression, in short, sometimes makes the mixed feelings less mixed than they really may be. Celebration of the intellect drives Auden to a distaste for the unconscious:

> ... discarding rhythm, punctuation, metaphor
> it sinks into a driveling monologue,
> too literal to see a joke or
> distinguish a penis from a pencil.

Granted, this is from a poem in praise of the god Terminus, who gives us "games and grammar and meters" and is the god of "walls, doors, and reticence." But Auden's aesthetic seems at points like these fruitlessly watertight, an aesthetic of the superintelligible defensively enclosing, peculiarly enough, his Troll-Fathers and Tusked-Mothers, who surely belong, one would think, to that realm where a pencil is a penis. To put Sycorax into sestinas is a distinctly odd vocation. However, in a brisk and cheerful self-portrait called "Profile," Auden tells us he is so obsessive a ritualist that even a pleasant surprise makes him cross, and that "without a watch / he would never know when / to feel hungry or horny."

Fenced in by rituals, grammar, meter, and watches, he may seem to be running a locked private zoo for his fearsome dragons, and a critic who wants spontaneity above all may quibble; but under the nooses and nets his vocabulary runs wild, his parades and escapades enliven the scene, his perfect conversation runs babbling along, Autolycus his quintessential spokesman:

> For a useful technician I lacked
> the schooling, for a bureaucrat
> the *Sitzfleisch:* all I had was the courtier's agility to adapt . . .

But even that snapper-up of unconsidered trifles grows old:

> No rheum has altered my gait, as ever my cardiac muscles
> are undismayed, my cells
> perfectly competent . . . But how glib all the faces I see about me
> seem suddenly to have become,
> and how seldom I feel like a hay-tumble.

The dismay and isolation that come with age have scarcely, ever been better-voiced than in this bravado of the out-of-date.

Whatever criticism we may make of Auden, he has been there before us and said it of himself, and more cleverly.

Finally, we find among these new poems, with the pleasure of recognition, those tireless entertainments Auden has been contriving for us for the past forty years. In the portrait of the "Rois Fainéants" we have one of his snapshots of history-as-it-really-was; in "Partition" a bureaucrat's look at history-as-it-really-is (in India, divided by "different diets and incompatible Gods," partition is accomplished by a London lawyer using out-of-date maps and incorrect census returns, "But there was no time to check them, no time to inspect / Contested areas. The weather was frightfully hot").

There are as well jolly moralities from Aesop (to be sung, with the frogs getting the double dactyls, to music by Hans Werner Henze) and other such divertissements; there are even, astonishingly in view of the age of the topic, new things to be said about the seasons:

> Lodged in all is a set metronome: thus, in May
> Bird-babes still in the egg click to each other Hatch!;
> June-struck cuckoos go off-pitch; when obese July
> Turns earth's heating up, unknotting their poisoned ropes,
> Vipers move into play; warned by October's nip,
> Younger leaves to the old give the releasing draught.

There is a Chaucerian impartial solicitude about it all, as there is in Auden's long description of a river-profile, natural and allegorical at once.

The rebelling critical appetite that still, unreasonably but unquellably, wishes that Auden's immense talent had been spent on the high serious, rebels equally at Pope and Byron and Skelton. Auden's long and revealing "Letter to Lord Byron," his couplets in the manner of Pope and Butler, his preference for *The Magic Flute* over *The Ring*, all station him for our pigeonholing, but he lightly eludes our cruder labels, and retorts by asking when Autolycus ever solemned himself.

Elizabeth Bishop

Elizabeth Bishop's poems in *Geography III* put into relief the continuing vibration of her work between two frequencies—the domestic and the strange. In another poet the alternation might seem a debate, but Bishop drifts rather than divides, gazes rather than chooses. Though the exotic is frequent in her poems of travel, it is not only the exotic that is strange and not only the local that is domestic. (It is more exact to speak, with regard to Bishop, of the domestic rather than the familiar, because what is familiar is always named, in her poetry, in terms of a house, a family, someone beloved, home. And it is truer to speak of the strange rather than of the exotic, because the strange can occur even in the bosom of the familiar, even, most unnervingly, at the domestic hearth.)

To show the interpenetration of the domestic and the strange at their most inseparable, it is necessary to glance back at some poems printed in *Questions of Travel.* In one, "Sestina," the components are almost entirely innocent—a house, a grandmother, a child, a Little Marvel Stove, and an almanac. The strange component, which finally renders the whole house unnatural, is tears. Although the grandmother hides her tears and says only "It's time for tea now," the child senses the tears unshed and displaces them everywhere—into the dancing waterdrops from the teakettle, into the rain on the roof, into the tea in the grandmother's cup.

> ... the child
> is watching the teakettle's small hard tears
> dance like mad on the hot black stove
> the way the rain must dance on the house ...

"Domestication, Domesticity, and the Otherworldly" first appeared in *World Literature Today*, Winter 1977.

> . . . the almanac
> hovers half open above the child,
> hovers above the old grandmother
> and her teacup full of dark brown tears.

The child's sense of the world is expressed only in the rigid house she draws (I say "she," but the child, in the folk-order of the poem, is of indeterminate sex). The child must translate the tears she has felt, and so she "puts . . . a man with buttons like tears" into her drawing, while "the little moons fall down like tears / from between the pages of the almanac / into the flower bed the child / has carefully placed in the front of the house."

The tercet ending the sestina draws together all the elements of the collage:

> *Time to plant tears,* says the almanac.
> The grandmother sings to the marvellous stove
> and the child draws another inscrutable house.

The absence of the child's parents is the unspoken cause of those tears, so unconcealable though so concealed. For all the efforts of the grandmother, for all the silence of the child, for all the brave cheer of the Little Marvel Stove, the house remains frozen, and the blank center stands for the definitive presence of the unnatural in the child's domestic experience—*especially* in the child's domestic experience. Of all the things that should not be inscrutable, one's house comes first. The fact that one's house always *is* inscrutable, that nothing is more enigmatic than the heart of the domestic scene, offers Bishop one of her recurrent subjects.

The centrality of the domestic provokes as well one of Bishop's most characteristic forms of expression. When she is not actually representing herself as a child, she is, often, sounding like one. The sestina, which borrows from the eternally childlike diction of the folktale, is a case in point. Not only the diction of the folktale, but also its fixity of relation appears in the poem, especially in its processional close, which places the almanac, the grandmother, and the child in an arrangement as unmoving as those found in medieval painting, with the almanac representing the overarching Divine Necessity, the grandmother as the elder principle, and the child as the principle of youth. The voice speaking the last three lines dispassionately records the coincident presence of grief, song, necessity, and the marvelous; but in spite of the "equal" placing of the last three lines, the ultimate weight on inscrutability, even in the heart of the domestic, draws this poem into the orbit of the strange.

A poem close by in *Questions of Travel* tips the balance in the other direction, toward the domestic. The filling station which gives its name to the poem seems at first the antithesis of beauty, at least in the eye of the beholder who speaks the poem. The station is dirty, oil-soaked, oil-permeated; the father's suit is dirty; his sons are greasy; all is "quite thoroughly dirty"; there is even "a dirty dog." The speaker, though filled with "a horror so refined," is unable to look away from the proliferating detail which, though this is a filling station, becomes ever more relentlessly domestic. "Do they live in the station?" wonders the speaker, and notes incredulously a porch, "a set of crushed and grease- / impregnated wickerwork," the dog "quite comfy" on the wicker sofa, comics, a taboret covered by a doily, and "a big hirsute begonia." The domestic, we perceive, becomes a compulsion that we take with us even to the most unpromising locations, where we busy ourselves establishing domestic tranquillity as a demonstration of meaningfulness, as a proof of "love." Is our theology only a reflection of our nesting habits?

> Why the extraneous plant?
> Why the taboret?
> Why, oh why, the doily? . . .
>
> Somebody embroidered the doily.
> Somebody waters the plant,
> or oils it, maybe. Somebody
> arranges the rows of cans
> so that they softly say:
> ESSO—SO—SO—SO
> to high-strung automobiles.
> Somebody loves us all.

In this parody of metaphysical questioning and the theological argument from design, the "awful but cheerful" activities of the world include the acts by which man domesticates his surroundings, even if those surroundings are purely mechanical, like the filling station or the truck in Brazil painted with "throbbing rosebuds."

The existence of the domestic is most imperiled by death. By definition, the domestic is the conjoined intimate: in American literature the quintessential poem of domesticity is "Snowbound." When death intrudes on the domestic circle, the laying-out of the corpse at home, in the old fashion, forces domesticity to its ultimate powers of accommodation. Stevens' "Emperor of Ice-Cream" places the cold and dumb corpse at the home wake in grotesque conjunction with the funeral baked meats, so to speak, which are being confected in the kitchen, as the primitive impulse to feast over the dead is seen surviving, instinctive and barbaric, even in our "civilized" society. Bishop's "First Death in Nova Scotia" places the poet as a child in a familiar parlor transfixed in perception by the presence of a coffin containing "little cousin Arthur":

> In the cold, cold parlor
> my mother laid out Arthur
> beneath the chromographs:
> Edward, Prince of Wales,
> with Princess Alexandra,
> and King George with Queen Mary.
> Below them on the table
> stood a stuffed loon
> shot and stuffed by Uncle
> Arthur, Arthur's father.

All of these details are immemorially known to the child. But focused by the coffin, the familiar becomes unreal: the stuffed loon becomes alive, his taciturnity seems voluntary, his red glass eyes can see.

> Since Uncle Arthur fired
> a bullet into him,
> he hadn't said a word.
> He kept his own counsel . . .
>
> Arthur's coffin was
> a little frosted cake,
> and the red-eyed loon eyed it
> from his white, frozen lake.

The adults conspire in a fantasy of communication still possible, as the child is told, "say good-bye / to your little cousin Arthur" and given a lily of the valley to put in the hand of the corpse. The child joins in the fantasy, first by imagining that the chill in the parlor makes it the domain of Jack Frost, who has painted Arthur's red hair as he paints the Maple Leaf of Canada, and next by imagining that "the gracious royal couples" in the chromographs have "invited

Arthur to be / the smallest page at court." The constrained effort by all in the parlor to encompass Arthur's death in the domestic scene culminates in the child's effort to make a gestalt of parlor, coffin, corpse, chromographs, loon, Jack Frost, the Maple Leaf Forever, and the lily. But the strain is too great for the child, who allows doubt and dismay to creep in—not as to ultimate destiny, oh no, for Arthur is sure to become "the smallest page" at court, that confusing place of grander domesticity, half-palace, half-heaven; but rather displaced onto means.

> But how could Arthur go,
> clutching his tiny lily,
> with his eyes shut up so tight
> and the roads deep in snow?

Domesticity is frail, and it is shaken by the final strangeness of death. Until death, and even after it, the work of domestication of the unfamiliar goes on, all of it a substitute for some assurance of transcendent domesticity, some belief that we are truly, in this world, in our mother's house, that "somebody loves us all." After a loss that destroys one form of domesticity, the effort to reconstitute it in another form begins. The definition of death in certain of Bishop's poems is to have given up on domesticating the world and reestablishing yet once more some form of intimacy. Conversely, the definition of life in the conversion of the strange to the familial, of the unexplored to the knowable, of the alien to the beloved.

No domesticity is entirely safe. As in the midst of life we are in death, so, in Bishop's poetry, in the midst of the familiar, and most especially there, we feel the familiar as the unknowable. This guerrilla attack of the alien, springing from the very bulwarks of the familiar, is the subject of "In the Waiting Room." It is 1918, and a child, almost seven, waits, reading the *National Geographic*, while her aunt is being treated in the dentist's office. The scene is unremarkable: "grown-up people, / arctics and overcoats, / lamps and magazines," but two things unnerve the child. The first is a picture in the magazine: "black, naked women with necks / wound round and round with wire / like the necks of light bulbs. / Their breasts were horrifying"; and the second is "an *oh!* of pain / —Aunt Consuelo's voice" from inside. The child is attacked by vertigo, feels the cry to be her own uttered in "the family voice" and knows at once her separateness and her identity as one of the human group.

But I felt: you are an *I,*
you are an *Elizabeth,*
you are one of *them.*
Why should you be one too?
. . . .
What similarities—
boots, hands, the family voice
I felt in my throat, or even
the *National Geographic*
and those awful hanging breasts—
held us all together
or made us all just one?

In "There Was a Child Went Forth" Whitman speaks of a comparable first moment of metaphysical doubt:

> . . . the sense of what is real, the thought if after all it should prove unreal,
> The doubts of day-time and the doubts of night-time, the curious whether and how,
> Whether that which appears so is so, or is it all flashes and specks?
> Men and women crowding fast in the streets, if they are not flashes and specks what are they?

It is typical of Whitman that after his momentary vertigo he should tether himself to the natural world of sea and sky. It is equally typical of Bishop, after the waiting room slides "beneath a big black wave, / another, and another," to return to the sober certainty of waking fact, though with a selection of fact dictated by feeling.

The War was on. Outside,
in Worcester, Massachusetts,
were night and slush and cold,
and it was still the fifth
of February, 1918.

The child's compulsion to include in her world even the most unfamilar data, to couple the exotica of the *National Geographic* with the knees and trousers and skirts of her neighbors in the waiting room, brings together the strange at its most horrifying with the quintessence of the familiar—oneself, one's aunt, the "family voice." In the end, will the savage be domesticated or oneself rendered unknowable? The child cannot bear the conjunction and faints. Language fails the six-year-old. "How—I didn't know any / word for it—how 'unlikely.' "

That understatement, so common in Bishop, gives words their full weight. As the fact of her own contingency strikes the child, "familiar" and "strange" become concepts which have lost all meaning. "Mrs. Anderson's Swedish baby," says Stevens, "might well have been German or Spanish." Carlos Drummond de Andrade (whose rhythms perhaps suggested the trimeters of "In the Waiting Room") says in a poem translated by Bishop:

> Mundo mundo vasto mundo,
> se eu me chamasse Raimundo
> seria uma rima, não seria uma solução.

If one's name rhymed with the name of the cosmos, as "Raimundo" rhymes with "mundo," there would appear to be a congruence between self and world, and domestication of the world to man's dimensions would seem possible. But, says Drummond, that would be a rhyme, not a solution. The child of "In the Waiting Room" discovers that she is in no intelligible relation to her world, and, too young yet to conceive of domination of the world by will or domestication of the world by love, she slides into an abyss of darkness.

In "Poem" ("About the size of an old-style dollar bill") the poet gazes idly at a small painting done by her great-uncle and begins yet another meditation on the domestication of the world. She gazes idly—that is, until she realizes that the painting is of a place she has lived: "Heavens, I recognize the place, I know it!" In a beautiful tour de force "the place" is described three times. The first time it is rendered visually, exactly, interestedly, appreciatively, and so on: such, we realize, is pure visual pleasure touched with relatively impersonal recognition ("It must be Nova Scotia; only there / does one see gabled wooden houses / painted that awful shade of brown"). Here is the painting as first seen:

> Elm trees, low hills, a thin church steeple
> —that gray-blue wisp—or is it? In the foreground
> a water meadow with some tiny cows,
> two brushstrokes each, but confidently cows;
> two minuscule white geese in the blue water,
> back-to-back, feeding, and a slanting stick.
> Up closer, a wild iris, white and yellow,
> fresh-squiggled from the tube.
> The air is fresh and cold; cold early spring
> clear as gray glass; a half inch of blue sky
> below the steel-gray storm clouds.

Then the recognition—"Heavens, I know it!"—intervenes, and with it a double transfiguration occurs: the mind enlarges the picture beyond the limits of the frame, placing the painted scene in a larger, remembered landscape, and the items in the picture are given a local habitation and a name.

> Heavens, I recognize the place, I know it!
> It's behind—I can almost remember the farmer's name.
> His barn backed on that meadow. There it is,
> titanium white, one dab. The hint of steeple,
> filaments of brush-hairs, barely there,
> must be the Presbyterian church.
> Would that be Miss Gillespie's house?
> Those particular geese and cows
> are naturally before my time.

In spite of the connection between self and picture, the painting remains a painting, described by someone recognizing its means—a dab of titanium white here, some fine brushwork there. And the scene is set back in time—those geese and cows belong to another era. But by the end of the poem the poet has united herself with the artist. They have both loved this unimportant corner of the earth; it has existed in their lives, in their memories and in their art.

> Art "copying from life" and life itself,
> life and the memory of it so compressed
> they're turned into each other. Which is which?
> Life and the memory of it cramped,
> dim, on a piece of Bristol board,
> dim, but how live, how touching in detail
> —the little that we get for free,
> the little of our earthly trust. Not much.

Out of the world a small piece is lived in, domesticated, remembered, memorialized, even immortalized. Immortalized because the third time that the painting is described, it is seen not by the eye—whether the eye of the connoisseur or the eye of the local inhabitant contemplating a past era—but by the heart, touched into participation. There is no longer any mention of tube or brushstrokes or paint colors or Bristol board; we are in the scene itself.

> ... Not much.
> About the size of our abidance
> along with theirs: the munching cows,

the iris, crisp and shivering, the water
still standing from spring freshets,
the yet-to-be dismantled elms, the geese.

Though the effect of being in the landscape arises in part from the present participles (the munching cows, the shivering iris, the standing water), it comes as well from the repetition of nouns from earlier passages (cows, iris), now denuded of their "paint" modifiers ("two brushstrokes each," "squiggled from the tube"), from the replication of the twice-repeated early "fresh" in "freshets" and most of all from the prophecy of the "yet-to-be-dismantled" elms. As lightly as possible, the word "dismantled" then refutes the whole illusion of entire absorption in the memorial scene; the world of the child who was once the poet now seems the scenery arranged for a drama with only too brief a tenure on the stage—the play once over, the set is dismantled, the illusion gone. The poem, having taken the reader through the process that we name domestication and by which a strange terrain becomes first recognizable, then familiar, and then beloved, releases the reader at last from the intimacy it has induced. Domestication is followed, almost inevitably, by that dismantling which is, in its acute form, disaster, the "One Art" of another poem:

I lost my mother's watch. And look! my last, or
next-to-last of three loved houses went . . .

I lost two cities, lovely ones. And, vaster,
some realms I owned, two rivers, a continent . . .

the art of losing's not too hard to master
though it may look like (*Write* it!) like disaster.

That is the tone of disaster confronted, with whatever irony.

A more straightforward account of the whole cycle of domestication and loss can be seen in the long monologue, "Crusoe in England." Crusoe is safely back in England, and his long autobiographical retrospect exposes in full clarity the imperfection of the domestication of nature so long as love is missing, the exhaustion of solitary colonization.

. . . I'd have
nightmares of other islands
stretching away frome mine, infinities

of islands, islands spawning islands,
like frogs' eggs turning into polliwogs
of islands, knowing that I had to live
on each and every one, eventually
for ages, registering their flora,
their fauna, their geography.

Crusoe's efforts at the domestication of nature (making a flute, dis-
tilling home brew, even devising a dye out of red berries) create a
certain degree of pleasure ("I felt a deep affection for / the smallest
of my island industries"), and yet the lack of any society except that
of turtles and goats and waterspouts ("sacerdotal beings of glass . . . /
Beautiful, yes, but not much company") causes both self-pity and a
barely admitted hope. Crusoe, in a metaphysical moment, christens
one volcano "*Mont d'Espoir* or *Mount Despair*," mirroring both his
desolation and his expectancy. The island landscape has been domesticated, "home-made," and yet domestication can turn to domesticity
only with the arrival of Friday: "Just when I thought I couldn't stand
it / another minute longer, Friday came." Speechless with joy, Crusoe can speak only in the most vacant and consequently the most
comprehensive of words.

Friday was nice.
Friday was nice, and we were friends.
. . . he had a pretty body.

Love escapes language. Crusoe could describe with the precision
of a geographer the exact appearances of volcanoes, turtles, clouds,
lava, goats, and waterspouts and waves, but he is reduced to gesture
and sketch before the reality of domesticity.

In the final, recapitulatory movement of the poem Bishop first
reiterates the conferral of meaning implicit in the domestication of
the universe and then contemplates the loss of meaning once the
arena of domestication is abandoned.

The knife there on the shelf—
it reeked of meaning, like a crucifix.
It lived . . .
I knew each nick and scratch by heart . . .
Now it won't look at me at all.
The living soul has dribbled away.
My eyes rest on it and pass on.

Unlike the meanings of domestication, which repose in presence and use, the meaning of domesticity is mysterious and permanent. The monologue ends:

> The local museum's asked me to
> leave everything to them:
> the flute, the knife, the shrivelled shoes . . .
> How can anyone want such things?
> —And Friday, my dear Friday, died of measles
> seventeen years ago come March.

The ultimate locus of domestication is the heart, which, once cultivated, retains its "living soul" forever.

This dream of eternal and undismantled fidelity in domesticity, unaffected even by death, is one extreme reached by Bishop's imagination as it turns round its theme. But more profound, I think, is the version of life's experience recounted in "The Moose," a poem in which no lasting exclusive companionship between human beings is envisaged, but in which a series of deep and inexplicable satisfactions unroll in sequence, each of them precious. Domestication of the land is one, domesticity of the affections is another, and the contemplation of the sublimity of the nonhuman world is the third.

In the first half of the poem one of the geographies of the world is given an ineffable beauty, both plain and luxurious. Nova Scotia's tides, sunsets, villages, fog, flora, fauna, and people are all summoned quietly into the verse, as if for a last farewell, as the speaker journeys away to Boston. The verse, like the landscape, is "old-fashioned."

> The bus starts. The light
> is deepening; the fog
> shifting, salty, thin,
> comes closing in.
>
> Its cold, round crystals
> form and slide and settle
> in the white hens' feathers,
> in gray glazed cabbages,
> on the cabbage roses
> and lupins like apostles;
>
> the sweet peas cling
> to wet white string
> on the whitewashed fences;
> bumblebees creep

inside the foxgloves,
and evening commences.

The exquisitely noticed modulations of whiteness, the evening harmony of settling and clinging and closing and creeping, the delicate touch of each clause, the valedictory air of the whole, the momentary identification with hens, sweet peas, and bumblebees all speak of the attentive and yielding soul through which the landscape is being articulated.

As darkness settles, the awakened soul is slowly lulled into "a dreamy divagation / . . . / a gentle, auditory, slow hallucination." This central passage embodies a regression into childhood, as the speaker imagines that the muffled noises in the bus are the tones of "an old conversation":

> Grandparents' voices
>
> uninterruptedly
> talking, in Eternity:
> names being mentioned,
> things cleared up finally . . .
>
> Talking the way they talked
> in the old featherbed,
> peacefully, on and on . . .
>
> Now, it's all right now
> even to fall asleep
> just as on all those nights.

Life, in the world of this poem, has so far only two components: a beloved landscape and beloved people, that which can be domesticated and those who have joined in domesticity. The grandparents' voices have mulled over all the human concerns of the village:

> what he said, what she said,
> who got pensioned;
>
> deaths, deaths and sicknesses;
> the year he re-married;
> the year (something) happened.
> She died in childbirth.
> That was the son lost
> when the schooner foundered.
>
> He took to drink. Yes.
> She went to the bad.
> When Amos began to pray

> even in the store and
> finally the family had
> to put him away.
>
> "Yes . . ." that peculiar
> affirmative. "Yes . . ."
> A sharp, indrawn breath,
> half-groan, half-acceptance.

In this passage, so plainly different in its rural talk and sorrow from the ravishing aestheticism of the earlier descriptive passage, Bishop joins herself to the Wordsworth of the *Lyrical Ballads*. The domestic affections become, for a moment, all there is. Amos who went mad, the son lost at sea, the mother who died, the girl gone to the bad—these could all have figured in poems like "Michael" or "The Thorn." The litany of names evoking the bonds of domestic sympathy becomes one form of poetry, and the views of the "meadows, hills, and groves" of Nova Scotia is another. What this surrounding world looks like, we know; that "Life's like that" (as the sighed "Yes" implies), we also know. The poem might seem complete. But just as the speaker is about to drowse almost beyond consciousness, there is a jolt, and the bus stops in the moonlight, because "A moose has come out of / the impenetrable wood." This moose, looming "high as a church, / homely as a house," strikes wonder in the passengers, who "exclaim in whispers, / childishly, softly." The moose remains.

> Taking her time,
> she looks the bus over,
> grand, other-worldly.
> Why, why do we feel
> (we all feel) this sweet
> sensation of joy?

What is this joy?

In "The Most of It" Frost uses a variant of this fable. There, as in Bishop's poem, a creature emerges from "the impenetrable wood" and is beheld. But Frost's beast disappoints expectation. The poet had wanted "counter-love, original response," but the "embodiment that crashed" proves to be not "human," not "someone else additional to him," but rather a large buck, which disappears as it came. Frost's beast is male, Bishop's female; Frost's a symbol of brute force, Bishop's a creature "safe as houses"; Frost's a challenge, Bishop's a reassurance. The presence approaching from the wood plays, in both these poems, the role that a god would play in a pre-Wordsworthian poem and the role that a human being—a leech-gatherer, an ancient soldier, a beggar—would play in Wordsworth. These human beings, when they appear in Wordsworth's poetry, are partly iconic, partly subhuman, as the Leech-Gatherer is part statue, part sea-beast, and as the old man in "Animal Tranquillity and Decay" is "insensibly subdued" to a state of peace more animal than human. "I think I could turn and live with animals," says Whitman, foreshadowing a modernity that finds the alternative to the human not in the divine but in the animal. Animal life is pure presence, with its own grandeur. It assures the poet of the inexhaustibility of being. Bishop's moose is at once maternal, inscrutable, and mild. If the occupants of the bus are bound, in their human vehicle, to the world of village catastrophe and pained acknowledgment, they feel a releasing joy in glimpsing some large, grand solidity, even a vaguely grotesque one, which exists outside their tales and sighs, which is entirely "otherworldly." "The darkness drops again," as the bus moves on; the "dim smell of moose" fades in comparison to "the acrid smell of gasoline."

"The Moose" is such a purely linear poem, following as it does the journey of the bus, that an effort of will is required to gaze at it whole. The immediacy of each separate section—as we see the landscape, then the people, then the moose—blots out what has gone before. But the temptation—felt when the poem is contemplated entire—to say something global, something almost allegorical, suggests that something in the sequence is more than purely arbitrary. The poem passes from adult observation of a familiar landscape to the unending ritual, first glimpsed in childhood, of human sorrow and narration, to a final joy in the otherworldly, in whatever lies within the impenetrable wood and from time to time allows itself to be beheld. Beyond or behind the familiar, whether the visual or the human familiar, lies the perpetually strange and mysterious. It is that mystery which causes those whispered exclamations alternating with the pained "Yes" provoked by human vicissitude. It guarantees the poet more to do. On it depends all the impulse to domestication. Though the human effort is bent to the elimination of the wild, nothing is more restorative than to know that earth's being is larger than our human enclosures. Elizabeth Bishop's poetry of domestication and domesticity depends, in the last analysis, on her equal apprehension of the reserves of mystery which give, in their own way, a joy more strange than the familiar blessings of the world made human.

Randall Jarrell

The Complete Poems

"We have lost for good," said Randall Jarrell, "the poems that would
have been written by the modern equivalent of Henry VIII or
Bishop King or Samuel Johnson; born novelists, born theologians,
born princes." We might add, born critics: because Jarrell, who was
fifty-one when he died in 1965, can be said to have put his genius
into his criticism and his talent into his poetry.

That talent, in the course of his life, grew considerably, and the
editors of these posthumous *Complete Poems* may have been right
to put the better poems first: the *Selected Poems* of 1955 are followed
by the collections of 1960 and 1965, and only after these groups are
we permitted to see the lesser rest (composed from 1940 through
1965). If we reconstruct, from this fanciful arrangement, the boy
Jarrell growing into the man Jarrell, we can see the progress of his
peculiarly double nature, one side of charming and comic, the other
vulnerable and melancholy.

The poems Jarrell wrote before World War II—roughly before he
was thirty—are on the whole forgettable, but they foreshadow his
continual risky dependence on history, folk tale, and art: many of the
later poems are retellings (of history or biography), redescriptions
(of a Dürer etching, a Botticelli canvas, the Augsburg Adoration), or
reworkings of a myth. That dependency in Jarrell never died; he was,
nobody more so, the eager audience to any book or piece of music
that captured his wayward interest; his poems in which the scene
is a library are hymns to those places where we can "live by trading
another's sorrow for our own."

His first steady original poems date from his experience in the

This review of Randall Jarrell's *Complete Poems* first appeared in the *New
York Times Book Review*, February 2, 1969.

111

Air Force, when the pity that was his tutelary emotion, the pity that was to link him so irrevocably with Rilke, found a universal scope:

> We died like aunts or pets or foreigners.
> (When we left high school nothing else had died
> For us to figure we had died like.) . . .
> In bombers named for girls, we burned
> The cities we had learned about in school.

Jarrell brings us his adolescent soldiers with their pitiful reality of high school—high school!—as the only notching-stick of experience; he brings us the veteran "stumbling to the toilet on one clever leg of leather, wire, and willow," with the pity all in the *faute-de-mieux* weird boastfulness of "clever"; he brings us the bodiless lost voices in the air—"can't you hear me? over, over—"; and, for all its triteness now, he brings us the death of the ball turret gunner.

The secret of his war poems is that in the soldiers he found children; what is the ball turret gunner but a baby who has lost his mother? The luckier baby who has a mother, as Jarrell tells us in "Bats," "clings to her long fur / by his thumbs and toes and teeth . . . / Her baby hangs on underneath . . . / All the bright day, as the mother sleeps, / She folds her wings around her sleeping child." So much for Jarrell's dream of maternity; but the ball turret gunner has a different fate: "From my mother's sleep I fell into the State, / And I hunched in its belly till my wet fur froze."

Jarrell often has been taken to task for his sentimentality, but the fiction, recurrent in his work, or a wholly nonsexual tenderness, though it can be unnerving in some of the marriage poems, is indispensable in his long, tearfully elated recollections of childhood. The child who was never mothered enough, the mother who wants to keep her children forever, these are the inhabitants of the lost world, where the perfect filial symbiosis continues forever. The nostalgia for childhood even lies behind Jarrell's aging monologists —the Marschallin, the woman at the Washington Zoo, the woman in the supermarket—and gives them at once their poignancy and their abstraction.

For all his wish to be a writer of dramatic monologues, Jarrell could only speak in his own alternately frightened and consolatory voice, as he alternately played child and mother. It has been charged that Jarrell's poetry of the war shows no friends, only, in James Dickey's words, "killable puppets"—but Jarrell's soldiers are of course not his friends because they are his babies, his lambs to the slaughter—

he broods over them. In his final psychic victory over his parents, they too become his babies as he, perfectly, in this ideal world of recovered memory, remains *their* baby:

> Here are Mother and Father in a photograph,
> Father's holding me . . . They both look so young.
> I'm so much older than they are. Look at them,
> Two babies with their baby.

His students are his children too, and the sleeping girl in the library at Greensboro receives his indulgent parental solicitude:

> As I look, the world contracts around you:
> I see Brünnhilde had brown braids and glasses
> She used for studying.

The student—"poor senseless life"—is nevertheless finally the pure and instinctual ideal:

> I have seen
> Firm, fixed forever in your closing eyes,
> The Corn King beckoning to his Spring Queen.

This guileless taste requires a guileless style, and Jarrell found it late, in the gossipy, confidential, and intimate manner of "The Lost World," his recollections of a childhood year in Hollywood:

> On my way home I pass a cameraman
> On a platform on the bumper of a car
> Inside which, rolling and plunging, a comedian
> Is working; on one white lot I see a star
> Stumble to her igloo through the howling gale
> Of the wind machines. On Melrose a dinosaur
> And pterodactyl with their immense pale
> Papier-mâché smiles, look over the fence
> Of *The Lost World.*

That childlike interest—in the cameraman, the artificial igloo, and the cartoon monsters—was the primitive form of Jarrell's later immensely attractive enthusiasm for all the pets he kept in his private menagerie. Nobody loved poets more or better than Randall Jarrell— and irony, indifference, or superciliousness in the presence of the remarkable seemed to him capital sins. In one of his last poems, "The

Old and the New Masters," he takes issue with Auden, arguing that in any number of paintings the remarkable sufferer or redeemer is not tangential but is rather the focus of the whole:

> ... everything
> That was or will be in the world is fixed
> On its small, helpless, human center.

Those lines could be the epigraph to these collected poems; and yet there are dimensions of Jarrell that we could wish for more of. One of his talents is to rewrite, in a grim way, nursery tales, so that we see Cinderella finally preferring the cozy female gossip of the fireside to life with the prince, or we see Jack, post-beanstalk, sitting in a psychotic daze by his rotting cottage, "bound in some terrible wooden charm . . . rigid and aghast." Another, and perhaps truer, Jarrell writes a disarming poem of pure pleasure ("Deutsch Durch Freud") on why he never wants really to know German; it's so much nicer only to know it halfway, via Rilke and lieder:

> It is by Trust, and Love, and reading Rilke
> Without *ein Wörterbuch*, that man learns German ...
> And Heine! At the ninety-sixth *mir träumte*
> I sigh as a poet, but dimple, as *ein Schuler* ...
> And my heart lightens at each *Sorge*, each *Angst* ...
> Till the day I die I'll be in love with German
> —If only I don't learn German ...

In lines like these, all of Jarrell's playful wit is coming to the surface, that wit which has dazzled us from the pages of his energetic criticism, but which often falters under the (very Germanic) melancholy of *The Complete Poems*. The refugees, children, recluses, soldiers, and aging women who inhabit his verse might have left more room in it for their satiric and resilient creator, but Jarrell kept his two sides very distinct. "One finds it unbearable," he remarked in an essay, "that poetry should be so hard to write," and he added that poets suffer their poetry as helplessly as anything else. He cannot be said, as a poet, to have invented new forms, a new style, or new subjects, in any grand way; but he made himself memorable as a singular man, at his most exceptional in denying his own rarity:

> How young I seem; I *am* exceptional;
> I think of all I have.
> But really no one is exceptional,

No one has anything, I'm anybody,
I stand beside my grave
  Confused with my life, that is commonplace and solitary.

So one late poem says, but it had begun, in a flash of the boyish Jarrell *brio*, with a woman in a supermarket "Moving from Cheer to Joy, from Joy to All." Zest, down to a zest for the names of detergents, stayed mixed, to the very last, with the tears of things.

The Third Book of Criticism

Randall Jarrell once wrote that his heart, confronted by the supermarket offerings of public media, was sad; but that same sad heart, offered a good book, reacted with an almost disorderly passion of gratitude, and these posthumous essays and reviews (all previously published) breathe on every page the pleasure of deprivation consoled, as if the child with his nose pressed to the sweetshop window (Yeats's phrase about Keats) had suddenly been given a cake.

The relish of a starved palate accounts for the energy of Jarrell's recommendations, and the hunger he awakens in his readers is an envy of that relish and a wish to taste with that strenuous tongue. Since taste is personal, Jarrell can occasionally disappoint; we may follow him to a book and find it less good than his account of it. But generally he incarnates his own definition of a critic in his first book of criticism, *Poetry and the Age* (1953), as "an extremely good reader—one who has learned to show to others what he saw in what he read."

The limits of this definition are also Jarrell's limits: he was, for better or worse, a member of no school of criticism; he was no theorist; he felt happier writing about the nineteenth and twentieth centuries than about earlier periods where what you see in what you read depends radically on historical information; he wrote always to "show to others" and not to muse to himself. He was not, in short, a Frye, an Auerbach, a Blackmur, an Auden.

On the other hand, his mind was anything but simple. No reader

This review of *The Third Book of Criticism* by Randall Jarrell appeared in the *New York Times Book Review*, January 4, 1970.

of poetry, however devoted, could fail to learn in generous amounts from his superlative essays on modern poetry (represented here by a "close reading" of Frost's "Home Burial" and a bewitching overview of Auden's whole career). It would be impossible for anyone, no matter how committed to theory or to historical scholarship, to condescend to the man who wrote these essays, or, to go back in time, to the man who could be so just, in *Poetry and the Age*, to Whitman and Marianne Moore at once. Jarrell is a worshiping evangelist of books, forever metaphorically lending us his most recent favorite, as in fact in life he recklessly lent his own library. He says endearingly that of the people he lent his *Crime and Punishment* to, "every fourth or fifth borrower returns it unfinished": fourth or fifth out of twenty? out of forty? Which of us has ever lent a book out even five times?

Jarrell's gratitude to his authors can sometimes seem indiscriminate. Why should he use such superlatives about Graves, we wonder; but somewhere the balance of things is always restored: "When you compare Graves with Wordsworth or Rilke, you are comparing a rearrangement of the room with a subsidence of continents." Jarrell sensibly says about his enthusiasm for writers less than the greatest, "You can write better stories than Kipling's, but not better Kipling stories." Minor writers, in short, can be loved as purely as major ones, and sometimes more easily.

Jarrell, in his criticism, had three special talents. He thought naturally in metaphor (a source of charm and jokes as well as a source of truth); he wrote, in almost every account, an implicit suspense story; and he saw books constantly as stories about human beings. In his flashes of likeness, William Carlos Williams' lines "move as jerkily and intently as a bird"; Wallace Stevens, if he were an animal, would be "that rational, magnanimous, voluminous animal, the elephant"; Theodore Roethke is "a powerful Donatello baby who has love affairs, and whose marshlike unconscious is continually celebrating its marriage with the whole wet dark underside of things"; the beatniks operate on "iron spontaneity"; Marianne Moore's poems have "the lacy, mathematical extravagance of snowflakes"; T. S. Eliot is "a sort of combination of Lord Byron and Dr. Johnson."

These telling accuracies are the blackberries in Jarrell's wood, and one can go wandering through his pages for these felicities alone, sometimes so perfect that they are like little poems in themselves, reminding us that Jarrell was, in his own mind, first and foremost a poet, and wrote his metaphorical criticism with the same pen that wrote his metaphorical poetry.

His talent for suspense is more difficult to illustrate, since it governs entire essays, but two examples may serve. Jarrell's famous powers of persuasion are set to make us believe, through a description of *The Death of Ivan Ilych*, that the most significant thing in the world is death, that death, in Tolstoy's words, "ruins all you work for . . . life for oneself can have no meaning." After Jarrell, with his harrowing sympathy, has forced us to a desolate acquiescence, he turns round and announces that Chekhov, in *Ward No. 6*, "detailedly contradicts this Tolstoyan analysis," and we are off, with relief breathing freely once again, hoping that after all "the pure immediacy of pleasure or pain, good or evil," is, or can be, "something ultimate."

The same suspense rules Jarrell's account, in this collection, of Auden's career. With Jarrell, we see Auden synthesizing "more or less as the digestive organs synthesize enzymes" his own order out of Marx, Freud, Groddeck, folk tales, science, and so on. What will Auden do next? Tune in to the next essay. What Auden did next (he turned godly) infuriated Jarrell, and the two essays on Auden in this collection, in their prejudicial view of Auden's "decline," may seem unfair. Nevertheless, there is no more brilliant short account to be found of Auden's matter and manner: Jarrell, even when hostile, was hardly ever inaccurate.

Jarrell's final virtue, and his most winning trait, was his unhesitating belief that though books may not be life, it is life that they are about. His own taste went unashamedly to the literature in which the connection of books and life is most explicit, and some of his flaws in judgment (like his unduly harsh dismissal of some late Stevens poems as "transcendental études") stemmed from his distrust, visible also in his rejection of late Auden, of abstraction in literature. But his appetite for event was inexhaustible. His list of topics in Kipling shows how humanly he absorbed a book of short stories (and who, after reading the list, would not hunger for the stories?): "A drugged, lovesick and consumptive pharmacist; an elderly cook and her lover's cancer; a providential murder committed by a brook; a middle-aged woman watching a wounded German pilot die in the underbrush," and so on. Kipling, he says, can make a list more interesting than the ordinary writer's murder; so can Jarrell.

The only theory that can be said to underlie Jarrell's fiercely sympathetic retelling of human predicaments is the Freudian one, significantly a theory of life rather than a theory of art. But the feeling that underlies all his writing is clear in what he said of one favorite volume, one of the many books with which, hour by hour, he assuaged his spiritual hunger, thirst, and pain: "I cannot look at my bound copy without a surge of warmth and delight: if I knew a monk I would get him to illuminate it." Readers of this collection may feel that a writer illuminated by Jarrell has no need of monks.

John Berryman

Dream Songs

A while ago, it became time to read Berryman. The *Dream Songs* were out, and readers discovered those poems, astonishing and beautiful if bizarre, where a new multiple-Berryman appeared in uninhibited dialogue with himself and his possible selves, a straight man in his own minstrel show, conducting his dreams in public, taking his pills and drinks onto the printed page with him, disavowing his creations all the while, making not confessions but harangues over his private public-address system, all in an eloquent lingua franca:

> Seedy Henry rose up shy in de world
> & shaved & swung his barbells, duded Henry up
> and p.a.'d poor thousands of persons on topics of grand
> moment to Henry, ah to those less & none.

Not quite less and none. By the end of *77 Dream Songs*, Henry, as part of nature, was part of us, as Stevens said of the poet, and his rarities were ours.

In *His Toy, His Dream, His Rest*, there come, almost frighteningly, several hundred more Dream Songs—an avalanche, eleven years of work in them. These ambitious poems take in the world of eleven years: the public world of Eisenhower, Nixon, and Kennedy; the newspaper world of Christine Keeler and Speck and Lana Turner's daughter; the inner world of poets—Eliot, Stevens, Williams, Yeats; the tragic world of lost friends—Delmore Schwartz, Randall Jarrell.

One figure of gross pathos speculates on these worlds—the speaker of these poems, whom Berryman, in another disavowing note

This review of John Berryman's *His Toy, His Dream, His Rest: 308 Dream Songs* appeared in the *New York Times Book Review*, November 3, 1968.

like the one that preceded 77 *Dream Songs,* calls "an imaginary character (not the poet, not me) named Henry, a white American in early middle age, sometimes in blackface, who has suffered an irreversible loss and talks about himself sometimes in the first person, sometimes in the third, sometimes even in the second; he has a friend, never named, who addresses him as Mr. Bones and variants thereof." It must be said that when Berryman breaks an arm, so does Henry; when Berryman goes to Dublin, so does Henry; Henry is not Berryman, but neither is Henry not-Berryman.

Berryman has come a long way to find Henry, and, in Henry, some liberated dimension of himself. In his early, very elegant, verse, he wrote most of the poems a twentieth-century young man can write— Yeats poems, Auden poems, Hopkins poems—all the while trying to write Berryman poems. It was no wonder that his fame waited on his first long original poem, *Homage to Mistress Bradstreet,* a poem standing now, as when it was written, as both true poetry and true Berryman, so many realizations thrust into it that we are still detaching them.

It is Berryman's American voice that speaks for the first time in the throat of Anne Bradstreet, as Berryman claims kin with the long line of American poets who must care for each other, since their worlds have unhanded them. The long self-portrait is full of faultless moments, one of them Mistress Bradstreet's description of her tireless "versing" to domesticate art to America:

> Versing, I shroud among the dynasties;
> quaternion on quaternion, tireless I phrase
> anything past, dead, far,
> sacred, for a barbarous place.

Her impulse is close to Henry's own, as he tirelessly writes down the record of his life and times, not in quaternions but in Berryman's newfound songs, three stanzas each, six lines a stanza, rhymed as he pleases, violated when he pleases. Anne Bradstreet, like Henry in his blackface, is an outsider, and knows that in her passions she is more an Indian than a colonist:

> ... My patience is short,
> I revolt from, I am like, these savage foresters
> whose passionless dicker in the shade, whose glance
> impassive & scant, belie their murderous cries
> when quarry seems to show.

It was an odd way for Berryman to find the colloquial—in the mouth of a seventeenth-century woman—but having found it he never quite let it go. His early sonnets (first printed in 1967, but written in the forties) had made stabs at the spoken language, but it came out derivative and Victorian, sounding here like Meredith, there like Hopkins. "Male American Midwest Colloquial"—if we can give a name to Berryman's native language—crept into his poetry bit by bit, displacing inch by inch his inherited voices.

The first Henry poems, appearing before *77 Dream Songs*, spoke that new language, crossed with blackface dialect:

> Henry sats in de plane & was gay.
> Careful Henry nothing said aloud
> but where a virgin out of cloud
> to her Mountain dropt in light
> his thought made pockets & the plane buckt.
> "Parm me, Lady." "Orright."

This is a considerably jauntier Henry than the one inhabiting *His Toy, His Dream, His Rest*. Too many deaths, public and private, have darkened the scene, too many suicides among them, and Henry is left, a "divided soul,"

> headed both fore & aft and guess which soul
> will swamp and lose:
>
> that hoping forward, brisk & vivid one
> of which will nothing ever be heard again.
> Advance into the past!
> Henry made lists of his surviving friends
> & of the vanished on their uncanny errands
> and took a deep breath.

Henry of the elegies—savage, rueful, petulant, lonely, and still irrepressible—is recognizably the Henry of the brilliant *77 Dream Songs*. But the mournful tone of this collection is fairly constant, and some of the best poetry comes in the seventh and last "Book," which concerns Henry's trip to Ireland—a poetry of leave-takings, farewell parties, ocean trips, solitary homesickness, letters from abroad, and transatlantic telephone calls made "only when drunk and at enormous cost."

Perhaps because these are dream songs and all is allowed, the socially unallowable reactions of rage, irritability, childishness, self-pity, gloom, pretense, and fear are permitted, are deposited, so to speak, in these truthful poems, which are, if we are to believe Berryman's touching title borrowed from Renaissance music, the toy, the dream, and the rest of their composer. The sense of mortality and loss that weighs these poems down sometimes also sinks them (notably in the painful elegies on Delmore Schwartz), but usually self-pity yields to the irony of one whose vices are leaving him:

> for years Henry had been getting away with *murder*,
> the Sheriff mused. There'll have to be an order
> specifically to stop climbing trees,
>
> & other people's wives . . .
> no drinks: that ought to cure him.

The progress of age helped him, to be not good but better. Behind this mask of acquiescence lies the wilder Henry, who began this book as a corpse in a grave (the first poems are labeled "Op. posth. no. 1." and so on to 14), resurrected himself, and then with second thoughts decided to dig back in, but ended up writing the book instead. And this revenant-Henry, in the next-to-last poem of the collection, murders his suicide-father, fulfilling the guilt felt in the most haunting of the 77 *Dream Songs*, "There sat down once a thing on Henry's heart," which ended:

> But never did Henry, as he thought he did,
> end anyone and hacks her body up
> and hide the pieces, where they may be found.
> He knows: he went over everyone, & nobody's missing.
> Often he reckons, in the dawn, them up.
> Nobody is ever missing.

In the sequel in *His Toy, His Dream, His Rest*, Henry sees his father's grave:

> who shot his heart out in a Florida dawn
> O ho alas alas
> When will indifference come, I moan & rave
> I'd like to scrabble till I got right down
> away down under the grass
>
> and ax the casket open ha to see
> just how he's taking it, which he sought so hard
> we'll tear apart
> the mouldering grave clothes ha & then Henry
> will heft the ax once more, his final card,
> and fell it on the start.

Henry, in the midst of suicides, stays alive because of the hunger he tells us was constitutional with him, "need need need / until he went to pieces. / The pieces sat up and wrote." These poems written by the pieces, "written in angry play," rehearse all the events of an "uneventful" life: Henry's three broken limbs ("one more to go"), Henry's debts, Henry's tenant ("the little scraggly-bearded jerk / has not paid his rent for two months"), Henry's foundation mail, Henry's ruined ladies with their "disabled fates" and their disabling letters, Henry's last "thirty years of mostly labour & scrounge," Henry's friends, Henry's trips, Henry's fear, nervousness, and irrational dislikes, Henry's poems, Henry's griefs.

Self-reproach fills the volume, but also, in the end, self-esteem, as Henry becomes the single inexhaustible subject. "Much to be done, much to be done," moans one of the poems; and much has been done. It is not that finding everyday speech in poetry is new; we have had it in Lowell, but severely and remotely; in Ginsberg, but dithyrambically. Here we have it in the ultimate familiarity of the dialogue of the mind with itself, in its banality ("Of course, praise is nice too"), in its self-babying ("an Excellent lady, wif whom he was in wuv"), and its folk-song lift ("Just being the same O"), and, with no falsity, in its sublimity:

> Applause was numerous but my orders were sealed:
> At forty nearly when I took them out
> I gave a joyless shout.

In the years since Henry read his orders, Berryman has become a poet writing of the scathing boundaries between the soul and its surroundings. " 'Tween what we see, what be, / Is blinds. Them blinds' on fire," says Henry's unnamed sage, and a daring passage through that barrier of fire distinguishes Berryman's comic and tragic work.

Robert Lowell

A Difficult Grandeur

In 1973 Robert Lowell, our greatest contemporary poet, published three volumes at once—*History, For Lizzie and Harriet*, and *The Dolphin*—and by that decisive self-presentation made us all once again confront his tumultuous and vexed career. The books were prudishly ignored by the National Book Award judges, who refused even to nominate the entirely new one, *The Dolphin*, for an award, but it later won the Pulitzer Prize for poetry, and reviews mirrored the mixed feelings reflected in the award-giving. *History* is a recasting, in chronological order and revised form, of the poems which appeared in *Notebook;* bracketing it are *For Lizzie and Harriet*, about Lowell's former wife and child, and *The Dolphin*, about his new wife and child. Personal history and the history of the race are Lowell's subjects, and the brutal force of the three books taken at once forced energetic postures of repudiation or championship from all his readers.

Lowell, though born of the Winslows, the Starks, and the Lowells, and perhaps our last intellectual New England poet, is nonetheless not a parochial Boston voice. The eccentricity of his life began, we may think, with his expulsion, for throwing stones, from the Boston Public Garden; it continued with his leaving Harvard for Kenyon College; it was marked by a conversion, though temporary, to Roman Catholicism, followed by imprisonment during World War II as a conscientious objector; it included successive periods of mental illness and successive marriages; and in its combination of reclusiveness and public action, it embodied its own contradictions. The books that issued from this life trace, at first obscurely and then

"The Difficult Grandeur of Robert Lowell" first appeared in *The Atlantic Monthly,* January 1975.

candidly (some have said exhibitionistically), the contours of Lowell's experience, and offer us a poetry of difficult grandeur.

In Lowell, the "mill of the mind" (as Yeats called it) grinds a diverse grain with a stony force. Perhaps the first and only question put to us by its incessant activity is why the grim books that make up his collected works should give us, in any sense, pleasure. Lowell's dramatic power has an edge of malice and, in his tragic moments, cruelty. Both malice and cruelty are countered by a quietism that took its extreme form in the early portrait of the shrine of Our Lady of Walsingham in "The Quaker Graveyard at Nantucket"—the face of the statue "expressionless, expresses God." This quietism later took the form of an expressionless, if biting, historical impartiality. But behind cruelty, malice, and deadly observation lies a covert idealism, sometimes self-indulgent and knowingly sentimental, sometimes pure. His commonest fantasies are of "tyrannizers and the tyrannized," whether Jonathan Edwards terrifying his congregation, or Stalin executing his friends; in our putatively democratic America, Lowell speculates on the use and abuse of power and kingship.

His sonnets throw up nearly indigestible fragments of experience, unprefaced by explanation, unexplained by cause or result; sudden soliloquies of figures from Biblical times to contemporary history; translations; diary jottings; stately imitations of known forms; the whole litter and debris and detritus of a mind absorptive for fifty years. His free association, irritating at first, hovering always dangerously toward the point where unpleasure replaces pleasure, nonetheless becomes bearable, and then even deeply satisfying, on repeated rereading. And if Verdun or Thomas More or Frank Parker is not in our sphere of reference, we can slide off to poems on the march on Washington, or private walks, or Emerson, or a Cambridge blizzard, or New York taxi drivers. The presence of the familiar, and the genuineness of its note, act to assure the genuineness of the rest.

Lowell is one of our most learned and widely read poets, liking encyclopedic reference for its own sake. He tells us that when he was a boy, he "skulked in the attic, / and got two hundred French generals by name, / from A to V—from Augereau to Vandamme." Any one of the two hundred might put in an appearance in *History*, and other, more private allusions to a family past jostle the large and casual mention of historical figures. Lowell has a formidable genius for the details of life, those details which made *Life Studies* an unrivaled family history in verse, and which, filling the pages of *History*, constitute an unspeakably dense poetic or secondary world. It is a world where, even after the publication of *Life Studies*, the Lowell ancestors refuse to disappear:

> They won't stay gone, and stare with triumphant torpor,
> as if held in my fieldglasses' fog and enlargement.

Like some crowded Tiergarten, Lowell's poetry exhausts all species. Since everything is here, we cannot exactly define the poet as a selective collector; he is rather the curator of the world, and it is only in the tone of regard with which this curator presents his specimens, whether alive or fossilized, that we can catch his likeness. That tone, though fierce, is measured. For him, the monuments of culture are not, as they were for Rilke, inexhaustible proof of the ecstatic potential of man; history has not for Lowell, as it had for Tennyson, a teleological shape; and family and home are not finally, as they are to Allen Ginsberg's monstrous piety, sacred. The disloyalty of Lowell-as-grandson in *Life Studies*, where we see him doodling moustaches on the last Russian Czar, plays a decisive role in Lowell's historical perspective. Though his poetry has been seen, with some truth in respect to the early books, as one rising out of disgust, preoccupied with the grotesque, and violent in its sensibility, these qualities are not its determining ones. He has learned, partly through the fitful tenderness first manifested in *Life Studies*, to tame the apocalyptic to the eternal dailiness of life. It is not that his Miltonic avidity for omnipotence has disappeared; but its direction has altered, and the temporal has obscured the prophetic. In fact, *History* and its companion volumes, with their tenderness toward the earth and its offerings, contain the first legitimate continuance of Shakespeare's sonnets since Keats, full of "Any clear thing that blinds us with surprise / . . . wandering silences and bright trouvailles." The closing poem in *For Lizzie and Harriet* demands quotation in any writing about Lowell's sonnets. In it he puts transcendence—all that demands aspiration, vengeance, order, justice, law, salvation— to rest, and chooses instead a Shakespearean recurrence:

> Before the final coming to rest, comes the rest
> of all transcendence in a mode of being, hushing
> all becoming. I'm for and with myself in my otherness,
> in the eternal return of earth's fairer children,
> the lily, the rose, the sun on brick at dusk,
> the loved, the lover, and their fear of life,
> their unconquered flux, insensate oneness. . . .

"My breath," says Lowell, "is life, the rough, the smooth, the bright, the drear."

Into his infernal scenarios enter the odd domestications of the universe, like the turtle discovered on the road, kept in the bathtub, then in the sink, where he refuses to eat:

> raw hamburger mossing in the watery stoppage,
> the room drenched with musk like kerosene—
> no one shaved, and only the turtle washed.
> He was so beautiful when we flipped him over:
> greens, reds, yellows, fringe of the faded savage,
> the last Sioux, old and worn. . . .

Lowell and his wife take the turtle to the river, watch him "rush for water like rushing into marriage." The "uncontaminated joy" of the turtle finding his proper food and element at last transforms the river for Lowell:

> lovely the flies that fed that sleazy surface,
> a turtle looking back at us, and blinking.

The turtle has some of the staunchness of the skunks in "Skunk Hour" (from *Life Studies*), but in that poem the poet cannot share in the cheerful animal life; his "ill-spirit sob[s] in each blood cell." In the vistas of the sonnets, however, the human species performs generic acts, like the lizard:

> The lizard rusty as a leaf rubbed rough
> does nothing for days but puff his throat
> on oxygen, and tongue up passing flies,
> loves only identical rusty lizards panting:
> harems worthy this lord of the universe—
> each thing he does generic, and not the best.

In the sonnets, Lowell embodies his maxims in fine-drawn descriptions, and views himself as not distinct from the lizard: "I, fifty, humbled with the years' gold garbage, / dead laurel grizzling my back like spines of hay." He moves ahead, "drawn on by my unlimited desire, / like a bull with a ring in his nose, a chain in the ring." The cause of our will to direction is only language: If seals should suddenly learn to write, "Then all seals, preternatural like us, / would take direction, head north—their haven / green ice in a greenland never grass." "The fish, the shining fish, they go in circles, / not one of them will make it to the Pole— / this isn't the point though, this is not the point." The "horrifying mortmain of ephemera" becomes in another view our only night on stage, as Lowell says in his poem about his ten-year-old daughter:

> Spring moved to summer—the rude cold rain
> hurries the ambitious, flowers and youth. . . .
>
> Child of ten, three quarters animal,
> threes years from Juliet, half Juliet,
> already ripened for the night on stage—
> beautiful petals, what shall we hope for. . . ?

If I quote such poems, it is because the inexhaustibility of the world, the eternal return of earth' fairer children, became Lowell's subject in the sonnets, expressed with full knowledge of the fragile in the inexhaustible. This poetry has no need of invitation or seduction to win us; it beckons by the comprehension of its atlas, historical and geographical, its representation of all we know.

It does not abandon its previous myths, but it subjects them to a relentless modernizing. Genesis is thrust into Darwinian time, as we see the beginning of the world:

> The virus crawling on its belly like a blot,
> an inch an aeon; the tyrannosaur,
> first carnivore to stand on his two feet,
> the neanderthal, first anthropoid to laugh—
> we lack staying power, though we will to live.
> Abel learned this falling among the jellied
> creepers and morning-glories of the saurian sunset.

Lowell believes equally in Abel and the dinosaurs; and he decides, in a bold throw of the dice, to give twentieth-century speeches to all his characters, even those lost in antiquity. So Clytemnestra becomes Lowell's mother, complaining about her husband:

> "After my marriage, I found myself in constant
> companionship with this almost stranger I found
> neither agreeable, interesting, nor admirable,
> though he was always kind and irresponsible."

Lowell himself appears as the young Orestes, in Clytemnestra's Christmas poem:

"O Christmas tree, how green thy branches—our features
could only be the most conventional,
the hardwood smile, the Persian rug's abstraction,
the firelight dancing in the Christmas candles,
my unusual offspring with his usual scowl,
spelling the fifty feuding kings of Greece,
with a red, blue and yellow pencil.... I
am seasick with marital unhappiness—"

The compulsion to rewrite history, to afford privileged glimpses
of the hidden moments of intimacy in public lives, to insert in the
book of history the commentaries of poets—Horace, Du Bellay,
Góngora, Heine, Baudelaire, Bécquer, Leopardi, Rilke, Rimbaud—to
modernize relentlessly in laconic colloquialisms, to assume familiarity, to impute motive—all this rules more of *History* than perhaps it
should.

Yet what fixes us in admiration of this poetry is the continual
presence of Lowell himself. He is at the shore, has eaten lobster,
watches his dying fire, and thinks how we still discover the dead
fires of druidic Stone Age men and quasi-mythical Celtic kings:

... The fires men build live after them,
this night, this night, I elfking, I stonehands sit
feeding the wildfire wildrose of the fire
clouding the cottage window with my lust's
alluring emptiness. I hear the moon
simmer the mildew on a pile of shells,
the fruits of my banquet ... a boiled lobster,
red shell and hollow foreclaw, cracked, sucked dry,
flung on the ash-heap of a soggy carton—
it eyes me, two pinhead, burnt-out popping eyes.

This is the quintessential beauty of the appalling exactly drawn. It
stands in counterpoint to the equal beauty of the beautiful exactly
drawn, in this "imitation" from Bécquer:

... The thick lemony honeysuckle,
climbing from the earthroot to your window,
will open more beautiful blossoms to the evening;
but these ... like dewdrops, trembling, shining, falling,
the tears of day—they'll not come back....

The vignettes of history spoken in Lowell's voice strike even more
sharply than the resurrected voices of history left to speak for
themselves. Here are the Pilgrims in New England:

... The Puritan shone here,
lord of self-inflicted desiccation,
roaming for outlet through the virgin forest,
stalking the less mechanically angered savage—
the warpath to three wives and twenty children.

As *History* moves to the modern era, Lowell speaks to his contemporaries, the dead poets—Eliot, Pound, Schwartz, MacNeice,
Frost, Williams, Jarrell, Roethke—and to the then still living Berryman. He speaks as well to the other admired dead, from F. O. Mat-
thiessen to Harpo Marx to Che Guevara. Each is allowed a remark,
an epigram, a moment of appearance, before the spurt of life dies
out: "The passage from lower to upper middle age / is quicker than
the sigh of a match in the water." Interspersed are other sighs of
aging, this one adapted from a letter by Mary McCarthy:

Exhaust and airconditioning klir in the city ...
The real motive for my trip is dentistry,
a descending scale: long ago, I used to drive
to New York to see a lover, next the analyst,
an editor, then a lawyer ... time's dwindling choice.

It was not to be expected that Lowell should forsake his autobiographical vein, but it is tempered often, in *History*, with episodes
of pure and detached observation, as an immortal eye, indifferent
to its own decay, makes notations of the disordered wonders of the
earth—the panorama, for instance, of Cambridge in a blizzard:

Risen from the blindness of teaching to bright snow,
everything mechanical stopped dead,
taxis no-fares ... *the wheels grow hot from driving*—
ice-eyelashes, in my spring coat; the subway
too jammed and late to stop for passengers;
snow-trekking the mile from subway end to airport ...
to all-flights-canceled, fighting queues congealed
to telephones out of order, stamping buses,
rich, stranded New Yorkers staring with the wild, mild eyes
of steers at the foreign subway—then the train home,
jolting with stately grumbling.

Such a passage rests in the present, in the isolation of perfect registering of sense, and prevents the worse isolation of the mind withdrawn
from sense:

> Sometimes, my mind is a rocked and dangerous bell;
> I climb the spiral stairs to my own music,
> each step more poignantly oracular,
> something inhuman always rising in me—

Lowell works, in his poems of sense, like those "star-nosed moles, [in] their catatonic tunnels / and earthworks . . . only in touch with what they touch."

There are morals that can be quoted or deduced from the poems in *History* and its companion volumes, but they are not what vivifies them. These poems live neither on ideology nor on logic—props thought to be the mainstays of an earlier Lowell; instead, they yield to the lawless free associations of the rocked and dangerous mind. The worst one can say of Lowell's later verse is that its connections are often at first sight baffling and its use of slang sometimes uncertain; but the awed formality of the early verse was a young man's evasion of his own language. Repudiating the "monotony of vision" inherent in unending attachment to the child he was, and yet knowing that child alive in himself till death, Lowell feels the thread of self as perpetual clue, while following the labyrinths of change, forcing works into shape, dismayed by the recalcitrance of words, wishing a real, not artificial, flame on the hearth:

> I want words meat-hooked from the living steer,
> but a cold flame of tinfoil licks the metal log,
> beautiful unchanging fire of childhood
> betraying a monotony of vision . . .
> Life by definition breeds on change,
> each season we scrap new cars and wars and women.
> But sometimes when I am ill or delicate,
> the pinched flame of my match turns unchanging green,
> a cornstalk in green tails and seeded tassel . . .
> A nihilist has to live in the world as is,
> gazing the impassable summit to rubble.

Of all styles, description is the most difficult to describe. Lowell freed himself from his large early abstractions, even from the categories of the individual soul that once seemed so natural. Taking on history as a discipline, Lowell refuses to be less than the world is.

Have we had a nihilist poet before this later Robert Lowell? Not a nihilist who is a disappointed idealist, but a philosophical nihilist, incorporating within truth both instinctual hope and equable resignation? How Lowell came to this nihilism is not clear; political and marital discouragement, the weariness of twenty years of cyclical mania and depression, and repeated, inevitable hospitalization would suffice, even without the blighting of Lowell's own generation by insanity, suicide, and tragedy. But the weariness is allowed to remain weariness, tending toward but never reaching that death whose "sweetness none will ever taste." "Life, hope, they conquer death, generally, always."

The comparative lack of fertility in Lowell's two weaker volumes, *For the Union Dead* and *Near the Ocean*—after their exquisite predecessor, the original *Life Studies*—warned us that Lowell had to find a new impulse of energy or die as a poet. It seemed impossible that he should go beyond *Life Studies*, with its finely modulated satiric memoir, "91 Revere Street," and its subsequent collection of family portraits. Though there were many beautiful poems in *Life Studies*, it was Part IV of that book, with its quality of sporadic memoir from a son not detached enough to be all-forgiving, but old enough to permit himself detachment, that immediately gained Lowell a new fame, a fame as misplaced in the adjective "confessional" as it was, in itself, deserved. It was not the confessions that made *Life Studies* so memorable; it was rather the quality of memory indelibly imprinted, a brilliance of detail almost unconsciously preserved in a store of words perpetually refreshed.

In *Life Studies*, a deliberate sparseness of syntax enhanced minute details, as daguerrotype succeeded daguerrotype, rendering the furniture, the cuckoo clocks, the lamps with doily shades, the hot water bottle, the golf-cap, the ivory slide rule, the Pierce Arrow, the billiards-table, the decor "manly, comfortable, / overbearing, disproportioned." If we believed in the confessions, it was because we were made to believe in their ambience. And all the forceful particularity of *Life Studies* reappears in Lowell's sonnets.

It is astonishing that anyone confronted with Lowell's three volumes of sonnets should still be praising *Lord Weary's Castle* over *History*. And yet it is done, for example, by a fellow poet who accuses Lowell of "self-exploitation" in *History*: "One senses the life lived in order to provide material for poems; one sees with horror the cannibal-poet who dines off portions of his own body, and the bodies of his family." There are flaws in *History*, of course, since there are no flawless books of poetry, but flaws die of themselves, in silence, and need no criticism for their extinction. A poet's necessary conversion of experience into art can hardly be called cannibalism, and if the accusation that "the life is lived in order to provide material for poems" is to be convincing, it must be proved. Poems are Lowell's life as much as his life is; perhaps more.

> Conscience incurable
> convinces me I am not writing my life;
> life never assures which part of ourself is life.

Lowell is not at his best in describing the chaos of present relation; *Life Studies* benefited from the haze, the selective screens of memory, which refined the *dramatis personae* into effigies of themselves, sepulchral statues fixed in eternally characteristic positions. The slip and flow of changing personal give-and-take is apparently not yet available to Lowell, and that truth is more damaging to his later poetry than any moral criticism. The lapses in the three books of sonnets spring from two sources—the cruel brevity of a fourteen-line form used for encyclopedic material, and the attempt to write of immediate personal interchange. When we lack Lowell's penumbra of information about Rome or the Enlightenment or the Chicago Convention, we miss the point; wishing for intimacy in the personal sonnets, we find sometimes simply the rags and tatters of conversation. "I am learning to live in history," Lowell says in *For Lizzie and Harriet,* and adds his definition: "What is history? What you cannot touch." Once it is irremediably past, and only then, does life give itself to the epiphanies of Lowell's verse, without losing itself as plight, and without divesting itself of dailiness. The shame of wrongdoing, the bitterness of the wronged, the claims of fidelity and the claims of change, must in life clash to a standstill, but nothing in the art of poetry serves justice as justice might urge in life. The extreme power, even of an apparently unjust position, cannot be gainsaid when it occurs. Here is Lowell, for instance, on the eternal problem of the subjection of women: In youth they were swallows, beautiful, capricious, full of movement and gaiety; they asked to be domesticated, to be put into nests, to be fed; now, oppressed by the drudgery of life, they metamorphose into stinging wasps: What are they but prostitutes? I quote the earlier version, called "Das ewig Weibliche":

> Serfs with a finer body and tinier brain—
> who asks the swallows to do drudgery,
> clean, cook, peck up their ton of dust per diem?
> Knock on their homes, they go up tight with fear,
> farting about all morning past their young,

small as wasps fuming in their ash-leaf ball.
Nature lives off the life that comes to hand;
yet if we knew and softly felt their being,
wasp, bee and bird might live with us on air;
the boiling yellow-jacket in her sack
of zebra-stripe cut short above the knee
escape . . . the nerve-wrung creatures, wasp, bee and bird,
felons for life or keepers of the cell,
wives in their wooden cribs of seed and feed.

Whatever our judgment of the social view of the poem, who can dismiss its powerful metamorphoses, its fuming wasps and boiling yellow-jackets, its lethal conjunction of seed and feed? Finally, the only test of a poem is that it be unforgettable, the natural held in the grip of vision. We know Lowell's vision, a powerful one that has forgone the comforts of nostalgia, of religion, seemingly of politics. In the sterner poems, he even forgoes love, though *The Dolphin* lingers in a forlorn hope for that subject even yet. Love itself bows to the eternal phenomenon of recurrence and fate:

I too maneuvered on a guiding string
as I execute my written plot.
I feel how Hamlet, stuck with the Revenge Play
his father wrote him, went scatological
under this clotted London sky.

But even within the rigid confines of the plot, still declaiming words fed by the prompter, the poet finds some liberties of choice and action hovering in possibility: To waver is to be counted among the living, he says, and "survival is talking on the phone." While death becomes "an ingredient of [his] being," he nonetheless watches, from night to morning, "the black rose-leaves / return to inconstant greenness." Writing and writing and writing, with an urgency showing no diminution, Lowell places himself, myopic and abashed, below his former epic assaults on heaven:

I watch a feverish huddle of shivering cows;
you sit making a fishspine from a chestnut leaf.
We are at our crossroads, we are astigmatic
and stop uncomfortable, we are humanly low.

Though this is not a comfortable poetry, it has the solace of truth in its picture of the misery, sense of stoppage, and perplexed desultoriness of middle age. "They told us," says Lowell, remembering the old motto, "by harshness to win the stars." That was, for a long time, his mode, the Luciferian embattled ascent, accompanied by an orchestration of clashing arms and wars in heaven. Now, making a net, as he says, to catch like the Quaker fishermen all the fish in the sea of life and history, even up to Leviathan, he works with no props but the mood of the occasion, with no sure guide but the inexplicable distinctiveness of personal taste. Foretelling the mixed extinction and perpetuity of his own poetic accomplishment, Lowell hangs up his nets in perpetuity. They are the equivocal nets woven and unraveled by a Penelope:

> I've gladdened a lifetime
> knotting, undoing a fishnet of tarred rope;
> the net will hang on the wall when the fish are eaten,
> nailed like illegible bronze on the futureless future.

The self-epitaph was premature, but not on that account false. The subjects of these poems will eventually become extinct, like all other natural species devoured by time, but the indelible mark of their impression on a single sensibility will remain, in Lowell's votive sculpture, bronzed to imperishability.

Ulysses, Circe, Penelope

Lowell's version of the Odyssey is a new instance of an obstinately recurrent literary confrontation to set against some memorable others. Each fastens on its own center: Atwood on Circe and the Sirens, Stevens on Penelope-as-meditation and Ulysses-as-knower, Pound on Circe's isle, Joyce on Ulysses-as-cuckold, Tennyson on the last fatal voyage, Dante on the sin of restless curiosity, Du Bellay on the amplitude of Ulysses' later years:

> Heureux qui, comme Ulysse, a fait un beau voyage ...
> Et puis est retourné, plein d'usage et raison,
> Vivre entre ses parents le reste de son aage!

This essay on "Ulysses, Circe, Penelope" appeared in *Salmagundi*, Spring 1977.

Each reimagined version embodies a different dream of truth or adequacy; none, in such partial glimpses, can be true to Homer. In Lowell's poem, Ulysses' adventures are reduced to one, as a marital triangle replaces Homer's broad society. Autobiography and gossip and the air of a *roman à clef* hover over the poem; can it remain a poem, and what sort of poem is it?

A poem moves, said Stevens, from an "ever-early candor to its late plural." After its initial flashback to the years before the Trojan war and to the war itself, Lowell's poem begins in the apparent candor of aubade, an expansive satisfaction in a young girl's bed. But there is no word for luxuriating in the possession of a mistress, and by using a marital adjective, Lowell's Ulysses is undone in his beginning: "What is more *uxorious*." The disabled dawn-piece that follows violates every usual convention. We do not see a young lover, a rejected sun, a spacious bedroom seeming to embrace the whole of reality, a wakeful mistress pleading that her lover continue his embraces. This aging Ulysses has only momentary sexual powers:

> The sun rises,
> a red bonfire
> weakly rattling in the lower branches—
> that eats like locusts and leaves the tree entire.
> In ten minutes perhaps,
> or when he next wakes up,
> the sun is white as it mostly is.

The bedroom is a prison, enclosed by "bars of sunlight, bars of shade." And Circe, sleepy, excuses herself from love. The posture is the oldest in the world, but the lyric, though it sets everything in order—sun, couple, time, and space—cannot make its posture rise to gesture and accomplishment. A reader might be kinder to this poem if it were more enterprising: "Oh Solomon, let us try again!" Or if its Ulysses were angrier at Circe, that delicious, sincere, sybaritic, but somnolent body. As it is, Ulysses is left inert and alone, and Circe's house, even in the privacy of morning, offers only ache and twilight.

The poem, from this opening, could go anywhere. As it is, it ends with Ulysses about to murder. Tennyson's Ulysses could not have murdered the suitors, and Du Bellay's Ulysses would have forgotten them. In Lowell, everything that has happened from that first dawn rises to the final violence, foreshadowed by Ulysses' destruction of Troy. Lowell is by no means the first to put murder into monodrama, but lyric identification with a murderer is rare. (If we know a murderer in lyric, we know him only as a murderer—as Porphyria's lover. But we know this Ulysses in many guises, and he grows on us as we read his restless repinings: "It's out of hand . . . Why am I my own fugitive?") No lyric poet except Lowell, so far as I know, has given rage so constant a right in poetry. Rather than making Lowell peculiar, his violence, barely repressed and often erupting, casts a backward question to his predecessors in lyric, asking why rage has so seldom appeared before. It is present enough in epics, novels, and plays, but lyric forms scarcely have allowed for it. In that history and science of feeling which poetry (according to Wordsworth) takes on as its task, Lowell has made a certain trajectory his own: the curve which begins in possibility and ends grimly in necessity. Here a grand human voyage, a grand exploratory adventure, narrows to the descent of a predatory shark closing in for the kill. Lowell's sense of doom might be Melville's:

> Found a family, build a state,
> The pledged event is still the same:
> Matter in end will never abate
> His ancient brutal claim.

Joining the failure and fear of the aubade to the menace and self-loathing pride of the end is the uneasiness of the middle of the poem. "Nothing, neither way," say the *disjecta membra* of the central sections. Leaves can choose to drop early and stay green on the ground, or to hold on and, even while on the tree, turn "prematurely brown." Circe offers a "mongrel harmony" of the ruthless and the yielding, drunkenness by day and "hysterical submission" by night (if we take Ulysses' men as surrogates for himself); in Circe's palace, Ulysses finds "derelict choice" confounded with necessity, compassion becoming terror, elation turning to quarrels, and over everything the simmering of dying bugs. Disliking the clichés of myth, disgusted at his followers, irritated even while charmed by Circe's "faded slang," her disorder, her discards, Ulysses leaves. Leaving, he has set his mind on dying; seeing the bugs, he displaces his own wish to die:

> This is mid-autumn,
> the moment when insects die
> instantly as one would wish for a friend.

Ulysses' monologue as he travels from Circe to Penelope looks back to "Returning" and thence to Ungaretti, who describes in his

"Canzone" an immobile Hades where no leaf is born or falls, nothing wakes or slumbers, and there is neither light nor shadow, nor past nor future. This is, says Ungaretti, "the crossing over, with sensual experience exhausted, of the threshold of another experience . . . the Pascalian knowing of being out of the null. Horrid consciousness. Its odyssey always has as its point of departure the past, always returns to conclude itself in the past."

Lowell's Ulysses will "return to conclude in the past," but he pauses for a moment between mistress and wife, detached from the illusions of erotic presence, to ask what drives him from place to place. Given the freedom of the universe by "the sea's great green golight," Ulysses finds himself propelled by another light, his own exhaustion, which, in driving him on, lights up the world. The third light guiding him is the moon he gazes on and follows over the ocean. The blind old man, in Coleridge's "Limbo," turns his "moon-like" countenance to the moon:

> . . . his eyeless face all eye;—
> As 'twere an organ full of silent sight . . .
> He seems to gaze at that which seems to gaze on him!

Like the old man, Ulysses catches the moon's likeness "in the split second of vacancy," and the inconstant moon seems at once like the Circe he forsook and also like a foreshadowing of his complaisant Penelope surrounded by suitors—"duplicitous / open to all men, unfaithful." The sexual venture is inherently doomed; Circe turns men to swine, yet they can only please her by being men. As hypnotized as their possessed Gadarene brothers, men allow their metamorphosis; repelled, she banishes them to her pigsties. The mutual contempt between the sexes is voiced by Ulysses from Circe's point of view: the one sex wants the other dependent, and then despises it for its dependency.

In the midst of his exhaustion, his drivenness, his survival "bleak-boned" into Circe's bestialization, Ulysses allows a brief pained glimpse of his earlier days, when he hoped by travel to become relativity's marvel, the voyager who returns younger than he left. Dirtied by the bilge of age, Ulysses of the green golight, the light of exhaustion, and the vacant light of the Circean moon, wishes he could believe in another light, the light of Resurrection "at the end of the tunnel." He thinks with nostalgia of the Christian doctrine of the Glorified Body (this Ulysses, like Lowell, is, it would seem, an ex-Christian; of course there are also disembodied shades in Hades). Perhaps Lowell is remembering Hopkins:

Man's spirit will be flesh-bound when found at best,
But uncumbered: meadow-down is not distressed
For a rainbow footing it, nor he for his bones risen.

Ulysses' wistfulness—"if faith can be believed"—is his momentary lapse into sentimentality before he lands in Ithaca, open-eyed and tight-lipped. Entering the house, "eyes shut, mouth loose," he is ready to stop traveling: he has "seen the known world," and can now shut his seeking eyes, relax his mouth for the kiss of greeting. In Ulysses' "just a step . . . just a step," Lowell remembers "Going to and fro" (*For the Union Dead*): "One step, two steps, three steps," Lowell had written in the earlier poem: "If you could get through the Central Park / by counting." That lyric continues with a flashback to days when the young poet collaborated with Lucifer, and blasphemously claimed that all the goings to and fro in the universe have one motive: Dante's "L'amor che move il sole e l'altre stelle":

> Ah Lucifer!
> how often you wanted your fling
> with those French girls, Mediterranean
> luminaries, Mary, Myrtho, Isis—
> as far out as the sphinx!
> The love that moves the stars
>
> moved you!
> It set you going to and fro
> and up and down—
> If you could get loose
> from the earth by counting
> your steps to the noose . . .

Myrtho and Isis (from Nerval's *Chimères*) are Muses and mesmerizers like Circe; Ulysses-Lowell's steps to the conjugal bed are his last "to," back from the "fro" of Circe. But Penelope is unimpressed: she "sees no feat / in his flight or his flight back— / ten years to and ten years fro." The suitors are put off by the "Tom, Dick, or Harry" who has crashed the party: "his uninvited hands are raw."

The murder of the suitors will be only the logical completion of male rapacity, begun in courtship and perfected in war. The first fatal aggression occurs in sexual possession itself; twenty years earlier Ulysses had "enticed Penelope / to dance herself to coma in his arms." Later, when he had made her pregnant, she seemed to him, in her starry-eyed dash toward him, "a cornered rabbit." At least this is how his murderous mind reinterprets their common past. Penelope has gotten used to her suitors, her salon, and as Ulysses finds himself outdoors and circling, he becomes the beast he perhaps had not become under Circe's rule. "He circles as a shark circles . . . / a vocational killer."

Is it Circe or Penelope who has brutalized him? or is it the combined pressures of the many antagonisms of living?

> When men the fiend to fight
> They conquer not upon such easy terms—
> Half-serpent in the struggle grow these worms,
> And does he grow half-human, all is right.

Or so said Meredith in his description of a marital triangle, feeling able to summarize in grand pentameters. Lowell's darting meters, abrupt and brusque, are less conclusive and more perplexed. For every given in Ulysses' approach, there is a taking-away: nobody knows him, yet he is too much remarked; his knees go forward, but his feet hold him back; his mouth is held in, but the lips are puffy; the lighthouse was a landmark, but now there is a marina; earlier male glory induced female sexual coma; a dash toward the predator is paradoxically the maneuver of a cornered prey; a well-furnished and well-lived life creates a deformity; a recognition turns out to be a mistake; a look in becomes a volte-face; ten years fro and ten years to, and then—to end all the jolts back and forth—mayhem. The last section of the poem justifies the poem.

Lowell has used some of these means before, but not at such length. Toward, back; toward, back; and Circe at the end has vanished utterly from the poem. We have come to the finale of the long effort. First there was the naming of the world; then, in a search for new names, came the "embarkation and carnival of glory," complete with marital triumph; next the war and the exploration of the world, the folly of following the Circean moon, seeing "the meanness and beacons of men"; finally, "bleak-boned with survival," the return, drawn by the myth of the unchanged home; what emotion is left to age but fury? Age finds in self the same prison that Ulysses found, at the beginning of the poem, in Circe's bed, so that in the menace of the perfectly aligned killing machine which Ulysses has become we see his new jail:

> his gills are pleated and aligned—
> unnatural ventilation-vents

closed by a single lever
like cells in a jail—

And there the description in this concluding poem breaks off, as it had begun, with Ulysses' circling. Encompassing all his flashbacks within the shark's surveillance, Lowell makes his final poem a long exercise in threat, a suspended streaking down to the kill. Even this energy is welcome after the tiredness of Ulysses' preceding soliloquy —but it leaves the sensibility no place to rest. The voice that speaks the last poem both is and is not Ulysses, both moves with his moves and yet criticizes his malevolence, his appearance

flesh-proud, sore-eyed, scar-proud
a vocational killer
in the machismo of senility,
foretasting the apogee of mayhem.

This is the voice that calls Ulysses "he": the voice that had disappeared in the fifth section where Ulysses, for once, speaks for himself and appears least the betrayer, least the coward, least the killer. There, in the central section of the poem, we hear the echo of the classic lyric voice, in sympathy with itself, or, at most, ironic toward itself. Tennyson's Ulysses, and Eliot's Prufrock and Gerontion are ancestors of this first-person Ulysses. But the other Ulysses, the third-person one, cannot be assimilated to the voices of dramatic monologues, for all the *style indirect libre* allowing us the privilege of acceding to his consciousness. Lowell is too ambivalent to merge with his creation: some cruel eye is marking Ulysses' jails, his shuttlings, his degeneracy, even his heartsickness.

If this poem is at first disturbing because of its ending on premeditated murder, it remains unsettling for more subliminal reasons. Lyrics are usually meditative poems. Even when they are addressed to a listener in a dramatic situation ("I wonder, by my troth, what thou and I / Did till we loved") they go on to meditate on the state of affairs invoked. They yield naturally to reflection, rumination, analysis—into the how, the why, the how long, the wherefore, the if only. Lyric assumes as a genre the value of introspection, the existence of some level of thought or judgment below or above the level of action. What is unnerving about Lowell's poem is the substitution of action—a subject linked to a predicate—for analysis. Interpretation is smuggled in here and there ("he *enticed* Penelope / to dance herself *to coma* in his arms"), but the phrasing of the typical sentence is all in vivid narrative. Moral judgment is subordinate to realist description: "He has seen the known world, the *meanness* and beacons of men." Though we are in some sense privy to Ulysses' mind, the poems stop short at the threshold of response: Circe may refuse to bestir herself for love—"I can't respond"—but Ulysses' reaction is suppressed. Even in the third section, which follows Ulysses' waking thoughts, the nature of the narrative—a continuing present tense—prevents any regression to a moment before, any recapitulation, any rethinking—we are simply hurried on from thought to thought with no global assessment of the predicament, no "placing" of Ulysses' experience with Circe against other adventures, against feelings for Penelope, against Ithaca. The briefest of flashbacks and "flashforwards" are the only placings permitted, and these are hardly more than gestures ("Young, his genius was stratagem; . . . he will die like others as the gods will").

The habitual present tense ("When this happens, then that happens" or "Often this happens"), the present tense of direct address ("For thou art with me"), or the present tense of a first-person poem ("I wake and feel the fell of dark") are all much more common in poetry than a present-tense poem in the third person of the *style indirect libre*. (Third-person description—"He travels on, a solitary man"—is something else entirely.) Lowell's lines, except for the moments of first-person utterance (at the end of section 3, and through all of section 5), read rather like stage directions, of the ample sort Shaw liked to give:

he lies awake and fears the servants
his heart is swallowed in his throat
they stand like two guests / waiting for the other one / to leave
her speech is spiced with faded slang
her discards lie about the floors
Ulysses circles
he enters the house
he looks / at her, and she at him admiring her
he circles as a shark circles / visibly in the window

The reader is the audience to this serial drama. And yet, when the poem has been read, what we have assisted at is not a drama but a reflection—a reflection on being old, on being at once unfit for a mistress and unfit for a wife. The poet has set in motion a meditation on rage as the emotion that lasts in all its vigor more than any erotic impulse, on the depravity and innocence of passion, on the symmetries of fate. Ulysses does not stand as an "objective correlative" for these sentiments; this author is not detached from his protagonist, but "lives along the line" with him, and the actions of the poem *are* the feelings of the man. "Things thought too long can be no longer thought," said Yeats; and perhaps there are no more thoughts that can be thought about the oldest situation in the world—husband of twenty years, wife of twenty years, young mistress. Where reflection would be trite, action can seem authentic. Even the title predicates nothing except conjunction: a wedge intervenes between husband and wife; or the three remain in eternal unresolved triangulation. They act out relation, and in act there is something secure, something that is irrevocable, beside which reflection seems insubstantial, trifling, of no consequence. That the actions themselves— Circe's indifferent seduction, Ulysses' irritable leavetaking, Penelope's complacent salon-holding—assert nothing of worth justifies, if anything can, Ulysses' final killer descent. The mixture of a judgment passed on Ulysses ("a vocational killer in the machismo of senility") and exaltation of his self-apotheosis ("flesh-proud, sore-eyed, scarproud . . . breaking water . . . He is oversize") suspends the poem momentarily in incoherence. Then the gods take over, their pendulum of fate coming to its predestined end: "ten years fro and ten years to." Moral judgment coexists with the necessitarian certainty that things could not have been otherwise. Self-loathing and a conviction of powerlessness cohabit in the last lines. Lowell forces a recognition of both.

Day by Day

Day by Day continues Robert Lowell's "verse autobiography [which] sometimes fictionalizes plot and particular"; it continues as well his struggle to break the icon—to dismember and reconstitute the English lyric. As self-portrait, it is linked backward to the guilty joy of Lowell's marriage to Caroline Blackwood, the birth of his

This review of Robert Lowell's *Day by Day* appeared in the *New York Times Book Review*, August 14, 1977.

son Sheridan, and his removal to England, all celebrated in *The Dolphin* (1973); this collection recounts the attrition of that marriage and looks ahead with foreboding. The domestic plot, centered in the exceptionally beautiful title-sequence, escapes the confines of that sequence and tinges the rest of the poems.

Writers have used lyric verse to write oratory, diaries, prophecies, natural history, philosophy, and theology. Since Lowell uses it to write autobiography, we expect from him what we ask of all literary autobiographies—subjectivity, vivid self-presentation, subtlety of analysis, and some detachment (whether scientific or ironic). On these counts alone Lowell ranks very high. He has largely given up one of the most solacing aspects of conventional lyric—that transcending of past and future in favor of an intense present moment of love, or grief, or happiness. Lowell forces us to read the emotions of the moment in the knowledge of emotions past and anticipated. Nothing is unshadowed; nothing is forgotten; no moment but reaches out to another on the farther shore. The burden of reading *Day by Day* comes from this weight of autobiography everywhere pervading a verse which is itself, paradoxically enough, almost transparent.

The transparency has been present, in part, since *Life Studies* (1959)—still, because of its title-sequence, Lowell's most famous book. In superficial ways, *Day by Day* resembles *Life Studies* and *For the Union Dead* (1964) in that its poems are more often personal than historical or political; and they are written in free verse rather than in the gorgeous couplet-quatrains of *Near the Ocean* (1967) or the sonnets of *Notebook* and its progeny *History, For Lizzie and Harriet,* and *The Dolphin* (1969–1973). But the free verse of *Life Studies,* like the strict verse of the later volumes, depended on those two reassuring bases of literature, the plot (for narrative consistency) and the narrative sentence (for local coherence). Plotted stories told in narrative sentences are deeply conventional, sanctioned by past practice, and comfortably sequential. Even in Lowell's most obscure moments, the presumption of story and sentence held fast, no matter how murky the story nor how rapid the utterance. He did not adopt those discontinuities of the modern poem and the modern line—collages, fragments, typographical dislocations, and unpunctuated reveries—which were the external signs of an attempted mimesis of inner, rather than outer, reality. Lowell was wedded, like Milton, to syntax, and was unwilling to forgo that powerful resource for the weaker glue of Poundian associativeness. *Day by Day* seems to me to have broken the hold of tidy narration and chronological sentences without abandoning conventional English writing—an altogether remarkable sleight of hand.

At the same time, this volume has all but dropped the former panoplies which gave Lowell's poems such a rich surface, and provided so many handles for critics. Historical panorama, visible allusiveness, family lore, theology, public causes, and so on have here mostly vanished. What is left is limpid—a wife, children, the seasons, ill health, acquaintances, friends living and dead, a walk, a photograph, a poetry reading, a dinner out, shaving, making love, insomnia, fishing. What remains in the way of allusion, which is considerable, is hidden: Lowell in an English sanitarium in depression, saying "I wish I could die," lapses into a childlike pang:

> The Queen of Heaven, I miss her,
> we were divorced. She never doubted
> the divided, stricken soul
> could call her Maria,
> and rob the devil with a word.

The close comes from Buonconte's story in the "Purgatorio" (used earlier in *Near the Ocean* and *History*); here it is not so much a glance toward Dante as part of Lowell's spontaneous exclamation in grief. As for religion, Lowell sees "in the bookcase, my Catholic theology, still too high for temptation." History has become, at least for the time being, an appurtenance to the present; the trees at Milgate Park (where Lowell and his wife lived in England) are "the yew row, planted under Cromwell"—where "Cromwell" is a system of dating rather than a historical personage. Lowell's "intemperate, apocalyptic terms" (as he called them in "Marriage") have been forsaken. Like his own "Watchmaker God," Lowell "loved to tinker," but "having perfected what He had to do / stood off shrouded in his loneliness." Those lines, from *History*, might be read analogically of *Day by Day*, as Lowell stands off and sees what life helplessly becomes.

Lowell's dislocation of narrative and meditative focus is delicately visible in a poem to his son, as Lowell remembers his own face in a lost photograph and sees the resemblance to his child's face now. The poem is almost disembodied in its simplicity:

> We only live between
> before we are and what we were.
> In the lost negative

you exist
a smile, a cypher,
an old-fashioned face
in an old-fashioned hat.

Three ages in a flash:
the same child in the same picture,
he, I, you,
chockablock, one stamp
like mother's wedding silver—
gnome, fish, brute cherubic force.

This from the poet who began at eighteen with hectic decorativeness ("when sunset rouged the sun-embittered surf"); who wanted
sonorities ("off 'Sconset, where the yawing S-boats splash / The
bellbuoy"); who needed religious myth ("Hide / Our steel, Jonas
Messias, in Thy side"); who invoked predecessors ("Look at the
faces—Longfellow, Lowell, Holmes and Whittier!"); who surrounded himself with revenants ("They won't stay gone"—all the
relatives in *Life Studies*); who plundered history (from Adam to Mc-
Carthy); who imitated fellow poets (from Homer to Ungaretti). The
old Lowell palette was full of colors, the perspective full of scenes,
the forms full of reminiscence; and the underlying aesthetic was
one of willed domination over the whole enormous baggage. And
even when the aesthetic of dominance broke under the exhaustion of
too much illness and middle age (in *For the Union Dead*), Lowell
held on, like a drowning man, to the coherence of an orderly
narrative:

Now the midwinter grind
is on me, New York
drills through my nerves,
as I walk
the chewed-up streets.

Day by Day, coming after the exuberance of the *Notebook* period
(when Lowell regained through medicine a stability of health), returns to those simple lines found in the late fifties, but leaves behind
that simple narration. Each portion of these rather long poems is
coherent in itself, but the leaps from part to part are unpredictable.
The poems carry the consolations of tradition into the unsettling
paths of a minutely reticulated mind. It is the lyrically familiar that
may win us at first, like Lowell's yearning and apprehensive down-
piece, "The Downlook":

For the last two minutes, the retiring monarchy
of the full moon looks down on the first chirping sparrows—
nothing lovelier than waking to find
another breathing body in my bed . . .
glowshadow halfcovered with dayclothes like my own,
caught in my arms.

Last summer nothing dared impede
the flow of the body's thousand rivulets of welcome . . .

Now the downlook, the downlook.

It may even please some to recognize, a few lines later, the echo of
Paolo and Francesca:

There's no greater happiness in days of the downlook
than to turn back to recapture former joy.

But for others, the unnerving ending will fix the poem like a hook
in the flesh:

How often have my antics
and insupportable, trespassing tongue
gone astray and led me to prison . . .
to lying . . . kneeling . . . standing.

This mysterious piece of lyric does not, according to the usual conventions, "belong" as an ending to the earlier sections; fear might
reasonably lead to self-criticism, but then a tidier righting of the
whole might be expected. Lowell has given up tidiness; it comes
from without, and he is remaining doggedly within. Accuracy and
fidelity to perception have rarely received such a desperate pledge
of faith. Only a poet who had so violently attempted to give the
ashheap of history a succession of intelligible aesthetic shapes could
now so passionately abandon himself to the randomness of felt fact,
mental and physical, where it may lead.

In the "Epilogue," which closes this book, Lowell's central line—
"We are poor passing facts"—contains both his current obliquity
of allusion and his flashing newness: "poor" for "Lear," "passing"
for Keats and Yeats—but "facts" for Lowell. The poem, which embodies his present poetics, may help this book to be read intelligently
and judged by its own aims:

Sometimes everything I write
with the threadbare art of my eye

seems a snapshot,
lurid, rapid, garish, grouped,
heightened from life,
yet paralyzed by fact.
All's misalliance.
Yet why not say what happened?

"Why not say what happened?" It is a subversive question because
it is the question of the sophomore in the creative-writing class. The
sophomore of course cannot say what happened even when he thinks
he is doing just that—what emerges from him is a mass of cliché.
But Lowell, to whom every word in the language has by now its
distinct musical value, can, with an accuracy to within a feather's
weight, "say what happened." In this concluding poem, Lowell
casts in his lot with genre-painting; and adapting a critic's words on
Vermeer ("the painter's vision is not a lens, / it trembles to caress
the light"), takes the Dutch painter for his model:

Pray for the grace of accuracy
Vermeer gave to the sun's illumination
stealing like the tide across a map
to his girl solid with yearning.
We are poor passing facts,
warned by that to give
each figure in the photograph
his living name.

Stealing like the tide over facts of feeling and of life, Lowell's verse
presses forward in obedience to that warning spoken by perception,
the artist's only conscience. There is no use denying that these
poems, like Lowell's historical or political or literary ones, need foot-
noting. One has to know (from previous work) his reading, his past,
and his present; and one has to reconstruct the scenario behind this
book—Lowell's life in Kent, his hospitalization in England, his wife's
sickness, their temporary stay in Boston, their separation, a reconciliation, a further rupture, a parting in Ireland, Lowell's return to
America. These episodes and others are the bases for the poems, but
Lowell is no more intent on sustained narrative here than he was in
Notebook, where he wrote in an "Afterthought":

It is not a chronicle or almanac; many events turn up, many
others of equal or greater reality do not. This is not my diary. . . .
The separate poems and sections are opportunist and inspired by

impulse. Accident threw up the subjects, and the plot swallowed them—famished for human chances.

These remarks, except for the last, are equally true of *Day by Day;* however, with the present sacrifice of plot and rhyme, Lowell embraces a new asceticism. His restless eye still notices and notices: the lust of the eye, as despotic as Wordsworth's, persists in him still. In "Shifting Colors," the most prophetic poem of *Day by Day,* we look toward a time when the lust of the eye, like lust itself, will have waned, as the poet becomes "weary of self-torture" and thinks of taking on a landscapist's art, remote, descriptive, unimpassioned:

> I seek leave unimpassioned by my body,
> I am too weak to strain to remember, or give
> recollection the eye of a microscope. I see
> horse and meadows, duck and pond,
> universal consolatory
> description without significance,
> transcribed verbatim by my eye.

Lowell's desire is the more believable because of the preceding "description without significance" of the "ageless big white horse," the meadow-creatures, and the pond:

> Ducks splash deceptively like fish;
> fish break water with the wings of a bird to escape.
>
> A hissing goose sways in stationary anger;
> purple bluebells rise in ledges on the lake.
>
> A single cuckoo gifted with a pregnant word
> shifts like the sun from wood to wood.

Though they use some features of literary language (metaphor, simile, the anthropomorphizing of nature), these lines have a beauty not explicable by conventional means; they are not examples of the pathetic fallacy, or of the round of the seasons, or of the pastoral life—they are nothing but what they are. They are placed, of course, in a poem full of feeling, but they would be beautiful quite without their setting. Commentators on Lowell have had, in the past, a jungle-thicket of language to map and civilize: now suddenly the terrain turns candid, lightened, yielding—while remaining a more cunning maze, in the end, than before. Mallarmé, says Lowell, "had the good fortune / to find a style that made writing impossible."

Mallarmé's dazzled page—the dream of language uttering itself—seems now what Lowell's art most desires.

If we ask for whom Lowell has forsaken his earlier models—the dramatic ones like Dante, Donne, and Milton, as well as the realistic ones like Bishop—the answer, both surprisingly and unsurprisingly, seems to me Horace. Lowell has "imitated" a good deal of Horace (making him, in the past, sound rather too vividly Juvenalian at times), so the present influence is in one sense not surprising. On the other hand, what is usually incorporated into English poetry from Horace is his epistolary style (from which Auden borrowed a good deal) or his nostalgia (Housman's "We are but dust and dreams"). Lowell is giving us in *Day by Day* something more like Horace's odes. The odes exhibit an extraordinary disconnection and compression (Horace too assumes an audience knowing all the history, personal and public, underlying his poems) and are distinguished above all other examples of Western lyric, even to the eye of an amateur in Latin, by their virtuoso balance of closely contained elements. Like a mortarless arch, they stand by the tension of force against counterforce. Though Lowell's terms are vastly different—intimate, colloquial, modern—Horace's experienced tone, though directly "imitated" only twice, is heard behind any number of passages in this book. I give only one, from "Seventh Year," in which Lowell, foreseeing the end of his marriage, thinks of other poets now dead—Longfellow, the New England Augustans, and Hart Crane—and sets their deadness, deaf to life, against his own latter days:

> To each the rotting natural to his age.
> Dividing the minute we cannot prolong,
> I stand swaying at the end of the party,
> a half-filled glass in each hand—
> I too swayed
> by the hard infatuate wind of love
> they cannot hear.

A more romantic poem would have ended with the penultimate line: Lowell's classical irony adds the deaf dead, the natural rotting, the sense of successive ages, the sideglance at Zeno's paradox of infinitely divisible time, the hard equation of love and infatuation, and the play on "swaying" and "swayed." The short, packed lines are Horatian, as are the level gaze and the *carpe diem*. And yet how new it seems, as though the notation for some harmony long lost had been rediscovered. This is not the only mode in this sumptuously varied book, but it is the newest and most imperial, comprehending, as it does in Horace, the pains of age, loss, and experience within a form governed by intellectual mastery, a steady eye, and a genius for the natural affinities of words.

Pudding Stone

Because it is the first work on Robert Lowell to appear since his death, Steven Axelrod's new book will be looked to for some first glimpse of a comprehensive view, consciously phrased in the light of the end of the poetic canon (only a few poems remain unpublished). The myth of Lowell's life and work proposed by Axelrod— my noun is not in itself a criticism, because all accounts of a career reveal an implicit myth—does not differ very much at first from the received ideas which by now encrust the Lowell canon: after apprentice work imitative of Tate in *Land of Unlikeness* (1944), Lowell becomes famous with his first notable book, *Lord Weary's Castle* (1946), which encompasses "three related themes . . . history, current events, and God." *The Mills of the Kavanaughs* (1951) is a mistake, *Life Studies* (1959) is the great watershed, *Imitations* (1961) is really a book of personal poems, not translations. Axelrod's recapitulations take on a personal shape when he turns to the later books. He praises *For the Union Dead* (1964), while admitting its "drought"; he is uncertain about *Near the Ocean* (1967), especially about its title poem; and he is positively impatient with *Notebook 1967–68* and its two recastings, first as *Notebook* (1970), then as *History* and *For Lizzie and Harriet* (1973).

For Axelrod, the quintessential Lowell is to be found in *The Dolphin* (1973); though he is polite to *Day by Day* (1977), he writes only sketchily about it. The poems receiving "major treatment" are, predictably, "The Quaker Graveyard in Nantucket," "Skunk Hour," "For the Union Dead," "Waking Early Sunday Morning," and the prologue and epilogue to *The Dolphin*. Lowell's religious, artistic,

This review of *Robert Lowell: Life and Art* by Steven Gould Axelrod appeared in the *New York Review of Books*, February 8, 1979.

and political engagements are recounted in some detail; the marriages are briefly mentioned. Various influences are proposed, with the chief drama of influence lying in the opposed attractions of Tate ("European," formalist, metrically regular and rhymed) and Williams ("American," open, metrically free and unrhymed). The general thesis of Axelrod's book, suggested by his subtitle, is that Lowell, after being too greatly preoccupied with art and symbols, achieved in *Life Studies* a "breakthrough" by writing about "direct experience and not symbols" (Lowell's words) and that "all of Lowell's subsequent work centered around his quest for the craft and inspiration to bring even more experience into his art, and his related quest to account for the place art makes in experience." Axelrod concedes that "art and experience continued to retain an important thin edge of distinctness for Lowell—art was experience that had been 'worked up,' imagined into form," but the tendency of this book is to blur that "thin edge," as Axelrod passes systematically from "life" to "art," episode by episode, through Lowell's decades of writing.

The inconceivable gap—no "thin edge"—which separates life from even the most apparently mimetic art does not figure in this book. Since only a few people in any given century manage to make art at all, there must be—it stands to reason—something very recalcitrant in life; unwilling to be made into art, it frustrates the most intense attempts by any number of would-be artists to give it beauty, shape, and significance. To put it a different way, art does not take to "life" as a very natural subject. Almost any preexistent convention suits art better, as Gombrich has suggested. To bring about even the slightest alteration in the conventions requires not so much the ability to reconceive life (whose stimuli, even in the most reclusive existence, are infinitely various) as the capacity to reconceive genre, prosody, or decorum.

Because Lowell's writing requires annotation (where 91 Revere Street is, what the March on the Pentagon was, who is buried in Dunbarton), it is not therefore more centrally about "life" than any other poetry. Even autobiography is not, except to the naive eye, more "about" life than any other genre. Its method of *being* about life, its tone, its conventions, differ; that is all. The most dissembling art is the art which appears to be a candid transcription of "experience." A genuinely candid transcription from experience, as we all know from our students, is likely to emerge as bathos, inertia, formlessness.

It is true that Lowell's early verse avoids the appearance of autobiography in favor of the symbolic, and that the verse of his twenties is inferior to the verse of his forties. But it scarcely therefore follows that it is a "wedding of art to experience" that makes the later poetry better. It is better—to speak tautologically—because it is better written. The early work contains pastiche, imitation, uncertainties of tone; the later work is *sui generis*, in full command of its registers, emancipated from its *grands maîtres*. But then, in all poets who get better as they pass thirty—and most do—the reason for the improvement is their increasing mastery of their own private language. To go behind what happens on the page to a theory of the marriage of art and life only begs the question of what is now being better done on the page.

Axelrod does not entirely ignore what happens on the page; he remarks, for instance, in connection with "For the Union Dead," that "every image in the poem echoes against other images," suggesting "the esemplastic power of the consciousness to connect even the most disparate-seeming of phenomena." He adds that "Lowell's characteristic poems have a remarkable power to evoke the historical moment in which they were conceived." This, the most cunning fiction of art, is rightly called "remarkable," but Axelrod's praise of it disappoints; he quotes newspapers and magazines, concludes (what may well be so) that Lowell was echoing common terms of political protest or social apprehension, and locates the "remarkable" power of historical evocation in such practices. The 1960s produced a mass of political poetry echoing just such local terms of fear and confrontation; but there is no "remarkable" power in that ephemeral writing. The clues to Lowell's success are not so easily unearthed.

There is no book of Lowell's that has not been disliked by somebody. Lowell himself genially disliked some of his poems enough to rewrite them. Not all metamorphoses of language worked; none worked permanently. The moment of pride in the achieved form became the moment of desolation, as the embodiment seemed, later, not only inadequate but inauthentic. Ulysses, in *Day by Day*, boasts that "things changed to the names he gave them." This is the effect of the prophet or the visionary rather than of the autobiographer. The next line takes away what the preceding one gave, as it continues, "then lost their names." The transforming power of the namer is impermanent; every few years, everything has to be named all over. The *locus classicus* for the renaming is the family romance; the scenario is rewritten every decade. The "blank" (to use Gombrich's term), the structure which has to be filled up over and over, is, in Lowell, a compulsion to "block" actors in a pattern of significant choreography. The actors themselves change (Caligula here, Robert Kennedy there, Charlotte Lowell somewhere else); the blocking patterns change (with simple agons of opposites being succeeded by more complex webs of family interrelations, which in turn give way to communally reinforcing acts, themselves supplanted by a sexual *pas de deux*); but the compulsion to arrange the data of literature and memory in new configurations remains.

Data—not "life" but data—are essential to the Lowell poem, which is rarely consistent in texture, but is instead as heterogeneous as pudding stone, full of bits and pieces of literature, history, private experience, popular culture, visual observation, and scholarly fallout. In this respect, Lowell resembles the poet who most influenced him, Milton. And the later verse does not differ very much in the use of data from the verse of the early or middle years; it is only that the data are his daughter's gerbils or his wife's letters instead of Roman history or neo-Thomism. The self, in Lowell's poetry, is defined by the data he moves among; the data are his cloak, his ambiance, he is constituted by them.

The question of the hospitality of lyric to data has been raised persistently in this century, and Axelrod mentions *Paterson* as a precedent for Lowell's incorporation of private letters in the later verse. But the *Cantos*, or *Paterson*, are not lyric, and they use data in a socially self-conscious and deliberately archaeological fashion, as fragments shored against ruins. Lowell's data are not primarily historical (though many are borrowed from classical and modern European history); they are symbolic. Cain, Nero, Caligula, Jesus, and Napoleon all serve equally as projections of Lowell himself; the data that are not immediately personally symbolic are domestic, and are of the sort one finds in a Renaissance portrait, identifying the interests and rank of the subject.

There was a degree of controversy about a recent Mary Cassatt exhibition at Boston's Museum of Fine Arts, and the questions raised there are pertinent to Lowell's poetry. The show juxtaposed domestic objects from Cassatt's house with paintings in which those same subjects—a tea set, a silver service—figured. The good intentions of the exhibition—to bring art closer to biography and thereby closer to the viewer—begged, once again, the central question: what had the data become in the picture? Cézanne's bottles, cherub, and skulls stand untransfigured now in his studio, all light fled from them. Deprived of their local symbolic and compositional place in the individual poem, Lowell's domestic and public data—his father's water-spotted book, his mother's Risorgimento coffin, the green-helmeted troops at the Pentagon, the Maine snowplow, the letters and conversational exchanges—would not only not be art, they would also not be "experience." We cannot go behind the art: the illusion that we can is art's most compelling hallucination.

The peculiar inertness of Axelrod's book stems from its refusal to face up to any of these questions. Lip service is paid, but in superficial ways, to Lowell's compositional powers. Imagery is doggedly pursued. Absurd ambiguities are "found"where none exist. The semblance of literary criticism is maintained while, to my mind, all that is essential goes unremarked. Three instances will have to suffice. "Fishnet," in *The Dolphin*, begins mysteriously and beautifully:

> Any clear thing that blinds us with surprise,
> your wandering silences and bright trouvailles,
> dolphin let loose to catch the flashing fish....

It is not that there is any one *right* thing to say about these lines, since every angle of vision produces a different angle of commentary. What is certain is that what Axelrod says—literal, heavy-handed, and mostly untrue—is the *wrong* thing to say:

> The image in these initial lines is complex. Literally, dolphins do assist fishermen in catching schools of albacore that swim alongside them . . . Further ambiguities proliferate in the syntax. To call attention only to the most crucial of these, does "let loose" modify "dolphin" adjectivally, so that the sentence is a verbless fragment in praise of her power? Or does "let loose" function as a verb, so that the sentence is a command to the dolphin (muse, Eros) to act? Perhaps the syntax must be read in both ways, a suggestion of the doubleness underlying the poem.

Axelrod's consistent failure to catch Lowell's tone appears characteristically in his comment on the mother skunk and her column of kittens at the end of "Skunk Hour." Lowell himself said of the skunks, "The skunks are both quixotic and barbarously absurd, hence the tone of amusement and defiance." Axelrod, missing the poet's amusement at the quasi-military order of the marching baby skunks, says, "Lowell's skunks are domineering and 'moonstruck,' a bestial, morally repugnant occupation army . . . They are the mili-

tant, brutish new order, commanding the ruins of the former civilization." The most grotesque of Axelrod's interpretations comes in
his discussion of the "burnt and decaying substances" which in his
view pervade "My Last Afternoon with Uncle Devereux Winslow":
"The clothing store," Axelrod announces with connoisseurship, "in a
fine combination of surface and symbol, is called 'Rogers *Peet's.*'"
Axelrod treats all of Lowell with the same evenhanded solemnity,
and misses, over and over, whatever is characteristic of some new
phase, thereby falsifying the mercurial shape of Lowell's career.

Lowell had little real humor to speak of (as he admitted in his elegy
on Berryman), but he was, as he got older, often amused, ironic, and
self-mocking in his verse. The aggressively serious young man who
wrote *Land of Unlikeness* could not encompass baby skunks and
sour cream. This is not necessarily a flaw; naturally prophetic or
religious poets do not, by and large, include self-mockery in their
poetic range. It is not that Lowell put more "life" into his later verse,
but that he put a different sort of art in it—an art which left room
for ruefulness, malice, slang, clumsiness, comedy, and irregularity.
When he looked back to the fledging author of that fiery and
denunciatory book of 1944, he saw no religious prophet, but a
homeless boy of twenty-five or thirty, caught in an over-prolonged
adolescence:

> too shopworn for less, too impressionable for more—
> blackmaned, illmade
> in a washed blue workshirt and coalblack trousers,
> moving from house to house.

It is no wonder that the names that that growing boy gave things
no longer sufficed the aging man. Unlike Yeats, Lowell had no
"half-read wisdom of demonic images" to satisfy age as they had
satisfied youth.

The lack of demonic images—or celestial ones—in Lowell is the
stumbling block for those who want their poets religious, and
consider the quest for the sublime a necessary and constitutive condition for the creation of lyric. Axelrod uncritically uses the word
"religious" of Lowell. There is a book to be written on Lowell and
religion, but he is in no sense a religious poet as the phrase is com-
monly used; those who dislike him find, above all in the later verse,
a relentless trivializing of life, as they see it, which seems to rob
existence of ardor, transcendence, and devotion. The literary equiva-

lent of sublimity of feeling is momentum, yearning, journey, climax, epiphany, vision. Lowell refuses them all. If the quest—even the failed quest—is one's model of meaning, then Lowell is incoherent. If verse-momentum—the Shelleyan drive—is one's model of yearning, then Lowell is fatigued. If prophetic energy of diction is one's model of poetic speech, then Lowell is prosaic. If "beginning, middle, and end" is one's model of aesthetic order, then Lowell is self-indulgent. If vision—even balked vision—is the end of art, then Lowell is inconsequential.

The odd and touching truth about Lowell is that he began his career with all those assumptions—that art sought a religious vision, that the artist should be a questing pilgrim, that his voice should be resonant with Hebraic denunciations, that enjambment would prove his yearning and momentum, that a poem should be a well-made object. "The Quaker Graveyard"—which so included all the expectable conventions that, like "Sunday Morning," it struck everyone as a true poem—secreted itself around Lowell's acceptance of this prescription for the utterance of anything which wanted to call itself poetic. The verse after 1967 is the secretion of a lurkingly opposite sense of poetry. Though it has something in common with Williams' day-by-day poetry written on prescription blanks, or with Frank O'Hara's poetry of "I do this, I do that," it does not share Williams' sanguine or despairing climaxes, or O'Hara's cheerfully extemporaneous tone. Whatever the speed of composition of Lowell's sonnets, they do not sound like casual utterances; they are dense and close-written.

And when Lowell turns, in *Day by Day*, to a poetry seemingly mused rather than written, it is ruminative, not spontaneous. Poetry, as it is implied in Lowell's late practice, is profoundly irreligious, reality-bound, ordered not by any structural teleology but by a confidence in free association, addressed not homiletically to an audience, but painfully to the self, private rather than public, closer to the epistolary than to the oratorical, as various as conversation in its tonal liberty, free to seem desultory and uncomposed, and, above all, exempt from the tyranny of the well-made. It is in this sense Chekhovian. In fact, reading the complete Lowell is rather like seeing Dostoevsky grow up to be Chekhov.

The final step in Lowell's evolution, and one that Axelrod misrepresents, was the abandon, as a metaphor for his poetry, of portrait-painting in favor of impromptu photography. Axelrod repeatedly describes the governing aesthetic in *Life Studies* as a photographic one:

> In "91 Revere Street," Lowell ironically surveys the wreckage
> of a self, family, and civilization (a wreckage he will photograph
> close up in the "Life Studies" sequence . . . The "I" remains
> relatively neutral and transparent, a camera eye . . . *Life Studies*
> gives us a world of characters in full view, with the conscious-
> ness of the poet reduced to the thickness of a camera lens.

But the title of *Life Studies* ("from the life or living model," a sense
"relating to Art," as the *OED* puts it) places Lowell's intent (as I
thought everyone knew) firmly in the area of family portraiture.
There is nothing random about the composition of these studies;
while they assume a naturalness (and even a nakedness) that we expect in works done in the "life class," they are subject to the modifica-
tion of the painter's compositional manipulation. The respectability
of the notion of "the sister arts," and the old axiom "*Ut pictura
poesis*" here conflict with Lowell's suggestion of the impropriety associated with painting from the undraped model. Just as every new
convention insists on its superior truthfulness by comparison with
the convention it replaces, so Lowell declares that his family, in his
portraits, will be naked, not swathed in decorous garments.

Lowell's intermediate convention, visible in *Notebook*, was that of
the sonnet-diary, presumably more "naked," less "composed," than
the usual sonnet-sequence. But his final aesthetic, to which he gave
deliberate emphasis by embodying it in his formal envoi, "Epilogue,"
threatened a last nakedness of convention, the album of snapshots,
"lurid, rapid, garish, grouped." His art, Lowell declares, is "threadbare," its plush worn off, its warp and woof revealed for all to see.
In "Epilogue," Lowell recited beforehand all the criticisms which
could be, and have been, voiced of his later work. He appears, under
the pressure of self-criticism, to draw back from the full implications
of amateurishness in the aesthetic of snapshots, and, in a *volte-face*
to the most sophisticated of painters, he couples himself with Vermeer, whose "grace of accuracy" he prays to have. Vermeer's girl is
not transcendent; she yearns, but is "solid with yearning." And the
sun's illumination in the painting is not referred to heaven, but to
earth and representation, as it is seen "stealing like the tide across
a map."
   This backward glance to the power of the painter's vision, as it
"trembles to caress the light," is paired with a backward glance to
"those blessed structures, plot and rhyme," the compositional resources comparable, in the poet's art, to balance of masses and hues

in the art of the painter. The "uncomposed" aesthetic of the "snap-shot" recurs, but that unkind name is replaced by the more dignified "photograph"—a Vermeer-like "writing with light." The stern ad-monition Lowell now obeys is that which warns him "to give / each figure in the photograph / his living name."

This adjuration, with its echoes of "the living God," carries an almost religious imperative. There is no longer time for named things to "change their name" and be renamed. The picture cannot be re-taken; "the line must terminate." In the obligation to "say what happened," the aesthetic of the photograph—the eye as lens, not as caressing brush—takes precedence, in an ascetic vow, over the more premeditated arrangements of portraiture. It is only another con-vention; but it contradicts, as Axelrod fails to see, the convention of *Life Studies.*

No doubt Lowell, if he proves durable as a poet, will create the taste by which he is to be admired. He lived long enough to see his repu-tation fluctuate, and to contemplate, with considerable irony, the several books written about him (of which Hugh Staples' remains the only distinguished one). It is too much to hope that any poet of Lowell's inventiveness should find any critics with an ear even approximating his own in fineness, but surely the editors of this book should have corrected Axelrod's more jarring sentences:

A cry for help is as hopeful as this sequence gets.

"The Quaker Graveyard" on its face remains a brutal clash of opposites.

Day by Day is a postultimate work.

[Lowell's South American poems] could scarcely have been what the CIA had in mind when it picked up his tab.

["The Quaker Graveyard"] is the longest and in my view most completely artful poem in the volume.

Part six of the poem presents the only existent alternative to human chaos.

Lowell rebels even against reverence, should it smack of smugness.

Instances could be multiplied indefinitely. The alternate form of diction that pervades the book could be called that of "English-course sentimentality." A representative passage, on *The Dolphin,* goes as follows:

On this level *The Dolphin* is about human freedom and growth. And it is supremely a poem about love, love that makes freedom meaningful, love that allows for human growth . . . In the largest sense Caroline as dolphin stands for Lowell's loving relationship to the universe. His opening himself to her represents his opening to the world outside himself . . . In *The Dolphin* Lowell marries a real woman named Caroline, and he also marries his life to his art. Founded on mutuality, the poem concerns events in his life and the way they become his art, and it also concerns art itself and the way art gives meaning (even existence) to his life.

Any poet—but more especially Lowell, with his hairsbreadth sense of words—deserves better from his commentators.

Last Days and Last Poems

The last years of Robert Lowell's life, when I knew him, were ones of almost emblematic location. He and his wife, Caroline Blackwood, were in Kent in a manor house called Milgate Park; when that house was sold, they lived at Castletown House in Ireland; he taught at Harvard one term each year, giving a course in nineteenth- or twentieth-century poetry and holding open office hours in which he commented on the writing of those presenting work; he was, during his last summer, in Maine with his second wife, Elizabeth Hardwick. In England and Ireland he was an expatriate; at Harvard he was at home by virtue of birth and name but exotic by virtue of his life and his poetry; in Maine he was returning to a scene long-familiar. In his final summer he went for the first time to Russia. After his sudden death on his return from Ireland to New York, there was a funeral at his childhood church, the Church of the Advent, not far from the Revere Street which appears in *Life Studies*. Finally, he was buried in the Winslow and Stark family cemetery, still in Dunbarton, New Hampshire, though moved from the original location described in several of his poems.

"Robert Lowell's Last Days and Last Poems" first appeared in *Robert Lowell: A Tribute*, edited by Rolando Anzilotti (Pisa: Nistri-Lischi Editori, 1979).

These various places—Boston, Maine, England, Ireland, New York—the old-fashioned, the urban, the rural, the foreign, the sophisticated—respond to facets of Lowell's complex character and appear in his last poems, collected in *Day by Day* (1977). In these poems Lowell becomes not only the New England poet of Boston, Dunbarton, and Maine, not only the American poet of New York, Washington, and Ohio, but also the expatriate poet of Kent and Ireland. Besides new places he added new experiences, writing for the first time at any length as the father of a son—a son uncannily resembling him. He wrote of physical illness—he was hospitalized briefly in January 1977 for congestive heart disease—and of the expectation, not unfounded, of his death.

Like the books which preceded it, *Day by Day* was attacked. "Slack and meretricious," one fellow poet said of the later poetry, accusing it of "the lassitude and despondency of self-imitation." In twenty years, he prophesied, no one would praise *Day by Day*, which would remain "a sad footnote to the corruption of a great poet." Without attempting to usurp the function of time, which will decide whether *Day by Day* is a stern and touching volume, as I believe it to be, or whether it deserves no such praise, I would like to dwell on a few of its poems and a few of its claims, beginning with its own description of itself. But I must look first, briefly, at its predecessors.

Lowell began as a writer of an obscure and oblique poetry, which struggled violently with murky feeling, invented baffling displaced sufferings like those in *The Mills of the Kavanaughs*, resisted interpretation, and discovered original resources in traditional forms. This poetry, in spite of its difficulty, attracted wide attention and praise, so much so that its very strength was the greatest obstacle to Lowell's poetic progress. *Life Studies* disappointed readers attached to Lowell's earlier "Catholic" manner, and the lean and loose-jointed poems which are now his most famous work had to wait some time for popular acceptance. Just as *Life Studies* entered the anthologies, Lowell returned to a species of formality, writing innumerable sonnets (collected in *Notebook* and subsequent volumes), compressing life with what seemed extraordinary cruelty and candor into a Procrustean and unyielding shape. These poems have not yet been assimilated—except in a voyeuristic way—into the American literary consciousness. "It takes ten years," Lowell said dryly of popular acquiescence.

Now he has ended, in *Day by Day*, as a writer of disarming openness, exposing shame and uncertainty, offering almost no purchase to interpretation, and in his journal-keeping, abandoning conventional structure, whether rhetorical or logical. The poems drift from one focus to another; they avoid the histrionic; they sigh more often than they expostulate. They acknowledge exhaustion; they expect death. Admirers of the sacerdotal and autocratic earlier manner are offended by this diminished diarist, this suddenly quiescent volcano. But Lowell knew better than anyone else what he had given up: "Those blessèd structures, plot and rhyme— / why are they no help to me now," he begins his closing poem, "Epilogue." He had been willing to abandon plot and rhyme in writing poems about things recalled—in order to make that recall casual and natural. But now, in his last poem, he wanted "to make something imagined, not recalled," and wished to return to plot and rhyme. But the habit of the volume held, and the last testament is unrhymed and unplotted, as unstructured apparently as its companions. Despairingly, Lowell contrasts himself with the "true" artists, the painter, feeling himself to be like Hawthorne's Coverdale, only an American daguerrotypist:

> Sometimes everything I write
> with the threadbare art of my eye
> seems a snapshot,
> lurid, rapid, garish, grouped,
> heightened from life,
> yet paralyzed by fact.

Lowell here anticipates all that could be said, and has been said, in criticism of his last book: that his art does not go clothed in the gorgeous tapestry of his earlier work, but is threadbare; that he is making capital of the lurid and garish episodes of his life—adolescent cruelty, family scandal, madness, three marriages; that his poems are rapid sketches rather than finished portraits; that he is hampered by his allegiance to fact without even the compensating virtue of absolute truthfulness, since all is heightened by compression and focus. After this devastating self-criticism, the only self-defense can be the anti-bourgeois question "Yet why not say what happened?"

Howard Nemerov has called the poet "the weak criminal whose confession implicates the others": and Lowell's "saying what happened" is not a cowardice of the imagination but a subversive heroism of the memory. "Memory is genius," Lowell said once at a reading, regretting how little remained even in his own prodigious memory, and regretting as well the poverty of language as a vehicle for the preservation of the past:

> How quickly I run through my little set
> of favored pictures . . . pictures starved to words.
> My memory economizes so prodigally
> I know I have suffered theft.

Abandoning the showy "objective correlatives" for his life which fill the earlier poetry, Lowell prays in his last poem for the "grace of accuracy," which he found in the Dutch realists, from Van Eyck to Vermeer. There is in this volume a painstaking description of Van Eyck's Arnolfini marriage portrait. The couple are not beautiful: the husband stands "long-faced and dwindling," the wife is pregnant; the husband "lifts a hand, / thin and white as his face / held up like a candle to bless her . . . / they are rivals in homeliness and love." In the background of the portrait, Lowell sees all the furniture of their common life: "The picture is too much like their life— / a crisscross, too many petty facts"; a candelabrum, peaches, the husband's wooden shoes "thrown on the floor by her smaller ones," the bed, "the restless marital canopy." This "petty" domestic inclusiveness is what Lowell now proposes to write about in place of his former metaphysical blazes, even in place of his former carefully casual "life studies." We know at least, then, that the aesthetic of the last work was not an unconscious or an unconsidered one. Whether it is, as some would say, a rationalization after the fact, justifying, *faute de mieux,* an exhausted invention, only history can tell; some will see in these pieces a shrewdness of choice and an epigrammatic wit that suggest consummate art.

These last poems, so random-seeming, were nonetheless composed with Lowell's characteristic severity of self-criticism. The worksheets, as always, are innumerable, incessant. Lowell lived for writing, was never happier than, as he said, when revising his revisions. Successive versions were exposed to the criticism of friends; spurred by questions, objections, suggestions, he would return eagerly to his drafts, and change, transpose, rewrite. "He loved to tinker," he said of God; it was equally true of himself. His brilliant adjectives were not achieved by chance; his inspired aphorisms took time to perfect themselves. His manuscripts may be the most interesting since Yeats's.

Lowell died in September 1977, at sixty. To honor his birthday, and commemorate his death, the Houghton Library of Har-

vard University exhibited a selection from his papers on deposit
there. His unremitting work appears in his earliest notebooks, in
the drafts for such famous poems as "The Quaker Graveyard"
(originally entitled "To Herman Melville") and "Skunk Hour"
(which had begun as a poem of personal desolation but had ac-
quired, late, its first three stanzas of tolerant, if biting, social description). The Houghton exhibit included a letter Lowell wrote, at
eighteen, to his father, declaring his vocation as a writer: "If I
fail at this, I would fail at anything else," he wrote, as I recall the
page.

How, then, are we to read these late poems? Not, certainly, for
the blessèd structures of plot and rhyme; not for the hard-driving
compression of the late sonnets; not for the transforming and
idealizing power of lyric; not for the diamond certainties of metaphysical verse; not for the retrospective and elegiac stationing of
figures as in *Life Studies;* not for the visionary furies of youth. One
afternoon in spring, I walked with Lowell through Harvard Yard.
"Did you see that Christopher Ricks had written a piece about me?"
he said. "No, what did he say?" I asked. "He said I'm violent,"
said Lowell with a mixture of humor and irony. "And Ehrenpreis
says you're comic," I said. "Why don't they ever say what I'd like
them to say?" he protested. "What's that?" I asked. "That I'm
heartbreaking," he said, meaning it.

And so he is. If this book is read, as it should be, as a journal,
written "day by day," as a fragment of an autobiography (Lowell
called his poems "my verse autobiography,") it is heartbreaking.
It records his late, perhaps unwise, third marriage; the birth of a
son; the very worst memories suppressed from *Life Studies,* memories of having been an unwanted child and a tormented adolescent;
exile in Britain and Ireland; the death of friends; clinical depression and hospitalization, lovemaking and impotence; distress over
age; fear of death. Against all this is set the power of writing—
"universal consolatory / description without significance, / transcribed verbatim by my eye."

Readers who demand something more than the eye's verbatim
transcript, who do not ask whether in fact there is anything more,
may not find these poems heartbreaking. But the Wordsworth who
said that the meanest flower that blows could give thoughts that do
often lie too deep for tears would, I think, understand the tears
underlying these "petty facts" of one man's existence. Let me quote
some of Lowell's memorable descriptions.

Of sexual impotence, recalling sexual capacity: "Last summer nothing dared impede / the flow of the body's thousand rivulets of welcome." "Rivulets" is, in its pastoral and Wordsworthian tenderness, the word carrying all the delicacy of reference. On depression: "a wooden winter shadow," with the paralysis of that state hiding in the word "wooden." On ants, and their pragmatic and logical errands: "They are lost case of the mind." On death: "My eyes flicker, the immortal / is scraped unconsenting from the mortal." On old age: "We learn the spirit is very willing to give up, / but the body is weak and will not die." On the anticipation of his own death and burial:

> In a church,
> the Psalmist's glass mosaic Shepherd
> and bright green pastures
> seem to wait
> with the modish faithlessness
> and erotic daydream
> of art nouveau for our funeral.

And yet, for all their air of verbatim description, these poems, like all poems, are invented things. They are invented even in little. Lowell once handed me a draft of a new poem, called "Bright Day in Boston." It begins, "Joy of standing up my dentist, / X-ray plates like a broken Acropolis . . . / Joy to idle through Boston." I was struck by the *panache* of standing up one's dentist, and said so; "Well, as a matter of fact," said Lowell sheepishly, "I actually *did* go to the dentist first, and *then* went for the walk." But in the poem, "the unpolluted joy / And criminal leisure of a boy"—to quote earlier verses—became fact, where in life they had been only wish. The life of desire is as evident in these poems as the life of fact. Medical prescriptions are both named and rejected: "What is won by surviving, / if two glasses of red wine are poison?" The Paterian interval becomes ever smaller: "We only live between / before we are and what we were." Lowell looks in terror to "the hungry future, / the time when any illness is chronic, / and the years of discretion are spent on complaint— / . . . until the wristwatch is taken from the wrist." These deathly truths, unrelieved by any prospect of afterlife or immortality, are, I think, what dismay many readers. How squalid and trivialized a view of death, they may feel— chronic illness, complaint, and that last hospital gesture, the wristwatch taken from the wrist. But over against that end, Lowell sets a flickering terestrial Eden: "We took our paradise here—how else love?" That "a man love[s] a woman more than women" remained for him an insoluble and imprisoning mystery: "A man without a wife / is like a turtle without a shell." "Nature," says Lowell who is part of nature, "is sundrunk with sex," but he would "seek leave unimpassioned by [his] body." That leave was not granted him: he stayed with women till the end of the party, "a half-filled glass in each hand— / . . . swayed / by the hard infatuate wind of love."

In this last accuracy the poet cannot even see himself as unique, unusual, set apart. There is the humility of the generic about this volume, in spite of its pride in its poetic work. As far as he can see, Lowell tells us, each generation leads the same life, the life of its time. No one in the present is wiser or more foolish than those in the past or the future. No fresh perfection treads on our heels; nor do we represent any decay of nature. This attitude distresses those who come to poetry for hope, transcendence, the inspiriting word. "Really," says Lowell to Berryman in his elegy for Berryman, "we had the same life / the generic one / our generation offered." First they were students, then they, as teachers themselves, had students; they had their *grands maîtres* as all young writers do, they had their "fifties' fellowships / to Paris, Rome and Florence," they were "veterans of the Cold War not the War." Thousands of other intellectuals of their generation had the same "generic life." If he were young now, say Lowell, he would be indistinguishable from the other young, listening to rock, "lost / in unreality and loud music."

In a class lecture on Arnold, Lowell once said that "Dover Beach" had been criticized, "in the old days of the New Critics," for not continuing the sea imagery in the last stanza; "But I think by then," Lowell went on, "you've had quite enough of it." His sense of the fluidity of life's events and of human response pressed him into some of the same discontinuity of imagery, and drew the disapproval of purists in structure. Lowell believed—I am quoting another class—that the poem "is an event, not the record of an event"; "the lyric claims to produce an event; it is this for which it strives and which it sometimes brings off." Like an event, the lyric can be abrupt, odd-shaped, irregularly featured, and inconclusive. The important thing is the presence of "exciting or strenuous writing"— what one finds in Henry James, he said, on every page, good or bad. Power and wistfulness stood, for Lowell, in inverse relation: he praised the "tender" poems at the end of Leaves of Grass while remarking nonetheless how different in tone Whitman's later poetry, written when he was ill, was from the poetry of his "great healthy days." We might say the same of Lowell's last collection. The impetuousness of the "manic statement" is gone: mania is now viewed with apprehension and horror: "I grow too merry, / when I stand in my nakedness to dress." Even poetry itself can seem to want conviction: it becomes merely a compulsive "processing of words," a "dull instinctive glow," refueling itself from "bits of paper brought to feed it," which it blackens.

In the transparent myth which opens *Day by Day*, a weary Ulysses tires of Circe, returns to a deformed Ithaca, to a Penelope corrupted by living well, and finds rage his only authentic and vivid emotion. A shorthand of reference is substituted for the luxuries of description, while a desultory motion replaces youth's arrowy energy. No one would deny that this poetry has destructive designs on convention. Lowell once quoted Eliot on Coleridge: "By the time he wrote the *Biographia Literaria* he was a ruin, but being a ruin is a sort of occupation." (T. S. Eliot actually wrote in *The Use of Poetry and the Use of Criticism:* "Sometimes, however, to be 'a ruined man' is itself a vocation.") The remark reveals a good deal about Eliot, but Lowell's citation is interesting in itself: it conveys the conviction of the artist-survivor that there is always something to be made of life, even of its orts and offal, its tired ends, its disappointments and disgusts, its ironies. The sense of the end of life must find some expression, even if in what Stevens called "long and sluggish lines." Without endorsing an imitative form, we can yet find in Lowell's casualness, his waywardness, his gnomic summaries, his fragmentary reflections, authentic representations of a sixty-year-old memory.

Not every poem, I suppose, succeeds in giving "each figure in the photograph / his living name." But the poet who had decided that "we are poor passing facts," felt obliged to a poetry of deprivation and of transient actuality, lit up by moments of unearthly pained happiness, like that in his last aubade:

> For the last two minutes, the returning monarchy
> of the full moon looks down on the first chirping sparrows—
> nothing lovelier than waking to find
> another breathing body in my bed . . .
> glowshadow halfcovered with dayclothes like my own,
> caught in my arms.

The poetry of "poor passing facts" entails the sacrifice in large part of two aspects of Lowell's poetry that had brought him many admirers: his large reference to European literature, through his allusions and translations (which he called "Imitations"); and his political protest. In that earlier grandeur of literary scope, as well as by the moral grandeur of defiance and protest, Lowell seemed to claim a vision and power for poetry that many readers were happy to see affirmed. Others were more pleased by the development, beginning in *For the Union Dead* and culminating in Lowell's final volume, of a humbler style, that of a man, in Rolando Anzilotti's fine description, "who confronts directly and with courage his own failures, his faults and despairings, without seeking comfort, without indicating solutions to cling to. Feeling is revealed with the subtlest delicacy and candor, in its essential being." "The eye of Lowell for the particular which becomes universal," Anzilotti contines, "is precise and perfect; . . . we are far away from the oratory, from the bursting out of emotion in tumultuous rhythms, that appeared in 'The Quaker Graveyard.'" This line of writing, as Anzilotti points out, remained in equilibrium with the national and moral concerns evident in *Near the Ocean* and *Notebook;* not until this final volume did the precise eye and the quotidian feeling become the dominant forces in Lowell's aesthetic. The allusions in this last collection come from an occasional backward glance to favorite passages—a line of Dante, a line of Horace—but the poetic mind turns less and less to past literature, more and more to the immediacy of present event. There is only one poem in the volume that springs from a political impetus; "Fetus," prompted by the trial, in Boston, of a doctor accused of making no effort to keep an aborted fetus alive. And even the poem quickly leaves its occasion behind and engages in a general meditation on death, that "black arrow" arriving like a calling-card "on the silver tray." It is perhaps significant that this poem is the least successful, to my mind, in the group, in part because Lowell no longer has to hand the moral sureness to condemn or approve the abortion. He sees only the grotesquerie of the medical procedure, of the trial court, and of the biological shape of "the fetus, the homunculus, / already at four months one pound, / with shifty thumb in mouth— / . . . Our little model . . ." A poem which, by its title, "George III," might seem to be prompted by Anglo-American relations turns out, in the event, to be in part a reflection on Nixon but even more a reflection on a fate Lowell feared for himself: a permanent lapse into madness, like George,

who whimsically picked the pockets of his page
he'd paid to sleep all day outside his door;
who dressed like a Quaker, who danced a minuet
with his appalled apothecary in Kew Gardens;

who dismayed "his retinue by formally bowing to an elm, / as if it were the Chinese emissary." George's later mania bears a strong resemblance to phases of Lowell's own illness:

addressing imaginary congresses,
reviewing imaginary combat troops,
. . . .
Old, mad, deaf, half-blind,
he talked for thirty-two hours
on everything, everybody,

read Cervantes and the Bible aloud
simultaneously with shattering rapidity . . .

Social forms disappear in this last phase of Lowell's writing, and public moral witness disappears with them. The solitary human being, his life extending only as far as the domestic circle, becomes the topic of attention. Epic ambition is resigned: the *Odyssey* is reduced to a marital triangle. The personal is seen as the locus of truth, insight, and real action.

And when Lowell writes about the personal, he spares himself nothing, not the patronizing doctor in the asylum addressing Caroline, "A model guest . . . we would welcome / Robert back to Northampton any time"; not the susurrus of public or private comment about madness having attacked him even in this third, scandalous marriage:

If he has gone mad with her,
the poor man can't have been very happy,
seeing too much and feeling it
with one skin-layer missing;

not a murderously detached self-portrait among the other mad:

I am a thorazined fixture
in the immovable square-cushioned chairs
we preoccupy for seconds like migrant birds.

After the scene-setting in the asylum comes the distracted interior monologue, much as it had in "Skunk Hour." But whereas in the earlier poem the poses struck were tragic, and then comic, redeemed in some way by the animal appetite of the skunks, the monologue in the asylum, forebodingly called "Home," is one of pure childlike pathos:

> The immovable chairs have swallowed up the patients,
> and speak with the eloquence of emptiness.
> By each the same morning paper lies unread:
> *January 10, 1976.*
> I cannot sit or stand two minutes,
> yet walk imagining a dialogue
> between the devil and myself,
> not knowing which is which or worse,
> saying,
> as one would instinctively say Hail Mary,
> *I wish I could die.*
> Less than ever I expect to be alive
> six months from now—
> *1976,*
> a date I dare not affix to my grave.
> The Queen of Heaven, I miss her,
> we were divorced. She never doubted
> the divided, stricken soul
> could call her Maria,
> and rob the devil with a word.

The grand drama of the manic has ended, and it is the depressive side of illness, without the illusions of mania, which gives its tone to these latter poems. As the horizon narrows, the smallest sensations of living—waking up alive, seeing the spring—suffice. "I thank God," says Lowell, "for being alive— / a way of writing I once thought heartless." Heartless because selfish, solipsistic— or so he thought when he was young, and had heart for all the world, or so it seemed. Recognizing the fury of political statement as a displacement of fury against parents, he can no longer permit its unmediated and thoughtless energy. In the poem to his mother, he admits, "It has taken me the time since you died / to discover you are as human as I am . . . / if I am." In the poem to his father, he confesses,

> It would take two lifetimes
> to pick the crust
> and uncover the face
> under our two menacing,
> iconoclastic masks.

His father refuses the sympathy proffered when Lowell implies that now he understands his father's life through the similarity of his own life to that of his father: "It can't be that, / it's your life," says his father, "and dated like mine." The failure of Lowell's father is reflected in his own failure, just as Lowell's childhood innocence is reflected in the innocence of his little son:

> We could see clearly
> and all the same things
> before the glass was hurt.
>
> Past fifty, we learn with surprise and a sense
> of suicidal absolution
> that what we intended and failed
> could never have happened—
> and must be done better.

The old paternal hope that the child's life will be lived better struggles with the conviction that each generation repeats the generic life of all its predecessors. The very motive for action is removed by such resignation to the common fate.

Nothing remains for Lowell, then, after he has jettisoned formal religious belief, social protest, a twenty-year marriage, even residence in America, except memory and the present moment. When asked why he wanted a formal funeral in the Episcopal church, Lowell said, "That's how we're buried"—that was the custom of the family. At the funeral his second and third wives, his grown daughter and his small son, and his three stepdaughters, sat in the first mourners' pew, existing side by side as they did in his life and his poetry. He is buried in Dunbarton next to his father and his mother. His parents' tombstones bear inscriptions he composed; in an odd flash of authorship, he had a signature incised, in cursive script, below the Roman lettering—"R. Lowell Jr." There were memorial services for him in New York, at Harvard, and in London. When Vozneszhensky came to America, he asked to be driven to Lowell's grave, and laid on it berries which had grown above the grave of Pasternak. Already there have been elegies, though none perhaps equal to the many elegies he wrote for the friends who preceded him in death.

In writing this last volume, Lowell pleased himself, listening with some inner ear to the inner life of the poem, deciding with mysterious certainty when it was finished, when it had found its equilibrium. I think that the instinctive principles on which he worked will become clearer with time. One writes poetry, he said, by instinct and by ear, and his own instincts and ear were pressing toward a poetry ever more unconventional, ever less "literary." He admired the way Coleridge, in his ballads, could be "showily simple and get away with it." He sought that ostentatious simplicity himself. He added that though Coleridge's verse epistle to Sara Hutchinson—the first version of the Dejection Ode—was embarrassing, yet it was "a long apologetic masterpiece—something is lost by making it an ode." What is lost is the spontaneity, the heartbreak, the domestic anguish —all that appears in Lowell's journal written day by day. No doubt it could all have been transformed into odes; that was his old manner. But the something that was lost in such a case now seemed to him more precious than the something that is found. His last book, however casual it may seem, is not a collection of unconsidered trifles. Lowell wrote justly: "My eyes have seen what my hand did." His metaphor for this book was not one of arrangement, but one of accumulation:

> This is riches:
> the eminence not to be envied,
> the account
> accumulating layer and angle,
> face and profile,
> 50 years of snapshots,
> the ladder of ripening likeness.

If, to Lowell in a Shakespearean mood, we are "poor passing facts," in a more Keatsian moment we resemble the "camelion-poet":

> We are things thrown in the air
> alive in flight . . .
> our rust the color of the chameleon.

"Not to console or sanctify," says Stevens, speaking of the aim of modern poetry, "but plainly to propound." The plain propounding—of things thrown in the air, alive in flight, and rusting in change to the color of dust—if too severe, for some tastes, is to others profoundly assuaging. We are lucky in America in our poetry of old age: Whitman's, Stevens', and now Lowell's. Such poetry never can speak to the young and form their sensibilities as can the poetry of passion and hope and revolutionary ardor; but it sums up another phase of life, no less valuable, no less moving, no less true.

Howard Nemerov

When Stevens wrote about his *Collected Poems* as "The Planet on the Table," he meant that a life's poetry, like a terrestrial globe, reproduces (though in a reduced scale) the whole world. The world as Howard Nemerov knows it is revealed, prophetically, in the title of his first (1947) volume, *The Image and the Law*. The world comes to us in images; the mind seeks a law in the heterogeneous information infiltrating the senses. A late poem shows Nemerov as a boy confronting "The Book of Knowledge," "a luxury liner on [a] sea unfathomable of ignorance," with poetry "as steady, still, and rare / As the lighthouses now manned and obsolete." These three things— our already immeasurable knowledge of the world, our nonetheless profound ignorance of its ways, and our landmarks and beacons in the productions of consciousness—are Nemerov's constant subjects:

> There is the world, the dream, and the one law,
> The wish, the wisdom, and things as they are.

Nemerov is chiefly a poet of "the wisdom," "the one law": his mind plays with epigram, gnome, riddle, rune, advice, meditation, notes, dialectic, prophecy, reflection, views, knowledge, questions, speculation—all the forms of thought. His wishes go homing to origins and ends. Any natural fact—a tree, for instance—becomes instantly symbolic in his eye's gaze: it seed summons up "mysteries of generation and death," its trunk and branches recall "the one and the many, cause and effect, generality and particulars," its movement from roots to trunk to branches will serve as a metaphor for "historical process," and so on—a method by which Yeats's great-

This review of Howard Nemerov's *Collected Poems* appeared in the *New York Times Book Review*, December 18, 1977.

rooted blossomer becomes distinctly more Emersonian and emblematic.

However, Nemerov has struggled increasingly, in the course of
his life, with his philosophical instincts, urging his poetry into moods
that will accommodate fact and dream as well as wisdom. There is
a touching poem ("Beginner's Guide") that recalls his persistent, if
never entirely successful, pursuit of the proper names—through
bird books, flower books, tree books, star books—of things as they
are, "to make some mind of what was only sense." Nemerov is not
innately hospitable to fantasy and imaginative waywardness, though
his wit is elusive, mischievous, and teasing. His masters in youth—
Stevens, Auden, Frost, and Yeats—shared in different ways his
discursive and philosophic stance. He is drawn to Breughel and Klee
for their allegories of dark whimsy. Nemerov's complaint about
Klee might be his own self-definition.

> He is the painter of the human mind
> Finding and faithfully reflecting the mindfulness
> That is in things, and not the things themselves.

Nemerov's paradox—"the mindfulness that is in things"—takes on
flesh in his many surprising lines that make us see the obvious-but-
till-now-unsaid. We have all, in the newspapers, read the engagements and the obituaries, but it remained for Nemerov to see that
the papers printed "segregated photographs / Of the girls that marry
and the men that die."

Nemerov revives old American themes, equaling his predecessors
on their own ground, and rivaling Dickinson and Frost as a poet of
the American autumn:

> Something that turns upon a hidden hinge
> Brings down the dead leaf and live seed together.

The "cryptically instructive" chambered nautilus becomes for him
the "divine and crippled norm," in which "A twist along the spine
begins the form / And hides itself inside a twisted house." Like
Lowell, he keeps a churchless Sabbath:

> Among the ashtrays in the living room
> [You] breathe the greyish air left over from
> Last night, and go down on your knees to read
> The horrible funnies flattened on the floor.

The morose humor that pervades the *Collected Poems* takes its rise from Nemerov's contemplation of various grim spectacles: the will's rebellion against necessity, history's repetitions, the pitfalls of the literary life, and the perpetual discrepancy between hope and event. Sometimes Nemerov's irony can itself seem contrived, a too orderly dismissal of life. But on the whole, the irony is mixed with a rueful pleasure, as Nemerov is distracted from wisdom by some natural phenomenon. He fends off his tendency to solemn periods with a jaunty colloquiality; while yearning toward his alphas and omegas, he can take time for a brilliant sketch of football players on television:

> Totemic scarabs, exoskeletal,
> Nipped in at the thorax, bulky above and below,
> With turreted hard heads and jutting masks
> And emblems of the lightning or the beast.

The world causes in Nemerov a mingled revulsion and love, and a hopeless hope is the most attractive quality in his poems, which slowly turn obverse to reverse, seeing the permanence of change, the vices of virtue, the evanescence of solidities, and the errors of truth. Dreams lie with death and mathematics, forgeries invade art museums, a green and silent cherry tree shades "the bloody stones, the rotting flesh" of its fruit, and the "translucency of leaf" of the ginkgo filters "a urinary yellow light." The sensibility mapped by such phrases is one permanently unsettled and bent on making a law out of its unease.

As the echoes of Nemerov's *grands maîtres* fade, the poems get steadily better. The severity of attitude is itself chastened by a growing humanity, and the forms of the earth grow ever more distinct, as by small increments of reality. Nemerov brightens his lonely algebraic world, beset by the First and Second Laws of Thermodynamics. In the fall, he now notices

> Acorns in neat berets, horse chestnuts huge
> And shiny as shoes inside their spiny husks,
> Prickly planets among the sweet gum's starry leaves.

These noticings thread veins of life through Nemerov's ruminations: his dandelions that puff and go to seed delicately ornament, like fanciful illuminations, his sterner text. If the ravens of unresting thought (as Yeats called them) swarm blackly through these pages, they find a series of living boughs on which to perch. The sadder poems about nature and life are, on the whole, the most memorable, but since one of the accidental services performed by any *Collected Poems* is to exert pressure on anthologies, anthologists of the future should not forget Nemerov's forceful, comic, and bitter topical poems, ranging from World War II to Vietnam, and embracing even such unpoetical matters as loyalty oaths.

Frank O'Hara

The Virtue of the Alterable

Frank O'Hara's charms are inseparable from his overproduction—
the offhand remark, the fleeting notation of a landscape, the Christmas or birthday verse, the impromptu souvenir of a party—these are
his common forms, as though he roamed through life snapping Po-
laroid pictures, pulling them out of his camera and throwing them
in a desk drawer sixty seconds later. And here they are—some over-
exposed, some underdeveloped, some blurred, some unfocused, and
yet any number of them succeeding in fixing the brilliance of some
long-forgotten lunch, or the curve of a body in a single gesture, or a
snowstorm, or a childhood movie. If these poems are photographic
in their immediacy, they resemble too the rapid unfinished sketches
done by an artist to keep his hand in or to remind him of some
perishable composition of the earth. If there were a movie equivalent
to a sketch, some of these poems would be better called verbal
movies—the "I do-this, I-do-that" poems, as O'Hara himself called
them.

The generic form of O'Hara's poems is conversation, the generic
punctuation the exclamation point, the generic population O'Hara's
friends, the generic landscape Manhattan and Fire Island, the generic
mythology the flora and fauna of art shows, radio shows, and movie
shows. Sureness and insouciance mark O'Hara's lines. But two aspects of his work tended to do O'Hara in: his radical incapacity for
abstraction (like Byron, when he thinks he is a child) and his lack of
a comfortable form (he veered wildly from long to short, with no
particular reason in many cases for either choice). The longest poems
end up simply messy, endless secretions, with a nugget of poetry

"The Virtue of the Alterable" first appeared in *Parnassus: Poetry in Review*,
Fall/Winter 1972.

here and there, slices of life arbitrarily beginning, and ending for no particular reason. "Dear Diary," says O'Hara, and after that anything goes. The perfect freedom any diarist enjoys—to put anything down that happened on a certain day only because at the head of the page there is that hungry date saying June 13, 1960—is what O'Hara claims for himself in the long poems. Beside these poems, even Ginsberg looks formal. The theoretical question O'Hara forces on us is a radical one: Why should poetry be confined in a limited or closed form? Our minds ramble on; why not our poems? Ramblings are not, to say the least, the native form of poets with metaphysical minds, but O'Hara, in his fundamental prescinding from the metaphysical, believes neither in problems nor in solutions, nor even in the path from one to the other. He believes in colloquies, observations, memories, impressions, and variations—all things with no beginnings and no endings, things we tune in on and then tune out of. Turn on the oscilloscope, attach the leads to the tuner, take gauge readings—these are the O'Hara processes. In one sense, there is no reason why a poem of this sort should ever stop. The inherent limitation seems not be a formal one within the poem, but an external one: the limited attention span of the poet or his reader. We can attend to life in this hyperattentive way for only a short time, and then our energy flags, so that like overexcited electrons we subside back into our low-energy orbits. The poet's language weakens, our response sags, and the poem loses us. And yet O'Hara was stubborn enough to wish, like Emily in *Our Town*, that life could always be lived on the very edge of loss, so that every instant would seem wistfully precious. Therefore the attitude of perpetual wonder, perpetual exclamation, perpetual naiveté. O'Hara had enough of all these qualities by nature (judging from their consistent presence from the earliest poems to the latest) so that this poise at the brink of life was no pose, but it does make me wonder how he would have endured that jadedness of age that, in their different ways, all old poets confront.

Some of O'Hara's poems are already deservedly famous, for the best reason in the world: nobody else has done anything like them in English. One reading of "Blocks" guarantees that the stunning last half will never be forgotten:

O boy, their childhood was like so many oatmeal cookies.
I need you, you need me, yum, yum. Anon it became suddenly
like someone always losing something and never knowing what.
Always so. They were so fond of eating bread and butter and

sugar, they were slobs, the mice used to lick the floorboards
after they went to bed, rolling their light tails against
the rattling marbles of granulation. Vivo! the dextrose
those children consumed, lavished, smoked, in their knobby
candy bars. Such pimples! such hardons! such moody loves.
And thus they grew like giggling fir trees.

The intense appeal of these lines comes from their having suppressed nothing of adolescence: the persistence of the childish in candy bars and giggles; the startling new growth "like fir trees"; the incongruous nursery scene of the mice in the children's bedroom eating their bedtime snack while the children suddenly discover themselves having hardons and pimples; the sudden flash of the personal ("I need you, you need me") combined painfully with its psychic results ("like someone always losing something . . . such moody loves"). Almost all other poems about adolescence have concealed one or the other of these facets of the state, whether out of shame or aesthetics one scarcely knows. An aesthetic that permits the coexistence of moody loves, hardons, mice, and candy bars has a good chance of being a new source of truth.

The same capaciousness appears in the ethereal poem "First Dances," where O'Hara touches in sequence a dancer's first attempt to lift a ballerina, a high-school dance, then, perhaps, his first gay dance:

1
From behind he takes her waist
and lifts her, her lavender waist
stained with tears and her mascara
is running, her neck is tired
from drooping. She floats she steps
automatically correct, then suddenly
she is alive up there and smiles.
How much greater triumph for him
that she had so despaired when his
hands encircled her like a pillar
and lifted her into the air
which after him will turn to rock
like boredom, but not till after
many hims and he will not be there.

2
The punch bowl was near the cloakroom
so the pints could be taken out of the
boys' cloaks and dumped into the punch.

> ... There were many
> introductions but few invitations. I
> found a spot of paint on my coat as
> other found pimples. It is easy to
> dance it is even easy to dance together
> sometimes. We were very young and ugly
> we knew it, everybody knew it.
> 3
> A white hall inside a church. Nerves.

The wholly intimate presence of the male dancer in the first section is suddenly dispensed with—"He will not be there"—and the agony and pleasure sketched so vividly in the second dance give way to a seriocomic summation ("We were very young and ugly") —and yet finally summary or dismissal is wholly scrapped and the primacy of recollection is allowed: "A white hall . . . Nerves." This invalidation of judgment is both dangerous and satisfying. After all, what difference does it make what happens later on or how the picture looks in retrospect or in second-order reflection? The final equation, First Dances = Nerves, is the truest.

O'Hara distrusts spectatorship, so that even his most cinematic self-filmings are expressed from the inside out, as though they were blood-pressure readings rather than a nurse's external observations on a chart, self-generated electrical impulses which record themselves without the interposition of a watching person. An evening is improvised, in "At the Old Place," and the gay-bar scene is sketched with no retrospective frame, noted down exactly as it happens. I'm not sure why this method succeeds, except that the mixture of frivolousness, bathos, high-pitched boredom, and self-satire is not one that men have allowed into poetry very often, if ever:

> Joe is restless and so am I, so restless.
> Button's buddy lips frame "L G T TH O P?"
> across the bar. "Yes" I cry, for dancing's
> my soul delight. (Feet! feet!) "Come on!"
>
> Through the streets we skip like swallows.
> Howard malingers. (Come on, Howard.) Ashes
> malingers. (Come on, J. A.) Dick malingers.
> (Come on, Dick.) Alvin darts ahead. (Wait up,
> Alvin.) Jack, Earl and Someone don't come.
>
> Down the dark stairs drifts the steaming cha-
> cha-cha. Through the urine and smoke we charge
> to the floor. Wrapped in Ashes' arms I glide.

(It's heaven!) Button lindys with me. (It's
heaven!) Joe's two-steps, too, are incredible,
and then a fast rhumba with Alvin, like skipping
on toothpicks. And the interminable intermissions,

we have them. Jack, Earl and Someone drift
guiltily in. "I knew they were gay
the minute I laid eyes on them!" screams John.
How ashamed they are of us! we hope.

The wish *not* to impute significance has rarely been stronger in
lyric poetry. It happened, it went like this, it's over. Why is it worth
recording? Because it happened. Why is what happened worth
recording? Because what else is there to record? And why should
we want to read it? Because what else is there to know except what
has happened to people? Such a radical and dismissive logic flouts
the whole male world and its relentless demand for ideologies,
causes, and systems of significance. The anarchic elasticity of
O'Hara's poetry depends entirely on his athletic effort to make the
personal the poetic—the personal divested of religion, of politics, of
mysticism, of patriotism, of metaphysics, even of idealism. One
might be reminded in part of Forster's ethic of personal relation, but
Forster shored up that ethos with innumerable arabesques of myth,
ranging from Pan to Brahma. O'Hara's designedly light explanation
of his theory of poetry (which he winsomely named "Personism")
rests on intimacy and immediacy:

> It was founded by me after lunch with LeRoi Jones on August 27,
> 1959, a day in which I was in love with someone (not Roi, by the
> way, a blond). I went back to work and wrote a poem for this
> person. While I was writing it I was realizing that if I wanted
> to I could use the telephone instead of writing the poem and so
> Personism was born. It's a very exciting movement which will
> undoubtedly have lots of adherents. It puts the poem squarely
> between the poet and the person . . . The poem is at last between
> two persons instead of two pages.

In another statement, later partially disavowed, O'Hara made a
more serious formulation:

> I don't think my experiences are clarified or made beautiful for
> myself or anyone else; they are just there in whatever form I can
> find them . . . It may be that poetry makes life's nebulous events

tangible to me and restores their detail; or, conversely, that poetry brings forth the intangible quality of incidents which are all too concrete and circumstantial. Or each on specific occasions, or both all the time.

Experiences, incidents, events—O'Hara's vocabulary betrays how impatient he was of any notion which would separate novel-writing and poetry-writing. He liked to cite Pasternak as an example of a writer who could do both, and we may guess that O'Hara suffered from a persistent wish for a longer form than his own poems afforded him. Without that long form, we are offered glimpses of relation, happy and sad, but no continuous curve of a life-spiral; like Roman candles, O'Hara's poems burst into a shower of bright particulars and then extinguish themselves, often enough in a few modest ashes, on the page.

O'Hara in some way refused to take his poems, I would guess, as seriously as he took life. "It's a pretty depressing day, you must admit," he wrote, "when you feel you relate more importantly to poetry than to life" (a feeling that underlies one of his most brilliant poems, "A Step Away from Them"). The greatest poets would have found that antithesis unthinkable and unsayable, and it works to the harm of O'Hara's poetry that he thinks poetry is *not* life. The shadowy, if immense, privileges he claims for art appear at their most impressive in his comic manifesto "Ave Maria":

> Mothers of America
> > let your kids go the movies!
> get them out of the house so they won't know what you're up to
> it's true that fresh air is good for the body
> > > but what about the soul
> that grows in darkness, embossed by silvery images
> and when you grow old as grow old you must
> > > > they won't hate you
> they won't criticize you they won't know
> > > they'll be in some
> > > glamorous country
> they first saw on a Saturday afternoon or playing hookey.

It is typical of O'Hara that the silver screen, however glamorous its images, cannot compete with the real thing, which is, of course, sex. The poem continues, in a child's experience of a wonderful *épanouissement* better than anything in the movies:

they may even be grateful to you
     for their first sexual experience
which only cost you a quarter
     and didn't upset the peaceful home
they will know where candy bars come from
      and gratuitous bags of
      popcorn
as gratuitous as leaving the movie before it's over
with a pleasant stranger whose apartment is in the Heaven on
 Earth bldg
near the Williamsburg Bridge
      O mothers you will have made the
      little tykes
so happy because if nobody does pick them up in the movies
they won't know the difference
     and if somebody does it'll be sheer
     gravy.

O'Hara's presentation of early sex as pure physical pleasure bestowed like the bribery of popcorn hovers on the edge of Romance. Would being picked up by a stranger in the movies really be that nice? Yes, maybe, sometimes, other times not, and the poem survives its loading of these particular dice only by its inveterate air of resolute comedy. O'Hara has a line in one poem about writing poetry to cheer people up, and there is an air of determined social duty about a lot of these poems, as though the balloon of group cheerfulness had to be batted back to the next player—over to you, Kenneth—and Kenneth Koch, himself equally noble in his obligations, serves a jaunty poem back, and so on through the clan, to Bill Berkson to John Ashbery, like Tinker to Evers to Chance. The important thing is to be quick on your toes, elastic and springy, especially springy.

It took O'Hara several years of writing to perfect his individuality. The reason he was not noticed early on is that most of his early work is his worst. John Ashbery, in his introduction to this volume, suggests a cabal of the anti-avant-garde who, ostrichlike, hid their heads against O'Hara's radiance:

It was not surprising that [O'Hara's] work should have initially proved so puzzling to readers—it ignored the rules for modern American poetry that had been gradually drawn up from Pound and Eliot down to the academic establishment of the 1940s.

If Dylan Thomas, who sounded not at all like Pound or Eliot, could be welcomed in America, so could anyone else, and this conspiracy theory is entirely untenable. O'Hara's poems got measurably better with the publication of *Mediations in an Emergency* (1957), and by the time he published *Lunch Poems* in 1964 he was well known. The early poems are often tiresomely insistent: the last of the twelve "pastorals," entitled "Oranges," reads in its conclusion (after five pages of ramblings):

> Marine breeze!
> Golden lily!
> Foxglove!
> In these symbols lives the world of erection and destruction, the dainty despots of society.
> Out of the cloud come Judas Agonistes and Christopher Smell to tell us of their earthy woe. By direction we return to our fulfilling world, we are back in the poem.
> Across the windowsill lies the body of a blue girl, hair floating weedy in the room. Upon her cypresses dance a Black Mass,
> the moon grins between their legs, Gregorian frogs belch and masturbate. Around the window morning glories screech of rape as dreadful bees, consummately religious, force their way in the dark.
> The tin gutter's clogged by moonlight and the rain barrel fills with flesh. Across the river a baboon blesses cannibals.
> O my posterity! This is the miracle: that our elegant invention
> the natural world redeems by filth.

A lot of this has been picked up from the more blasphemous French poets, and the strain is felt. The confused antagonism between art ("elegant invention") and sex ("filth") is almost buried in a welter of lurid images, and the soapbox is not far away. In the early verse exclamation points attempt over and over a rape of the reader, and even in "A City Winter," the title poem to his first volume, O'Hara sounds like bad George Meredith:

> I plunge me deep within this frozen lake
> whose mirrored fastnesses fill up my heart.
> where tears drift from frivolity to art
> all white and slobbering, and by mistake
> are the sky. I'm no whale to cruise apart
> in fields impassive of my stench, my sake,

my sign to crushing seas that fall like fake
pillars to crash!

The miracle is that even while O'Hara was writing trash like this
there was growing a small pile of poems far more unassertive, self-
deprecatory, and self-admiring, at once combining pain and joy,
one disarmingly entitled "Autobiographia Literaria":

> When I was a child
> I played by myself in a
> corner of the schoolyard
> all alone.
>
> I hated dolls and I
> hated games, animals were
> not friendly, and birds
> flew away.
>
> If anyone was looking
> for me I hid behind a
> tree and cried out "I am
> an orphan."
>
> And here I am, the
> center of all beauty!
> writing these poems!
> Imagine!

This was written in 1949 or 1950, when O'Hara was twenty-three or
twenty-four, and even that early O'Hara had found the poignant
way of talking to the world that he brought to perfection in "A True
Account of Talking to the Sun on Fire Island," written in 1958:

> I picked up a leaf
> today from the sidewalk.
> This seems childish.
>
> Leaf! you are so big!
> How can you change your
> color, then just fall!
>
> As if there were no
> such thing as integrity!
>
> You are too relaxed
> to answer me. I am too
> frightened to insist.

Breathless and marveling, as he says of himself in an early verse letter to Bunny Lang, O'Hara patrols the paths of the world, hoping to unclutter himself of cynicism and false sophistication, tempted by fantasy and yet shamed by it. One of the most finished of the early poems is a transparent look inward to the fascination of the movies:

> The cinema is cruel
> like a miracle. We
> sit in the darkened
> room asking nothing
> of the empty white
> space but that it
> remain pure. And
> suddenly despite us
> it blackens. Not by
> the hand that holds
> the pen. There is
> no message. We our
> selves appear naked
> on the riverbank
> spreadeagled while
> the machine wings
> nearer. We scream
> chatter prance and
> wash our hair! Is
> it our prayer or
> wish that this
> occur? Oh what is
> this light that
> holds us fast? Our
> limbs quicken even
> to disgrace under
> this white eye as
> if there were real
> pleasure in loving
> a shadow and caress
> in a disguise!

The medium of the poem is so simple that the title—"An Image of Leda"—comes almost shockingly to reinterpret our attachment to movies. Hypnotized and repudiatory at once, the poem holds its double feelings in a momentary tranced suspension, quickening from reflection to vicarious action and then subsiding in withdrawal.

These small triumphs succeed in their pure colloquial strength, and even such random samples as these few quotations from the early poetry demonstrate that O'Hara's native gifts for simplicity and a fresh view, though scarcely noticeable in the bulk of less completely achieved poems, were nonetheless present from the beginning.

There is scarcely a poem lacking striking lines in this volume, and almost never a poem, no matter how bad in general, lacking some wonderful words from O'Hara's tumultuous vocabulary. Chasubles and buzz saws, zebras and tendrils, yawns and ponies, gullies and rattletraps, Afghanistan and Broadway, Prussian leather and Mack trucks, the U.S. Senate and Spenser's False Florimell—all join the proliferating herbage of O'Hara's acquisitive mind. There is everywhere a breakdown of logical categories, sometimes only in a false imitation of Dada, but later in the volume in a true attempt to synthesize all of American experience, taking even a wider field than Whitman (though Whitman, to do him credit, wanted a poetry that could have room for all the names of the drinks served in all the taverns of America, as he said in *An American Primer*). O'Hara follows Whitman and Williams in writing urban pastoral, but neither Whitman nor Williams took the pleasure in the city that O'Hara did:

> I love this hairy city.
> It's wrinkled like a detective story
> and noisy and getting fat and smudged
> lids hood the sharp hard black eyes.
>
>   the country is no good for us
> there's nothing
>   to bump into
>   or fall apart glassily
> there's not enough
>   poured concrete
>   and brassy
> reflections . . .
>   New York
> greater than the Rocky Mountains

Whitman and Williams suffer from a rueful attachment to the natural world precluding any full assent to city life. But the sun has to chide O'Hara for not looking up more:

> I know you love Manhattan, but
> you ought to look up more often.

Impulsive and appetitive, OHara rakes in friends, paintings, and evenings-out with the same impartial joy. Tedious though the in-group references (to Bill and Kenneth and Janice and Edwin and Vincent and so on) can be, they are genuinely invoked to make the real precious, an experiment that is at least worth trying. In one of the most beautiful of many beautiful love poems, "Having a Coke with You" (1960), there is a praise of consummated life which always, for O'Hara, must (the highest compliment) transcend art; and this consummation is here the most banal of acts, having a Coke. Having the Coke, O'Hara can scorn to change his state with kings (in this case Marini, Duchamp, Leonardo, or Michelangelo). These quintessential hyperboles of love begin partly tongue-in-cheek, but suddenly gather to a crystallization of liberated insight, and conclude in happiness:

Having a Coke with You

is even more fun than going to San Sebastian, Irún, Hendaye,
  Biarritz, Bayonne . . .
partly because in your orange shirt you look like a better happier
  St. Sebastian
partly because of my love for you, partly because of your love for
  yoghurt . . .
and the portrait show seems to have no faces in it at all, just paint
you suddenly wonder why in the world anyone ever did them
                                                      I look
at you and I would rather look at you than all the portraits in
  the world
except possibly for the *Polish Rider* occasionally and anyway it's
  in the Frick
which thank heavens you haven't gone to yet so we can go
  together the first time
and the fact that you move so beautifully more or less takes care
  of Futurism
just as at home I never think of the *Nude Descending a Staircase* or
at a rehearsal a single drawing of Leonardo or Michelangelo that
  used to wow me
and what good does all the research of the Impressionists do them
when they never got the right person to stand near the tree when
  the sun sank
or for that matter Marino Marini when he didn't pick the rider as
  carefully
as the horse
              it seems they were all cheated of some marvellous
    experience

which is not going to go wasted on me which is why I'm telling you about it.

The happy marriage in this poem of the paintings, the trees, the Coke, the past, the present, the lovers, and the artists shows how unerringly the jumble in O'Hara's sensibility could sort itself out into shapely forms.

Though the *journal intime* can be sometimes more gripping for the diarist than for us, yet in the late poems there are signs that O'Hara could take the full measure of himself, America, and the arts better than any other of his contemporaries except perhaps Lowell and Ginsberg. In "Answer to Voznesensky and Evtushenko" he forsakes the winsome, the cute, and the childish, and launches into a grand manifesto resisting the conventional picture of America transmitted by contemporary Russian poets, reminding them in scorn of their great ancestors Mayakovsky and Pasternak:

> We are tired of your tiresome imitations of Mayakovsky
> we are tired
>   of your dreary tourist ideas of our Negro selves
> our selves are in far worse condition than the obviousness
> of your color sense
>   your general sense of Poughkeepsie is
> a gaucherie no American poet would be guilty of in Tiflis . . .
>   how many
>   of our loves have you illuminated with
> your heart your breath
>   as we poets of America have loved you
> your countrymen, our countrymen, our lives, your lives, and
> the dreary expanses of your translations
>   your idiotic manifestos.

The accomplished swings between the grand and the minute, contempt and love, keep us teetering on a bravado always just avoiding the ridiculous on the one hand and the sentimental on the other, a version of public poetry which does not abolish the private. O'Hara would like a world where nothing excluded anything else, where a conversation can coexist with a private fantasy, as it does in his almost seamless abutting of a private recollection of a movie (*Northern Pursuit*) with a search for remedies for Allen Ginsberg's stomach:

> . . . Imagine
>   throwing away the avalanche

so early in the movie. I am the only spy left
in Canada,
         but just because I'm alone in the snow
doesn't necessarily mean I'm a Nazi.
                Let's see,
two aspirins a vitamin C tablet and some baking soda
should do the trick that's practically an
                Alka
Seltzer. Allen come out of the bathroom
             and take it . . .
    Ouch. The leanto is falling over in the
firs, and there is another fatter spy here. They
didn't tell me they sent
         him. Well, that takes care
of him, boy were those huskies hungry.
              Allen,
are you feeling any better?

All of these poems are demonstrations—demonstrations of what mind is by what mind does, its remarkable double and triple tracks, so that a question about old movie scores leads to a full-dress recollection-fantasy even while one is collecting vitamin tablets, getting down the baking soda, uncapping the aspirin, and hollering to Allen in the bathroom, all the while having second-order reflections on movie-making. The number of possible tracks is theoretically limitless and it seems as though in some poems O'Hara pushes the possibilities beyond intelligibility. But when the technique works, spontaneity fills the room like helium, and the poem takes off with pure buoyancy.

The reason O'Hara can be truly aerial is that he genuinely has no metaphysical baggage. No religion, no politics, no ideology, no nothing. It is only partially a joke when he calls these lines "Metaphysical Poem":

When do you want to go
I'm not sure I want to go there
where do you want to go
any place
I think I'd fall apart any place else
well I'll go if you really want to
I don't particularly care
but you'll fall apart any place else
I can just go home
I don't really mind going there

but I don't want to force you to go there
you won't be forcing me I'd just as soon
I wouldn't be able to stay long anyway
maybe we could go somewhere nearer
I'm not wearing a jacket
just like you weren't wearing a tie
well I didn't say we had to go
I don't care whether you're wearing one
we don't really have to do anything
well all right let's not
okay I'll call you
yes call me

These relational intricacies are the only metaphysics O'Hara admits, and their probable transiency prohibits the sublime relational
metaphysics, whether deluded or not, of the Keatsian "holiness" of
the heart's affections. Happiness yes, holiness only maybe. Dismay
followed by elation, comfort succeeded by loneliness, anger giving
way to a shrug, apathy followed by quickening—these are O'Hara's
dimensions and out of them he creates his poetic space. There are
ominous sighs in the later poems, sighs especially about America,
that make us wonder whether O'Hara could have kept up the verve
and bounce and amplitude of his best poems, but even a sad poem
wafts up, often enough, a comic energy. An old Russian in America
reminisces unhappily,

> . . . meanwhile back in my old
> country they are renaming everything so
> I can't even tell any more which ballet
> company I am remembering with so much
> pain and the same thing has started
> here in American Avenue Park Avenue South
> Avenue of Chester Conklin Binnie Barnes
> Boulevard Avenue of Toby Wing Barbara
> Nichols Street where am I what is it
> I can't even find a pond small enough
> to drown in without being ostentatious
> you are ruining your awful country and me
> it is not new to do this it is terribly
> democratic and ordinary and tired

When the democratic and the ordinary get tired for O'Hara, there
remains no substratum he can deck with his fantastic tinsel of reference. O'Hara was, as he said himself, "the opposite of visionary,"

and all he asked was "grace to be born and live as variously as possible." When variety in the real is the only value, the Chameleon is God, that Chameleon that, in the poem called "Etiquettes Jaunes," O'Hara had been unable to reconcile with integrity. By the time we finish the *Collected Poems* we at least know that that particular ethical problem has disappeared. Integrity, cherishing the variety of the self and the world, persists through O'Hara's mercurial poems, ebbing and flowing with "the tender governing tides of a reigning will." "Alterable noon," he says, "assumes its virtue," and that virtue of the alterable adorns him too as he saunters through the world, a step away, as he truthfully notes, from the variety he records. Guessing, observing, looking, reading, comparing, reflecting, loving, writing, and talking, he takes us through life as though he were the host at a spectacular party. We may regret the equableness and charm of our guide, and wish him occasionally more Apollonian or more Dionysian (the sex poems aren't very good, though they try hard and are brave in their homosexual details), but there is no point wishing O'Hara other than he was. The scale he works in is deliberately, at least by past ideological standards, very small. Klee might be the painter who seems comparable, in his jokes, his whimsical collocations, his tenderness, his childlike naiveté, his sprightliness, his muted levels of significance, his sentiment. In O'Hara, modern life is instantly recognizable, and a modern ethos of the anarchically personal receives its best incarnation yet. If it satisfies some portion of us less than a more panoramic ambition, we are self-betrayed in recognizing the frailty of our own supports. We cannot logically repudiate ideology and then lament its absence (though Stevens made a whole poetry out of just that illogic). O'Hara puts our dilemma inescapably before us for the first time, and is therefore, in his fine multiplicity and his utter absence of what might be called an intellectual syntax, a poet to be reckoned with, a new species.

Allen Ginsberg

Planet News, 1961–1967

Allen Ginsberg, the *wunderkind* who took off after his years at Columbia on an ecstatic and shocked Magic Mystery Tour of America and of himself, is back from Asia and Europe, once more in America, but focusing, as his new title has it, on the planet. "Think of the planet!" I. A. Richards once said, and his audience rather flinched at being asked to think of anything so large.

Ginsberg does not flinch, but it can be argued that he has taken a wrong turn in abandoning the domestic for the planetary. His own word for this collection is "picaresque," and it is that, but the *pícaro* has lost the early rage of *Howl* and instead dispassionately distributes dishonors:

> And the Communists have nothing to offer but fat cheeks and
> eyeglasses and lying policemen
> and the Capitalists proffer Napalm and money in green suitcases
> to the Naked,
> and the Communists create heavy industry but the heart is also
> heavy.

Instead of scrambling to a private sanctuary, Ginsberg evangelizes America, exerting pure will power, declaring all by himself the end of the Vietnam War (in his role as unacknowledged legislator of the world), casting himself as the descendant of Blake, Christopher Smart, Whitman, and Williams.

Ginsberg's public mission—to give news of the planet—is wistfully accompanied by his private news-of-the-day: how he is un-

This review of Allen Ginsberg's *Planet News, 1961–1967* appeared in the *New York Times Book Review*, August 31, 1969.

likely ever to have a child, how he is afraid of women ("Like a homosexual capitalist afraid of the masses"), how he is "rueful of the bald front of my skull and the grey sign of time in my beard," how he is snarled at by the public, how he is still haunted by his dead mother ("And my mother's skull not yet white in the darkness . . .—GO / BACK!").

The poems are full of horrifying omens:

> The cat vomited his canned food with a
> mix of inch-long worms
> that arched up over the
> dread plop—
> I threw it in the garbage bag aghast—
> cockroach crawls up the bath tub Yosemite wall,
> rust in the hot water faucet, a sweet smell
> in the mouldy chicken soup,
> and little black beings in the old bag of flour
> on the pantry shelf last week

But the comic obverse in Ginsberg's life is a movie-sequence of zig-zag travel:

> Today I saw movies, publishers, bookstores, checks . . .
> I saw politicians we wrote a Noise Law!
> . . . I rode in a taxi!
> I rode a bus, ate hot Italian Sausages, Coca Cola, a chiliburger,
> Cool-Aid I drank—
> All day I did things!

Ginsberg's daily-life poems, with their fermenting specificity, are a repository of the data of American life in the fifties and sixties, and may on that account become unintelligible to the next, non-Pepsi, generation. His current project—a long chronicle-in-progress, "These States," is represented here by an extract called "Wichita Vortex Sutra," a "mind collage," which is depressingly nowhere near so good as his sublime elegy for his mother, "Kaddish," which showed how good a long poem he could write.

In this collection, the shorter poems, with their impressive grip on exact description, are the best. They remind us of how Ginsberg sees everything—railroad, cloverleafs, Dino Sinclair signs, "tiny human trees" in the plains, newspaper stories and their reduction of the real to the ("continued from page one") verbal, football fields, J.Edgar Hoover, and, above all, himself. For his contemporaries, he

is the biographer of his time—its high schools, its streets, its telephones, its monsters ("television was a baby crawling toward that
deathchamber"), its bland head counts, its drugs, its cops, its cities,
its freeways, and most of all its short-cut language.

The publishers' ad for this book says "Celestial vulgar humor!
Solemn experience! Blake & Whitman ride again! Hare Krishna!
Waves of Queer Bliss! An ecological thrill!" and so on. The blurb-
writer, whether it is Ginsberg or somebody aping him, is selling the
book short, It hasn't the naive joys and bitter accusations of *Howl*,
and there is no single piece in it so good as "Kaddish," but neither
is it a book to be ashamed of. Touting it so nervously belies Ginsberg's own comic seriousness and embarrasses his apologetic
honesty.

The Fall of America

The fall of America is not Ginsberg's real subject in this book, in
spite of his title. He has two subjects: the state of America and the
state of his life, the first now almost eclipsing, on the pages, the
second. Balked by the roadblock of middle age, Ginsberg marks
time around it, baffled, like other poets, by the moment when poetry
thins out, everything is already known, and everything has stopped
happening.

Too many times the cycle of life has turned all the way through to
death; Neal Cassady is dead, Jack Kerouac is dead, it is only a matter
of time for everyone else. Friends are now what they will be for
good; no one will change. Everything has been encountered: sex,
love, friendship, drugs, even fame, even the boundary-dimensions of
self. War has come and gone; peace has come and gone; a moon-
landing has come and gone. After Europe and India, after the
Orient, what is left to do but to come back to America, an America
already endlessly crisscrossed in the past, in cars, in buses, on trains,
on planes—the interchanges, the highways, the cities, the airports,
the bars, the lecture halls, the apartments.

This review of Allen Ginsberg's *The Fall of America: Poems of These States,
1965–1971* appeared in the *New York Times Book Review*, April 15, 1973.

Motion, in the face of this fixity, becomes more imperative: more and more places, more trips, more excursions, more visits; and noise, to fill the silence, rises more and more intrusive, in radios, headlines, TV, singers, rock, gospelers. An addictive sociability coexists now in Ginsberg with a pall of solitude; willed prophecy inhabits a religious void; and of empty necessity topographical description supersedes familial drama.

Ginsberg's version of the crisis of middle life is everywhere in the *Indian Journals* (1962–63):

> I wanted to be a saint. But suffer for what? Illusions? . . . Next the rest of India & Japan, and I suppose later a trip: England, Denmark, Sweden & Norway, Germany, Poland, Russia, China & then back home again. And that'll be the end of that world, I'll be about 50, the relatives'll all be dead by then, old ties with the boys of yore be loosed or burnt, unfaithful, in so many decades it's best to let it all go—is Jack drunk? Is Neal still aware of me? Gregory yakking? Bill mad at me? Am I even here to myself? I daren't write it all down, it's too shameful & boring now & I haven't the energy to make a great passional autobiography of it all . . . I guess I have nothing to contribute to general edification by this vague haphazard slow motion death.

Like Oblomov, he says, he lies "in morphined ease" in Benares, wondering "what possible poem to imagine any more":

> Now seem the thrills of scanning the scaly dragon dream universe
> equal in endlessness boredom to passing my moons playing Cards
> in third class trains circling the equator.

"Washed up desolate on the Ganges bank, vegetarian & silent hardly writing," Ginsberg ends the *Indian Journals* saying:

> Now all personal relations cold exhausted.
> I'll be on impersonal curiosity hence flying round the world.

The poems written in India, some of them published in *Planet News* (1968), fix on the life of beggars and lepers:

> Today on a balcony in shorts leaning on iron rail I watched the
> leper who sat hidden behind a bicycle
> emerge dragging his buttocks on the grey rainy ground by the
> glove-bandaged stumps of hands,

one foot chopped off below knee, round stump-knob wrapped
    with black rubber
pushing a tin can shiny size of his head with left hand (from
    which only a thumb emerged from leprous swathings)
beside him, lifting it with both ragbound palms down the curb
    into the puddled road,
balancing his body down next to the can & crawling forward on
    his behind
trailing a heavy rag for seat, and leaving a path thru the street
    wavering
like the Snail's slime track—imprint of his crawl on the muddy
    asphalt market entrance—stopping
to drag his can along stubbornly konking on the paved surface
    near the water pump.

Concentration and exactness of focus are, when he is able to summon them, among Ginsberg's undeniable powers. "Kaddish," his elegy for his mother, is full of visualized moments comparable to the presented isolation of the leper; and Ginsberg's shorter poems, like the wonderful "American Change," depend equally on making us see, to paraphrase Yeats, "as though a sterner eye looked through our eye." Ginsberg had cried to the crowds at Sather Gate in Berkeley: "I have a message for you all—I will denote one particularity of each!" and for years he believed, with Blake and Yeats, that it was necessary that "eye and ear . . . silence the mind / With the minute particulars of mankind."

The trouble with the present book is that the minute particulars of mankind seem to be vanishing from Ginsberg's latest verse in favor of the minute particulars of geography. In the *Indian Journals* Ginsberg declared that since we now know that visions are "no longer considerable as objective & external facts, but as plastic projections of the maker & his language," we must stop being concerned with these "effects," eliminate subject matter, and concentrate on language itself. With a penitence we can only regret, he admits, "I seem to be delaying a step forward in this field (elimination of subject matter) and hanging on to habitual humanistic series of autobiographical photographs—although my own Consciousness has gone beyond the conceptual to nonconceptual episodes of experience, inexpressible by old means of humanistic storytelling . . . As my mind development at the year moment seems blocked so also does my 'creative' activity, blocked, revolve around old abstract & tenuous sloppy political-sex diatribes & a few cool imagistic

photo descriptions (which contain some human sentiment by implication)."

In *The Fall of America*, then, we see the disappearance or exhaustion
of long-term human relations, an unwillingness to continue the "old
means of humanistic storytelling," a persistent wish (evident since
Howl) for some "non-conceptual episodes of experience," and a
theory of poetry intending to "include more simultaneous perceptions and relate previously unrelated (what were thought irrelevant)
occurrences."

Under these pressures, Ginsberg has become a geographer, and
his one inexhaustible subject is the earth and what it looks like. There
are precedents for this sort of subject in the past, though then, it is
true, the earth looked rather more natural. Drayton's "Polyolbion,"
for instance, meanders unhurriedly through England, describing
rivers and mountains, woods and dales, shepherds, nymphs, and
worthies of past history. Ginsberg's effort is not far distant in its
kind from Drayton's: Ginsberg has it in mind to write a long "poem
of these states" (incorporating earlier poems like "Wichita Vortex
Sutra"), which will finally sum up the physical and spiritual map
of America—its natural rivers, mountains and coastlines, its man-
made cities, superhighways, and dams, its media (radio, TV, magazines, newspapers, movies), its social life (bars, universities, dance-
halls), its political activity (especially its isolationism, suspicion, and
hatred of foreigners), its poets and musicians (including rock and
pop) its mythology (comics and S.F.), its graffiti, its religion (a
poisonous fundamentalism), its banks, its wars, its violence, its
secret police, its history, its seasons—in short, the whole of our
common life. This text of the common life is crossed, less often
than one could wish, with the text of the life of Ginsberg.

Mostly, the conclusions of the Ginsberg census are apocalyptic
ones. America is going to fall because of its sins, chiefly the sins
of crushing its dissidents and conducting war:

> Jerry Rubin arrested! Beaten, jailed, coccyx broken—
> Leary out of action—"a public menace ... persons of tender
>   years ... immature judgment ... psychiatric examination ..."
> i.e. Shut up or Else Loonybin or Slam
>
> Leroi on bum gun rap, $7,000 lawyer fees, years, negotiations—
> SPOCK GUILTY headlined temporary, Joan Baez' paramour
>   husband Dave Harris to Gaol
> Dylan silent on politics, & safe—having a baby, a man—

Cleaver shot at, jail'd, maddened, parole revoked
Vietnam War flesh-heap grows higher.

The indictment is made repeatedly through the book, because *The Fall of America* is really a daily newspaper—a "chronicle tape-recorded scribed by hand or sung condensed, the flux of car bus airplane dream." What spontaneity gains, reiteration loses. But as soon as that easy criticism rises to the lips, a countertruth stills it: it may be boring to read the map aloud—West Coast to East, East to West, "L.A. to Wichita," "Kansas City to St. Louis," "Bayonne Turnpike to Tuscarora," and so on, but it is true that Ginsberg lights up territory when it is land familiar to me, and so maybe the ideal reader of this poem is someone who knows Kansas City and Wichita and Salt Lake and Bixby Canyon and Sonora Desert as I do not. "Know me, know my map," says Ginsberg: it's not an unfair demand for a poet to make.

Ginsberg's avalanche of detail is like the rain of dust and lava that preserved Pompeii—here lies America, in literally thousands of its emanations, recorded in such minute particularity that quotation from this time-capsule (because it would have to go on so long) is impossible. I still tend to prefer the shorter poems, because they allow some drawing of breath for relief from Ginsberg's ardent atlas. And I like best the poems where Ginsberg is still visited by evanescent flashes of his old humor, too often now in abeyance.

There are faults in the book: the Eastern mantras get in the way, for instance. It is one thing to end an English poem with "Shantih, shantih, shantih," but to end "Om Om Om Sa Ra Wa Bu Da Da Ki Ni Yea," and so on for three more lines is disaster. Then, too, Ginsberg strikes certain prophetic attitudes whose irony is their own undoing:

Oh awful man! What have we made the world! Oh man capitalist
exploiter of Mother Planet!

The book allows sentimental confessions ("When he kissed my nipple / I felt elbow bone thrill") and masochistic self-abasement (in "Please Master") unaccompanied by (so far as I can see) any redeeming poetic value, except a programmatic confessional one.

But Ginsberg belongs, if we accept Blake's two categories of the Prolific and the Devouring, to the Prolific: there will always be more of him, and more of his excesses, than we can quite want. On the other hand, he is never negligible, and he is often (the only true test) unforgettable. This book, for instance, in the midst of a lot of ephemeral poetry, contains the supreme summing-up of this decade, a perfectly finished fourteen-page poem wittily called "Ecologue." Ginsberg has bought himself a farm and lives there in a tragicomic mixture of live animals, killed animals, cows who eat his Blakean sunflowers, batteries that fail, detergent-fouled creeks, the Pleiades, the day's radio news, memories of the dead, books, rain, returnable Ginger Ale bottles, quarrels, abashed recollections of Marie Antoinette playing milkmaid, bugs on the potatoes, thoughts of Ezekiel and the F.B.I., Indian Summer, and the *New York Times.*

The poem has all the earnestness and absurdity of the commune movement in it, the despair of a "return to nature" combined with a horror of "civilization": it walks a tightrope between the intimate and the international, it embeds in every phrase (except, perhaps, in its rather strained prophetic beginning) the incompetent New Yorkers trying out country life. But it pits against that initial comic incongruity the tale-within-a-tale of the poet frightened by death and ennui back into the company of the hillsides and the stars.

It belongs, in its fine casual descriptiveness and open personal truth, with Ginsberg's slowly cumulative Indian Summer poem "Autumn Gold: New England Fall," a poem that passes from depression to almost Emersonian sight, from the wrenched admission that "even sex happiness [is] a long drawn out scheme / To keep the mind moving" to the beautiful visions near the end.

> Entering Whatley,
> Senses amazed on the hills,
> bright vegetable populations
> hueing rocks nameless yellow,
> veils of bright Maya over New England,
> Veil of Autumn leaves laid over the Land
> Transparent blue veil over senses,
> Language in the sky.

Sadness, and not his intermittent hysteria, underlies Ginsberg's most eloquent poems. Though he is recognizably the native heir of Emerson, Whitman, and Williams, he was not born with their regenerative sporadic optimism; nor does he participate, like Whitman, in heroic human action, nor descend, for that matter, as far as Whitman into despair. "Elegy," said Coleridge in his "Table-Talk," "is the form of poetry natural to the reflective mind . . . Elegy presents everything as lost and gone or absent and future." Ginsberg, a naturally elegiac poet, is at present repressing his own elegiac spirit, attempting a poetry where, to quote Coleridge again, "all is purely external and objective, and the poet is a mere voice." The elegiac side of Ginsberg still seems to me the winning one, but it may be that in the sparseness of middle age Ginsberg needs the plurality of notations and enumerations accumulating to fill these pages. It is nothing new for a poet to need filler: what else was play-writing to Tennyson or thinking up *A Vision* for Yeats?

It may be that later, in the subsidence and condensation of this tireless relief-map of America, we will have from Ginsberg the sort of quintessential late poetry of old age that we have already received from Yeats and Stevens. For the present, we cannot begrudge Ginsberg his painstaking record of his microcosm, "empty-lov'd America."

James Merrill

Braving the Elements

The time eventually comes, in a good poet's career, when readers actively long for his books: to know that someone out there is writing down your century, your generation, your language, your life—under whatever terms of difference—makes you wish for news of yourself, for those authentic tidings of invisible things, as Wordsworth called them, that only come in the interpretation of life voiced by poetry. With an impatience that picks up *The New Yorker* to see if there is a new poem, that goes to poetry readings to glean another sheaf, Merrill's readers have been assembling this book of poems in their minds in order to possess it before it emerges between covers.

Merrill has become one of our indispensable poets, earning that final unquestioned role of a sibling in our family, so that it no longer matters what exactly he does or what ups and downs he shows; since we take the latest news from his quarter as another entry in our common journal, we trust him, we accept wrong turnings as readily as right ones, certain that he knows his own way and will find it.

In *Braving the Elements* Merrill has found a use, finally, for all his many talents. His surreptitious fondness for narrative, which issued rather badly in his early novel *The Seraglio* (1957) and his later sketch for a novel *The (Diblos) Notebook* (1965), has now found a clear medium in his wonderful short narrative lyrics; his almost unnaturally exquisite gift for euphony has become unobtrusive but no less exquisite, in fact more so; his ironic and wayward humor has been allowed to appear in poetry as well as in prose; his single best subject—love—has found a way of expressing itself masked and unmasked at once, instead of hiding almost mummified in swathings

This review of James Merrill's *Braving the Elements* appeared in the *New York Times Book Review*, September 24, 1972.

of secrecy. Secrecy and obliquity were Merrill's worst obstacles in his early verses; though his tone was usually clear, the occasion of the tone was impossibly veiled: who are these people? what relation are they in? what has just happened to provoke this response? what is the outcome?—all these questions led to the murkiest answers, if to any answers at all.

The trouble was not reticence: after all, without once mentioning his personal griefs in the odes, Keats made us know them almost by heart. But in Merrill's earliest poetry he stood at several removes from his own experience, or, to put it another way, he still called poems by titles like "The Black Swan," Kite Poem," "The Parrot," "Periwinkles," "Marsyas," and "The Power Station." The confusing thing about these "objective" poems was the cloudy weight of displaced feeling they bore, all out of proportion to their ostensible subjects. Clots of pain or brittle arabesques of suffering equally hovered unexplained; chaotic dreams assumed their own authority; catastrophes and resolutions alike veered uneasily between social staccato and pregnant pause; and the "intellectuality" for which the poems were sometimes praised was more a matter of labyrinthine syntax than of penetrating thought. But always, in spite of these lapses, a beautiful and radiant cadence rippled its way through Merrill's pages: his verse, like a brook, tumbled over the obstructions set by his rather frigid subjects and had a concurrent voice of its own, infinitely clearer and surer of itself than the poems in themselves seemed to warrant.

In a way, no beginning is more promising, since bad poets usually begin full of subjects but lacking contour; good poets begin all contour looking for a content. When content remains dim, euphonies are useless; but when talent for content grows to equal talent for contour, the union of Truth and Beauty that is all we ask of poems can take place. Merrill's *Nights and Days* (1966) ended with a fine presaging "narrative" poem called (after Cavafy) "Days of 1964," and this new volume continues the form with "Days of 1971" as well as other poems ("After the Fire," "Strato in Plaster," "Up and Down," "Days of 1935," and so on).

These, Merrill's best new ventures, are autobiographical without being "confessional": they show none of that urgency to reveal the untellable or unspeakable that we associate with the poetry we call "confessional." These poems are gripping because they are quiet and conversational: it is as though a curtain had been drawn aside, and we were permitted a glimpse of the life inside the house, a life that goes on unconscious of us, with the narrator so perfectly an actor in his own drama that his presence as narrator is rendered transparent, invisible.

The unpredictability of life itself seems to flicker capriciously in some of these pieces; in others, the equal predictability of life shines in a contemplated steadiness. Among the first sort, the unpredictable ones, "After the Fire" remains entirely present long after it has been heard or read, and it can serve as an example of the form Merrill has brought to a high perfection. There has been a fire in the house that Merrill lived in with his lover in Greece, and from America he has ordered repairs: now he returns to Greece to find everything changed.

> Everything changes; nothing does. I am back,
> The doorbell rings, my heart leaps out of habit,
> But it is only Kleo—how thin, how old!—
> Trying to smile, lips chill as the fallen dusk.

Kleo was the servant; her old mother has "gone off the deep end" and calls out to the whole neighborhood that Kleo's son is "a *Degenerate!* a *Thieving / Faggot!* just as Kleo is a *Whore!*"

> I press Kleo's cold hand and wonder
> What could the poor yiaya have done
> To deserve this terrible gift of hindsight . . .

In fact, Kleo *was* once a "a buxom armful," and her son Panayioti "cruised the Naval Hospital." The mixture of the dismaying, the nostalgic, and the funny mounts with Merrill's visit to Kleo's house, where the forty-year-old son greets him with outrageous warmth in outrageous French, all the time wearing Merrill's bathrobe and slippers. Merrill's gaze takes in other relics from the fire, and he suddenly realizes the truth:

> It strikes me now, as happily it did not
> The insurance company, that P caused the fire.

The fire destroyed forever the house as it was when Merrill lived there with "love-blinded gaze": the love affair, like the original color of the walls, is "hidden now forever but not lost / Beneath this quiet sensible light gray." Interrupting this almost unstable mixture of loss and survival, the grotesque and the painful, the old senile grandmother shrieks out, in a sudden access of rationality,

"It's Tzimi! He's returned!"
—And with that she returns to human form,
The snuffed-out candle-ends grow tall and shine,
Dead flames encircle us, which cannot harm,
The table's spread, she croons, and I
Am kneeling pressed to her old burning frame.

These poems are a potpourri of all the odors of the past, or rather vials for those essential oils which, as Emily Dickinson said, are wrung. Nothing is simple any longer: the rapt words of love in "The Fire Screen" (1969), vows, claims, even farewells ("I love you still, I love you") subside into a detachment touched by judgment but touched also still by love. The life which first saw itself bound and hemmed in and which fled to Greece, light, sensation, and love now begins to shrink back into a semblance of its first dimensions, the efflorescence gone but resurrected in a fidelity striated with irony but yet not ironic. Somehow Merrill still arranges to see Strato, his Greek:

Strato, each year's poem
Says goodbye to you.
Again, though, we've come through
Without losing temper or face.

The painful grace Merrill finds to modulate the whole bizarre experience with Strato-as-chauffeur in "Days of 1971" can be appreciated only as the whole poem spins its way through its ten "sonnets." At ease, with social aplomb, Merrill narrates the journey from Paris through France and Italy to Greece, affection and self-knowledge, tenderness and ridicule all mixing to illustrate what Merrill calls "Proust's Law":

a) What least thing our self-love longs for most
Others instinctively withhold;

b) Only when time has slain desire
Is his wish granted to a smiling ghost
Neither harmed nor warmed, now, by the fire.

That smiling ghost writes this book, and curiously he is nevertheless Merrill's most substantial incarnation. He stands in these poems at the point where Yeats could say, "Dear shadows, now you know it all." As if in spectral fulfillment, old portions of life rise up to be concluded: in Merrill's novel *The Seraglio* the mother of the protagonist has given up wearing her jewels: "the jewels waited in a vault for Francis's bride." Now, as the elements of life assert them-selves, Merrill has fled Byzantium and its exotica, and there is no bride: the strongbox in the vault yields up (in the poem "Up and Down") an emerald ring, and the mother addresses her son:

> "He gave
> Me this when you were born. Here, take it for—
>
> For when you marry. For your bride. It's yours."
> A den of greenest light, it grows, shrinks, glows,
> Hermetic stanza bedded in the prose
> Of the last thirty semiprecious years.
>
> I do not tell her, it would sound theatrical,
> *Indeed this green room's mine, my very life.*
> *We are each other's; there will be no wife;*
> *The little feet that patter here are metrical.*
> But onto her worn knuckle slip the ring.
> Wear it for me, I silently entreat,
> Until—until the time comes. Our eyes meet.
> The world beneath the world is brightening.

As the social comedy of the obsequious bank attendants yields to the green-lit troth in the vault, we acquiesce, compelled, in the mixed media of life.

Merrill has arrived at an instantly recognizable personal voice—even its awkwardnesses are genuine. He refuses to give up either side of his language—the pure concentrate of distilled essence, pres-ent since his beginnings, and the more recent importation of casual talk, even down to slang and four-letter words. The forms Merrill has used before—dream, myth, ballad, sacred objects—re-emerge on these pages with greater or lesser success. For all its pathos (a rich neglected little boy fantasizing his own Lindbergh-like kidnap-ping by surrogate-parent criminals he falls in love with), I cannot really admire "Days of 1935," since, like most literary ballads, it wavers uncertainly between its own sophistication and the naiveté of its predecessors. On the other hand, Merrill's best mythical poem yet closes the collection. Called "Syrinx," it arises as a variation on the Pascalian notion that man is a "thinking reed." Pascal meant the metaphor as a sign of human frailty; Merrill uses it to remind us of the human capacity for art. In Ovid, the nymph Syrinx, pur-sued by Pan, was changed into a reed, from which Pan made his pipe; here, the reed-flute is played upon by the great god Pain:

... he reaches for me, then

Leaves me cold, the great god Pain,
Letting me slide back into my scarred case

Whose silvery breath-tarnished tones
No longer rivet bone and star in place

Or keep from shriveling, leather round a stone,
The sunbather's precocious apricot

Or stop the four winds racing overhead
                    Nought
        Waste   Eased
                    Sought

It is not for nothing that Merrill has read Herbert: Herbert, I think, would recognize the punning names and formation of these yearning, despairing winds; Merrill's sexual apricot, ripe and shriveled at once, is not far from Herbert's heart: "Who would have thought my shrivel'd heart / Could have recover'd greennesse?" It is hard to know where Merrill will go from here—whether he will set himself to a Proustian remembering and give us more vignettes of the past, or whether some new convulsion of life will wreck the fine equilibrium by which, in this book, the four racing winds are held and viewed.

Divine Comedies

Since he published his *First Poems,* James Merrill's energies have been divided between successive books of increasingly brilliant lyric poems (the most recent, *Braving the Elements,* in 1972) and attempts in larger fictional forms—two plays (1955 and 1960) and two novels (1957 and 1965). The flashes and glimpses of "plot" in some of the lyrics—especially the longer poems—reminded Merrill's readers that he wanted more than the usual proportion of dailiness and detail in his lyrics, while preserving a language far from the plainness of journalistic poetry, a language full of arabesques, fanci-

This review of James Merrill's *Divine Comedies* appeared in the *New York Review of Books,* March 18, 1976.

fulness, play of wit, and oblique metaphor. And yet the novels were not the solution, as Merrill himself apparently sensed.

In his new collection, where most of the poems have a narrative emphasis, Merrill succeeds in expressing his sensibility in a style deliberately invoking Scheherazade's tireless skein of talk: the long poem, "The Book of Ephraim," which takes up two-thirds of this volume, is described as "The Book of a Thousand and One Evenings." In explaining how he came to write this novelistic poem, Merrill recapitulates his struggle with fiction:

> I yearned for the kind of unseasoned telling found
> In legends, fairy tales, a tone licked clean
> Over the centuries by mild old tongues,
> Grandam to cub, serene, anonymous.
> Lacking that voice, the in its fashion brilliant
> Nouveau roman (including one I wrote)
> Struck me as an orphaned form.

He once more tried his hand at writing a novel, but it lost itself in "word-painting":

> The more I struggled to be plain, the more
> Mannerism hobbled me. What for?
> Since it had never truly fit, why wear
> The shoe of prose?

His narrative forms in verse allow Merrill the waywardness, the distractions, the eddies of thought impossible in legends or in the spare *nouveau roman*, and enable the creation of both the long tale and of a new sort of lyric, triumphantly present here in two faultless poems, sure to be anthologized, "Lost in Translation" and "Yannina."

Divine Comedies marks a departure in Merrill's work. He has always been a poet of Eros, but in an unwritten novel, about "the incarnation and withdrawal of / A god," "the forces joined / By Eros" come briefly together and then disperse:

> Exeunt severally the forces joined
> By Eros—Eros in whose mouth the least
> Dull fact had shone of old, a wetted pebble.

And Merrill's servant in Greece, whose name (Kleo) he had never seen written, turns out to be named not Cleopatra, as he had thought,

but Clio; she is not the presiding surrogate for Eros but the incarnation of the Muse of history, Merrill's new patroness:

> "Kleo" we still assume is the royal feline
> Who seduced Caesar, not the drab old muse
> Who did. Yet in the end it's Clio I compose
> A face to kiss, who clings to me in tears.
> What she has thought about us all God knows.

If the divinity of youth was Eros, the divinity of middle age is Clio;
if the metaphor for being thirty was embrace, the metaphor for being
fifty is companionship; and if the presence in the mind was once
love, it is now death.

Quickened by the thought of death, which so resists the rational intelligence, the imaginations of poets react and react and react, pressing back (to use Stevens' phrase) with all the inventions, illusions,
conjectures, wiles, seductions, and protests of which they are capable.
Nothing so compels poets to complication: and if what they conjure
up to talk to them from the dark is a voice recognizably their own
but bearing a different name, they (and their readers) are peculiarly
consoled by the reflected Word. So Milton found his own best voice
speaking back at him under the names of Phoebus Apollo and St.
Peter; so Dante fell into colloquy with his elder self, Vergil; so
Yeats invented his "mysterious instructors" who dictated to him and
his wife his elaborate system of history and the afterlife; and so
James Merrill, in his divine comedies, communicates with an affable
familiar ghost named Ephraim, first evoked at the Ouija board in
Stonington twenty years ago, and a frequent visitor since.

In his 1970 volume, *The Country of a Thousand Years of Peace*
(literally Switzerland, but since Merrill's friend Hans Lodeizen had
died there, also metaphorically the country of the dead), Merrill
published his first Ouija poem, in which a candid, if ineptly expressed, stanza offers the motive for listening to "voices from the
other world":

> Once looked at lit
> By the cold reflections of the dead
> Risen extinct but irresistible,
> Our lives have never seemed more full, more real,
> Nor the full moon more quick to chill.

These lines give at least some notion of the origins of "The Book of Ephraim." It is a poem in twenty-six sections, each beginning with a different letter of the alphabet, from A to Z, exhausting the twenty-six capital letters of the Ouija board. And yet, for all its ninety pages, the Book is not finished, scarcely even begun, its dramatic personae—living, dead, and invented—hardly glimpsed, and only partially listed, its tale of an unfinished novel still untold, its gaily inventive theology linking this world to the otherworld barely delineated.

Merrill casually and mockingly praises his own "net of loose talk tightening to verse" through his surrogates among the dead. Ephraim ("A Greek Jew / Born AD 8 at XANTHOS"), who communicates of course in the caps of the Ouija board, tells Merrill,

> . . . POPE SAYS THAT WHILE BITS
> STILL WANT POLISHING THE WHOLES A RITZ
> BIG AS A DIAMOND.

Instead of Vergilian solemnity, this guide to the otherworld uses social chitchat:

> U ARE SO QUICK MES CHERS I FEEL WE HAVE
> SKIPPING THE DULL CLASSROOM DONE IT ALL
> AT THE SALON LEVEL.

For rationalists reading the poem, Merrill includes a good deal of self-protective irony, even incorporating in the tale a visit to his ex-shrink, who proclaims the evocation of Ephraim and the other Ouija "guests" from the other world a *folie à deux* between Merrill and his friend David Jackson. But once the "machinery"—not here the sylphs and nymphs of *The Rape of the Lock*, but the ghosts of dead friends and other revenants—is accepted as a mode of imagination, what then can be said of the import of this strange poem?

It is centrally a hymn to history and a meditation on memory— personal history and personal memory, which are, for this poet at least, the muse's materials. The host receives his visible and invisible guests, convinced that Heaven—the invisible sphere—is "the surround of the living," that the poet's paradise is nothing other than all those beings whom he has known and has imagined. Through Ephraim,

We, all we knew, dreamed, felt and had forgotten,
Flesh made word, became . . . a set of
Quasi-grammatical constructions . . .
   Hadn't—from books, from living—
The profusion dawned on us, of "languages"
Any one of which, to who could read it,
Lit up the system it conceived?—bird-flight,
Hallucinogen, chorale and horoscope:
Each its own world, hypnotic, many-sided
Facet of the universal gem.

These "facets of the universal gem" shine throughout "The Book of Ephraim," which aims at being a poem of a thousand and one reflecting surfaces. The irregularities and accidents of life are summed up in the fiction of reincarnation which animates the book's theology: people pass in and out of life as the bodies in which their spirits are incarnated die of heart attacks, in fires, or by less violent means; spirits get placed in unsuitable bodies; and in the crowded world of the afterlife a constant influx of souls makes for an agitated scene. Merrill's father, dead and between lives, gets through on the board:

           Then CEM gets through,
High-spirited, incredulous—he'd tried
The Board without success when Nana died.
Are we in India? Some goddam fool
Hindoo is sending him to Sunday School.
He loved his wives, his other children, me;
Looks forward to his next life.

The next life of Charles Merrill, announces Ephraim, is in Kew:

YR FATHER JL.I he goes on (we're back
In the hotel room) WAS BORN YESTERDAY
To a greengrocer: name, address in Kew
Spelt out.

This social comedy between otherworld and this world is one tone of "The Book of Ephraim": another is reminiscence of a simpler ego:

Götterdämmerung. From a long ago
Matinee—the flooded Rhine, Valhalla
In flames, my thirteenth birthday—one spark floating
Through the darkened house had come to rest

214

Upon a mind so pitifully green
As only now, years later, to ignite . . .
The heartstrings' leitmotif outsoared the fire.

Still another tone juxtaposes the eternal confrontation of youth and age, Eros and entropy, Prometheus and the eroding Parthenon:

Leave to the sonneteer eternal youth.
His views revised, an older man would say
He was "content to live it all again."
Let this year's girl meanwhile resume her pose,
The failing sun its hellbent azimuth.
Let stolen thunder dwindle out to sea.
Dusk eat into the marble-pleated gown.

Merrill's company of the dead comes in late exchange for the abandoned dream of the immortal couple, echoed through the book in Wagnerian terms, in Tristan's *"höchste Lust,"* and in Brünnhilde's choice of love over Valhalla: *"Nie Liebe liesse ich nie, mir nähmen nie sie die Liebe."* These sublimities remain, icons unattainable but not disallowed, at the edges of this deliberately social and tempered poetry. Wanting consuming passions, Merrill says, he has found only refining ones.

Merrill's lines, in their exquisite tones, are often painful to read. Though they keep their beautiful poise on the brink of sense and feeling, and aim here at the autumnal, or the ironic, they keep echoes, undimmed, of the past: Merrill is not yet, and I think will never be, a poet free of sensuality, love, and youth, actual or remembered. Enshrined with Brünnhilde in the section (Q, of course) of Quotations in "The Book of Ephraim" is Spenser's transcendent dream of the Garden of Adonis, where in "immortal blis . . . Franckly each paramour his leman knowes," in an equable and unfallen counterpart of Wagner's doomed couples.

"The Book of Ephraim," for the most part, refuses the postures thought appropriate to age—stoicism, resignation, disbelief, patience, or cynicism. The mild conviviality of Merrill's unearthly symposium is boyish in its welcome to comedy, sympathy, and nostalgia at once; and the poet's naive enthusiasm for "learning" from Ephraim the ins and outs of behavior and fate in the otherworld is so different from Dante's and Yeats's gloomy reverence for their guides that we are moved to delight by the refraction of these "divine comedies" from their more religious antecedents.

On the other hand, "The Book of Ephraim" is not really a comic poem. When Merrill and Jackson protest Ephraim's offhand tone about death, and say "Must *everything* be witty?" Ephraim answers, in a phrase that could be applied to the whole poem,

AH MY DEARS

I AM NOT LAUGHING   I WILL SIMPLY NOT SHED TEARS.

If life is "a death's head to be faced," it is also, in this poem, the repository of counterpointed treasures.

The claim of this long poem to moral significance rests in the way it balances two entirely opposite truths about middle age. One is the truth of perceived fate, as it declares itself in the simplest of sentences: *This is who I am; This is where I live; This is the person I live with; My father is dead; I will not fall in love again.* The other is the truth of received experience, as it glitters in a cloud of witnesses—all the things seen, the people met, the places traveled to, the books read, the faces loved, the lines written, the events lived through, the events imagined, the past absorbed—the past not only of personal life but of cultural history as well. The glowing dialectic of restriction of present life and expansion of experienced soul animates these pages into a visionary balancing of scales, now one pan up, now the other. Merrill's imagination has always been mercurial, airy, and darting, but here the counterweight of death adds a constant pull toward grief.

"The Book of Ephraim" might seem to risk the accusation of triviality, in its apparent refusal to take large issues seriously:

> Life like the periodical not yet
> Defunct kept hitting the stands. We seldom failed
> To leaf through each new issue—war, election,
> Starlet; write, scratch out; eat steak au poivre,
> Chat with Ephraim.

But under this briskness lies a wasting ennui:

> The whole house needs repairs. Neither can bring
> Himself to say so. Hardly lingering,
> We've reached the point, where the tired Sound just washes
> Up to, then avoids our feet.

In this repetitive routine, Merrill is free to admit all the flotsam and jetsam floating in his mind, and to let us judge that mind as we will.

Because Merrill is a poet whose devotion goes to the Absolute under the form of the Beautiful, his range, like that of the Beautiful itself, is diverse: the Good and the True do not really participate in a spectrum of more and less in quite the same way. From bibelots to Beatrice, from embroidery to altarpiece, goes the scale, and Merrill's tone modulates along with its object. Like Proust and Nabokov, two other sensibilities more attached to the Beautiful than to the Scientific, the Philosophical, the Ethical, or the Ideological, Merrill avoids being polemical or committed, in the ordinary sense of those words. By taking conversation—from lovers' exchange of vows to friends' sentences in intimacy—as the highest form of human expression (in contrast to the rhapsode's hymns, the orator's harangues, or the initiate's hermetic colloquies with the divine) Merrill becomes susceptible to charges of frivolity, at least from readers with a taste only for the solemn. But this espousal of the conversational as the ultimate in linguistic achievement is a moral choice, one which locates value in the human and everyday rather than in the transcendent.

It is no accident that Merrill appropriates for himself Keats's image of the chameleon poet, as delighted by an Iago as by an Imogen; he draws out a constantly changing veil of language like the endless scarves of silk from the illusionist's hands, now one color, now another, scattering light in rainbow transparency over and under his subject. And yet the severity of death fixes a new, unwavering color on the apparently boundless earlier sympathy with the attractions of experience:

> Already I take up
> Less emotional space than a snowdrop.
> . . . Young chameleon, I used to
> Ask how on earth one got sufficiently
> Imbued with otherness. And now I see.

Though the other poems in this collection share the conversational immediacy of "The Book of Ephraim," they also, in their persistent elegiac tone, seem to be fragments from a modern version of *The Prelude*. "Lost in Translation," of which the putative subject is Merrill's putting together, as a child, a complicated jigsaw puzzle with the aid of his governess, is really a gorgeous combination of Popean diversity of surface talk and Wordsworthian rumination on the past, and on the powers and lapses of memory. It is an easier poem than "Yannina," an elegy for Merrill's father set in the Turkish town of Yannina, once ruled by Ali Pasha, who becomes in the poem the surrogate for Charles Merrill. We see Ali flanked by "two loves, two versions of the Feminine": one the "pious matron" Frossíni, drowned at Ali's order for having refused compliance; the other Vassilikí, pictured with Ali sleeping in her lap. Byron (whose ottava rima Merrill here borrows and rings changes on) visited Ali, and found him "Very kind . . . indeed, a father." Merrill continues,

> Funny, that is how I think of Ali.
> On the one hand, the power and the gory
> Details, pigeon-blood rages and retali-
> Ations, gouts of fate that crust his story;
> And on the other, charm, the whimsically
> Meek brow, its motives all ab ulteriori,
> The flower-blue gaze twining to choke proportion,
> Having made one more pretty face's fortune . . .
>
> Ali, my father—both are dead.

Around this center vacillate feelings about the Oriental multiplicity of Yannina—its provincial promenade cluttered with sellers' booths, a magician's tent, loudspeaker music—and feelings about the two women, the wronged matron and the complaisant concubine. The scene on the promenade resembles the London Fair in *The Prelude,* but the human jumble of sight and sound, so inimical to the recoiling Wordsworthian sensibility which required solitude and massive forms, is the food of life to Merrill, who needs movement, color, the vulgar and the passionate together. As for the two women, one, the wronged Frossíni, has become a secular saint:

> And in the dark gray water sleeps
> One who said no to Ali. Kiosks all over town
> Sell that postcard, "Kyra Frossíni's Drown,"
> Showing her, eyeballs white as mothballs, trussed
> Beneath the bulging moon of Ali's lust.
> A devil (turban and moustache and sword)
> Chucks the pious matron overboard.

Frossíni's fate is half farce, half martyrdom; and "her story's aftertaste / Varies according to the listener," especially when her garish memorial postcard is placed against the skillful, still preserved, painting of Ali and Vassilikí—"almost a love-death, höchste Lust!" In the end, though, both versions of the feminine—"one virginal and tense, brief as a bubble, / One flesh and bone"—go up in smoke, and the poem dips momentarily into ghoulish images of death:

> Where giant spits revolving try their rusty treble,
> Sheep's eyes pop, and death-wish ravens croak
>   ... At the island monastery, eyes
> Gouged long since to the gesso sockets will outstare
> This or that old timer on his knees.

The empty sockets would seem to betoken the end of Ali and his women, and of the blushing girls and radiant young men courting on the promenade as well:

>   Where did it lead,
> The race, the radiance? To oblivion
> Dissembled by a sac of sparse black seed.

This is Merrill's most complicated retelling of his family history. But since living, of itself, perpetuates nothing, he turns, almost reluctantly, to his pain and his pen at home, far from Yannina, and invites us to enter with him, in fantasy, the magician's tent on the promenade where a woman can be sawed into two, then miraculously healed, a reassuring myth to set over against Frossíni's fate:

>   A glittering death
> Is hefted, swung. The victim smiles consent.
> To a sharp intake of breath she comes apart...
> Then to a general exhalation heals
>
> Like anybody's life, bubble and smoke
> In afterthought.

Afterthought may, in comparison to life, be only "bubble and smoke," but afterthought is also the domain of art, where a dreamy eternity envelops Ali. In afterthought, the "elements converge":

> Glory of windless mornings that the barge
> (Two barges, one reflected, a quicksilver joke)
> Kept scissoring and mending as it steered
> The old man outward and away,
> Amber mouthpiece of a narghilé
> Buried in his by then snow white beard.

In this universe, the poet's reflective mind meets and internalizes all the Oriental opulence of Ali and his town, the prudishness and pathos of Frossíni, the luxuriousness of Vassilikí, and the recurrent chorus of the courting couples on the promenade: "What shall the heart learn, that already knows / Its place by water, and its time by sun?" It also accepts the ghastly permanence of the dead bodies visible in the monastery underground burial-place, and the dying animals turning on spits. But it believes that in writing it can make "some inmost face to shine / Maned with light, ember and anodyne, / Deep in a desktop burnished to its grain." The lights have vanished along the lake in Yannina, but

> Weeks later, in this study gone opaque,
> They are relit. See through me. See me through.

The pun, like most of Merrill's plays on words, is serious, and the elegy has gone as far as a poem can go in attempting to take into its stylized world of "bubble and smoke" the fleshly lusts of Ali and the theatrical immolation of Frossíni, the Vanity Fair of the world and the gruesome end of the sexual impulse. It is an odd, crowded, and baroque elegy, with a remarkable joining of filial and paternal spheres.

It remains to be seen how Merrill, whose inventiveness is to be trusted, will continue with such narrative poems and, perhaps, with more installments of "The Book of Ephraim." Mozart, according to Ephraim, has been currently reincarnated as a black rock star: it makes one want more news from that source.

Mirabell: Books of Number

James Merrill's *Mirabell: Books of Number*, which won the National Book Award for 1978, is the middle volume of a trilogy composed with the aid of a Ouija board. The Ouija board is a symbol system that offers potentially unlimited combinations of letters and numbers, affirmations and denials; it can stand, we might say, for lan-

This review of James Merrill's *Mirabell: Books of Number* appeared in *The New Yorker*, September 3, 1979.

guage itself. The first installment of Merrill's trilogy, "The Book of Ephraim" (printed in *Divine Comedies*, in 1976), exhausted the letters of the board; it was composed in twenty-six sections labeled "A" through "Z." The current volume uses up the numbers of the board in ten books going from zero to nine. The final volume, to be called *Scripts for the Pageant*, is left with "Yes" and "No." The Ouija board is a shared system, used by the dead and the living, in which tradition, in the person of the dead, meets an individual talent—or, in this case, the joint talents of the poet and his friend David Jackson. Together, as JM and DJ, in their house at Stonington, where the action of *Mirabell* occurs, they transcribe the rapid gestures of a blue-willow cup that they use instead of a planchette. The messages from "the other side," all in the uppercase of the board, are edited by Merrill—compressed, made intelligible, made into poetry. The books of the trilogy consist of board messages interspersed with commentary and colloquy by the poet.

The pages of the books are typographically unnerving, as blocks of otherworldly uppercase—looking, as a friend remarked, like a computer printout—alternate with blocks of mortal lowercase. The uppercase, in the board's peculiar spelling—"before" becomes "B4," "you" becomes "U"—is sometimes a ten-syllable line (when dead people talk), sometimes a fourteen-syllable line (when the spirits, who enact "a fall from metrical grace," take over). Human talk is always decasyllabic, in "this rough pentameter, our virtual birthright." From time to time, a lyric form, like a strain of music, appears. The talk of the dead and of the living alike tends to rhyme in couplets and quatrains, but that of the spirits does not rhyme. The spirits, who are here represented chiefly by one among them bearing the number 741, seem to be in part what Milton would have called the fallen angels, and are first conceived of as black batlike creatures. At the center of the third book, 741 metamorphoses into a peacock, and he is later given the name Mirabell, supposedly after the "strut and plumage" of Congreve's hero, but also after "Merrill." Mirabell, "a paragon of courtly gentleness," here replaces the earlier Ephraim as familiar spirit. Ephraim was chatty, conversational; he was comfortable in iambic pentameter, since he was human ("A Greek Jew / Born AD 8 at XANTHOS . . . / a favorite of TIBERIUS . . . Died / AD 36 on CAPRI throttled / By the imperial guard for having LOVED / THE MONSTER'S NEPHEW [sic] CALIGULA"). However, Ephraim spoke rather rarely, and his book is narrated mostly by Merrill. Mirabell, on the other hand, speaks in ungainly syllabics, and the poet's interpolated lines serve as connective tissue between

Mirabell's speeches and the speeches of the dead. The dead, principally, are Wystan Auden and Maria Mitsotáki, a childless Greek
friend of Merrill's, whom he celebrated in a lyric, "Words for
Maria" (1969), and who died of cancer.

Mirabell is a poem about the dead in part because it is a poem of
the single life and childlessness; since there is no question of poster-
ity, life is composed of oneself and one's friends, the dead as much
as the living. The four bound together round the Ouija board—JM,
DJ, Wystan, Maria—are chosen for their lessons because of their
childlessness. To Auden's question "Why the four of us?" Mirabell
answers, "KEEP IN MIND THE CHILDLESSNESS WE SHARE   THIS TURNS
US / OUTWARD TO THE LESSONS & THE MYSTERIES." The scale of the
poem is both domestic and cosmic. The domestic life includes day-
by-day details of life in Greece and in Stonington, the visits of
friends, the deaths of parents, an operation. The cosmic life, presided
over in Manichean fashion by two gods—Chaos, the god of feeling, and an inexorable "God B" (for "biology")—is evolutionary,
hierarchical, mythological, and intermittently purposive. God B's
successive projects have included Atlantis, the centaurs, and Eden;
he "is not only history but earth itself." The literary tradition in
which the poem falls includes all works written by men to whom
the angels speak outright: Dante, the four Apostles, Buddha, Mohammed, and, in later days, Milton, Blake, Victor Hugo, and Yeats.
Merrill himself diffidently admits to doubts about "all this / warmed
up Milton, Dante, Genesis," fearing "Allegory in whose gloom the
whole / Horror of Popthink fastens on the soul"; he worries about
being "cast / Into this paper Hell out of Doré / or Disney." On the
other hand, the quintet of Merrill, Jackson, Auden, Maria Mitsotáki,
and Mirabell is said to be an example of the "vital groupings of
five," who do "V work"—the work of mind and heart (primarily
poetry and music)—encouraged, according to Mirabell, by loves
that do not envisage the production of bodies:

> LOVE OF ONE MAN FOR ANOTHER OR LOVE BETWEEN WOMEN
> IS A NEW DEVELOPMENT OF THE PAST 4000 YEARS
> ENCOURAGING SUCH MIND VALUES AS PRODUCE THE BLOSSOMS
> OF POETRY & MUSIC, THOSE 2 PRINCIPAL LIGHTS OF
> GOD BIOLOGY. LESSER ARTS NEEDED NO EXEGETES:
> ARCHITECTURE SCULPTURE THE MOSAICS & PAINTINGS THAT
> FLOWERD IN GREECE & PERSIA CELEBRATED THE BODY.
> POETRY MUSIC SONG INDWELL & CELEBRATE THE MIND . . .
> HEART IF U WILL.

Few painters or sculptors enter this life of the mind, Mirabell adds, since they, "LIKE ALL SO-CALLED NORMAL LOVERS," exist for no purpose other than to produce bodies. This Platonic myth is mocked by Mirabell's listeners: "Come now, admit that certain very great / Poets and musicians have been straight." But the claim, however whimsical, has been made, and the whole of Merrill's trilogy can be seen as a substitution of the virtues of mind and heart—culminating in music and poetry—for the civic and familial and martial virtues usually espoused by the epic.

We might hesitate to think of *Mirabell* in epic terms, since it learns at least as much from Pope and Byron as from Dante. But in its encylopedic instructions about the history of the cosmos and its cast of characters from Olympus (if we may so locate the spirits) and from Hades as well as from earth, its traits are epic ones. For all its rueful tone as it fears and doubts its own matter and method, it goes irrepressibly along, piecing together shards of myth from all cultures—Akhnaton rubs shoulders with Mohammed and centaurs, while Mother Nature, in conjunction with the Sultan God B, presides over all. The hymn to nature in the seventh book articulates the ebb and flow of loyalty— now to mind, now to nature— implicit in the whole poem. Fearful of the power of the senses, Merrill, like some modern metaphysical, asks what rational instruments they have robbed him of—"What have you done with / My books, my watch and compass, my slide-rule?"—but nature answers with her own fascination of texture, whether in constellations or in bodies, "those infinite / Spangled thinnesses whose weave gosling and cygnet / Have learned already in the shell."

When Merrill contemplates what he has done in writing this book, he complains to Auden that the result is maddening:

> It's all by someone else!
> In your voice, Wystan, or in Mirabell's.
> I want it mine, but cannot spare those twenty
> Years in a cool dark place that *Ephraim* took
> In order to be palatable wine.
> This book by contrast, immature, supine,
> Still kicks against its archetypal cradle.
>   ... I'd set
> My whole heart, after *Ephraim*, on returning
> To private life, to my own words. Instead,
> Here I go again, a vehicle
> In this cosmic carpool. Mirabell once said

He taps my word banks. I'd be happier
If *I* were tapping them. Or thought I were.

Auden replies in a magisterial defense of convention, tradition, and fable. On convention:

> THINK WHAT A MINOR
> PART THE SELF PLAYS IN A WORK OF ART
> COMPARED TO THOSE GREAT GIVENS   THE ROSEBRICK MANOR
> ALL TOPIARY FORMS & METRICAL
> MOAT ARIPPLE!

On tradition:

> AS FOR THE FAMILY ITSELF MY DEAR
> JUST GAPE UP AT THAT CORONETED FRIEZE:
> SWEET WILLIAMS & FATE-FLAVORED EMILIES
> THE DOUBTING THOMAS & THE DULCET ONE
> (HARDY MY BOY WHO ELSE? & CAMPION).

On the superiority of fable to facts:

> FACTS JM WERE ALL U KNEW TO WANT,
> WRETCHED RICKETY RECALCITRANT
> URCHINS   THE FEW WHO LIVE GROW UP TO BE
> IMPS OF THE ANTIMASQUE.

In fable, "A TABLE / IS SET & LAMPS LIT FOR THE FEASTING GODS." Auden concludes that, given time, facts themselves take on the livery of fable, and become material for art. The poem ends as Mirabell withdraws in favor of a stern-voiced angel Michael, speaking in long, irregular lines: he will be the next instructor, an unfallen rather than a fallen one, as Merrill proceeds into the *Paradiso* of his "Divine Comedies."

"Ephraim" is, on the whole, a cheerful book, constructed around a mythology of reincarnation: most people live on, over and over, even if in someone else's body. In *Mirabell*, Merrill and Jackson discover that their dead companions Auden and Maria will not be reincarnated, but will dissolve into their elements, having first been stripped of their earthly connections. The end of the book celebrates "Maria's Himmelfahrt" and Auden's. Goodbyes are said, of a careful lightness:

How

We'll miss you! We'd imagined—I know   CIAO

JM had imagined a thousand and one nights of conversation with these indispensable voices. But the Ouija board meets the law of dissolution, and in the last episode Auden and Maria seem to have disappeared, leaving behind only a snapshot—"Young, windblown / Maria with dark glasses and Gitane"—and a book "by Wystan / Face up . . . all week / Open to Miranda's villanelle." *Mirabell* is a a book of long farewell to the parental figures of Auden and Maria, a book that holds on to the dead as long as possible. They are the people who call JM and DJ "MES ENFANTS" (Maria, known as "Maman") or "MY BOYS" (Auden). When these voices fall silent, there will be no one to whom the poet is a child. Though Merrill's mother is alive, she is deliberately left out of the trilogy, as "Ephraim" explains:

> All of which lights up, as scholarship
> Now and then does, a matter hitherto
> Overpainted—the absence from these pages
> Of my own mother. Because of course she's here
> Throughout, the breath drawn after every line,
> Essential to its making as to mine.

The deaths of David Jackson's parents preface the appearance of Mirabell. In the usual biological cycle, parents die after their children have become parents; the internalizing of the parental role, it is believed, enables the parents to be absorbed into the filial psyche. In the childless world of *Mirabell,* the disappearance of parents, or parental friends, is the disappearance of the parental and therefore of the filial; JM and DJ can no longer be "boys," but must put on the mortality of the survivor. However much the sweetness of posthumous conversation with Auden and Maria may be prolonged—with analyses of their character, examples of their wit, descriptions of their lives—the end of the exchange is envisaged from Maria's first warning, at the end of Book 1: "I HAVE MORE TO LOSE." In Merrill's myth, Maria will become a plant, not a human being; the radiation she endured as a treatment for cancer reduced her human soul to the vegetative level. Auden will be "stripped, reduced to essences, joined to infinity," like one of his beloved minerals:

> What must at length be borne
> Is that the sacred bonds are chemical.

The "seminar" of the participants round the Ouija board is itself such a "stripping process," since Mirabell, Wystan, and Maria will gradually fade away. Merrill's work in creating the trilogy is a comparable "stripping":

> Art—
> The tale that all but shapes itself—survives
> By feeding on its personages' lives,
> The stripping process, sort of. What to say?
> Our lives led *to* this. It's the price we pay.

If the artist needs new resources in middle age, it is not because the old ones are exhausted. On the contrary, the old ones, accumulating exponentially, seem to forbid the acquisition of the new. At some point the writer begins his replay in slow motion of all the eclectic litter and learning that crowds his mind: unburdening himself, he discharges, in an art relatively random by contrast to that of his earlier years, portions of everything he knows. So the board throws up bits and pieces of Merrill's reading (as *A Vision* threw up Yeats's, as *History* threw up Lowell's), and one of the difficulties with the trilogy is that no one of us duplicates Merrill's reading bank, any more than we duplicate Blake's or Milton's. The jumble that is any fifty-year-old memory poses for a reader the problem of other minds; the encyclopedic modern poem, from the *Cantos* on, presses the question almost intolerably.

Though the allusive density of *Mirabell* makes the poem at first difficult, the test of such a poem is not in the first reading (though if there is not enough pleasure in that, the reader is lost for good), but in the reading that takes place once the scheme, the family relations, and the life histories in question have become natural and familiar. In this poem Merrill is enterprisingly (with some incidental wreckage) enlarging his theater of operations. He avoids for lines on end the effortless jeweled effects for which he has been known, and he has turned aside from lyrics of the personal life to narrative, to mythological and metaphysical "explanations" of a discursive order ruled not by "feeling" or by "beauty" but by "truth." He is writing in voices other than his own. These undertakings are not wholly new: Merrill said as far back as 1962: "If I am host at last / It is of little more than my own past. / May others be at home in it."

But the past of the earlier volumes was on the whole a selective one, careful of its references, arranged in exquisite forms, and restricted to crises of feeling. Two poems in *Nights and Days,* of 1966, appear to anticipate the trilogy. In a sequence of reflections on love called "The Thousand and Second Night," "the rough pentameter / Quatrains give way, you will observe, to three / Interpolations, prose as well as verse," reflecting on "mind, body, and soul (or memory)." The second instance is the inquiry into the nature of Eros in a long sequence called "From the Cupola." The poet adapts the myth of Eros and Psyche, and is himself both Psyche's poet (like Keats) and Psyche herself, receiving letters from the unknown Eros. Two caricatured evil sisters mock Psyche's claim to an invisible lover, but Psyche's real anxiety derives not from their realist cynicism but, rather, from her own distrust of love's distorting idealism. She is consoled by her poet in Audenesque cadences:

> Psyche, hush. This is me, James
> Writing lest he think
> Of the reasons why he writes—
> Boredom, fear, mixed vanities and shames;
> Also love.
> From my phosphorescent ink
> Trickle faint unworldly lights.

By the end of *Mirabell* the faint unworldly lights have brightened into the radiance of enlightenment. But in his pursuit of truth Merrill has by no means forgotten his earlier homage to the senses. The daily life described in *Mirabell,* which offers itself as one realized version of human existence, is attentive to the senses, to friendship, to domesticity, to art—all the elements found in Merrill's lyrics —as well as to the dead, for whom the poet has had to invent his trilogy. "The dead," "Ephraim" tells us, "are the surround of the living."

Merrill's argument for the senses denies the old propriety that would distinguish the aesthetic from the sensual. (In this, he resembles Keats rather than his other master, Auden.) A continuity between the aesthetic and the sensual is at the heart of Merrill's work, from the earliest lyrics on—as if it were inconceivable that a love of textures, shapes, lines, light, and color should not also be a love of faces and bodies, even if "one falls back, soiled, blurred." Merrill's primary intuition is that of the absolute ravishment of the senses. As they combine and mingle, the senses create, in the order of flesh, interrelations and reinforcings that are like the elements of an artwork. Yet Merrill's interest in the translation of the data of the senses into the nonpictorial forms of verse and music poses difficulties. Language cannot imitate reality in any easily describable way; and the well-known pitfalls of testifying in verse to the more sensuous of the world's pleasures—pitfalls that are clearest in early Keats and Hopkins—argue against a too literal rendering of sensuality. Language, an abstract medium, is always in allegorical relation to perception and sensation.

In arguing that the sensual and the spiritual are indivisible, Merrill places his trust in the affections as a middle term. Faithlessness and infidelities are acts not of the flesh but of the spirit, and they occur when affection doubts or betrays its own powers. The certain loss of all "sacred bonds" underlies Merrill's verse. But as disbelief and death depopulate his real and imagined worlds, Merrill compensates by a poetry of exuberant mythology and a symposium of incarnate and discarnate voices. The eclectic banquet of youth is replaced in middle age by a Proustian feast of memory. In the fiction of *Mirabell*, the blessings of conversation replace the blessings of sensuality. The audible conversation of tongues—life's addendum to the sensual conversation of bodies—gives way to the inaudible ghostly converse of the dead and the disembodied, as language, letter by letter, assembles itself through the Ouija board. As narrator of, and Prospero to, the whole pageant, Merrill, though fictionally the child of the "father of forms and matter of fact mother" on "the other side," is the adult progenitor of all that happens. The providential and parental figures of Mirabell, Auden, and Maria are only the creatures of his creation.

We might ask whether Merrill's case, at least in the trilogy, is too special to be susceptible of translation into our own terms. Does this flood of transcriptions from another world, this massive treatise on "science" and "history," imply anything for us? Merrill's implicit protest against the censorship of feeling by our relentless ironic intellectualizing of life (he speaks here for all reflective people) takes the form of a defiant mythology—though, in a charming revenge exacted by the time we live in, the mythology must couch itself in "scientific" terms. The mysterious instructors told Merrill to write "Poems of Science." He went home and waited, but nothing happened, since his "word bank" was unfurnished with material. He resorted to potted science (Isaac Asimov, Lewis Thomas) and to remembered childhood myths, inventing macrocosmic and subatomic perspectives from which nothing can be hidden to the enlightened eye. Merrill's mythology attempts to ask what work we can find for that part of the mind hitherto occupied in inventing religious systems. Unlike Robert Lowell, who considered the really interesting people in history to be the emperors, the kings, and the politicians, Merrill thinks that the most attractive souls are those who thought up Edens and afterlifes, saints and satyrs.

It is surprising that Merrill, a poet of infinite finish, should come down so decisively in favor of large mythological outlines and of expository theology. Or perhaps it is not so surprising. The epic poetic of the trilogy demands the large, and even the prosaic. Whereas the lyric is discontinuous, and rejects the narrativity that (however much it may be submerged) links the successive events of drama and fiction, the epic goes beyond narrativity to an encyclopedic account of all things in heaven and earth. The instructors promise to return Merrill to his "chronicles of love and loss" after the trilogy is done, but he will not be the same poet who set down the first lines of "The Book of Ephraim"—the stretching and straining of this large effort cannot be forgotten in a contraction to lyric shapes.

The lessons of *Mirabell* are the unpopular ones of middle age. Most people, the poem tells us, are unevolved, and remain in an animal unawareness, in which they grow, couple, reproduce themselves, and die. Some souls evolve beyond this—into thought, vision, and art. (They are the souls "cloned" in the "Research Lab" of the spirits and sent into the world to do the "V work" of civilization—creating religions, symphonies, temples, cultures, poems.) There is no permanent culture; ours is one of successive attempts by God B to order chaos. The achievements of mind always seem to excel their material origins: hence the myth of inspiring Muses, mysterious instructors, visions, and oracles. The honey of generation is an opiate; the childless have freer access to the spiritual life. Everyone dies. The conversation of friends is precious. As parents and friends die, we dwell more and more on the dead. Our minds become a repository of all we have read, learned, been brought up on. We begin to think in larger terms—about history, about the survival of the planet, about genius.

But it is not for these or other worthy observations in their bald sense that we prize *Mirabell*. It is, rather, for the intimate and solid circumstantiality in which those truths are based. We know the death of parents not propositionally but circumstantially, in the long, particular narration of the death of David Jackson's parents, in "stupor, fear, incontinence," and their burial in a "raw trench." We know the loss of friends as Merrill accustoms us, through a

hundred and seventy-eight pages, to the tender and solicitous rail-
lery of Auden and Maria, and then, once we look forward to hearing
them indefinitely, strikes the knell of their disappearance. We come
to prize even the most frail creations of culture as Merrill's myths
link the oldest constructions, like Atlantis and Eden, named rather
than evoked, to the creation, metamorphosis, and humanizing of
the bat-peacock Mirabell. First an inhuman other, Mirabell becomes,
through "this world of courtesy"—the board of communication—
someone who can love ("I HAVE COME TO LOVE U"), someone self-
conscious and aesthetically reflective. In his becoming we see the
coming-to-be of every conscious creature, through language and
love:

> B4 OUR MEETINGS I WAS NOTHING   NO TIME PASSD   BUT NOW
> YR TOUCH LIKE A LAMP HAS SHOWN ME TO MYSELF & I AM
> ME: 741! I HAVE ENTERED A GREAT WORLD   I AM FILLED
> WITH   IS IT MANNERS?

There are stretches of flats in the exposition of the mythology, yet
its density shares with all systems—from Leviticus to *The Book of
Mormon* and Melville's cetology—a sheer willingness to bore. The
visionary mind has its own pedantries. Just as complicated poets, like
Milton, have to learn to be simple, so Merrill, natively compact,
has here decided to learn a discursive plainness.

Before the concluding speech of the archangel Michael, who announces the next act of the comedy, Merrill speaks in his own voice
of the world's diversity, as he glances out to numberless brilliances
of light over the water:

> The message hardly needs decoding, so
> Sheer the text, so innocent and fleet
> These overlapping pandemonia:
> Birdlife, leafplay, rockface, waterglow
> Lending us their being, till the given
> Moment comes to render what we owe.

Merrill has offered a self-definition through metaphor in the course
of the poem: his metal is silver (Auden's is platinum), his element
air, his mineral crystal, his color "cold lavender." In themselves,
these specifications are definitive. By middle age, one knows what
one is. If Merrill reminds us sometimes of Ariel, he is yet an Ariel
making a deliberate gesture toward an enlarging of style in his refusal to be exclusively beautiful. By its admission of the learning,

conversation, and random use of language that underlie the crystal-
lizations of lyric, Merrill's poem pays homage to the riches of un-
ordered literary experience:

MANS TERMITE PALACE BEEHIVE ANTHILL PYRAMID JM
IS LANGUAGE   USE IT   STIR THE THINKERS & DETER THE REST.

Language "of such a depth, shimmer, and force" is the "life raft"
that carries the poet over the flood of sensation. *Mirabell* is more
a diary, in fact, than a planned "system": each section encompasses
whatever rises to the surface at a given moment of composition. The
mind whose word banks and image banks are here tapped is not
in any way a typical one. It is preternaturally knowing, and eclec-
tically read; it strikes attitudes; it is fond but acutely critical; it likes
puns perhaps more than it should; its relativism is both despairing
and elated. It never lacks fit language—silky and astringent by turns,
lustrous and decorative one moment, attenuated and scholastically
drab the next, candid or esoteric as its author decides.

What is in the American mind these days—the detritus of past
belief, a hodgepodge of Western science and culture, a firm belief
in the worth of the private self and in the holiness of the heart's
affections, a sense of time and space beyond the immediate—is here
displayed for judgment. Somewhat less general in reference, perhaps,
is Merrill's examination of what, as a personal aim, can replace self-
reproduction in childbearing. Once the biological purpose of life is
even theoretically put aside as a justification of living, we must
(theological justification having been abandoned long since) advocate something like Merrill's civilizing "V work." The Arnoldian
doctrine of the saving remnant seems in this poem to have a new
defender; but Merrill dwells, as Arnold does not, on the parallel
necessity of private affection. Love and civilization here go hand
in hand, the work of art and science refining life in public as the
bonds of affection refine life in private. *Mirabell* is Merrill's hymn
to the spiritual evolution that seems possible, if precarious, now that
biological evolution has invented man; its dark undersong is
Hiroshima in the realm of science, and subhuman stupidity in the
realm of the private life.

What Merrill once said of Eugenio Montale—that his emotional
refinement is "suprisingly permeable by quite ordinary objects:
ladles, hens, pianos, half-read letters"—is true of Merrill himself.
The claim of ordinary objects and ordinary events on lyric is a mark
of the democratic sense in every modern poet of quality—from the

priestlike Eliot down through the alchemizing Merrill—that the things of the world can lend a myth (as Crane said of the Brooklyn Bridge) to God. The tendency of modern American lyric poets to reclaim whole tracts of language and experience ceded in the nineteenth century to novels or nonfictional prose continues in Merrill. It is this tendency that has caused us to outstrip our parent stock in England. If to play so free with tradition one poet needs the Ouija board, and another, like Ginsberg, needs visions, and another, like Eliot, needs Buddhism, those who are not poets can only conclude that the work of creation proceeds by its own means.

W. S. Merwin

These books invoke by their subtitles the false distinction between prose and poetry: the real distinction is between prose and verse, since both are books of poems, with distinct resemblances and a few differences. There are more allegories, parables, and fables in the eighty-odd pieces that make up the book of prose, but that only makes for more narrative and less reflection. The prose pieces come with their dramatic title, *The Miner's Pale Children*, to preclude our criticism: if we ask why they are not more robust, they answer by a single eloquent finger pointing to sunless caverns where they were born: peaked and huge-eyed, like wizened English workhouse children, they stand in speechless reproach in the schoolyard, rebuking by their mere subterranean etiolation the boisterous ruddiness of the terrestrial.

The trouble with the analogy is that nobody tells us why the father of these pieces hasn't let them play in the sunshine more. There is maybe even a complacency in their fragility, as if to say that they are more sensitive than those huge galumphing children with their tans. I do not know for sure whether one has the right to reproach a poet for his subject, but Merwin has been maintaining his starved and mute stance so long that one has a relentless social-worker urge to ask him to eat something, anything, to cure his anemia.

And then, relenting in face of a single poem, singly perceived, and not part of the litany of hunger, one grants Merwin his talent for the desolate and the dismembered. He is a voice singing out of empty cisterns and exhausted wells with the toneless cry of *The Waste*

This review of W. S. Merwin's *The Miner's Pale Children: A Book of Prose* and *The Carrier of Ladders: A Book of Poems* appeared in the *New York Times Book Review*, October 18, 1970.

Land. He often seems a lesser Eliot, taking one of Eliot's tonalities to its logical conclusion, a hollow man finding his hollow divinities:

> in the abandoned fountain a dead branch points upwards
> eaten out from inside as it appears to me
> I know a new legend
> this is the saint of the place his present form another blessing in
>   absence.

The prose pieces are mostly too long to quote, but one of the shortest, "From a Mammon Card," can give some idea of the intricacies of the others:

> Those who work, as they say, for a living, are not to calculate how much they make an hour and then consider what they claim to own, remembering that there was a time when they made less per hour, and then consider that what they claim to own is perhaps all that remains of what they sold that many hours of their life for, and then try to imagine the hours coming again.

There are tenuous allegories of wish and incomprehension: a "June couple" imagine the "little place beside the water" that they would like to own, each confecting a private vision (his has tan imitation-brick shingles, with a screen porch, while hers is "a low stone building, one big dormer in its thatch roof"), and while each says raptly in separate chorus "Mine," the separation yawns invisibly between them, and the piece ends.

There are parental neglects and reparations. (A mother, frightened of her grown-up daughter, continues "to look after her, but from a distance," so much so that by the time she gets up courage to look inside the bedroom, she finds "that the girl has left without a word two days before.") Other stories, more dreamlike, with the attendant disadvantages, revolve around incomprehensible journeys, uninhabited ports, fragmented bodies, chilling rites of passage, inexplicable ordeals, and surreal tasks (like "unchopping a tree"—a minute set of directions on how to put a chopped-up tree back together again).

There are also painstaking and self-flagellating dissections of memory, grief, fear, and personality: "You are the second person . . . You make a pathetic effort to disguise yourself in all the affectations of the third person, but you know it is no use . . . No, you insist, it is all a mistake, I am the first person. But you know how unsatisfactory that is. And how seldom it is true." The first person would

234

be "the orphan's mother who never lived but is longed for," and it seems to be an orphan who has written both this spectral book and its companion volume in verse.

Merwin's abstraction cloaks the human cause of these poems, but desolation and abandonment shading into terror are more common than any other feeling. On the other hand, one feels that these poems were written not so much from sentiments requiring expression as from obsessive counters demanding manipulation. These counters are a set of words, found here and in Merwin's earlier volumes, that act for him as a set of talismans: endlessly he pushes them around into different spatial arrangements, festoons them with different decorations, but they are almost always there, central, demanding, repetitive, exacting.

The Merwin dictionary has nouns of ill-omen (pain, grief, fear, pallor, extinction), obsessive objects (gloves, hands, clocks, watches, bandages, shrouds, eyes), exhausted adjectives (hollow, empty, faint, deaf, blind, blank, frozen, lost, broken, hungry, dead), and constellations of negation (speechless, colorless, nameless, windless, unlighted, unseen, unmoved, unborn). Is it ill-will in a reader to want to force-feed these pale children till they, when cut, will bleed? Even Merwin would seem to want a change: he prays,

> Send me out into another life
> Lord because this one is growing faint
> I do not think it goes all the way.

There are poems when a new life may seem to be beginning, and some of these are very beautiful, especially "Snowfall," where, after a vision of death in the night a vision of communion intervenes in the day:

> ... this morning
> I see that the silent kin I loved as a child
> have arrived all together in the night
> from the old country
> they remembered
> and everything remembers
> I eat from the hands
> of what for years have been junipers
> the taste has not changed
> I am beginning
> again.

In his elusive pallors, Merwin sometimes comes near a flawless balance of cadence and meaning. Some of his poems of deprivation and winter share a place in "the pre-history of the mind" with the February poems of Wallace Stevens, but they lack Stevens' obdurate persistence in the natural—his squirrels, his forsythia, his scrawny bird cry. On the other hand, Merwin has not subscribed to the falser poetic consolations of Eliot: he inhabits a dimmer world than either Eliot or Stevens, but there is a faint cast of sentimentality over his poems that persuades the reader that he could, by taking thought, add a cubit to his stature and raise sturdier offspring.

Adrienne Rich

Diving into the Wreck

Adrienne Rich's memorable poetry has been given us, a book at a time, for more than twenty years. Four years after she published her first book, I read it in almost disbelieving wonder; someone my age was writing down my life. I felt then, as I feel now, that for each reader there are only a few poets of whom that is true, and by the law of averages, those poets are usually dead or at least far removed in time and space. But here was a poet who seemed, by a miracle, a twin: I had not known till then how much I had wanted a contemporary and a woman as a speaking voice of life:

> Strength came where weakness was not known to be,
> At least not felt; and restoration came
> Like an intruder knocking at the door
> Of unacknowledged weariness.

When I look back through *A Change of World* (1951), I try to remember which of the pages so held me and why; and I find four sets of poems I greet with the sense of déjà vu. One set had simply lovely lines, seeming today almost too decorative, too designed, but presenting to me then the poetry of the delicately apprehended and the exquisitely remembered, poetry of "the flecked leaf-gilded boughs," and "paths fern-fringed and delicate," ornamented with "whisking emerald lizards." I did not mind, in some of these solacing poems, echoes of Auden or Yeats, feeling that what was beautiful was beautiful no matter who invented it; but there was, it was true, an ominous note which kept being interlaced with the poised rhythms.

"Ghostlier Demarcations, Keener Sounds" first appeared in *Parnassus: Poetry in Review*, Fall/Winter 1973.

237

A second group of poems set the status quo against some threatened future time; yet the danger was contained, and in fact the
action of containing danger was gravely obligatory, a sacred trust.
The poems articulated their own balance between danger and decorum in imagery of rebellion (which usually lost) against tradition
(which usually won, at least tonally). The speaker for tradition in
one poem is "the uncle in the drawing room"; gesturing toward
"crystal vase and chandelier," knowing the "frailties of glass," he
points seriously to the duties of the custodians of culture:

> Let us only bear in mind
> How these treasures handed down
> From a calmer age passed on
> Are in the keeping of our kind.
> We stand between the dead glass-blowers
> And murmurings of missile-throwers.

The poet-observer creating the uncle may see him ironically in part,
but there is no denying the ethical imperative of his last claim.
Equally subversive of tradition, but yearningly attached to its honor,
"For the Felling of a Tree in Harvard Yard" ends ambiguously on a
double set of responses:

> The second oldest elm is down.

> The shade where James and Whitehead strolled
> Becomes a litter on the green.
> The young men pause along the paths
> To see the axes glinting bold.

> Watching the hewn trunk dragged away,
> Some turn the symbol to their own,
> And some admire the clean dispatch
> With which the aged elm came down.

Though revolution may end this poem, nostalgia rules it, nostalgia
for the "roots enormous in their age," for "the great spire . . .
overthrown." In 1955 I read this poem purely as elegy (no doubt
confusing it in my undiscriminating admiration with "Binsey Pop-
lars" and the spreading chestnut tree) and I was unable as yet, myself, to conceive of revolutionary impatience. But even now its tone
seems to contain far more of the pang of elegy than of the briskness
of destruction. So the poems played with fire, yet did not burn: I
must have liked that.

The third set of poems that moved me then were poems on the identity and lot of women. I had no conscious thoughts on the topic, the natural order of the universe seeming then to be the inequality of man and woman; and yet some strains of discord in the book must have seemed an external documentary to those inarticulate strains in myself. On the one hand, woman was to be Patience on a monument, a Hermione-statue always there when her husband chose to come back:

> She who has power to call her man
> From that estranged intensity
> Where his mind forages alone,
> Yet keeps her peace and leaves him free,
> And when his thoughts to her return
> Stands where he left her, still his own,
> Knows this the hardest thing to learn.

Hard it may be, but learn it she must, says "An Unsaid Word"; and it assumes that there is no such "estranged intensity" where *she* could be mentally foraging alone, and whence he might forbear to call *her* back. And yet, in other poems, the imperative of exploration, separation, and private discovery is equally felt:

> Each his own Magellan
> In tropics of sensation . . .
> These are latitudes revealed
> Separate to each.

In still other poems, needlework, that laborious confection of female artistry, becomes the repeated symbol of the ambiguously triumphant womanly lot. While their lords left for "harsher hunting on the opposite coast," Norman ladies

> sat at home
> To the pleasing minor airs of lute and hautbois,
> While the bright sun on the expensive threads
> Glowed in the long windless afternoons.

But what is left of the Anglo-Norman battles but the Bayeux tapestry, which "prove[d] / More than the personal episode, more than all / The little lives" ("Mathilde in Normandy"). And, in spite of the seductive evenings in "The Kursaal at Interlaken," the female speaker, while playing her social role, nonetheless casts longing eyes toward a solitary virginity:

> Jungfrau, the legendary virgin spire,
> Consumes the mind with mingled snow and fire.

This sentimental image, though there is no reason to doubt its sincerity, cannot equal, in poetic success, the trivialities so adeptly and ironically sketched earlier in the poem:

> What is the world, the violins seem to say,
> But windows full of bears and music boxes,
> Chocolate gnomes and water-color mountains,
> And calendars of French and German days—
> Sonntag and vendredi, unreal dimensions,
> Days where we speak all languages but our own?

The Jungfrau, no matter how symbolically laden, loses out, and that loss means that this poem wished to be what we would nowadays call a feminist poem and had not the emotional force to carry it off. The impulse toward a feminist stance arises in "The Kursaal" because the speaker is not in love with her lover:

> You will perhaps make love to me this evening . . .
> Reality would call us less than friends
> And therefore more adept at making love.

But most of A Change in World is written by a girl in love, a girl "receiving marvels, signs":

> There is a streetcar runs from here to Mars.
> I shall be seeing you, my darling, there,
> Or at the burning bush in Harvard Square.

This seems too easy an apotheosis now, but it seemed bold at first reading and drew me by the same authority as the lines in "For the Conjunction of Two Planets" which imperiously declared for myth against astrophysics:

> Whatever register or law
> Is drawn in digits for these two,
> Venus and Jupiter keep their awe,
> Warders of brilliance, as they do
> Their dual circuit of the west—
> The brightest planet and her guest.

Not only was our feminism only an occasional shadow over our expectation of the ecstatic, our sense of permanent location in our lot was only incipient, too. The fourth set of poems that kept me standing in the library stacks reading this new and revelatory book was the set about Europe. In *A Change of World* Rich struck all the notes of her generation's inchoate responses to Europe: an attachment, a disloyalty; beauty, decadence; the perfect, the tired; art, the artificial. Alienated by a lengthily educated childhood from the American scene and yet invisibly, visibly, and irrevocably American, the students who went abroad like Rich wandered tranced in the deceptive paradises of the transatlantic escape.

Six books later, almost two decades older, Rich's readers encounter *Diving into the Wreck*. If we suspend knowledge of what came between, we may ask what has happened to the girl of 1951, that girl who wanted everything suffused by the delicate and the decorative, who questioned her passivity even while exhorting herself to that virtue, who mourned change and yet sensed its coming, who feared her own alienation in her native country, who, above these cares and anxieties, took pains that all her poems should turn out right, that there should be no ragged edges, that chimes should chasten discords—what has become of her? She has forgotten, or repudiated, her dream of Europe: Beethoven makes a fugitive appearance in the new book, but even he is not permitted to represent nineteenth-century European high culture; Rich calls her Beethoven poem "The Ninth Symphony of Beethoven Understood at Last as a Sexual Message." Passivity, too, is repudiated in principle, but returns in surreptitious forms, as life is consumed by that which nourished it:

> Time takes hold of us like a draft
> upward, drawing at the heats
> in the belly, in the brain
>
> ... the mirror of the fire
> of my mind, burning as if it could go on
> burning itself, burning down
>
> feeding on everything
> till there is nothing in life
> that has not fed that fire

The overtones here come from Williams' "Burning the Christmas Greens," but Williams' poem is about the desire for change which consigns the greens to the fire, while Rich is helplessly suspended in the fires of time and thought. The old decorativeness reappears in the intricate ending, but this time not in the service of a scrim-curtain prettiness. As for the questions of female identity and the rival claims of change and tradition, they have merged into one inextricable and apparently insoluble problem. In the first book, change could be chosen or not; here, Rich utters ruin (and resurrection) as inevitable law:

> I don't know who we thought we were
> that our personalities
> could resist the failures of the race.
>
> Lucky or unlucky, we didn't know
> the race had failures of that order
> and that we were going to share them
>
> Like everybody else, we thought of ourselves as special . . .
>
> Next year it would have been 20 years
> and you are wastefully dead
> who might have made the leap
> we talked, too late, of making
>
> which I live now
> not as a leap
> but a succession of brief, amazing movements
> each one making possible the next

It is easier to believe in the failures of the race than in the amazing movements, and in fact the fine title poem of this volume proposes, with resolute courage, the exploration of those failures:

> I came to explore the wreck.
> The words are purposes.
> The words are maps.
> I came to see the damage that was done
> and the treasures that prevail.

These declarative pallors give way to a rich sense of the state of the wreck, in which we recognize an old vitality:

> I am she: I am he
>
> whose drowned face sleeps with open eyes
> whose breasts still bear the stress
> whose silver, copper, vermeil cargo lies

obscurely inside barrels
half-wedged and left to rot
we are the half-destroyed instruments
that once held to a course
the water-eaten log
the fouled compass

There is a visible continuity between the phosphorescent wreck and the orderly gardens and villas of early Rich, but the complacency of tone, so earnestly assuring the intellectual resolution of the early poems, is conspicuously stricken from this new exploration.

Oddly, it is not stricken from other poems, where complacency has become an unthinking assault on plain reasonableness. Because this new volume has provoked such hostile and intemperate criticism, it is probably just as well to mention its most extreme poem: a poem called "Rape," which begins by announcing that "There is a cop who is both prowler and father," and ends by claiming that as you describe your rape to him, "your details sound like a portrait of your confessor" (who has been carefully described in SS terms, as, with boots on, gun in hand, "he and his stallion clop like warlords"). This cliché (the cop whose eyes "grow narrow and glisten" as "his hand types out all the details") is unworthy of a poet, as is the incrimination of all men in the encapsulation of brothers and fathers in the portrait of this rapist super-cop. Rich would be the first to object to an equally stereotyped description of women—as shrew, as castrating mother, or whatever. The poem, like some others, is a deliberate refusal of the modulations of intelligence in favor of an annulling and untenable propaganda, a grisly indictment, a fictitious and mechanical drama denying the simple fact of possible decency (there are decent cops and decent fathers, and decent brothers, too, but they have no place in the consciousness producing this poem).

It is not hard to imagine someone writing a poem like "Rape," but it is hard to see how such poems pass muster months later when a volume is being gathered for publication. The truth of feeling ("I felt this way, I wrote it down") has never been coterminous with the truth of art. And since the truth of art has always been Rich's securest claim on our attention, even in her tidiest poems, it gives a reader a wrench of pain to see her play false to her own standard. But criticism has so fastened on these lapses that the tense fineness determining the tactics of many of these poems has been ignored. Unwelcome though some of Rich's sentiments may be to

those who do not share her recent activist feminism and other political activities, it would be unfair to let ideological differences obscure the presence, felt and conveyed in these poems, of finely
discriminated emotions—of the numbed, the stricken, the defrauded,
the miserable. Rich feels all of these and finds metaphors for them,
this "living in the cave," as one poem has it. The poem seems to be
about being a mother with children, but it will do for any one with
dependents:

> These things around me, with their
> daily requirements:
> > fill me, empty me
> talk to me, warm me, let me
> suck on you
>
> Every one of them has a plan that depends on me
>
> stalactites want to become
> stalagmites
> veins of ore
> imagine their preciousness
>
> candles see themselves disembodied
> into gas
> and taking flight
>
> the bat hangs dreaming
> of an airy world
>
> None of them, not one
> sees me
> as I see them.

This ending may seem reductive to others, but I do not believe
the poet need grant consciousness equivalent to her own to those
surrounding her, especially if those people are children with their
indisputable "daily requirements" and their innocent but monstrous
egotism. And yet the virtue of the poem is the respect accorded
those "other minds"—they are real, they have dreams, wishes, plans,
hopes. Are we not all urged to contemplate our own preciousness,
to aspire to the condition of luminousness, to dream of life outside
the cave, to hope to grow up to stand on our own two feet (like
stalagmites) instead of hanging dependently (like stalactites)? Who
would want anything else for her children but those dreams, those
plans? And yet—that the means to all these ends should be the
one consciousness "arranging all in one clear view" gives that consciousness at least the right to wish that someone else could see

the whole geography, flora and fauna, of the cave, to bear her company. There are many poems of this sort, in which the poet's grief does not encroach upon the rights of others, and the feminist consciousness is mitigated by the real demands of life: the final perplexity of the poem is the misery of contending rights and needs in human existence.

The complicity of women in their own plight is, in the better poems, admitted: though a man depends on a woman for "protection" as she on him, and though "it all seems innocent enough, this sin / of wedlock," there is something in her perpetual self-abnegating servitude that atrophies one portion of the woman—yet she participates in the infliction of that atrophy:

> your wife's twin sister, speechless
> is dying in the house
> You and your wife take turns
> carrying up the trays,
> understanding her case, trying to make her understand.

Fair enough. For someone who finds the present world "a world masculinity made / unfit for women or men" poetry will often express "the phenomenology of anger." And yet the desolate poems seem to me better than the ones preoccupied with fantasies of murder (becoming a human acetylene torch, and so on). I do not know why this should be, but the poetry of pure anger is a relatively rare phenomenon. The dialogue with men, which provokes Rich's anger (a dialogue dating from adolescence, perpetuated through courtship, desiccated in marriage, renewing itself in affairs, exploding in betrayal or abandonment) is artificial when uninflected by grief, loss, and incredulity. When Rich is genuinely "trying to talk with a man" (the title of one poem) she allows for mixed emotions; out in the desert with the man, she recapitulates with exhausted irony the whole long trip that has brought them to this ghost town:

> What we've had to give up to get here—
> whole LP collections, films we starred in
> playing in the neighborhoods, bakery windows
> full of dry, chocolate-filled Jewish cookies,
> the language of love-letters, of suicide notes,
> afternoons on the riverbank
> pretending to be children

Which of us, at forty, will not wince at the fluoroscopic truth of that list: we can name our own LP's, our fantasy PTA neighborhood self-projections, our parents' cookie jars, our dramas of love and self-pity, our slides into regressive and delusory role-playing. Critics who represent Rich's recent poetry as the utterance of exaggerated feminism alone seem not to have read these plainspoken passages, returning throughout this book, passages showing (in the jargon of today) where we are all at.

There is more to look at in *Diving into the Wreck*, notably its last poem; but first, in order to see the place of this book in Adrienne Rich's continuing writing, writing unflaggingly done through youth, marriage, motherhood, solitude, employment, political engagement, and fame, we must look back to earlier works. Except for youth, any one of these phrases, not to speak of all of them, can be destructive of writing: we recall Jane Austen's years of silence when her father had to give up his house and take the family into lodgings; we remember Sylvia Plath's hectic early-morning sleepless composition before her babies awoke. A writer who persists, phase after phase, usually has some intrinsic and compelling self and style demanding expression. If we try to isolate the self and style which appeared in *A Change of World* and which have continued, through age and variation, all the way up to *Diving into the Wreck*, we are asking, really, which are Rich's best poems, how her voice makes itself both remarkable and beautiful.

Rich hit her stride, and wrote her first "perfect" poem in her second volume, *The Diamond Cutters* (1955). The poem in question, "The Middle-Aged," is one of a distinguished group, including "The Tourist and the Town," "Lucifer in the Train," "The Wild Sky," "Villa Adriana," and "Landscape of the Star," which all, in some way, deal with homelessness; and that homelessness, with its accompanying ache of filial nostalgia, is the new theme, coming into the ascendant, which distinctly marks *The Diamond Cutters* as an advance over the first volume. Sometimes the pain of departure and separation is overt and unmediated:

> Imperceptibly
> That landscape altered; now in paler air
> Tree, hill and rock stood out resigned, severe,
> Beside the strangled field, the stream run dry.

In a passage that recalls the (independently conceived) Plath poem "The Colossus," we see another child reconstructing the parental domain:

We come like dreamers searching for an answer,
Passionately in need to reconstruct
The columned roofs under the blazing sky,
The courts so open, so forever locked.

And some of us, as dreamers, excavate
Under the blanching light of sleep's high noon,
The artifacts of thought, the site of love,
Whose Hadrian has given the slip, and gone.

Moon explorers, in a desolate new landscape, long for their terrestrial home:

We speak the names we learned as we were bred,
We tell of places seen each day from birth—
Obscure and local, patois of the Earth!

Finally, identifying herself with the Magi for whom "the palaces behind have ceased to be / Home," Rich walks, on Christmas morning, in "an unaccustomed city" and says bravely that though this is the "night that calls all travellers home, / The prodigal forgiven and the breach / Mended for this one feast," for her, denied this solace, there is another; the passage is prophetic:

Yet all are strange
To their own ends, and their beginnings now
Cannot contain them . . . Once-familiar speech
Babbles in wayward dialect of a dream.

Our gifts shall bring us home: not to beginnings
Nor always to the destination named
Upon our setting-forth. Our gifts compel,
Master our ways and lead us in the end
Where we are most ourselves.

All of these poems of exile, separation, breach, and, most explicitly, the deprivation of native speech, are both made and marred by their sense of shivering phantomhood; like Lucifer, the poet is banished—to the moon, to "ashen prairies of the absolute," to a ruined villa, to an endless desert journey. But recovery, though hoped for, and vowed, and even prophesied, is still spectral, unseen—recovery as anodyne, not fact. But "The Middle-Aged" has mastered its exile and has taken the larger view: no longer outcry alone, it includes analysis as well. If it has a fault, it is that it bends backward, away from its companions; it tries so bravely not to be bitter that it is not bitter enough. Nonetheless, it points to the attempt at the conquering of experience which is the ground of the aesthetic. Here is Rich on the suffering of being young:

> To be young
> Was always to live in other people's houses
> Whose peace, if we sought it, had been made by others,
> Was ours at second-hand and not for long.
>
> They were so kind;
> Would have given us anything; the bowl of fruit
> Was filled for us, there was a room upstairs
> We must call ours: but twenty years of living
> They could not give. Nor did they ever speak
> Of the coarse stain on that polished balustrade,
> The crack in the study window, or the letters
> Locked in a drawer and the key destroyed.
> All to be understood by us, returning
> Late, in our own time—how that peace was made,
> Upon what terms, with how much left unsaid.

When I copied that poem down in 1955—I still have the copy, and have retyped it time and again for others—I did not know why, since I liked all the other poems too, I liked this one the best. Now I would say that it holds its position of preeminence among the companion poems that share its theme not only because of its analytic mastery of the situation, but also because of its simplicity. All of the paraphernalia—Lucifer, Hadrian, the Mare Crisium, the Magi, Constable, San Miniato al Monte—have been swept away, and we meet the bowl of fruit, the upstairs room, the secondhand peace, the affliction of the young who have "to live in other people's houses." There is a lot to be said, I suppose, for objective correlatives, but Magi treks and moon journeys go rather far afield and threaten to render the experience more fancifully than accurately, as the correlative becomes more interesting to the poet than its origins.

The shape of *The Diamond Cutters* suggests that Rich may need to write explicit *cris du coeur* as sketches, so to speak, for more contained and disciplined later poems. It is odd that some readers will so placidly receive and even praise unmediated cries of filial longing, but will become irrationally damning about a single cry of unmediated anger. These hysterias only prove that Rich is touching intense and widely diffused feelings; a poet could hardly ask for more. In her poems, Rich sees more deeply than in her recent prose propaganda; poetry makes her more reflective and more self-corrective, less inflexible, more pained.

In *Snapshots of a Daughter-in-Law* (1963) we find that marriage has turned the earlier filial exile-in-space into something considerably more bitter—separation under the same roof, a sense of separate-and-not-equal lives bequeathed to men and women, with women's only claim that of a more genuine insight into Nature:

> . . . has Nature shown
> her household books to you, daughter-in-law,
> that her sons never saw?

The silent isolation of minds in marriage is followed by a choking, deprived speech. The central poem in this volume is without doubt "A Marriage in the Sixties," a poem still hoping for the best and yet unwilling to dissemble the worst:

> Today we stalk
> in the raging desert of our thought
> whose single drop of mercy is
> each knows the other there.
> Two strangers, thrust for life upon a rock,
> may have at last the perfect hour of talk
> that language aches for; still
> two minds, two messages.

"My words," says Rich, watching those words drop unheard and neglected, "reach you as through a telephone / where some submarine echo of my voice / blurts knowledge you can't use" ("The Lag"). In this volume Rich's lines loosen up into free verse; we may assume various influences, from Eliot to Lowell to Plath, but since the modern movement as a whole was on its way toward dispensing with rhyme, it was inevitable that Rich should forsake her sweetness, cadence, and stanzas once her life began to refuse its earlier arrangements. Nervous, hardened, noting harshly that only cutting onions can provoke her unwept tears into her eyes, she moves under a "load of unexpired purpose, which drains / slowly." Rich's effects now depend only on metaphor, juxtaposition, and adroit lineation; she vomits up "dead gobbets" of herself, "abortive, murdered, or never willed" for new recognition; she crawls out of her cocoon like a fish attempting the grand evolutionary trick of becoming a bird:

like a fish
half-dead from flopping
and almost crawling
across the shingle,
almost breathing
the raw, agonizing
air
till a wave
pulls it back blind into the triumphant
sea.

At about this time, Rich's dilemmas make for unresolved poems, ending in the defeat of the fish or a flight of a naked man across roofs of houses:

Was it worth while to lay—
with infinite exertion—
a roof I can't live under?
—All those blueprints,
closing of gaps,
measurings, calculations?
A life I didn't choose
chose me:—even
my tools are the wrong ones
for what I have to do.
I'm naked, ignorant,
a naked man fleeing
across the roofs.

The weakness of the book is its explicitness and its irresolution. The nerves it touches are raw and recognizable; but it leans on words like "ache" and "agonizing" which preempt our responses. "If Rich were a great poet," said a friend reading these poems, "which of us could bear to read her?" Rich's transcriptions of pain, wholly accurate, are to be prized even if only as documentaries: and these unhappy limbo poems ending in stalemate are an honorable and possible form, but a whole book of them inevitably sets the reader on a slide downhill at the bottom of which he anticipates a crash. And yet the crash is staved off for one more book, Rich's most beautiful and accomplished single volume, *Necessities of Life* (1966).

If, as Rich's early pattern suggests, blunter poems are followed by subtler ones, *Necessities of Life* derives its power from its absorption of all past phases into its present one. In "Autumn Sequence," Rich forces herself to that generosity toward past selves:

> Generosity is drying out,
>
> it's an act of will to remember
> May's sticky-mouthed buds
> on the provoked magnolias.

But that act of will makes this volume almost an obituary; at least it is the obituary of a whole section of life. The title poem—a second talisman to join with "The Middle-Aged"—shows a new self emerging and seeking a new place in the world:

> Piece by piece I seem
> to re-enter the world: I first began
>
> a small, fixed dot, still see
> that old myself, a dark-blue thumbtack
>
> pushed into the scene,
> a hard little head protruding
>
> from the pointillist's buzz and bloom.

We cannot help noticing how free from compulsion Rich's images have become. The early poems were so neat in their useful skeins of imagery; if a color appeared in the upper left of the tapestry, it was sure to reappear, economically but predictably, in the lower right. Now precision of feeling and exactness of recollection govern the correlative, and though the visual reference apparent in the thumbtack and the pointillist is maintained, it is allowed considerable freedom. In adolescence come passion and ambition, melting the pigments:

> After a time the dot
>
> begins to ooze. Certain heats
> melt it.
>   Now I was hurriedly
>
> blurring into ranges
> of burnt red, burning green,
>
> whole biographies swam up and
> swallowed me like Jonah.
>
> Jonah! I was Wittgenstein,
> Mary Wollstonecraft, the soul

of Louis Jouvet, dead
in a blown-up photograph.

There is a hiatus in the poem at this point, as though the self-devouring of adolescence were nameable, but the other-devouring of marriage and child-rearing were not. The "hard little head" become photograph loses its painterly dimension and becomes a dry bulb waiting out its time of deprivation, "gone underground" like Herbert's flower, through "all the hard weather":

Till, wolfed almost to shreds,
I learned to make myself

unappetizing. Scaly as a dry bulb
thrown into a cellar

I used myself, let nothing use me.
Like being on a private dole

Sometimes more like kneading bricks in Egypt.

In this poverty of slavery—and the comparisons tell us that even the "privileged" life of a Cambridge wife and mother can feel like that—the poem reaches its central minimal state in an exhausted miserliness keeping others at bay:

What life was there, was mine,

now and again to lay
one hand on a warm brick

and touch the sun's ghost
with economical joy,

now and again to name
over the bare necessities.

This beautiful passage, though it could perhaps not have been written before Stevens' poetry of poverty, has the touch of the physical in it that Stevens' poetry lacked: that warm brick and its ghostly heat did not inhabit Stevens' universe. Those "certain heats" of adolescence have dwindled to this ghostly form: passion and ambition alike almost expire in this daily kneading of the bricks, this being "wolfed almost to shreds" by others. But the devouring demand has, with time, eased; a tentative green shoot rises from the root cellar; "Who would have thought my shrivel'd heart / Could have recover'd greennesse?" Herbert asks under similar conditions.

But Rich's resurrection is not Herbert's cyclical one; she will never again be a flower. However, she can be a cabbage, an eel, something sturdy and slippery at once (and female and male at once, the androgynous imagery suggests):

> So much for those days. Soon
> practice may make me middling perfect, I'll
>
> dare inhabit the world
> trenchant in motion as an eel, solid
>
> as a cabbage-head. I have invitations:
> a curl of mist steams upward
>
> from a field, visible as my breath.

Encouraging, brisk lines: they tell what every depleted mother must feel when the haze and stumbling of physical and psychic tiredness finally lift after a decade of babies. But where is the new society to join, when child-bearing is over? Where but among the old wives?

> houses along a road stand waiting
>
> like old women knitting, breathless
> to tell their tales.

In these lines, acquiescence and rebellion compete: that the little dark-blue thumbtack should come to this; that the girl who dreamed of being Wittgenstein should join the garrulous crones. And yet, what else can the normal lot be; given the submission of the soul in all those years of Egyptian bondage, given the confines of the root-cellar, is it not enough to sit on the doorstep and knit?

That was as far ahead as Rich could see in 1962, and, as always, she told us life as she saw it. It is with an almost desperate vertigo that we come from this poem and others like it to the poems of violent change in the later books, when Rich feels picked up and thrown by life into jangling new positions, unforeseen, unasked-for, but welcomed as they come. The more reproachful of her critics have assumed that her revolutionary stances are chosen and there-fore blameworthy; I see them rather as part of the inexplicable on-goingness of life, to be reported like the rest. Better a change than the falsely "mature" acceptance of the unacceptable, a stance that Rich falls into off and on in *Necessities of Life*, notably in the in-creasingly expedient "literariness" of the poem "After Dark" on her father's death, and in the forced ending of the fine poem "Like

This Together," where she declares that love can be kept alive by our working at it, that the dry scaly bulb can be pried into life:

> Only our fierce attention
> gets hyacinths out of those
> hard cerebral lumps,
> unwraps the wet buds down
> the whole length of a stem.

This "solution" won't work for a destroyed city, and a destroyed city is the problem of this poem:

> They're tearing down, tearing up
> this city, block by block.
> Rooms cut in half
> hang like flayed carcasses,
> their old roses in rags,
> famous streets have forgotten
> where they were going. Only
> a fact could be so dreamlike.
> They're tearing down the houses
> we met and lived in,
> soon our two bodies will be all
> left standing from that era.

These lines have that power of the best sort of metaphor, that they pierce equally in two directions, until we scarcely know whether we are flinching from the tearing up of Cambridge or from the decay of a marriage. The death of Rich's husband since the poem was written gives the last line an edge it did not have in the writing; but even without that added wreckage, all the king's horses and all the king's men cannot put this Cambridge together again, and the final forced hyacinths are an evasion of reality.

The two books preceding *Diving into the Wreck* are waiting out some murky transition: the most explicit poem in *Leaflets* (1969) jettisons every past except the residual animal instinct of self-preservation, and every future except death; comparing herself to "the red fox, the vixen" and denying any connection to the ascetic New England settlers (like the Israelities, a "chosen people") with their "instinct mortified in a virgin forest," Rich says:

> what does she want
> with the dreams of dead vixens,
> the apotheosis of Reynard,

the literature of fox-hunting?
Only in her nerves the past
sings, a thrill of self-preservation . . .
and she springs toward her den
every hair on her pelt alive
with tidings of the immaculate present . . .
She has no archives,
no heirlooms, no future
except death
and I could be more
her sister than theirs
who chopped their way across these hills
—a chosen people.

This vixen ("wise-looking in a sexy way," in Rich's unfortunate description) has none of the vitality of torn-down Cambridge, and so is allegorical rather than convincingly metaphorical, but this rather weak poem makes the clear point of the book; jettison the past, live in sex and the present, forget the mind, tradition, and sublimation. "All our high-toned questions / breed in a lively animal" Rich had said in "Two Songs," and now the animal is trying to get rid of the questions; but of course they are bound to recur. That they recur in angry declarations (quoted at length by unsympathetic critics) rather than as questions does not make them any the less the old questions. And so I do not terribly mind if Rich writes, "I have learned to smell a *conservateur* a mile away: / they carry illustrated catalogues of all that there is to lose" (a couplet that enraged one reader), because all that these lines mean is that Rich is still bothered by tradition and its claims. How much more can we ask of a living poet than that he should be engaged with the old questions and new ones? Must we always approve his answers if we are to admire his work?

The Will To Change (1971) takes too much credit to itself in its title. Change is our lot whether we will it or not, and though we like to think we have willed what has happened, a sterner eye might see us as motes blown by the zeitgeist. In fact, Rich does see the roots of mystery in human states. In an anti-Wordsworthian version of a Wordsworthian thought ("O mystery of man, from what a depth / Proceed thy honors!") she sees the "depth" as the Freudian upstream of a river. Addressing someone else, she writes unsparingly of his present state, reserving condemnation by the imputation of mysterious damage done long ago. The slow, accretive metaphors describing the river in the poem "Study of History" mirror ecological despair and are a harrowing picture of a mind so silted over and trampled upon that it can barely make its clouded way through the narrows of present experience:

> Out there.   The mind of the river
> as it might be you.
>
> Lights   blotted by unseen hulls
> repetitive shapes passing
> dull foam crusting the margin
> barges sunk below the water-line with silence.
> The scow, drudging on.
>
> Lying in the dark, to think of you
> and your harsh traffic
> gulls pecking your rubbish   natural historians
> mourning your lost purity
> pleasure cruisers
> witlessly careening you

(I pause only to say that Rich's "music," so praised by her earlier reviewers and so ignored by many of her later ones, reaches its height of accomplishment in lines like these, as "hulls," "dull," "crust," "sunk," and "drudge" play one note, while "margin" and "barges" play another, both soon to be reinforced by "gulls" and 'rubbish" for the first, and "dark" and "harsh" for the second. The unobtrusiveness of these choices, choices perceived as such only when we ask why the lines adhere so to each other, is worth all the prettiness sacrificed in favor of their reticence.)

After the description of the river comes the Freudian exculpation:

> but this
> after all
> is the narrows and after
> all we have never entirely
> known what was done to you upstream
> what powers trepanned
> which of your channels diverted
> what rockface leaned to stare
> in your upturned
> defenseless
> face.

The ending may be sentimental, but the river and the mind to which it corresponds are heavy with truth. But *The Will To Change* as a volume is tortured by its own frequent disbelief in language. In "Snow" Rich asks herself:

> was it a whole day or just a lifetime
> spent studying crystals
>
> on the fire escape while the 'Sixties
> were running out

As the snow crystals melt, as every unique "star [becomes] a tear," Rich asks about the adequacy of a common language:

> if no two are alike
> than what are we doing
> with these diagrams of loss

The impotence of language forces recurring descriptions of itself:

> this name traced on a window
>
> this word I paste together
> like a child fumbling
>
> with paste and scissors
> this writing in the sky with smoke
>
> this silence
>
> this lettering chalked on the ruins
> this alphabet of the dumb
>
> this feather held to lips
> that still breathe and are warm

In search of a new style Rich refuses the old structural model of problem-and-resolution and lets all the crystals turn to tears:

> the mind of the poet is changing
>
> the moment of change is the only poem

The refusal of articulation is most complete at the beginning of "Shooting Script," the remarkable fifteen-page poem closing *The Will to Change*. I am not certain that "Shooting Script" is one poem, beginning as it does with fragmented single images, continuing with a translation of the Persian poet Ghalib, and going on to entire poems recognizably Rich-like. Composed from November of 1969 through July of 1970, "Shooting Script," for all its awkwardness, still seems to mark a conclusive new beginning, as the first poem in which Rich is willing—in fact is compelled as by a vow—to let her descriptions float entirely free, uncoerced by any will to make things neat and orderly, whether for herself or for her readers. It is ironic that a volume labeled *The Will To Change* should abandon the will to shape, but Rich's new poetic—the faithful transcription of what the new generation calls "vibes," without faking them together into premature sense—is announced in the third poem of the volume, "Planetarium":

> I am bombarded yet   I stand
> I have been standing all my life in the
> direct path of a battery of signals
> the most accurately transmitted most
> untranslateable language in the universe . . .
>   I am an instrument in the shape
> Of a woman trying to translate pulsations
> into images   for the relief of the body
> and the reconstruction of the mind.

In "Shooting Script," composed in "midwinter and the loss of love," those pulsations are allowed to occur, or rather to resurface from the past, like potsherds from a dig. The painful task of "reconstruction of the mind" forbids any convenient alterations which might force the shards to fit together; the heap of broken fragments must instead be patiently accumulated, patiently sorted and recorded; only at night can one allow a dream of a primitive wholeness, the wholeness of a more direct and primitive sort of people, those who originally made the pots. The poem using the metaphor (number 5 of "Shooting Script") tells us once more of the post-Wordsworthian experience of the civilized man meeting the solitary reaper: "Will no one tell me what she sings?" But the immediacy of the song, of the potter's wheel, is hidden from the poet, who can only "dream of the unformed, the veil of water passing over the wet clay, the rhythms of choice, the lost methods." Rich has abandoned the sentimental fantasy of being a purely animal vixen, but she still wishes for a hypothesized primitive physical human self, like the villagers whose ancestors made the pots:

> Of simple choice they are the villagers; their clothes come
> with them like red clay roads they have been walking.
>
> The sole of the foot is a map, the palm of the hand a letter,
> learned by heart and worn close to the body.

In the new primitivism the poet must abandon her magic lantern and give up "the temptations of the projector": but in fact the projector itself had come to grief, refusing to move on to the next slide, projecting one image "over & over on empty walls." One must "see instead the web of cracks filtering across the plaster":

> To read there the map of the future, the roads radiating
> from the initial split, the filaments thrown out from
> that impasse.
> To reread the instruction on your palm; to find there how
> the lifeline, broken, keeps its direction.
> To read the etched rays of the bullet-hole left years ago
> in the glass, to know in every distortion of the light
> what fracture is.

Giving up the prism, the lens, the map, and pulling herself up by her own roots, Rich, as *The Will To Change* closes, eats the last meal in her own neighborhood and prepares, deprived of all instruments, to move on, guided only by the fortuitous cracks in the plaster, the innate lifeline, the traumatic rays of the bullet-hole. She could hardly have been more frank; from formalism to—not freedom, but, as always—a new version of truth. If this is a revolution, it is one bound like Ixion on the wheel of the past—environmental past in the plaster, genetic past in the lifeline, traumatic past in the bullet-hole. And if it is revolution, it is one which does not wish to deny the reality of past choices and past modes of life. Putting off in her boat, Rich watches "the lights on the shore I had left for a long time; each one, it seemed to me, was a light I might have lit, in the old days." Houselights and hearthfires, abandoned, remembered, light the departure.

And so, in *Diving into the Wreck*, the old questions are still mining like moles underneath: tradition, civilization, the mind and the body, woman, man, love, writing—and the war added as a metaphor, so far as I can see, for illustration of the war between the sexes rather than for especially political commentary. In the most meditative and searching poem (besides the title poem) in *Diving into the Wreck*, Rich forsakes distinctions between men and women, for the most part, and sees us all as crippled creatures, scarred by that process of socialization and nurture which had been, when she began writing, her possession, her treasure; tapestries, Europe, recorders, Bach —the whole edifice of civilization, of which she now sees the dark side—war, exploitation, and deadening of instinct. The fable of

civilization and its discontents is drawn from the account of the taming of a savage child told in *The Wild Boy of Aveyron* by J-M Itard.
The poem begins in a reminiscence of "The Middle-Aged"—"They
were so kind; / Would have given us anything":

> In their own way, by their own lights
> they tried to care for you
> tried to teach you to care
> for objects of their caring.

The seductive interchange by which parents barter "care for you"
in exchange for your "caring" for "objects of their caring" is glossed
by Rich's pun. Other details from "The Middle-Aged" (and other
poems) seem to haunt this beginning, as we see the list of things
the parent-figures, who captured the wild child, want to make him
care for: the "polished balustrade" of the earlier poem becomes
"glossed oak planks"; the "letters locked in a drawer and the key
destroyed" become "locks, keys / boxes with coins inside"; the "dead
glass-blowers" whose precious works the uncle in the drawing room
still protected reappear in "glass / whirled in a fire / to impossible
thinness": but the deepest slight to civilization comes in the vision
of a book seen through savage eyes:

> they tried to make you feel
> the importance of
>
>> a piece of cowhide
>> sewn around a bundle
>> of leaves impressed with signs
>
> to teach you language:
> the thread their lives
> were strung on

The repudiation of the pattern of parental lives leads to the repudiation of books, their life-thread. And yet, this poem uses the medium
it distrusts, attempting to

> Go back so far there is another language
> go back far enough the language
> is no longer personal

The possibility is enough to justify the attempt, and it is an attempt not half so strange as it has been made, by some critics, to ap-

pear: what else have artists attempted to find in returning to motifs drawn from tribal painting and sculpture but some level at which language is no longer personal? Rich's myth is now the primitive— therefore her notions of trips in solitary kayak-like skiffs, of caverns, of the primeval forest, of indigenous villagers. The long exposure of most women to the more primitive experiences still remaining in civilized life—menstruation, intercourse, pregnancy, miscarriage, childbirth, nursing, toilet training, and child-rearing—make any woman feel as if she has spent ten or fifteen years in a Cro-Magnon cave. It is natural to ask what the irremediable substructure of life is, and what is overlaid upon it: not a new question, but a perennial one in any attempt to get at the truth of human relations.

The wild child was discovered with many scars, bearing witness, as Itard writes, "against the feebleness and insufficiency of man when left entirely to himself, and in favor of the resources of nature which . . . work openly to repair and conserve that which she tends secretly to impair and destroy." Rich writes another of her cavern poems on Itard's hint, entering "that part of the brain / which is pure survival":

> The most primitive part
> I go back into at night
> pushing the leathern curtain
> with naked fingers
> then
> with naked body
>
> There where every wound is registered
> as scar tissue
>
> A cave of scars!
> ancient, archaic wallpaper
> built up, layer on layer
> from the earliest, dream-white
> to yesterday's, a red-black scrawl
> a red mouth slowly closing . . .
>
> these scars bear witness
> but whether to repair
> or to destruction
> I no longer know

It is not suprising that the poem, although some later tidying up is done, can get no further in insight than this. Since the efficient moral is, or ought to be, in Itard's view, better care of the child, "the attention of scientists, the solicitude of administrators, and the protection of the government," Rich is surely within her rights to flash on her screen of language a question from Vietnam (from a war waged by scientists, administrators, and the government):

> is the child with arms
> burnt to the flesh of its sides
> weeping eyelessly for man

Diving into the Wreck ends asking:

> why do the administrators
>
> lack solicitude, the government
> refuse protection,
>
> why should the wild child
> weep for the scientists
>
> why

Though the official reproof from the poet is directed against those faceless bureaucracies, the primary offenders are still the parents— those first administrators and original governors, who inflict, by their scientific "teaching the child to care for what they care for," a conditioning regardless of individual needs, and inflict thereby those first scars which determine in large part the rest. The forcefulness of *Diving into the Wreck* comes from the wish not to huddle wounded, but to explore the caverns, the scars, the depths of the wreckage. At first these explorations must reactivate all the old wounds, inflame all the scar tissue, awaken all the suppressed anger, and inactivate the old language invented for dealing with the older self. But I find no betrayal of continuity in these later books, only courage in the refusal to write in forms felt to be outgrown. I hope that the curve into more complex expression visible in her earlier books will recur as Rich continues to publish, and that these dispatches from the battlefield will be assimilated into a more complete poetry. Given Rich's precocious and sustained gifts, I see no reason to doubt her future. The title poem that closed *The Diamond Cutters* says that the poetic supply is endless: after one diamond has been cut, "Africa / Will yield you more to do." When new books follow, these most recent poems will, I think, be seen as the transition to a new generosity and a new self-forgetfulness.

Of Woman Born:
Motherhood as Experience and Institution

> I told myself that I wanted to write a book on motherhood because it was a crucial, still relatively unexplored, area for feminist theory. But I did not choose this subject; it had long ago chosen me.

These mixed motives—to enlarge "feminist theory" and to express a personal experience of a fateful kind—account for the title of Adrienne Rich's book. Motherhood as experience appears in autobiographical episodes interspersed through much longer reflections attempting to analyze motherhood as a social institution. It is impossible to discuss either the autobiography or the analysis without raising the problem of partisan writing.

The autobiography is retold by a convinced feminist, reinterpreting her past in the light of her present convictions. All autobiographies construct a myth of explanation; some are more complex than others; some authors are conscious of the limitations of their myths (as Yeats was in discussing his "masks"). Though Rich is conscious that she has not always interpreted her life as she now does, her present myth is not offered as provisional; instead, the current interpretation of events of the past forty years, from childhood to liberation, is offered as the definitive one. The gist of it runs as follows:

> I don't remember when it was that my mother's feminine sensuousness, the reality of her body, began to give way for me to the charisma of my father's assertive mind and temperament; perhaps when my sister was just born, and he began teaching me to read.

> This "perfect" daughter [herself], though gratifyingly precocious, had early been given to tics and tantrums, had become permanently lame from arthritis at twenty-two; she had finally resisted her father's Victorian paternalism, his seductive charm and controlling cruelty, had married a divorced graduate student, had begun to write "modern," "obscure," "pessimistic" poetry, lacking the fluent sweetness of Tennyson, had had the final

This review of *Of Woman Born: Motherhood as Experience and Institution* by Adrienne Rich appeared in the *New York Review of Books*, September 30, 1976.

temerity to get pregnant and bring a living baby into the world. She had ceased to be the demure and precocious child or the poetic, seducible adolescent. Something, in my father's view, had gone terribly wrong.

It is not surprising that a woman who, at this stage in her life, represents her father as seducer, cruel controller, intellectual critic of her first poetic attempts, and angered despot, should find herself protesting the control that a society which she regards as male-dominated, and therefore cruel, exerts over women. It is not suggested in these pages that a woman with a different sort of upbringing—or a woman with the same upbringing who interpreted it differently—might have arrived at different political or cultural feelings.

The autobiography, though sketchy and scanty because of its subordinate (though controlling) position in the book, continues. Rich had three sons, and was anesthetized for all three hospital deliveries; after the third birth she had a tubal ligation. For many years she was a "full-time mother"; she ended the marriage; her husband committed suicide; her children are now grown. Since her undergraduate years she has published poetry; during the years when she had small children, she experienced as "primal agony" the conflict between the constant care of children and the attempt to create an individual self. The autobiographical construct ends with a new sexual orientation and a new reconciliation with the mother: "For those of us who had children, and later came to recognize and act upon the breadth and depth of our feelings for women, a complex new bond with our mothers is possible."

Rich interprets history as a phylogenetic analogue to her own ontogenetic myth. Once there were "prepatriarchal" periods of human culture which "shared certain kinds of woman-centered beliefs and woman-centered social organization." (By these terms Rich does not mean either "matriarchy" or "gynecocracy," those two unsubstantiated institutions; instead she means matrilocal social organization—in which the husband enters the woman's family, and the woman, in marrying, does not lose her mother, sisters, and female relatives—and, more dubiously, goddess-worship.) In "prepatriarchal" times, while men hunted, "women became the civilizers, the inventors of agriculture, of community, some maintain of language itself." Then, in the feminist version of the Fall, society extirpated the worship of the Mother-Goddess in her various forms, instituted monotheism, and devised the patriarchal family "with its super-naturalizing of the penis, its division of labor by gender, its emotional, physical, and material possessiveness, its ideal of monogamous marriage until death, . . . the obedience of women and children to male authority, the imprinting and continuation of heterosexual roles." To the patriarchal system, represented by "rapism and the warrior mentality," "the death-culture of quantification, abstractions, and the will-to-power," Rich opposes the "maternal" or "nurturant" spirit, now oppressed and confined in institutionalized motherhood.

Both of these myths—the personal narrative and the historical reconstruction—refuse full existential reality to men. The Svengali-father is matched by the warrior-rapist-abstract-power-hungry generations of patriarchal males. It is disheartening to see any of our ruling ideologies ("those lower forms of religious instinct," as Octavio Paz calls them) able to seduce a poetic mind, able to make a poet choose (in Paz's terms) "the rhetoric of violence." In Rich, the rhetoric of violence is accompanied by a rhetoric of sentimentality, as though, in having chosen to ally herself with a female principle in opposition to a putative male one, she has adopted a language of un-critical deliquescence:

> There was, is, in most of us, a girl-child still longing for a woman's nurture, tenderness, and approval, a woman's power exerted in our defense, a woman's smell and touch and voice, a woman's strong arms around us in moments of fear and pain.

There is, of course, no such thing as a sentimental emotion; emotions are felt or not felt, and that is all. It is the language of expression which is or is not sentimental. To find language better than that of greeting-card verse to express the sentiments of love is the poet's task: the rest of us are not equal to it. In lapsing so often into cliché in this volume, Rich has failed her own feelings.

And yet, for all the impatience it provokes, the book has a certain cumulative force, not so much on account of its theorizing as because of its undeniable feelings and its unarguable social facts. Some of these are frequent in feminist publications (the fact, whatever its origin, of male control of women's reproductive choices; male definition of women in art, theology, education, and so on); others, mostly dealing with motherhood, are less familiar. As Rich remarks, there is remarkably little written at all about motherhood. Most of what exists, in documentary and in narrative, has been written by male doctors, psychologists, sociologists, or anthropologists. The scanty testimony of females is still being unearthed. A few contemporary accounts have recently appeared. The reason for the dearth of information and analysis, of course, is that motherhood is profoundly uninteresting to men. They have no expectation of engaging in it, their fellow males have not experienced it, it is not a subject of male conversation, nor an object of male achievement. Men do not read books on motherhood. They will not read this one.

This is a great pity. The corresponding ignorance in women occurs, I suppose, in relation to war: but women do not live in close proximity to barracks, while men do live in the houses where motherhood is experienced. Only in certain stereotyped ways (such as pain or death in childbirth, or the attraction felt toward a daughter) has the experience of motherhood or parenthood engaged the male imagination. Oddly enough, Rich did not, at least when she was a young mother, see her children as a subject which could engage the female imagination:

> Once in a while someone used to ask me, "Don't you ever write poems about your children?" The male poets of my generation did write poems about their children—especially their daughters. For me, poetry was where I lived as no-one's mother, where I existed as myself.

This remark is one of many, scattered throughout the book, which are arresting and provoking. Is solitude so conceived—"When I write, I am a self which is no-one's mother"—even possible after childbearing? Is it a delusion that writing mothers practice on themselves, a perpetuation of a fantasy of intact girlhood? Rich does not say, "Poetry was where I lived as no-one's daughter, as no-one's wife." Is there something about the relation with children, in contrast to relations with adults, which makes it unavailable to the writer? Is it simply that one can separate oneself from other adults, but not from children?

Rich's vocabulary of selfhood is troubling in its assumptions: "Institutionalized motherhood demands of women maternal 'instinct' rather than intelligence, selflessness rather than self-realization, relation to others rather than the creation of self." Rich is here speaking of the ideals held up to mothers by society, and her disjunctions imply that she endorses her set of opposing terms—intelligence, self-realization, the creation of self. But how is the self realized and created except by relations to others; and why is a "selfless" realization not so self-actualizing as a "selfish" one? Even the notion of "selflessness" is, as we know, a suspect one. The relation of altruism to self-interest, the relation of "instinct" to "intelligence," are questions begged in such quick summaries. Elsewhere, Rich endorses a concept of "intelligence" which would include something she calls, rather melodramatically, "thinking through the body": "There is an inexorable connection between every aspect of a woman's being and every other; the scholar reading denies at her peril the blood on the tampon." Rich's concept—that an inclusive consciousness is to be preferred to a disembodied or repressed one—is one endorsed in every century anew, and found too painful by most inhabitants of every century except for the greatest artists. But Rich's language ignores the honorable history of this idea, and espouses inclusiveness as a "new form of thinking" to be practiced by women, who will thereby free themselves from the death-culture of abstraction and quantification. Why not tell women to imitate Keats or Shakespeare? There are models for such "thinking through the body"; that they are men does not vitiate their usefulness.

The things to remember, against all this rhetoric, are the other, undeniable sentences. Of motherhood, says Rich, "I could remember little except anxiety, physical weariness, anger, self-blame, boredom, and division within myself: a division made more acute by the moments of passionate love." It is useful to have it said forcefully that the *institution* of motherhood (the nuclear family, the mother's exclusive responsibility for the children) is not identical with bearing and caring for children. It is a plain fact about mothers that "our wildcat strikes have most often taken the form of physical or mental breakdown." It is a truth ignored by child-rearing manuals that "motherhood without autonomy, without choice, is one of the quickest roads to a sense of having lost control": "Some women express this by furiously and incessantly cleaning house, which they know will be immediately disorganized by small children; others, by letting the house go utterly to pieces since any kind of order seems hopeless." More sinister, though quieter, are the deeper disorders of the psyche: "the woman who serves her family their food but cannot sit down with them, the woman who cannot get out of bed in the morning, the woman polishing the same place on the table over and over."

Rich avoids a confrontation with the differences, even in modern

America, between ethnic and economic groups in their perception of the difficulties and satisfactions of motherhood, differences mentioned by Jessie Bernard and Mirra Komarovsky. In criticizing, implicitly or explicity, women who do not share her views—who would prefer anesthetized childbirth in hospitals, who are phlegmatic enough to enjoy routine, who are socially timid and prefer the company of children to the stress of being with other adults, who do not perceive men as exemplars of rapism and the warrior mentality—Rich seems to attribute stupidity, bad faith, or self-delusion to all women not yet radical. There are no doubt real elements of historical and social evil which contribute to the oppression of women. Selfish or unprincipled doctors, puritanical clergy, prejudiced professionals, vanishing fathers, brutal husbands are all real agents of the suffering of women. On the other hand, the puritanical regrouping of women without men, the new theology of male evil, the prejudices of radical feminism, the rewriting of history do not offer a solution to the problems they confront.

Too often the argument here collects only the evidence which seems attractive. The wish is the father to the deed. Of all the anthropological "evidence" randomly assembled, the single worst item, to my mind, came in Rich's discussion of puberty rites. "In becoming a man," she says, "it is necessary to expunge all susceptibility to the power of women." A quotation follows:

> The youths of the East African tribe of the Kikuyu fear that the first sexual intercourse after initiation will be fatal. For this reason, bands of fifteen or twenty newly initiated youths range the country together, fall upon some old woman, rape her and then put her to death with stones. According to Reik, this old woman is a symbol of the mother.

A horrifying story. An old woman raped by "fifteen or twenty youths" and then stoned to death. Rich's footnote directs the reader to *Dark Legend: A Study in Murder* (1941), by Frederick Wertham. Now Frederick Wertham is no authority on anything. His source is Reik's *Ritual* (1931). Reik reads:

> Chazac reports of the Kikuyu of West Africa that they believe that the first coitus which the newly circumcised youths perform leads to their death or that of their partner . . . [Therefore], fifteen or twenty men collect together, seize some old women in a lonely spot, misuse them sexually, and then kill them.

The Kikuyu have been translated to West Africa, and the old woman is now "some old women," and the means of killing is indefinite. Reik gives as *his* source a 1910 article by the aforesaid "Chazac." Though the reference is incorrect (the 1910 volume of *Anthropos* is not ii, as the English version of *Ritual* says, but v, and the author's name is Cayzac, not Chazac), the essay can be found. "Chazac" turns out to be a missionary of the Congregation of the Holy Spirit, writing on the religion of the Kikuyu (who are retranslated to East Africa). Father Cayzac identifies himself as one of the "chercheurs d'évolution morale et religieuse": this places him as one of those early colonizers who justified colonial rule by announcing that it improved the savages. The savages had therefore to be described as savage, at least before the advent of Christianity and benevolent European rule.

Yet the Kikuyu seem relatively harmless in all that Cayzac can relate of them from his own experience. However, what of long ago before the present vigilant government arrived? "Il existait naguère," he says earnestly, "une coutume barbare, qui disparaît depuis l'arrivée d'un gouvernement vigilant":

> Or donc, voici ce qu'on a pensé: La première fois qu'un nouveau circoncis aura des rapports avec une femme, ce sera la mort de l'un ou de l'autre . . . Réunis en une bande de quinze ou vingt, les nouveaux circoncis surprennent quelque vieille femme en un lieu écarté, abusent d'elle, et l'assomment ensuite à coup de pierre! . . . Les jeunes circoncises, pour la même raison, sont sauvées de la mort par un petit incirconcis, mais lui n'est pas immolé, n'étant pas censé un être humain.
>
> (There existed hitherto a barbarous custom, which disappeared after the arrival of a vigilant government. Now here is what people thought: the first time that a newly circumcised man had sexual relations with a woman, it would be the death of one or the other of them . . . Joined in a band of fifteen or twenty, the newly circumcised men surprise an old woman in a remote spot, abuse her sexually, and then kill her with a blow from a stone! . . . The young circumcised women, by the same token, are saved from death by a little uncircumcised boy, but he is not killed, since he is not considered to be a human being.)

The total absence of any authority for this story, and the suppression, in all of the quoted accounts, of the rape of a young uncircumcised man by the recently circumcised women, give proof of the game of rumor appearing as anthropological "evidence." The selectivity of quotation throughout is a fault common to all ideologically motivated writing. It will be said that all writing is ideologically motivated. To that remark there is no response.

Rich says of *The First Sex* by Elizabeth Gould Davis that though it is "at times inaccurate, biased, unprofessional—all these charges do not really dismiss it . . . [Davis tries] to prime the imagination of women living today to conceive of other modes of existence." The same might be said of Rich's own book. The value of it does not lie in its remarks about women's historical role or their function in religious cults of antiquity, where better authorities (like Sarah Pomeroy's recent book, *Goddesses, Whores, Wives, and Slaves*) can be found.

Its value lies in reminding us that different conceptions of motherhood are possible; that motherhood is not necessarily congenial in the same way to every woman; that the "failures" of mothers in past generations were often socially caused; that infanticide and abortion are first of all crimes that society has induced women to perform against their own sentiments; that every mother, before she was a mother, was a woman with a body and a mind of her own; that motherhood is only "one part of female process . . . not an identity for all time"; that "motherhood has a history, it has an ideology"; that, in 1973, more than six million children under the age of six in the United States had mothers who worked fulltime outside the home; that men excluded women from medicine; that "an indifference and fatalism toward the diseases of women . . . persists to this day in the male gynecological and surgical professions"; that birth itself "is neither a disease nor a surgical operation"; that a woman should be able to choose her own style of giving birth; that men may for a long time, as the roles of parenthood change, "need a kind of compensatory education in the things about which their education as males has left them illiterate"; that "the cathexis between mother and daughter is the great unwritten story." But it would have been preferable if the whole book had been as cogent as these remarks. Freud, according to Rich, was "terribly limited both by his culture and his gender." What Rich finds true of Freud is of course true of herself.

Sylvia Plath

Although this book is by no means Sylvia Plath's best, it represents a chapter of her poetic life. In these poems, written between 1960 and late 1961 and antedating *Ariel*, the poet plays Pygmalion to her own Galatea, willing herself into shape, struggling against the inherited outlines of her predecessors. There are very grotesque stages along the way, as in some larval metamorphosis: the roaring-ram disguise of Dylan Thomas; babbling exclamatory whispers-in-the-potting-shed after the manner of Theodore Roethke; duets between heaven and earth in Stevensian orchestration; and many plaintive familial brutalities learned from Lowell. What exhausting costumes these were, and how heavy, and how distasteful to Sylvia Plath's soul we can only judge from her persistent attempts to shed these skins, and finally, in *Ariel* and some later poems, to transcend them. Meanwhile, she rages about in these disguises like some rebellious adolescent dressed in unsuitable clothes.

There were problems in Sylvia Plath's life deeper than the problem of poetic inheritance, more fundamental exhaustions than these tireless searches for the right wedding garment. Some critics have invoked the word "schizophrenia" in talking about these poems, but Plath's sense of being several people at once never here goes beyond what everyone must at some time feel.

There are three selves present, for instance, in "Two Sisters of Persephone": Persephone, herself, has already chosen the realm of death with Pluto; the second sister has chosen a work of bone-dry intellect, where her squint eyes go rat-shrewd and her meager frame goes root-pale; the third sister has chosen to be the bride of the sun, and lies "bronzed as earth . . . lulled near a bed of poppies," where she "bears a king." Though the preference among these selves

This review of Sylvia Plath's *Crossing the Water: Transitional Poems* appeared in the *New York Times Book Review*, October 10, 1971.

might seem made distressingly naive by the serene picture of the third sister, the poem ends not with the bride but with the intellectual one "turned bitter / And sallow as any lemon . . . wry virgin to the last." The bride remains a daydream of romance. Persephone herself, except in the title of the poem, is never mentioned at all, and yet it is she who creates the powerful undertow which drowns, finally, the other two selves.

There are poems in this volume written, one might say, by each of the three sisters. Persephone's are the best. Nevertheless, the bride-turned-wry-virgin has some triumphant lines, dismissing her husband, her marriage, and even, finally, herself:

> He was bullman earlier,
> King of the dish, my lucky animal . . .
> He kept blowing me kisses.
> I hardly knew him.
>
> He won't be got rid of:
> Mumblepaws, teary and sorry,
> Fido Littlesoul . . .
>
> Mud-sump, happy sty-face.
> I've married a cupboard of rubbish . . .
> Hogwallow's at the window.
> The star bugs won't save me this month.
> I housekeep in Time's gut-end
> Among emmets and mollusks,
> Duchess of Nothing,
> Hairtusk's bride.

In another poem of split selves, a total neutrality or willed absence of affect creates a self of plaster, agreeable to the outside world which rewards plaster saints, but horrifying to the authentic self:

> I shall never get out of this! There are two of me now:
> This new absolutely white person and the old yellow one,
> And the white person is certainly the superior one.
> She doesn't need food, she is one of the real saints.

At first the symbiosis seems possible, but eventually the plaster saint becomes more and more impatient with the slovenly and unmanageable "real" self, and, helpless though the imprisoned soul may be, she begins to plan her revenge:

Now I see it must be one or the other of us.
She may be a saint, and I may be ugly and hairy,
But she'll soon find out that doesn't matter a bit.
I'm collecting my strength.

Though a poem like this seems a textbook illustration of R. D. Laing crossed with Women's Lib, it fails to authenticate Laing, consciousness-raising, or itself. To find the genuine Plath, it is not enough to say that she is the ugly and hairy id repressed by the saintlike superego. On the contrary, she is not at all exclusively a libido in search of liberation. Her rage, though it may come from the most primitive levels, is not primitive in its most natural utterance: an undeniable intellect allegorizes the issues before they are allowed expression. Even in the famous "Daddy," the elaborate scheme of Prussian-and-Jew has been constructed to contain the feelings of victimization, and the decade-by-decade deaths in "Lady Lazarus" are as neat a form of incremental repetition as any metaphysical poet could have wanted.

In some way Sylvia Plath sensed that her sensual or appetitive impulses were not the single-minded component she would have liked them to be. And yet, in her wish to be physical and uncomplicated, she wrote poems pretending a buoyant sense of physicality, playing herself false in them, as in this poem about pregnancy:

I'm a riddle in nine syllables,
An elephant, a ponderous house,
A melon strolling on two tendrils.
O red fruit, ivory, fine timbers!
This loaf's big with its yeasty rising.
Money's new-minted in this fat purse.
I'm a means, a stage, a cow in calf.
I've eaten a bag of green apples,
Boarded the train there's no getting off.

Only the last line is grim enough to wake a reader's response. The rest is pure silliness. Still, in sympathy one wants to say that the aridity of the intellect in dealing with life, and its pure insufficiency to metabolic processes, is enough to send anyone round the bend in this particular fashion, to turn a woman into a talking melon.

Plath would like, in distrust of mind, to trust nature, and yet she ends, in the volume, by refusing nature any honorable estate of its own. "The horizons ring me," she says in the opening words of this volume, and this awful centripetal sense binds nature into a compass much smaller than it deserves. The poet's eye bounds the limits of the world, and all of nature exists only as a vehicle for her sensibility. The wind stops her breath "like a bandage"; the sky exists as her "ceiling" with an "old star-map" on it; the night sky is "only a sort of carbon paper" poked through with holes; the new moon looks like "the skin seaming a scar." Some such scrim-curtain of pain veils all images of the natural world in reductive metaphors, till we ask whether there ever was, in Sylvia Plath at this time, a genuine sense of something existing that was not herself. (Later, her children became real other beings to her, if we can judge from the poems in *Ariel*.)

There are moments when the imposition of self on the world attains a beautiful if deceptive, coherence:

> Black lake, black boat, two black, cut-paper people . . .
> A snag is lifting a valedictory, pale hand;
> Stars open among the lilies.
> Are you not blinded by such expressionless sirens?
> This is the silence of astounded souls.

But on the other hand, nature undomesticated becomes purely soulless; in the Canadian wilderness, the rocks "offer no purchase to herbage or people." The withdrawal of affect annihilates not only nature, but people, who become, seen on their holidays, "grownups coffined in stockings and jackets, / Lard-pale." They exist only insofar as they are criticized; they exist only to be criticized. They are not allowed independence, they have no solidity, they are stick-figures to prove a point about how horrible Whitsun holidays are.

Too often in this volume a metaphor is chosen and used without any full sense of its own unalterable solidity apart from the poet's use of it. It is understandable that a writer, surveying her less successful poems, should think "It is as though they are my stillborn children." But then, as she takes up the metaphor of the mother of the stillborn, she invests the poem with a kind of ghastly friskiness that is not in any way what a real mother of the stillborn would say about her children, leaving us to wonder why Plath invoked the parallel in the first place:

> These poems do not live: it's a sad diagnosis . . .
>
> O I cannot understand what happened to them!
> They are proper in shape and number and every part.

They sit so nicely in the pickling fluid!
They smile and smile and smile and smile at me . . .

They are not pigs, they are not even fish,
Though they have a piggy and a fishy air—
It would be better if they were alive, and that's what they were.

Pigs and fishes, alive or not, are not what the mother of a dead child wishes her child were. This falseness to the wellsprings of life from which metaphors are drawn, though it can serve certain sur- realistic purposes, palls in the long run and endangers several poems in this book. Thus, a woman who has had a face-lift thinks of her operation as a successful suicide-and-resurrection, and says of her old self:

They've trapped her in some laboratory jar.
Let her die there, or wither incessantly for the next fifty years . . .
Mother to myself, I wake swaddled in gauze,
Pink and smooth as a baby.

This, we can say with hindsight, is less the poem of a woman hav- ing a face-lift than the poem of a woman fantasizing a harmless form of suicide. Metaphor here acts to conceal rather than to clarify.

Sylvia Plath's ruthlessness toward her own work is clear in her relentless advance, in *Ariel* and other posthumously published poems, toward a purer selfhood. To criticize the poems in *Crossing the Water* is to share in her own evident self-criticism of them: she went on to do better. But even here there are some poems which justify themselves without apology, and the fact that they are among the most clinical and harsh shows the direction, never fully traveled, in which her verse was going. Some of these poems are sensational and primitive, like the one in which a surgeon describes his work:

It is a garden I have to do with—tubers and fruits
Oozing their jammy substances,
A mat of roots. My assistants hook them back.
Stenches and colors assail me . . .
I worm and hack in a purple wilderness.

But Plath's verse had another, less lurid, direction as well, appear- ing in the best poem of this collection, "Parliament Hill Fields." It is, so far as I can deduce, a poem spoken by a mother to her dead child, and she presents her feelings, both admirable and less admirable, in drained lines which aim at no self-display:

> The tumulus, even at noon, guards its black shadow:
> You know me, less constant,
> Ghost of a leaf, ghost of a bird.
> I circle the writhen trees. I am too happy.
> These faithful dark-boughed cypresses
>
> Brood, rooted in their heaped losses.
> Your cry fades like the cry of a gnat.
> I lose sight of you on your blind journey,
> While the heath grass glitters and the spindling rivulets
> Unspool and spend themselves. My mind runs with them,
>
> Pooling in heel-prints, fumbling pebble and stem.

It is a moment of admission equal to Emerson's on the death of his son: "This calamity . . . does not touch me; something which I fancied was a part of me, which could not be torn away without tearing me . . . , falls off from me and leaves no scar." "I suppose it's pointless to think of you at all," says Plath: "Already your doll grip lets go." These helpless lines of lack and silence remain to enrich this volume beyond glitter and flash, pointing to a depth opening toward *Ariel*.

Charles Wright

The Transcendent "I"

> I was born on the 25th of August in 1935 . . . in Hardin County,
> Tennessee, in a place called Pickwick Dam . . . My father worked
> for the TVA at the time as a civil engineer . . . In the tenth grade
> I was sent to a school that had eight students . . . My last two
> years of high school were at an Episcopal boarding school with
> the unlikely name of Christ School, in Arden, N.C.

This summary of the early career of the poet Charles Wright comes
from an interview during a visit to Oberlin, transcribed and published in *Field* (Fall 1977). Wright went on to Davidson College
("four years of amnesia, as much my fault as theirs"), then spent four
years in the Army (three of them in Italy) and two years at the
University of Iowa. As he said to his audience, this represents "pretty
much the biography of almost everyone here . . . We all went through
more or less the same things." The connections between that life
lived in Tennessee and North Carolina and the poems that have
issued from it—*The Grave of the Right Hand* (1970); *Hard Freight*
(1973); *Bloodlines* (1975); *China Trace* (1977)—are intermittently
evident, but the effort of the poetry is to render them tenuous, often
invisible. Because Wright's poems, on the whole, are unanchored to
incident, they resist description; because they are not narrative,
they defy exposition. They cluster, aggregate, radiate, add layers
like pearls. Often they stop in the middle, with a mixed yearning and
premonition, instead of taking a resolute direction backward or
forward. It may be from the Italian poet Eugenio Montale (1896–   )
that Wright learned this pause which looks before and after; Wright
recently issued his translation, done in the sixties, of Montale's

This essay first appeared in *The New Yorker*, October 29, 1979.

powerful 1956 volume entitled *La Bufera e altro (The Storm and Other Poems)*.

The translation offers an occasion for a glance at both Montale and Wright; the conjunction helps to define what sort of poet Wright has become. Montale wrote *La Bufera* during the postwar years, and his pauses in the midst of event come as often as not in the midst of nightmare: "The Prisoner's Dream" shows a speaker imprisoned in a time of political purges, tempted, like everyone else, to "give in and sign," but instead waiting out the interminable trial, addressing from prison his fixed point of reference—a dreamed-of woman who represents beauty, justice, truth:

> And the blows go on, over and over . . . and the footsteps;
> and still I don't know, when the banquet is finally served,
> if I shall be the eater or the eaten. The wait is long;
> my dream of you is not yet over.

This poetry, though it implies a better past and an uncertain future, incorporates them in the burning-glass of the present. It renounces, as forms of articulation, narrative, the succession of events, the sequence of action and reaction. The spatial form, one of many in Montale, is for Wright the most natural. It can be seen in "Spider Crystal Ascension," his poem about the rise of the Milky Way at night. The galaxy, full of energy, resembling a cosmic and eternal spider-web made of crystal, is watched, as death might be watched, by the temporary inhabitants of an earthly lake:

> The spider, juiced crystal and Milky Way, drifts on his
>   web through the night sky
> And looks down, waiting for us to ascend . . .
>
> At dawn he is still there, invisible, short of breath,
>   mending his net.
>
> All morning we look for the white face to rise from the
>   lake like a tiny star.
> And when it does, we lie back in our watery hair and rock.

The spider looks, we look, he drifts through the sky, we rock in the lake, his net is patient, we will be caught from our lake one day and ascend with him, he is crystal, we are flesh, he can electrocute, we are mortal, the end is foreseen but not yet accomplished. This arrested motion, this taking thought, though it is congenial to Wright, requires nevertheless certain sacrifices.

The first sacrifice is autobiography. The autobiographical sequence

"Tattoos," which appeared in *Bloodlines*, solved the problem of reference by appending, at the end of twenty poems, a single note on each one: a sample note reads "Automobile wreck; hospital; Baltimore, Maryland." Instead of a first-person narrative of the crash and its surgical aftermath, Wright produces a montage of sensations:

> So that was it, the rush and the take-off,
> The oily glide of the cells
> Bringing it up—ripsurge, refraction,
> The inner spin
> Trailing into the cracked lights of oblivion.

In *Bloodlines* these verses are encountered with no title, no explanation; the note is to be read later, and then the poem reread, from the crash to the hospital:

> Re-entry is something else, blank, hard:
> Black stretcher straps; the peck, peck
> And click of a scalpel; glass shards
> Eased one by one from the flesh;
> Recisions; the long bite of the veins.

It is easy to see how interminable, predictable, and boring a plain narrative might appear after this "jump-cut" (Wright's words) monitoring of sensation. The problem of affixing closure to sensation and perception (since of themselves they have no closure but unconsciousness) has bothered Wright a good deal. The automobile wreck finds closure in sententious question-and-answer, with echoes of Williams and Berryman:

> And what do we do with this,
> Rechuted, reworked into our same lives, no one
> To answer to, no one to glimpse and sing,
> The cracked light flashing our names?
> We stand fast, friend, we stand fast.

The danger of this three-stanza form, as Wright realized, is that it is unduly "comfortable":

> Three stanzas is good because you can present something in the first, work around with it a bit in the second and then release it, refute it, untie it, set fire to it, whatever you want to, in the third. And that's its main problem for me. I felt I'd explored enough of what could be done, so I changed it for the next [long] poem.

The words Wright uses for the functions of that third stanza are all in some way linear, logical, causal: the problem can be "released," "refuted," "untied," torched. In any case, the problem goes away. The premise is that of syllogism in the realm of mind, action in the realm of morals. The premise, by extension, implies a world of meaning ranging from solutions to revolutions. The interesting thing about Wright's development is that he found he could no longer work within such a frame.

His next experiment, in the second sequence in *Bloodlines* (a wonderful poem called "Skins"), was to abandon the three equal pieces—presentation, complication, and conclusion—of "Tattoos" for a set of seamless meditations, each fourteen lines long. Though these have of course affinities with sonnets, they are sonnets that go nowhere, or end where they began: either the second half of the poem repeats the first, or the last line reenters the universe where the first line left it. Even the poems which seem to evolve in a linear way show only a moment in a life-cycle itself endlessly repeated; they are therefore more fated than free, as in the case of the sixth and most beautiful meditation, about the metamorphosis of a mayfly:

Then

Emergence: leaf drift and detritus; skin split,
The image forced from the self.
And rests, wings drying, eyes compressed,
Legs compressed, constricted
Between the dun and the watershine—
Incipient spinner, set for the take-off . . .
And does, in clean tear: imago rising out of herself
For the last time, slate-winged and many-eyed.
And joins, and drops to her destiny,
Flesh to the surface, wings flush on the slate film.

This is almost too ravishing in sound and sight, in its mimetic instability between the grotesque and the exquisite, to be thought about. The mind of the reader is delayed by the felicities of the slate wings on the slate water-film, by the dun detritus of chrysalis played off against the watershine, by the flesh flush on the surface, by the conjugation of drift and force, compression and incipience, and by the brief cycle of wings drying, rising, dropping. This sensual music precludes thought, almost; but the subject of metamorphosis is so old and so noble, the flesh as chrysalis so perennial a metaphor, that the conceptual words—image, self, imago, destiny—work their own subsidiary charm in the long run. In spite of the ephemeral nature of the cycle, Wright rescues by his vocabulary a form of transcendence. ("The nitty-gritty of my wishes . . . would be to be saved, but there's no such thing.")

Wright has talked about the "sparring match I had for about ten years with the Episcopal Church, in which I was raised, in which I was tremendously involved for a short amount of time and from which I fled and out of which I remain. But it had a huge effect on me":

> It's a very strange thing about being raised in a religious atmosphere. It alters you completely, one way or the other. It's made me what I am and I think it's okay. I can argue against it, but it has given me a sense of spirituality which I prize.

There are other names for this "sense of spirituality": it might just as well be named a sense of euphony, a sense for the Platonic or the seraphic. It is no doubt what attracted Wright to Montale. Montale preserved an exacerbated but inflexibile fidelity to a principle itself exigent, even aggressive, in its purity and fierceness. This principle is figured in his absent "Clizia," named after the nymph who so loved the sun that she was metamorphosed into the sunflower forever faithful to radiance no matter how distant its path. Clizia burns through *The Storm* as a presence, even in absence, not to be put by, no less a Fury than an angel, sometimes rainbow, sometimes lightning-bolt, sometimes in tatters, sometimes in flames. The world is more often than not at odds with her: sometimes the ambience is vicious, sometimes simply obstructive. In "Hitler Spring," as Mussolini and Hitler appear together, Clizia must exist in the midst of "the sirens, the tolling bells / that call to the monsters in the twilight / of their Pandemonium." In "The Eel," Clizia is sister to those ambitious swimmers into unpromising landscapes:

> The eel, whiplash, twisting torch,
> love's arrow on earth, which only
> our gullies and dried-out, burned-out streams
> can lead to the paradises of fecundity;
> green spirit that hunts for life
> only there, where drought and desolation gnaw,
> a spark that says everything starts
> where everything is charred, stumps buried.

The eel's world, full of momentum, is the paradoxical one of inception in extinction. The mystery of such motion defies linearity, and consequently allies itself with those Christian paradoxes of the dying grain and the lost life saved, antithetical to the prudential and the providential alike, since foresight and backward glances have nothing to do with illumination, conversion, metamorphosis.

Wright's aim in translating Montale has been to be idiomatic, within his own idiom as well as within Montale's. Robert Lowell's "imitation" of "The Eel" is more fluent and more condensed:

> The eel, a whipstock, a Roman candle,
> love's arrow on earth, which only
> reaches the paradise of fecundity
> through our gullies and fiery, charred streams;
> a green spirit, potent only
> where desolation and arson burn;
> a spark that says everything
> begins where everything is clinker.

Wright attempts greater fidelity, at the cost of some loss of naturalness (and, I have been told, of accuracy). Surely both Lowell and Wright, with their Italianate "paradise of fecundity," are themselves bettered by John Frederick Nims, who substitutes "edens of fertility." Montale—compressed, allusive, oblique, full of echoing sound—is relatively untranslatable; his poems swell awkwardly as they take on English under anyone's hands, and his infinitely manipulable Italian syntax begins to hobble, hampered by stiff English clauses. Wright's translations, as he says, taught him things:

> I feel I did learn . . . how to move a line, how to move an image from one stage to the next. How to create imaginary bridges between images and stanzas and then to cross them, making them real, image to image, block to block.

These are not—though they may appear to be—idle concerns. If conclusions are not the way to get from A to B, if discursiveness itself is a false mode of consciousness, if free-association in a surrealist mode (to offer the opposite extreme) seems as irresponsible as the solemn demonstrations of the discursive, what form of presentation can recreate the iconic form of the mind's invention? It is really this question that Wright takes up in *China Trace* and subsequent poems. Chinese poetry, as it entered twentieth-century literature through Waley and Pound, came to stand for an alien but immensely attractive combination of sensation and ethics, both refined from crudeness by their mutual interpenetration. Suggestion and juxtaposition seemed adequate to replace statement, as Pound's petal-faces on the Métro-bough would claim. Wright's trace—*vestigium*—of China is in part a homage to Pound, but it also pursues, yet once more, the problem of the potential complacency of stanzas, especially of repeated stanzas. Who is to say that today's poem, like yesterday's, should have three stanzas? or one stanza of fourteen lines? And yet to insist that every form is a nonce form—good for only one use and then to be discarded—is to falsify what we know of recurrences and rhythms in the mind's life.

For *China Trace,* says Wright,

> I decided, rather arbitrarily, that no poem was going to be longer than twelve lines. In the first section I wanted to have an example of each length of poem from one to twelve lines but I *couldn't* write a four line poem. It was the hardest thing. They always came out sounding like a stanza that needed another stanza, or two more stanzas.

This probem is less superficial than it may seem. Aside from light verse, gnomes, or riddles, poems in English often have either two or three stanzas, chiefly because thought and feeling often proceed either by comparison or antithesis (resulting in two stanzas) or by statement, complication or amplification, and resolution (yielding three stanzas or divisions). Perception, unsupported by reflection, tends to seem truncated, unfinished, uncommented upon. That analytic restlessness which causes the second, and even the third, stanzas to be written is absent in the Chinese lyrics—compact, single, coherent—favored by Waley, and hovering over *China Trace.* But in spite of Wright's deliberate variety of form, a principle of repetition has its way in the design of the book: each of its halves is prefaced by the same citation from Calvino's *Invisible Cities,* envisaging the day when, knowing all the emblems, one becomes an emblem among emblems. This Yeatsian notion stands side by side with a Chinese epigraph, about the ambition "to travel in ether by becoming a void," or, failing that, to make use of a landscape to calm the spirit and delight the heart. In these epigraphs Wright reveals his own disembodied ethereality in coexistence with his pure visual sense.

The poems in *China Trace* are frosty, clear, descriptive, seemingly dispassionate, wintry even in spring. Even in April,

> [I] know I want less—
> Divested of everything,
> A downfall of light in the pine woods, motes in the rush,

Gold leaf through the undergrowth, and come back
As another name, water
Pooled in the black leaves and holding me there, to be
Released as a glint, as a flash, as a spark . . .

Throughout the volume Wright persistently imagines himself dead, dispersed, re-elemented into the natural order. ("And I am not talking about reincarnation at all. At all. At all.") In focusing on earth, in saying that "salvation doesn't exist except through the natural world," Wright approaches Cézanne's reverence for natural forms, geometrical and substantial ones alike. *China Trace* is meant to have "a journal-like, everyday quality," but its aphorisms resemble *pensées* more than diary jottings, just as its painters and poets (Morandi, Munch, Trakl, Nerval) represent the arrested, the composed, the final, rather than the provisional, the blurred, or the impressionistic. *China Trace* is in fact one long poem working its desolation by accretion; it suffers in excerpts. Its mourning echoes need to be heard like the complaint of doves—endless, reiterative, familiar, a twilight sound:

There is no light for us at the end of the light.
No one redeems the grass our shadows lie on.

Each night, in its handful of sleep, the mimosa blooms.
Each night the future forgives.
Inside us, albino roots are starting to take hold.

The entire life-cycle—light, dark, blooming, sleep, guilt, forgiveness, pallor, growth—takes place each night, and no phase is inextricable from its opposite. In a linear view, by inexorable necessity, the "first minute, after noon, is night" (Donne's version). Wright, in opposition, urges in "Noon" the extension of life, altered, into our perception of death:

Extension that one day will ease me on
In my slow rise through the dark toward the sweet wrists of the
rose.

The "me" here defined is a biological, not a spiritual, entity:

The dirt is a comforting, and the night drafts from the sucker
vines.
The grass is a warm thing, and the hollyhocks, and the bright
bursts from the weeds.

> But best of all is the noon, and its tiny horns,
> When shadows imprint, and start
> their gradual exhalation of the past.

Wright is not innocent of influence; one recognizes Whitman, Pound, and Stevens, as well as Berryman and Williams, among his predecessors. On the other hand, he is obsessed with sound rather more than they were. Sound adds to his poems that conclusiveness which logic and causality confer on the poetry of others: "Mostly I like the sound of words. The sound, the feel, the paint, the color of them. I like to hear what they can do with each other. I'm still trying to do whatever I can with sound." The tendency of sound to despotism does not go unrecognized. "Sometimes I think [Hopkins'] sound patterns are so strong that you miss what he is saying." Wright's poems would be endangered if they were constructed on a more casual base, but he seems to work with infrastructures which are powerfully organized; the one for "Skins," in all its twenty items, is spelled out in the interview in *Field*. These sub-scaffoldings may in the long run drop away, but they keep the poems from being at the mercy of whims of sound.

If *China Trace* can be criticized for an unrelenting elegiac fixity, nonetheless its consistency gives it incremental power. Its deliberateness, its care in motion, its slow placing of stone on stone, dictate our reading it as construction rather than as speech. It is not surprising that as a model Wright has chosen Cézanne, that most architectural of painters:

> I like layers of paint on the canvas. I also know after I'm tired of lots of layers on the canvas, I'm going to want just one layer of paint and some of the canvas showing through . . . I've been trying to write poems . . . the way a painter might paint a picture . . . using stanzas in the way a painter will build up blocks of color, each disparate and often discrete, to make an overall representation that, taken in its pieces and slashes and dabs seems to have no coherence, but seen in its totality, when it's finished, turns out to be a very recognizable landscape, or whatever. Cézanne is someone who does this, in his later work, to an almost magical perfection.

Wright's eight-poem sequence "Homage to Cézanne" builds up, line by line, a sense of the omnipresent dead. Wright's unit here is the line rather than the stanza, and the resulting poem sounds rather like the antiphonal chanting of psalms: one can imagine faint opposing choruses singing the melismatic lines:

> The dead fall around us like rain.
> They come down from the last clouds in the late light for the
>   last time
> And slip through the sod.
> They lean uphill and face north.
>   Like grass,
> They bend toward the sea, they break toward the setting sun.

Wright does this poetry of the declarative sentence very well, but many poets have learned this studied simplicity, even this poetry of the common noun. What is unusual in Wright is his oddity of imagery within the almost too-familiar conventions of quiet, depth, and profundity. As he layers on his elemental squares and blocks of color, the surprising shadow or interrupting boulder emerge as they might in a Cézanne:

> High in the night sky the mirror is hauled up and unsheeted.
> In it we twist like stars.

To Wright, death is as often ascent as burial; we become stars, like Romeo, after death, as often as roses. The modern unsheeted mirror reveals the Tennysonian twist of the constellations round the pole-star, in this Shakespearean image of the posthumous—or so we might say if we look at Wright for his inheritances as well as for his originality.

Wright claims, like all poets, a return to original nature: the refusal to particularize his individual existence implies his utterance of universal experience, predicable of everyone. Everyone's dead are ubiquitous: we all "sit out on the earth and stretch our limbs, / Hoarding the little mounds of sorrow laid up in our hearts." On the other hand, the oracular mode sacrifices the conversational, and Wright evanesces under the touch in his wish to be dead (or saved), to enlarge the one inch of snowy rectitude in his living heart into the infinite ice of the tomb. In "Virginia Reel" he stands among family graves, in "the dirt their lives were made of, the dirt the world is, / Immeasurable emptiness of all things," and sees himself as a "bright bud on the branch of nothing's tree." A hand out of the air, like one of Montale's spirit-talons from an angel, touches his shoulder, and

> I want to fall to my knees, and keep on falling, here,
> Laid down by the articles that bear my names,
> The limestone and marble and locust wood.

The hunger for the purity of the dead grows, in these poems, almost to a lust. So far, as a poem quoting Dickinson's gravestone says, he has been "Called Back" by the bird songs and flowers of the world; but the ice-edged and starless cloak of night outshines his bougainvillea and apple blossoms. The eternal and elemental world is largely unrelieved, in *China Trace* and after, by the local, the social, the temporary, the accidental, the contingent. Some very good poetry has incorporated riotous, and occasionally ungovernable, irruptions of particularity; the "purer" voice of finely ascetic lyric has a genuine transmitter in Wright. His synoptic and panoramic vision, radiating out from a compositional center to a filled canvas, opposes itself to the anthropocentric, and consequently autobiographical or narrative, impetus of lyrics with a linear base. If there is nowhere to go but up from making the unsupported line your unit, the dead your measure of verity, and the blank canvas meticulously layered with single cubes of color your creative metaphor, Wright's poetry is bound to change. As it stands, it is engaged in a refutation of the seductions of logic, of religion, and of social roles. By its visionary language it assumes the priority of insight, solitude, and abstraction, while remaining beset by a mysterious loss of something that can be absorbed and reconstituted only in death.

The spiritual yearning in Wright is nowhere rewarded, as it sometimes is in Montale, by a certain faith in an absolute—damaged no doubt, elusive surely, disagreeable often, but always unquestioned and recoverable. The difference in part may be historical. Montale, who fought in World War I and saw the shambles of postwar Italy give rise to Mussolini, faced pressing social evils that demanded a choice of sides; he refused to join the Fascist party and lost his job in consequence. Virtue made visible by its denunciation of the evils of Pandemonium can appear emblematic, allegorical, winged, embattled. Without a historical convulsion, tones of poetry subside into perplexity, sadness, elegy. Wright's debt to Montale, attested to by original poems as well as by these early translations, is more than stylistic: the disciple exhibits that desire and hopelessness we associate with Montale at his most characteristic. Montale's description (in *Auto da Fé*, 1952) of the solitude of the artist can stand as a program for Wright:

Man, insofar as he is an individual being, an empirical individual, is fatally alone. Social life is an addition, an aggregate, not a unity of individuals. The man who communicates is the transcendent "I" who is hidden in us and who recognizes himself in others. But the transcendent "I" is a lamp which lights up only the briefest strip of space before us, a light that bears us toward a condition which is not individual and consequently not human . . . The attempt to fix the ephemeral, to make the phenomenon non-phenomenal, the attempt to make the individual "I" articulate, as he is not by definition, the revolt, in brief, against the human condition (a revolt dictated by an impassioned *amor vitae*) is at the base of the artistic and philosophic pursuits of our era.

Wright's verse is the poetry of the transcendent "I" in revolt against the too easily articulate "I" of social engagement and social roles. Whether one "I" can address his word to other, hidden "I's" across the abyss of daily life without using the personal, transient, and social language of that life is the question Wright poses. Remembering Montale's eel venturing into the rocks and gullies of a scorched earth, I would hope to see in Wright's future poetry a more vivid sense of the social and familial landscape in which the soul struggles. "Life itself," Montale wrote, "seems like a monstrous work of art forever being destroyed and forever renewed." While Montale foresaw a popular art—utilitarian and almost playful—for the masses, he also predicted (and incarnated) a "true and proper art, not very different from the art of the past, and not easily reduced to cliché." The creators of this art—and for Montale, who translated Eliot, Eliot would be a case in point—though they may seem hermetic, isolated, and inaccessible, are not really such:

It is these great isolated personalities who give a meaning to an era, and their isolation is more illusory than real . . . In this sense, only the isolated speak, only the isolated communicate; the rest—the mass-communication men—repeat, give off echoes, vulgarize the poets' words.

In making Montale better known, Wright makes his own aims better understood, and his remote and severe writing more accessible.

Dave Smith

"Oh I Admire and Sorrow"

Faced with Dave Smith's "high-pilèd books," I scarcely know where
to begin in describing his rich writing. Perhaps the best place is with
four poems published in *APR* (March/April 1976). His work is that
of a man writing dense verse out of hard moments. The ecstatic in
Smith is brother to despair. "That Moment, Which You Could Love,
What of It?" asks one new poem, by its title stopping the willing
rush toward faith offered in its ending. A "bitch of a day" in its
gray overcoat of dusk, "self's sickness," the burning bush reduced to
"one snaking tongue"—and even there, "You try, can't hold it. The
window's iced." Into this exhaustion—aborted grass, snow fouled
with ice—comes the radio-borne voice of "the opera-woman no one
ever expects," but she disappears into static as the poet, sitting next
to his fish-tank, idly traces tracks in spilled salt on his table. Suddenly, the static over, the aria comes through clear again:

> Suddenly
> the fierce blaze of light, her
> cry riding the one long note
> of your breath, the overcoat
> left in a corner, and you
> know a pale surge in the earth,
> something trackless, nor of wires
> received, envelops you, is
>
> and is gone with the shift she
> rides, the opera-woman,
> straining notes like moments

" 'Oh I Admire and Sorrow' " first appeared in *Parnassus: Poetry in Review*,
Spring/Summer 1977.

so rare nothing dies. Who
would not risk everything
for this, even as darkness rushes
over the fish, the salt, the snow?

This is Smith working at his characteristic speed-up of mass. After mentioning, at some more leisurely pace, the dusk, the overcoat, the voice, tracks in the salt, the aquarium, the opera-woman, he rises to marshal them all in a rapid acceleration which makes the reader feel rushed-in-upon, like someone driving into a snowstorm when all the flakes seem to converge at a point on the windshield. This technique of massed structuring adds to the pathos of individual phrases like "a pale surge in the earth" or the fine irrationality (however carefully prepared for) of the sequence "the fish, the salt, the snow." I am not happy at the Stevensian coinage "opera-woman," but I like the poem in which she (whether real singer or Muse) appears. Smith's ethic here is a Romantic one ("Who would not risk everything for this"—the cry, the pale surge, the rare moment); and the same passion for existence at its best appears in another *APR* poem, one recording the moment in which a boy first notices, in a girl his own age, the phenomenon of breasts,

breasts
only slightly larger than his own, thinking of her
who is inexplicably older but was not

not an hour before: to have seen that then like a purple
bruise (that strange) through the gaunt, stretched neck-
loop of her T-shirt stained by wrestling, I tell
you I felt the tick of grass.

The discomfort one feels in breaking off a quotation from Smith is a measure of his Faulknerian power: it is unfair to this good poem to stop here, since the poet could justly protest that I have left out the fine subsequent echo of "tick" in "itch," and the repetition of "tick" in "ticking," and the reiteration of the breasts in "those hard nubs inviolate," and so on through this poem of "that throb of passage." This is entirely true: interrupting the passage breaks the throb, falsifies Smith's wonderfully constructed momentum, and "corrects" into reflection what is, on the page, a pressing re-creation of the advent of sexual consciousness. The fantasy of omnipotence which springs within the adolescent after this "spot of time" gives the poem its title and its ending: the title, "Over the Ozarks, Because I Saw Them, Stars Came," anticipates the conclusion:

> After that I slept, improbably
> dreaming I stood at the center of being, and woke
> in the dark, godless and afraid, alive.

Smith's way with surprises of language appears in "improbably," "godless," and "alive."

His best work so far comes in poems where he is conceiving so much that he cannot possibly—at least not yet—bring it all into focus. There is an ambitious poem called "Night of the Chickens, North of Joplin," which describes (not autobiographically, it is about someone else) drunkenness, night driving, memories of a girl lost, memories of a dead father riding the rails, running into chickens on the road, breaking the headlights on the chickens, trying to drive without headlights, being guided by the lights on the houses and roadhouses paralleling the route, being sideswiped, trying to follow another man's car lights, and being evaded by him out of fear. All of this is sketched with the utmost condensation and with frightening drunken velocity:

> And suddenly
> you can't recall her name and there is no moon
> and though you are skidding the chickens seem
> to want to die and do, absurdly breaking
>
> both headlights. Now you find you must feel the road
> and how to get along it, no more blundering through
> the hummocks of darkness, but working from house-
> light to houselight, speeding to trail one
>
> that passes, to steal his light and glide in.
> It doesn't work. He's afraid too.

By the time the poem touches bottom, "there is nowhere to go, only the going / absurd as the life of a chicken on a shack-lined / road in Missouri." So far so good. But then Smith begins to talk of "the necessary foolishness of raging for love," and offers nostrums:

> To get through,
> sing a chorus for each roadhouse and rail-sign.
> Sing the song of a girl's thigh in moonlight.

Faulknerian reminiscence is invoked in rather too many words: "Do not expect / honor, compassion, restraint, direction / from anyone here. We are all strangers."

That Smith can provoke sharp disappointment is a measure of the satisfactions he gives. The rich immersions of his imagination are revealed when we consider that these latest poems—which are not about his first subject, the fishermen of Virginia—seem as fully thought through as the poems drawing powerfully from his childhood in Portsmouth and Poquoson. *Bull Island* (1970) contained a number of poems on the life of a fishing village in the Virginia tidewater; *The Fisherman's Whore* continued this powerful geographic and social portrait and added some family poems; *Cumberland Station* includes both these strains with a broader canvas. The new poetry is autobiographical, but not necessarily rooted in the family or in the locales of Smith's early life. There seems no reason, given Smith's steady advance in art, to doubt that other powerful books will follow these.

Cumberland Station contains several sorts of poems. The ones I like least are some semi-allegorical ones toward the middle of the book, with names like "The Divorce," "The Testimony of Wine," "The Delivery," "The Sex of Poetry," and "The Dome Poem." "The Delivery" begins, "This is a poem about Nature. No use trying / to hide it." "The Sex of Poetry" begins, "She unzips her skirt," and tells us, "If she has a name it is false." "Dome Poem" says "a poem is a kind of country, full / of tent stays and lines you always kick / at night." Smith's explicitness falls flat, as his more reticent work does not. In the dome poem he does find one gorgeous stanza of indirect equivalency:

> . . . what we must have is so simple
> it constantly sits there like a shadow's
> shadow on water, bones and tendons slyly
> hidden so only the maker knows how it is
> done, and it smiles and says simplify, simplify.

Thoreau's allegories are moving because they have the natural force of natural fact behind them, and Smith looks for the same degree of support from materiality; but the material in these allegorical poems too often seems cooked up to support the allegory. "The Divorce" is the worst offender, a dreary parable in which, since the husband's and wife's kisses taste of dead trout, the wife goes to a dentist (a new lover):

> As each session ended,
> the dentist would climb off her, remove and clean his drill.

"Daddy" waits out the sessions, but "one day, summoning courage,"

> he asked Mommy how her teeth were. Mommy broke her
> dinner plate on her forehead and said that's the last
> time I eat dead trout. You go get your own dentist.

This doesn't seem either very clever or very funny, and the profit in inventing the parable seems to be nil—no new light on marriage or divorce, no notable new gains in language or structure.

The landscape and fishing poems, on the other hand, are exquisite. The real test of such poems is whether they can touch a reader who has never lived in the out-of-doors, who has never fished, who has never lived in that masculine society they evoke. The mystique of the male initiation (in the first hunt, in camping, in fishing) can seem, in less profound poets, perilously silly, but Smith's presence in these events is purely human, not gender-bound. In "The Last Morning" he wakes up early on the last morning out camping; others are still asleep; he goes down to the river to wash his clothes and he hangs them up to dry. As he sits naked beside the river, he could be anyone, aboriginal, at the beginning of American time:

> It is then across water a wolverine
> comes to drink and a trout dimples
> the silence like the soul rising. I
>
> begin to hear not far away the crash
> of dammed water and a beaver's bark.
> I think unaccountably of an early snow,
> children with black, hungry eyes, men
> cutting arrows where the elders bud.

The Indian quiet is reflected in Smith's finely turned lines, vaguely primitive in their echoing Anglo-Saxon four-beat pulse. (One of Smith's poems is called "The Scop," and the epigraph to his second volume is taken from "The Seafarer.") The beautiful closing chiasmus of "The Last Morning" is so gentle it could go unnoticed—but as "bud" echoes "cut," so "elders" has some affinity with "arrows," just enough to give the last line a conclusive frame. Smith's fondness for certain sounds—especially the dull "u" (here in "cut" and "bud," but frequent throughout his work, so much so that he has written a whole poem—"How One Thing Leads to Another"—on the word "cusp")—marks him as a true poet to whom sounds are masters, not servants.

Smith dwells on strenuousness and on obliteration—the strenuousness of building, fishing, giving birth; the obliteration of shipwreck, disease, drunkenness, unemployment, death. In these receptivities he most resembles Hopkins: "Oh I admire and sorrow!" In his successful poems, he is generally a heavy poet, serious, burdened, sometimes angry, full of life's effort. Even effects as delicate as those in an early description of fog ("in Points South") are motivated by the effort of moving through obscurity:

> first thin wisps curling
> like lace into the lowest
> limbs of the pines whole
> patches of froth blindingly
> coming.

The senseless events of life (floods, rot, disuse) move Smith as much as virtue (hard work, salvaging, giving birth). His brilliant sense of reality lights up even his densest work; in spite of a frequent murk— a deliberate murk, the confusingness of perception—one feels a promise of touching ground, beaching on some shore of the understood. But Smith did not always have the wisdom to keep conceptual bedrock a promise and a finding. In *Bull Island*, privately printed at his own Back Door Press, he was unable to refrain from giving the show away. One poem actually ends, "Ain't that life?" Others are simply heavy-handed in their offering of a "message": "It's clear I do not / belong to you now"; boats are too old "for bearing men / safely through the tides / of a life's dim dreams"; "I have come here meaning / for my son to see / how the earth was rent / by his grandfather"; "the marsh . . . wears its stains / like a fisherman"; "I dreamed you touched me / and I did not care"; "There is no net / I can make of rope to catch / the thing I have lost." And yet, *Bull Island* does not perform its descriptions in order to frame its messages: on the contrary, the poetical energy is in the descriptions, and the commentaries seem afterthoughts.

The Fisherman's Whore, uneven though it is, knows its own path, goes ahead surefootedly, correcting weaknesses in the poems it reprints from *Bull Island*. The lines about the old boats, for instance, now become a description of

> ulcerous hulks too old
> for bearing men safely
> through the last sharp tides
> of the unforgotten ways.

A phrase like "a life's dim dreams" has been recognized for what it is, unassimilated Yeats—and in fact the whole poem from which it comes has been tightened, its rifts more fully loaded with ore. There are moments of pure flawlessness in *The Fisherman's Whore*: one is the close of a poem describing a fire in the night. Smith is a child, still; he wakes up to see that the man across the street has been lucky, losing neither of his two houses to the fire. As the poem continues, the child perceives everything as apparently unchanged: the neighbor is, as usual, weaving a trap; his wife is hanging out the wash; their dog laps "from the ruts of the fire trucks." It is only now, writing the poem, that the poet realizes that the landscape had been added to:

> I saw how little had been changed by fire,
> only the tool shed limp as a black dress
> in a heap which left a new, tidy hole
> in the landscape. And now I remember
> seeing also, as if for the first time,
> the slate grey hand of the sea, where
> far off the figures of boats crossed,
> wove, and sank as they burned in the sun.

The candor and simplicity of the lines are suitable to the child, but nobody writes verse so expertly as this without a great deal of practice. The wonderful personification of the "slate grey hand of the sea"; the precision of naming (not "boats," but "the figures of boats"); the gifted adaptation of the Keatsian "and now" which brings a poem into a fateful present; the linking of the present "and now" with the verb of memory "I remember" knitting together the writing and the recalling; the irrational echo of the trap-weaving in the weaving of the boats; the odd conjunction of the fire in the night and the boats burning in the daylight; the rendering of the child's satisfaction of vision as he notices the "new, tidy hole in the landscape"; all of these felicities, which could not proceed except from a wholly natural alliance of sight and insight, announce a poet already capable of great control.

However, Smith has trouble, in *The Fisherman's Whore*, with managing his violence. There is a lady who eats her lover; there is a girl with a bullet in her chest and a mention of green body bags; a man hangs himself; a man is killed by being stabbed with a screwdriver; there is an imagined rape. Smith struggles to find a way of incorporating into verse the sudden incursion of violence into life and its permanent aftermath, to contain the fact of horror in language without playing it false. He succeeds best by indirection in the fine Civil War poem, "The Bullets of Camden, North Carolina." The bullets here have lodged in trees, which are forever after useless for lumber. The chastity of language, in its perfectly steady "deepening," matches the wound eternally deforming the growth layers of the tree; the poem silently and invisibly enacts the ineradicable scarring of war. Smith draws no parallels, appends no message. His parable stands intact:

> A deepening works within ancient pines,
> slowly rises the shadow soft shimmer,
> wind or something worse than wind,
> all drawn close, as water draws to ice,
>
> around the bark's wounds thickened, edged,
> time's scab now utterly hard, that coil
> unable to free itself, imbedded, eaten,
> perfectly pure in the wood's green blood,
>
> but not so the pine's swollen flank, tissue
> rippled and warped forever, so, cut,
> planed, the slender boards are blemished
> by dark whorls like an onion's heart, warts
>
> growing deeper and older on the fine steel
> until even roots and their frail saplings
> distant from the trunk as grandsons know
> the scar's mark like an ancient disease.
>
> The tree I climbed as a child in Camden
> still stands, gnarled by its wounds,
> linking a wind-swept tribe that cannot be
> cut down for kitchens or floors or anything.

In fact, Smith's Civil War poems are the first worthy successors to Melville's *Battle-Pieces*. I will resist the temptation to quote an Indian "re-doing" of the Camden bullets in a beautiful poem about a piece of petrified wood showing the "bruise of a warrior's first spear hurtled," and go on instead to a new Civil War poem, "On a Field Trip at Fredericksburg." Smith goes to the battlefield at Fredericksburg; presumably a school field trip has brought some children there at the same time. Smith remembers old photographs of child-soldiers (some of them only fifteen) taken by Matthew Brady. A child asks Smith the name of the yellow flower she holds in her hand. There is a tourist plaque describing the historical significance of the battlefield. Smith thinks of the enormous increase in killing in nuclear war. He thinks too of peaceful uses of meadows; Audubon could have made a "field trip" to Fredericksburg looking for the birds of America. Out of these pieces of experience a poem takes shape, beautifully following the drift of experience and reflection, seeing the natural population of birds, dandelions, and children give way to Brady's blackened corpses after battle. For all its waywardness of progress, the poem is as tight as a theorem:

> The big steel tourist shield says maybe
> fifteen thousand got it here. No word
> of either Whitman or one uncle
> I barely remember in the smoke
> that filled his tiny mountain house.
>
> If each finger were a thousand of them
> I could clap my hands and be dead
> up to my wrists. It was quick
> though not so fast as we can do it
> now, one bomb, atomic or worse,
> one silly pod slung on wing-tip,
> high up, an egg cradled
> by some rapacious mockingbird.
>
> Hiroshima canned nine times their number
> in a flash. Few had the time
> to moan or feel the feeling
> ooze back in the groin.
>
> In a ditch I stand
> above Marye's Heights, the book-
> boned faces of Brady's fifteen-year-old
> drummers, before battle, rigid
> as August's dandelions
> all the way to the Potomac
> rolling in my skull.
>
> If Audubon came here, the names
> of birds would gush, the marvel
> single feathers make
> evoke a cloud, a nation,
> a gray blur preserved
> on a blue horizon, but
> there is only a wandering child,
> one dark stalk snapped off
> in her hand, held out to me.
> Taking it, I try to help her

hold its obscure syllables
one instant in her mouth,
like a drift of wind
at the forehead, the front door,
the black, numb fingernails.

If there is a flaw in the poem, it comes in the echo of Crane's "Broken Tower" in the last stanza ("its voice / An instant in the wind"). There are many daring flashes: the demotic beginning ("maybe / fifteen thousand got it here"); the surrealistic fantasy ("If each finger were a thousand of them / I could clap my hands and be dead / up to my wrists"); the dismissive meiosis for the atomic bomb ("one silly pod"); the substitution of birds for the soldiers in blue and gray uniforms("a gray blur preserved / on a blue horizon"); the unobtrusive symbols (the drummers, "rigid as August's dandelions," yield to "one dark stalk snapped off," and the hint of death in the "drift of wind / at the forehead, the front door"). Smith's uncle (too young, even if he were a granduncle, to have himself fought in the War) is Smith's family link to the scene—he may have been the child of one of the dead, we are not told. But for some reason Smith becomes the voice of those dead at Fredericksburg, and his "naming" for the child of one element in the landscape becomes a modest surrogate for his work as a poet, as he helps her "hold . . . obscure syllables / one instant" in her mouth. It is inevitable, in criticism, to "place" the poem as a *gestalt* before talking about its details, but this procedure plays Smith false, since his most characteristic quality is an unexplained plunge *in medias res*. An irresistible curiosity draws us into the vortex of the poem after the poet has said "fifteen thousand got it here," or "You cannot get him easily, or you can so / easily what you get will be hardly / anything you'd want," or "For years I've watched the corners for signs," or "He can only drink tea now, screwed and filed"—all openings of poems in *Cumberland Station*. One is by no means sure of having unraveled the antecedent scenarios for all these poems even after having read them several times.

In *Cumberland Station* Smith tries so many different kinds of poems that only an account which took notice of them one by one would serve. He takes on the voices of the watermen, a constraint on his own voice prompted by a wish for a simplicity of language not wholly native to him. He is an ornate poet by instinct and by youth, as Hopkins was. The brutal plainness of Hopkins' last sonnets is still not in his grasp, but he really does rival the sheer weight and mass

of, say, Hopkins' fragment of an epithalamion. In a spectacular
mediative poem marred only by its ending (another ritual "slap
[of] a tune" like his chorus for the roadhouses), he takes us to
uninhabited Smith Island off the coast of Virginia, where he beaches
his rowboat and runs, then stumbles, over the beach, over the hulls
of abandoned boats, until he trips and falls into the mess of a
rotting turtle, a "storm-proof charnel house for crabs." The poem is
almost shamelessly imitative of Hopkins (it actually speaks of
"wimpling winds," borrowing boldly from the windhover's "wimpling wing") but it is the sort of borrowing amply justified by the
results. "Am I at home here?" the poet begins—and "here," though
meaning Smith Island, also turns out to mean "with the dead," "with
death," "alone."

> Scrambling from
> deck to deck, on the shells of dead
> fishermen's boats, I feel the families
> pulling back alive while tides bubble
> through stoved-in sterns. Silence
> in this junkyard of currents rots,
> reeks, absorbs bleached carcasses of
> trout, jellyfish, lung-busted oysters,
> sea-going Bugeyes with impeccable
> equality. The elements are everywhere
> rising, meager flecks of flesh decomposing
> on spears of wood, glittery chips
> wedged like gold in the ventricles of weed.

It is difficult to say why this is so intensely satisfying. Perhaps it is
Smith's seigneurial way with language. Like Whitman, from whom
he has learned so much, he can be simply true, talking of families
and dead fishermen; he can be distantly elegant, talking philosophi-
cally of death's "impeccable equality"; he can be colloquial (a "Bug-
eye" is a fishing boat); and he can be grandly metaphysical ("the
elements are everywhere rising"), not to speak of brilliantly visual.
Surely the most beautiful single lines in this passage are the last
four, but they would have their import severely damaged if they
were shorn from the human material preceding them.

Smith's descriptive powers are not restricted to static scenes: he
is equally good at motion. Into the rotting head of the turtle come
the sand crabs: Smith, who has fallen down by tripping over the
turtle, sees the biological interaction from a worm's-eye view, and
the turtle shell becomes a protective cave:

A being empties all over
again heart, fish-stuffed gut, still
threshing bones, its jaw snapping nothing
where I lay full-length as Gulliver. Sun
bleeds through the rear slope of his
house, warming sand crabs who come waving
one weak claw, gropers digging their
wind-beaten, juice-stewing bodies, tiny
silhouettes making cave shadows against
what weirdly transforms from heroic swimmer
to storm-proof charnel house for crabs.

We gradually sense that we are reading a fable about generations, that the young live in the charnel-house protection of the ancestral dead. The dead become "what they never thought of— / what the ghostly radar of crabs homes at . . . a new temple." And the crabs enter, "claws high, no grief, no joy imagined." It simply happens. We all "eat and breed and age in hoods / we surrender to the meat of the living." Smith enters equally into the opportunism of the crabs and the practical use of the dead turtle, finding his sermons on islands bearing his name. It would be ungenerous to mind too much when the ending weakens.

Smith, incidentally, writes good poems about being a husband and father. *The Fisherman's Whore* ends with a two-part poem about his wife's pregnancy and the birth of his daughter (more successful, to my way of thinking, than the slightly sentimental song for his son preceding them). In *Cumberland Station*, there is a poem called "The Gift of the Second Snow" in which Smith has been feeling somehow hemmed in by an "abstract hurt," and by "writing hard things." Then the second snowfall finally stops: the sun comes out and "frothed against the glass / until I would let it in." It makes the world come right ("no thorns / I could feel snagged in any metaphysics / I spread out"). Smith's wife puts her arms around his neck "like a whispered joy":

Then I had to let out
the dog, turn off the TV,
give up my good excuse
to go on writing
hard things

and it was just then the children came
swaddled up like small pines, glittery,
speckled for their own celebrations,

their eyes pumping up
what was left of my heart,
so we went out for hotdogs,
and went all night on our
bellies under the black
locusts, until you
fell with me, soggy
in bed, in love,
in the dark.

Not very complicated, but not false: and the description of the children is the best thing in it, with Smith's characteristic trouvailles which ring so unexpectedly true—small children in snowsuits do look like small pines, and when flecked with snow do look like small Christmas trees, "glittery, / speckled for their own celebrations." There are, one way or another, lots of ancestors in Smith's poems and I hope there will be more children. He is a family poet by nature, as much as he is a landscape poet.

Smith's wish to end on an upbeat, in song, though it is human enough, is still his Atalanta's apple. It is no pleasure to say that life will probably cure him of happy endings: "Worst will the best. What worm was here, we cry, / To have havoc-pocked so, see, the hung-heavenward boughs?" His own predecessor Hopkins went much the same route as Smith seems to be taking: seeing everything "all in a rush with richness" till life undid for him the dapple of the world. Smith has not yet been taken into that sybilline evening where "only the beak-leaved boughs dragonish / Damask the tool-smooth bleak light, black / Ever so black on it." For the moment, he is still watching his children being born:

> ... cars
> begin to thud toward the first light,
>
> and as the shrouding shadows cramp,
> already there is a mothering wind
> unhooding like an angel in a room,
> and a father dropping doorkeys
>
> in the unimaginable dawn, a man
> who rubs his eyes and grins as
> steam breaks through a stationhouse
> and all creation steps down safe.

He is watching the bluefish run:

Bluefish are pouring at me in squads.
I haul two, three at a time, torpedoes, moon-shiners,
jamming my feet into the splintered floor, battling
whatever comes. I know I have waited
a whole life for this minute.

He is listening to rural fiddlers:

We come at last
into the unfretting wish to be nothing else,
for there rises from bow's graze and struck strings
not only land's lute, but eerie rapture
stunning the sailor
who feels at first daybreak a peace slicing wrist-labor
as if before storm or prayer.

What will this poet of plenty write when he becomes a poet of
deprivation? It is a question that leads to poems like Whitman's "As
I Ebb'd with the Ocean of Life," and Hopkins' Dublin verse. We
come nearest to this mood in the title poem of the new volume.
Cumberland Station (now defunct) in Cumberland, Maryland
seems to Smith the grave of his family. First "Big Daddy" died, then
an uncle, then a cousin:

I come here alone, shaken
the way I came years ago to ride down
mountains in Big Daddy's cab. He was
the first set cold in the black meadow . . .

This time there's no fun in coming back. The second
death. My roundhouse uncle coughed his youth
into a gutter. His son, the third, slid on the ice,
losing his need to drink himself
stupidly dead. In this vaulted hall
I think of all the dirt poured down
from shovels and trains and empty pockets.
I stare into the huge malignant headlamps
circling the gray walls and catch a stuttered
glimpse of faces stunned like deer on a track.

Smith's indignation still refuses to take this glimpse of stunned
doomed faces as the norm of life. He is a poet of the utmost ambition
and the utmost care; his poems make other poems seem loose, unfinished; he is prolific; and he is in his mid-thirties, an age where
most poets have only just begun to find a voice.

Louise Glück

Even now this landscape is assembling.
The hills darken. The oxen
sleep in their blue yoke,
the fields having been
picked clean, the sheaves
bound evenly and piled at the roadside
among cinquefoil, as the toothed moon rises:

This is the barrenness
of harvest or pestilence.
And the wife leaning out the window
with her hand extended, as in payment,
and the seeds
distinct, gold, calling
Come here
Come here, little one

And the soul creeps out of the tree.

"All Hallows" appeared on the first page of Louise Glück's *The House on Marshland* (1975). If there were echoes of Stevens and perhaps of Sexton, they were assimilated into a new voice. "All Hallows" is about bearing a child—or so it seems to me—but it is saturated by the poet's sense of her own birth. A mother has paid some unspeakable price into an invisible hand, has enabled the gold seeds, and the child victim is sold into bondage, enticed into the world. When a human couple takes on the unknown in the form of a baby, it is a time of "harvest or pestilence": their spring flowering is over, and, after the fashion of an archetypal Nativity, the baby is born in the cold. The "toothed moon," a savage jack-o-lantern, rises

"The Poetry of Louise Glück" first appeared in *The New Republic*, June 17, 1978.

in a sinister ascendancy, a parody of the Christmas Star. The deceptive title and peaceful beginning lead to the frightened child-soul
leaving its tree nest, beckoned by the evil fairy-tale voice—"*Come
here / Come here, little one.*" The helplessness of the child, the complicity of its mother, the cannibal jaws of the moon, make the title
"All Hallows" in one sense a blasphemy; but the pity for the child,
the uncertainty whether this is harvest or pestilence, the sense of a
waiting landscape, all make the title, in another sense, the most
reserved of benedictions. The whole poem trembles on a verge: "And
the soul creeps out of the tree." Nativity, said Shakespeare, crawls to
maturity: where Shakespeare saw the crooked eclipses, Glück sees
the toothed moon.

A powerful re-seeing of family life animates many of the poems
in *The House on Marshland*, down to its last poem, "The Apple
Trees," spoken by a woman to a man who is leaving her; he is the
father of her child. In a dream, she holds the child up to him, saying,
"See what you have made"—

> and counted out the whittled ribs,
> the heart on its blue stalk.

As a mother's view of her child, this is unnerving: she sees him as
artifact and X-ray plate, with the dispassionate eye of a woodcarver
or a radiologist.

In that dispassionate eye so stiffened against the distortions of
love, Glück exerts a clear sovereignty that attracts assent rather
than inquiry. One scarcely wants to ask the secret of certain impeccable lines:

> And the deer—
> how beautiful they are,
> as though their bodies did not impede them.
> Slowly they drift into the open
> through bronze panels of sunlight.

Glück's rhythm yearns toward the deer: we think of the isolate
Mariner pained by "the many men, so beautiful," as we see that this
speaker, "impeded" by her body, envies the natural paradise of the
deer, drifting through sun as through some etherealized version of
the Ghiberti doors. And yet, at the end, these natural messengers, if
I read the poem aright, are superseded by a wounded, disembodied
consciousness:

> . . . they come before you
> like dead things, saddled with flesh,
> and you above them, wounded and dominant.

The perverse dramatist of this poem has perhaps learned something from Sylvia Plath. But Glück's tone owes nothing to Plath, it is not Lawrentian or clinical (Plath's extremes), but rather, as one auditor said after Glück's Harvard reading in 1977, "unearthly."

In fact there is something "disembodied, triumphant, dead"—Whitman's words—about Glück's usual voice (barring some uncollected songs, in a more demotic manner, which are not successful). She sees experience from very far off, almost through the wrong end of a telescope, transparently removed in space or time. It is this removal which gives such mythological power, in *The House on Marshland*, to the account of her parents' lives and of her own childhood, and makes their family constellation into a universal one:

> Father has his arm around Tereze.
> She squints. My thumb
> is in my mouth: my fifth autumn.
> Near the copper beech
> the spaniel dozes in shadows.
> Not one of us does not avert his eyes.
>
> Across the lawn, in full sun, my mother
> stands behind her camera.

In this brilliant poem, "Still Life," Glück reconstitutes the over-exposed Kodak shot in every reader's photograph album, revealing the impossibility of family relations, the aversion and separation in the poses family life makes us strike; if we were animals, we would curl up out of the sun, out of postures, and be spared these stiff and unnatural configurations.

Glück's poems of family life tend to avoid the biographical, as a way of avoiding the inevitably helpless "I." Lyric has, historically, voiced a prayer or a complaint, both presupposing a listener, the "thou" of remedy. But if there is no "thou," the voice can make no leap to another ear, can scarcely conceive of itself as subject. An inflexible statement of what is must replace protest, plea, confiding, intercession, and defense. Glück resolutely gives the blank title "Poem" to her *ur*-poem of family life, with its inescapable images of man, wife, spring, a house, and an unborn child:

In the early evening, as now, a man is bending
over his writing table.
Slowly he lifts his head; a woman
appears, carrying roses.
Her face floats to the surface of the mirror,
marked with the green spokes of rose stems.

It is a form
of suffering: then always the transparent page
raised to the window until its veins emerge
as words finally filled with ink.

And I am meant to understand
what binds them together
or to the gray house held firmly in place by dusk

because I must enter their lives:
it is spring, the pear tree
filming with weak, white blossoms.

The only unexpected component in this complex is the man's writing. He is a poet, and doubles for Glück herself in this archetypal tale. The woman's face in the mirror takes on the contours of an icon or a mandala, as she becomes a Muse and her mirrored reflection causes that writing which takes on the function of life, as ink replaces blood. The conundrum of marriage is set for the unborn child, a conundrum she can never solve; the house is immobile in the constricting universe; and once again, nature, unbidden, sends forth those weak blooms vulnerable to the first frost, the first too-rough airs of heaven. Such a poem appears to exhaust one form of life, and thereby earns its title: there is a house, a couple, suffering, "what binds them together," reproduction, a child, an utterance in ink: what else could there be? And the tale of life unrolls unstoppably on: the child who enters the parents' lives must go to school and propitiate the mysterious teachers, intent on silencing the children into the classroom order.

The first day of school is not an unattempted topic (though school itself appears less in poetry than one might expect): but Glück's "The School Children" takes it more seriously than any previous description I can recall:

The children go forward with their little satchels.
And all morning the mothers have labored
to gather the late apples, red and gold,
like words of another language.

And on the other shore
are those who wait behind great desks
to receive these offerings.

How orderly they are—the nails
on which the children hang
their overcoats of blue or yellow wool.

And the teachers shall instruct them in silence
and the mothers shall scour the orchards for a way out,
drawing to themselves the gray limbs of the fruit trees
bearing so little ammunition.

Glück's is post-Freudian poetry; its wide-eyed and appalled gaze takes seriously the gulfs and abysses of the child's experience, an experience shared by the mother for her departing child. Glück's mothers are in the last phase of fertility; the orchards—which are the mothers themselves—are yielding only a few late apples of maternity and love, "so little ammunition" to fortify the children with, before the mothers turn into barren gray limbs. The children make the first great crossing—from the shore of the mothers to the shore of the teachers—and it is a sacrificial rite, the yearly tribute to the Minotaur. The nails are waiting for the children, the mothers are trapped in the orchards. There is no prayer, no protest, no outcry, even: only the primal simplicity of the narrator.

This narrator, who holds us with her tale of deadly ill so quietly told, is Glück's great resource. The telling is oblique but not self-mocking; divinatory, like that of a Fate, who can see the apples "like words of another language," mute signs to the teacher that the child is used to an Eden of nourishment, not a world of desks and nails and silence. The Fate impersonally pities both mothers and children, seeing the uneven battle, the pathetic armor of the children's "little satchels," and the timid insufficiency of their ammunition.

Here and there, Glück's tome of doom modulates into something less deathly, as it does in "Flowering Plum" and "Brennende Liebe"; it lifts for a moment in the discovery of love, punning, in her Moses-fable "The Undertaking," on her own name—"everywhere you turn is luck." A benevolent euphony, in such happy moments, tunes her lines. But any light supervenes on some unimaginable incarceration in the dark: "The darkness lifts, imagine, in your lifetime." It is like the opening of the camps after the war: captives resigned to a lifetime of imprisonment hear the unhoped-for creak of widening gates. It is not surprising that even this expansive freedom, of spring and love, is soon incorporated into Glück's fateful sense of meaningless life-rhythms. Glück has some of Stevens' bitterness about the child-ish onslaughts of the spring, and some of Williams' naive power in encompassing birth and death in one breath. This, from the poem "For Jane Myers," is one quick sequence of love, reproduction, and execution:

> Look how the bluet falls apart, mud
> pockets the seed.
> Months, years, then the dull blade of the wind.
> It is spring! We are going to die!

Insight is of no use in spring; the bluet's power makes us follow the bluet's cycle:

> And now April raises up her plaque of flowers
> and the heart
> expands to admit its adversary.

By a single word—"plaque"—Glück confers on April all the monu-mentality of an allegorical goddess, stationed irresistibly on the heart's pathway.

Since *The House on Marshland*, Glück has published a memorable sequence, *The Garden* (1976), prolonging her fixed glance and con-clusive style into a linked series of poems. Sections of *The Garden* could stand alone, but each gains by juxtaposition. From its begin-ning in a rebirth of love to its diminished ending in death, *The Gar-den* combines Glück's almost posthumous tone with moments of quick proximate sympathy. From the one immobile focus she can say that "the past, as always, stretched before us, / still, complex, impenetrable"; from the other, fluid point of view she can still feel temped by the garden's "ecstatic reds" and feel certain that to be like the statues, stone animals, beyond harm, is "terrible." *The Gar-den* speaks from the abstract knowledge of past losses ("one after the other, all supportable") but its present losses are made so exact that they are felt as if for the first time. Glück's eclectic mythology, combining Eden, feather-cloaked gods, classical stone animals, and a helmeted sun, ends with a Christian ghost, a spirit sitting on its own headstone, "a small rock." "The tomb in Palestine," according to Stevens, "is not the porch of spirits lingering"; but Glück's ghost, like the gospel angels, lingers in the cemetery. The body is forgotten by the relentless village, its faint searchlights scanning the rows of gravestones. The land, once a garden, has become Keats's stubble plains—here, Glück's "sheared field"; the "poor body" has only its buckled shadow, having lost its spirit. The body waits to be claimed, like Jesus' by the Marys.

The remoteness of what was once common is Glück's central subject: the irreality of life in the maternal orchard once one has passed through the doors of what Ginsberg once called in horror "the vast high school," but what Glück names elementary school; the incomprehensibility of the parents' marriage in the eyes of the child; the elements of daily life, "the bread and milk . . . on the table," ungraspable once one has left the land of the living. The very table at the end of *The Garden* would evanesce were it not for the weight of the daily bread; the house would disappear without its wooden doors; Glück poses "weight" and "wooden" against the shadowy otherness of the dead body and formless spirit alike.

Lamentations, Glück's most recent sequence, retells in four parts a portion of what *The Garden* had told in five, but it fatally separates the woman into two: the woman she had been with the man, and the body that will bear a child. It is the child, with no one to turn to but its parents, who makes them into the only authority. And from this premise, everything else must follow: these primal parents become human, their white flesh becomes the *tabula rasa* for those wounds which will give rise to the hieroglyphs of language; and God leaves Eden for Heaven, enabling his creatures for the first time to conceive, through their imagining of him, earth seen from the air. This parable, beginning with copulation and an indigenous God, passing on through splitting and panic to birth and authority, and ending with language and estrangement (though with an uneasy joy in wide-ranging consciousness), will be read differently by different readers, who may recall, while reading Glück, Blake's ambiguous Genesis-parable stationing the angels, in the form of stars, as our surrogates.

Two recent lyrics, "Thanksgiving" and "The Drowned Children," are allusive in Glück's enigmatic manner, hopeless, staving off tears with finish and surface. In the bitter "Thanksgiving" the "summoned prey" come to eat, knowing that they will be eaten, once tracked down and located by their hoofprints in the snow:

> They have come again to graze the orchard,
> knowing they will be denied.
> The leaves have fallen; on the dry ground

the wind makes piles of them, sorting
all it destroys.

What doesn't move, the snow will cover.
It will give them away; their hooves
make patterns which the snow remembers.
In the cleared field, they linger
as the summoned prey whose part
is not to forgive. They can afford to die.
They have their place in the dying order.

In this ritual, eaters and eaten have their roles: the part of the eater
is not to relent, the part of the eaten is not to forgive; all is order,
all is a dying order. It may be an allegory of the generations. Nature
is as meticulous as the feasters: before it destroys, it sorts. The summoned prey, the sorted leaves, the lethal wind, the treacherous snow,
the waiting predators, the dying order: all this is prefaced by the
name of America's most genial family feast.

I put last Glück's chilling explanation of the event always considered the most unnatural of all—the death of children, in this case
by drowning:

You see, they have no judgment.
So it is natural that they should drown,
first the ice taking them in
and then, all winter, their wool scarves
floating behind them as they sink
until at last they are quiet.
And the pond lifts them in its manifold dark arms.

But death must come to them differently,
so close to the beginning.
As though they had always been
blind and weightless. Therefore
the rest is dreamed, the lamp,
the good white cloth that covered the table,
their bodies.

And yet they hear the names they used
like lures slipping over the pond:
What are you waiting for
come home, come home, lost
in the waters, blue and permanent.

"You see," Glück says ingenuously, "they have no judgment. / So it
is natural that they should drown," should resume their fetal con-

dition—blind, weightless, suspended in water. Weightless again, but now in the pond, they wait in the water hearing their parents' fruitless calls, "lost / in the waters, blue and permanent." Glück's last line evades analysis: is it an accident that I link *blue* and *permanent* with ink? It is hard to fix the speaker's relation to the children: she wants death to have been easy for them, she wants them to think of their brief earthly life as a dream; but yet she wants them still to hear the beckoning earthly voices, passing above them like lures over fish suspended just below the surface. It is as though Glück were a mother excusing their fault, hoping they were not hurt and do not miss her, and yet unwilling that they should forget her utterly or be deaf to her voice. We are made to remember, with her, the last moment, the floating scarf, surrealistically prolonged; and we bequeath them, with her, to the pond's colder maternity. But that last act, against all reason, is the call "come home, come home."

Glück's cryptic narratives invite our participation: we must, according to the case, fill out the story, substitute ourselves for the fictive personages, invent a scenario from which the speaker can utter her lines, decode the import, "solve" the allegory. Or such is our first impulse. Later, I think, we no longer care—in, for instance, "Thanksgiving"—who are the prey and who the predators: we read the poem, instead, as a truth complete within its own terms, reflecting one of the innumerable configurations into which experience falls. Glück's independent structures, populated by nameless and often ghostly forms engaged in archaic or timeless motions, satisfy without referent. They are far removed from the more circumstantial poetry written by women poets in the last ten years, but they remain poems chiefly about childhood, family life, love, and motherhood. In their obliquity and reserve, they offer an alternative to first-person "confession," while remaining indisputably personal.

The leap in style from Glück's relatively unformed first book, *Firstborn* (1968), to *The House on Marshland* suggests that she is her own best critic. I would hope she might follow the advice Keats and Stevens gave themselves, and write a long poem: "All kinds of favors," said Stevens, "drop from it."

Broadsides

The Broadside Press in Detroit—run singlehandedly by Dudley Randall without subsidy or grants—issues books of poems by black writers. The small eloquent volumes and single broadsides now make a sizable pile, and have been joined by tapes, anthologies, posters and an assortment of other things—an associated British series, an African cookbook, the beginning of a series of writings by black critics, and children's books. Though Randall's is not the only black press, it is the most imaginative; its inexpensive broadsides are the next thing to "pomes pennyeach," to borrow Joyce's words.

"I try," says Randall, who is a poet and a reference librarian, "to make the format of the Broadside harmonize with the poem in paper, color and typography," and the famous *We Real Cool* of Gwendolyn Brooks (Broadside No. 6) is, for instance, "lettered white on black to simulate scrawls on a blackboard." The instant appeal of broadsides is an old story and suggests that the world would prefer reading poems in the ways poets write them—one by one. It is almost a shame that books of poetry exist at all, and sinful that anthologies and Collected Works should betray the poems they print by jamming them together and running them into one another. The volumes that Randall publishes at the Broadside Press are almost the next best thing to broadsides; they are short, spare, wide-margined, well-designed and immediately readable. They are also, for readers of poetry, indispensable for hearing black America in its several voices.

If poetry is what you read for your sense of life, then novels and sociology won't do: black life in America can only be told to readers of poetry, black and white, by poetry itself. From these

"Good Black Poems, One by One" first appeared in the *New York Times Book Review*, September 29, 1974.

313

books, each a fragment of a life, life rises to our eyes. The reinforce-
ment of each separate book by the others in the Broadside Series
gives the whole the character of a communal voice, and the chorus
of the ensemble makes up one strain of that poetry of earth which,
as Keats said, is never dead. The scattered black voices of the past—
Hughes, McKay, Toomer, Cullen—seem not have had such a broad
base, even in the days of the Harlem Renaissance, as black poets
now have and will, it seems, continue to have.

A black press, though it seems a self-evident necessity these days,
may not have seemed so in 1965 and 1966, when Randall gathered
his first six Broadsides. In the collection as it now stands two principles of selection can be observed: a strong principle of hospitality to
different points of view and different styles of writing, and an
equally strong principle of aesthetic judgment. "I restrict the publications to poetry," Randall wrote in 1970 in the *Black Academy
Review*, adding "(which I think I understand and can judge not
too badly)." It is an understatement; a nationalist press (and there
have been innumerable ones) almost always fatally goes under to
propaganda. Randall must have resisted any number of well-
meaning but unbeautiful manuscripts. In almost all of the Broadside
volumes, even the slightest, there are lines that remain as only poetry
remains. Even in the poems written by William Thigpen, a poet
killed at twenty-three:

> Black baby stands naked clothed
> in smog colored sunlight
> pot-bellied, bow-legged and hungry
> crying, dying but alive.

Even in Pearl Lomax's picture of "Neighbor 1," a poem by a
twenty-four-year-old writer:

> Every morning
> he sweeps the porch
> with fluttering brown
> broom stick arms.
> steady strokes
> that push ugly clouds
> of rust and dry shit
> into the cool air.
> later, the porch
> will be thick with screaming
> children

314

and tiny pigfaced dogs
who mingle their
small stinking bodies
among the weeping babies
with an intimacy
that speaks of beds soggy
with human sweat
and dog sweat
and urine.
and then he will be sitting
smiling indulgently
holding his broom
like a thin golden scepter.
but for now
the porch is empty
and he is sweeping slowly
with a gentle push
that is almost
a caress.

"To leave our print, our image on the world, you'll find that 24 hours in a day is like seconds in a fast minute," says Don Lee, the best-known Broadside poet, in his introduction to *We Walk the Way of the New World*. Blacks will buy Broadside books to see their print, their image on the world, to watch the print—of a baby, of a neighbor—developing into visibility; but they knew the scenes already, for them it is a ratification, a confirmation. For a reviewer who is white, the scenes in the Broadside books are a series of prints, a movie, a choir, surpassing, as poetry for those who read it surpasses any other conveying of life, the images in stories, on TV, in the newspapers. The sunlight that clothes the naked baby, the baby dying alive—these things cannot be said except in words, and the mediating force of poetry allows emotion its full language. A photograph, even a movie, of "Neighbor 1" would be hard put to touch so lightly the mingled squalor and civility of life.

But these are the incidental graces of the series. The explosive center of the press's output is the poetry of Don Lee, who changed his name to a Swahili name, Haki R. Madhubuti. Lee's poems, written in a rapid, jerky, intense speech-rhythm in almost Morse shorthand, have sold over 100,000 copies without any large-scale advertising or mass distribution, a phenomenon which (like the success of Ginsberg's *Howl*) means that something is happening. Lee is not

Rod McKuen or Lois Wyse; he does not sell comfortable sentimentality. He sells on nerve, stamina, and satire. In him the sardonic and
savage turn-of-phrase long present in black speech as a survival
tactic finds its best poet; here it is in his elegy for Coltrane ("Don't
Cry, Scream"):

> the ofays heard you &
> were wiped out spaced.
> one clown asked me during,
> *my favorite things, if*
> you were practicing.
> I fired on the motherfucker & said.
> "i'm practicing."

These clean cool acid vignettes run side by side with the staccato
rhythms of Lee's long poems, most of them too long to quote, de-
pending as they do on quick sharp changes of focus in devastating
snapshots—like the much-anthologized "But He Was Cool or: he
even stopped for green lights":

> super-cool
> ultrablack
> a tan/purple
> had a beautiful shade
>
> he had a double-natural
> that wd put the sisters to shame.
> his dashikis were tailor made
> & his beads were imported sea shells
> (from some blk/country I never heard of)
> he was triple-hip.

The downfall of the super-cool is one of Lee's themes, and he
pursues it smartly; but there is likely to be some change from satire to
sympathy—not a bad turn—in his current alignment with the Pan-
Africanists. Lee can do, besides long poems, tiny epigrams:

> in 1959
> my mom
> was dead at the
> age of
> 35
> & nobody thought it
> unusual; not even
> me

He catches, before they vanish, words of conversation, undeniably
exact; "Big Momma" (his grandmother?) speaks to him:

> . . . the way niggers cut each other up round
> here every weekend that whiteman don't haveta
> worry bout no revolution . . . anyhow all he's
> gotta do is drop a truck load
> of dope out there
> on 43rd st. & all the niggers & yr revolutionaries
> be too busy getten high & then they'll turn round
> and fight each other over who got the mostest.

Because Lee's impartial accuracy catches survival as well as suc-
cumbing, his poems dispense faith along with satire. As he leaves
"Big Momma" he sees a derelict bearing out her gloom; but last
and best he sees her own resilience:

> touching the snow lightly i headed for 43rd st.
> at the corner i saw a brother crying while
> trying to hold up a lamp post,
> thru his watery eyes i cd see big momma's words.
>
> at sixty-eight
> she moves freely, is often right
> and when there is food
> eats joyously with her own
> real teeth.

The whole of "Big Momma" is even more touching and funny than
its parts, and there are many more poems like it in Lee's six collections. The sales of Lee's books will continue as long as his spurts of
anger, of derisive force, of bitter warning, and of undeniable hope
continue to find a mirror in the black readers who wait for each new
collection, but it is time for a wider public to hear his voice. David
Llorens, who wrote so well about Lee in *Ebony* a few years ago,
died at thirty-four in an automobile accident; Lee needs another
critic equally good.

A mixture of two accessible arts—photography and jazz—lies behind the rhythms, visual and aural, of these precious and irretriev-
able moments of documentary record. The image rules in these
new black poems, but not in the imagist way, with its deliberate suppression of emotion or statement. Here the image rules because, as
the only escape from the stoic or the satiric, it speaks purely. The

image is the hardening of complaint (the patient past) into accusation; it is permanent, like sculpture, irrefutable, like a photograph. Endurance, hope, nostalgia, poignancy, heartbreak—those emotions so often present in older black poets—have all taken on a sterner guise now, and the hatred also present in the older poets ("my life-long hate," McKay called it) has risen to a dominant note. Yeats once said that you could refute Hegel but not a saint or the Song of Sixpence, and the same is true of hate; it appears because it is. "I study hatred with great diligence," said Yeats, "For that's a passion in my own control." Many of these poets could say the same, among them Sonia Sanchez.

To hear Sanchez's flat, measured, controlled tones on the Broadsides tapes of her two books is to hear not the inflammatory but the concluded, a hatred bent to work, a hatred derisive even of the blues:

> blues ain't culture
>   they sounds of
> oppression . . .
>   when i hear billie's soft
> soul / ful sighs
>   of "am i blue"
>   i say
> no.   sweel / billie
>   no mo.
> no mo
>   blue / trains running on
>   this track
>   they all been de / railed.

Sanchez's new collection, *A Blue Book for Blue Black Magical Women*, finds in the Black Muslims a place to work; a rage for communal order causes her to "vomit up the past":

> i vomited up the waters
> that had separated me
> from Dahomey and Arabia
> and Timbuktoo and Muhammad
> and Asia and Allah.

Vomiting up "the stench / of the good ship *Jesus*," Sanchez finds a place where the frightened little girl "hidden behind black braids and stutters" can rest, and work; and write? perhaps.

Etheridge Knight's *Poems From Prison* (read on a tape made in prison) began a documentary, continued in his *Belly Song* and in the Broadside anthology, *Betcha Ain't: Poems From Attica,* of black prison life. It is only the beginning of a history of the feelings of black prisoners and addicts in our penal colonies, a history bound to be continued. "I boil my tears in a twisted spoon! / And dance like an angel on the point of a needle," says the addict. In a grand poem already anthologized by Dudley Randall in his excellent collection, *The Black Poets* (1971), Knight tells of his family ("The Idea of Ancestry"): "Taped to the wall of my cell are 47 pictures: 47 black / faces. . . . / They stare / across the space at me sprawling on my bunk. I know—mine." Another poem immortalizes a moment of prison despair; "Hard Rock Returns to Prison From the Hospital for the Criminal Insane":

> Hard Rock was "known not to take no shit
> From nobody," and he had the scars to prove it:
> Split purple lips, lumped ears, welts above
> His yellow eyes, and one long scar that cut
> Across his temple and plowed through a thick
> Canopy of kinky hair.

Hard Rock goes under, lobotomized, as the poem knows he will, but the lumps and the welts stay in the poem unrepaired and unrepentant. Knight's other side voices a longing no less deep than the yearning of the spirituals it remembers in its wish for Mississippi.

> One day we shall all go back—
> we shall surely all go back (down home . . .
> and the shame will leave our children's eyes (down home . . .

Misery, impatience, urgings, loneliness, refusals, love, and terror rise from the pages of Audre Lorde's *From a Land Where Other People Live* (nominated for a National Book Award). The events that mark all these books of poetry—the children burned in Birmingham, the assassinations of the Kennedys and King and Malcolm X—are here too:

> Malcolm was shot dead
> and I ran to reread
> all that he had written
> because death was becoming such an excellent measure
> of prophecy
> As I read his words the dark mangled children

came streaming out of the atlas
Hanoi Angola Guinea-Bissau Mozambique Pnam-Phen
merged into Bedford-Stuyvesant and Hazelhurst Mississippi
haunting my New York tenement that terribly bright summer
while Detroit and Watts and San Francisco were burning.

In Lorde's poems, "elementary forces collide in free fall": she has
a freer and less programmatic emphasis than Sanchez or Lee, though
she is no less pained. Her poems express uncertainties about choices
and roles, the difficulties and falterings of motherhood and living.
A rich long poem, "Moving Out" ("I am so glad to be moving /
away from this prison for black and white faces") is full of the
grotesque tyrannies of cooperative living:

last month a tenant was asked to leave
because someone saw him
wandering one morning up and down the tenth floor
with no clothes on
having locked himself out the night before
with the garbage
he could not fit into the incinerator
but it made no difference
the floor captain cut the leads to his cable TV
and he left covered in tangled wires of shame
his apartment was reconsecrated by a fumigator
I am so glad I am moving.

Lorde's freedom from norms of "poetic" language gives her an
acute simplicity. She spares herself not at all, seeing, for instance
her own inevitable obsolescence in the flourishing of her children:

... I shall be buried with the bones of an eagle
with a fierce detachment
and legends of the slain buffalo ...

A phoenix named Angela
nests in my children's brain
already
the growing herds of bison unnoticed
are being hunted down the federal canyons
of Yellowstone Park.

Lorde's poems, like others in the Broadside series, depend less on
ambiguity or irony than on the force of earnestness and plain speech.

320

The news of the day, in these poems, blends imperceptibly into the personal scarred phrase:

> Six black children
> burned to death in a day care center
> on the South Side
> kept in a condemned house
> for lack of funds
> firemen found their bodies
> like huddled lumps of charcoal
> with silent mouths and eyes wide open.

The last two lines of speechless vision are all that distinguish the poem from the evening news: but they are enough, a simile that is not even a simile, simile as fact. The almost artless voices of the black poets distrust a concealing rhetoric, and practice instead only the mute rhetoric of contiguity: the condemned house, the firemen, the huddled lumps. The convergence of causes to the final effect is rhetoric enough.

In the Broadside poets the false notes are few. The series is a powerful amassing of evidence given public life. It seems inevitable that the weight of feeling so intolerable and yet so inescapable in the lives of American blacks will find voice some day in a black poet as great as Whitman, who will gather up all the separate strands represented by these many volumes, who will speak for Muslims and non-Muslims, for the sufferers of past generations and the new militants, for rural and urban families alike; who, by his own comprehensiveness, will hear what Whitman called the "varied carols" of separate Americans and resume them in his own. Great poets tend to rise from a base of common thought, as Whitman needed all the nationalistic verse preceding his own, as well as Emerson's divine example. In its expansion, the Broadside Press has provided, it may be, that base. It only remains for libraries and schools to disseminate these poets, so that Dudley Randall's poets find that "great audience" without which, said Whitman, no great poems can arise.

Ammons, Berryman, Cummings

The mystery of e. e. cummings' great aborted talent is not solved, only deepened, by his *Complete Poems*. His brave quixotry, still proclaiming itself in his 1968 volume as it had forty-five years earlier in *Tulips and Chimneys*, has made him one of the poster gurus of a new generation: "one's not half two. It's two are halves of one," says the motto shining poignantly on a brilliant yellow-orange background, with a single flower as shy adornment of this revealed truth. In fact, cummings' first and last lines are nearly always, as in this case, his memorable ones, and most of his poems sag in the middle. While we all go round remembering "nobody, not even the rain, has such small hands," or "the single secret will still be man," or "there's a hell of a good universe next door, let's go," we rarely recall what led up to these declarations. Something is wrong with the relation of parts to wholes in cummings: we do not receive, as Coleridge thought we should, "such delight from the *whole*, as is compatible with a distinct gratification from each component *part*." Cummings was capable of stunning parts, and these parts glitter on the page like sparklers, float up like scraps of hurdy-gurdy music —but the sparks don't organize into constellations, the music falls apart into notes and remains unorchestrated. "Our genuine admiration of a great poet," Coleridge says, "is a continuous *under-current* of feeling; it is everywhere present, but seldom anywhere as a separate excitment." Whether this is true or not, it is certain that for the most part cummings provides only separate excitments, and is for that reason beloved of the young, who vibrate to his local effects and ask no more.

The disintegrative impulse was specially strong in cummings, and it is a wonder that he could put wholes together at all, he so much

"Poetry: Ammons, Berryman, Cummings" first appeared in *The Yale Review*, Spring 1973.

liked tinkering with words to take them apart, the dismemberment interesting him more, in some conspicuous examples, than the reintegration:

```
                                        r-p-o-p-h-e-s-s-a-g-r
                          who
       a)s w(e loo)k
       upnowgath
                   PPEGORHRASS
                          eringint(o-
    aThe):l
          eA
             !p:
    S                                                    a
                          (r
       rIvInG                           .gRrEaPsPhOs)
                                                      to
       rea(be)rran(com)gi(e)ngly
       ,grasshopper;
```

Infinite amusement: scatter the alphabet across a page and watch the letters scramble to get back together again into words. But the energy to reintegrate lies in the preexistent word: the energy to disintegrate arises from the michievously scissored poet, who is willing to allow a resurrection if he is permitted to dissect. His unreadable-aloud poems are cummings' most original and charming contribution to English verse. Though he may have learned the technique from the French, still he immortalized it in English, proving once and for all that rhythm and meter, and even sound, are not indispensable in poetry. Cummings' iconoclastic mind must have reveled in his avant-garde visual arrangements, while his painter's eye sensed their satisfying punning contours:

```
       l(a

       le
       af
       fa

       ll

       s)
       one
       l

       iness
```

I wish there were more of these exquisite and fragile triumphs. But, as Frost says, the truth keeps breaking in, or ought to, and cummings' mind was abysmally short on ideas, however long on gently frivolous games with letters. For some reason, one a biographer may eventually reveal, cummings violently mistrusted mixed feelings, or mixed ideas. Ambivalence was not a possibility to him, and everything had to be all or nothing. Where Keats could hear in the nightingale both ecstasy and requiem, where Frost could hear the hard "diminished thing" in the oven bird, cummings was unwilling to have any birdsong that was not unequivocally joyful:

"o purple finch
            please tell me why
this summer world(and you and i
who love so much to live)
            must die"
"if i
      should tell you anything"
(that eagerly sweet carolling
self answers me)
            "i could not sing"

So there it is. Song can't tell, and certainly can't tell of death, but must go on imperturbably carolling a babble of sweet sound. And the bird has the last word: cummings does not want or will not permit Hardy's turning from "the blessed Hope" of the aged darkling thrush to his own somber and unconvinced mind. It could be said that cummings has the right to be born an optimist, as Hardy to be a pessimist, and that such preferences are radically a matter of temperament. But cummings' optimism excludes too much; pain is scanted, and the perpetual analogy of man's life to the seasonal cycle awakes in the reader angry logical resistance instead of the faith-filled acquiescence cummings must have hoped for. "Given much mercy," says cummings, "more than even the / mercy of perfect sunlight after days / of dark," he

will climb; will blossom: will sing(like
april's own april and awake's awake)

"Oh you will, will you?" we rudely reply, and this response is fatal to anything cummings wished for from us. We know that, but try as hard as we can no willing suspension of disbelief arises, and so we appear ungenerous Scrooges, hissing "bah, humbug" to the spirit

of mercy, blosoming, life, love, and april which has dared to dis-
turb our cynical universe. This myth of the sensitive poet immured in
a greedy and unreceptive world was, not surprisingly, adopted by
cummings himself, as he established himself in a saved little en-
clave with his appreciative reader where they together could look
out and repudiate all the damned everyone else, the Scrooges, the
"mostpeople":

> The poems to come are for you and for me and are not for most-
> people—it's no use trying to pretend that mostpeople and our-
> selves are alike. Mostpeople have less in common with ourselves
> than the squarerootofminusone. You and I are human beings;
> mostpeople are snobs (*New Poems*, 1938).

It is not hard to see who is the snob here. Such a position is certainly constricting to a poet, and it provoked in cummings that affectation of superior wisdom which is one of the most irritating
things in his verse:

> seeker of truth
>
> follow no path
> all paths lead where
>
> truth is here

It is true that Emerson wrote things nearly as bad, but he had more
intellect (or genius) to use on the exotic Indianisms and Orientalisms
from which such poetry springs. Good poems often acknowledge,
as interior appeals, the regions they eventually dismiss, but cummings gives no temptations houseroom. Others are in error, and *he*
points the way to truth, allying himself, in a disarming want of
modesty, with those humble supporters the sun, the moon, the stars,
and the earth: these primal things say Why and Who and Be and
Now and May, but "the greedy the people" (in the poem so named)
ally themselves, chary and wary and busy and cunning and craven
as they are, with Because and Which and Seem and Until and Must.
The world is so clearly divided into the Good and the Bad, and
cummings is so sure which is which and whose side he is on, that
we are left gasping. Of course we too are against the greedy, and
so on, and that is why it is so hard to object to cummings. We cannot
exactly deny his "values," and we are all, I suppose, in favor of the
sun, the moon, and the stars. We may, however, doubt that these
sublime objects do exactly utter the imperatives cummings attributes

326

to them. How much truer and more painful, even if we do not agree
with its espousal, is Wordsworth's stoic farewell to Why, Who, Be,
Now, and May:

> I, loving freedom, and untried,
> No sport of every random gust,
> Yet being to myself a guide,
> Too blindly have reposed my trust . . .
> Me this unchartered freedom tires;
> I feel the weight of chance-desires.

In the same poem, Wordsworth gave full acknowledgment to the
wish for an ethos like cummings':

> Serene will be our days and bright,
> And happy will our nature be,
> When love is an unerring light
> And joy its own security.

Cummings seems never to have felt any misgivings about his
creed—or, if he felt them, he only raised his voice more defiantly in
his utopian affirmations. The affirmations become, in the *Complete
Poems,* ever more stereotyped, until one could write a cummings
poem oneself simply by juggling the cummings syntax and the cummings counters: young, new, yes, frail, love, bright, dream, doom,
flower, moon, small, deep, touch, least, sweet, brief, guess, kiss, lost,
and on and on and on.

The murderous devaluation of intellect in cummings has yet to
be explained. Perhaps it comes from seeing all those Cambridge
ladies living in furnished souls; perhaps intellect stood in cummings'
mind for his parents. In any case, a guerrilla war against intellect
is being conducted almost perversely all through the *Complete
Poems:*

> —the best gesture of my brain is less than
> your eyelids' flutter which says
>
> we are for each other
>   . . . not
> all matterings of mind
>
> equal one violet

Cummings protests so much (far more than Wordsworth ever
did) that nature is better than mind that the brain and the mind in

his poetry take on sinister potential. His willed atrophy of both is matter for regret, especially since his satiric talent was the product of a sharp malicious intellect enjoying its own precision. If cummings had not been so afraid of what are now called "negative feelings," we might have had less slush about love and april and more wit; if he had kept in mind more often the ironic circumstances under which "love" is conducted, we might have had more poems like the immortal one about the necking couple:

> may i feel said he
> (i'll squeal said she
> just once said he)
> it's fun said she
>
> (may i touch said he
> how much said she
> a lot said he)
> why not said she
>
> (let's go said he
> not too far said she
> what's too far said he
> where you are said she)
>
> may i stay said he
> (which way said she
> like this said he
> if you kiss said she
>
> may I move said he
> is it love said she)
> if you're willing said he
> (but you're killing said she
>
> but it's life said he
> but your wife said she
> now said he)
> ow said she
>
> (tiptop said he
> don't stop said she
> oh no said he)
> go slow said she
>
> (cccome?said he
> ummm said she)
> you're divine!said he
> (you are Mine said she)

Aggression and pathos arise together here as they cannot in cummings' sentimental verse. Early in the *Complete Poems* two cummings-selves elbow each other for room: the cummings who sketches, with brilliant economy, low-life Paris—madams, whores, sailors, bars, sidewalks; and then there is the cummings, inheritor of the troubadours, who sings ballades of love. In many of the poems of *Tulips and Chimneys* (1923) cummings allows both selves a say, but somehow, in later years, a disjunction took place, and the pretty and the miserable ceased to communicate with each other in his verse. His delighted humor (visible in poems like "my sweet old etcetera" and "nobody loses all the time") thinned mysteriously; his dancing rhythms ("anyone lived in a pretty how town") were given less and less play; his caprices of letter-jokes became less joyous and more contrived; his satire (especially on women) became uglier; and only the dogged sentimentality remained, spreading like a proliferating growth until it crowded out the rest, pretending its name was love and joy when its name really was fear of all that the earlier self had justly tried to include. The final dwarf of cummings is a disappointment to American letters. He remains a poet who is best represented by his anthologized self—by olaf glad and big, by the little lame ballon-man, by uncle sol, by the little couple on the wedding-cake, by ignorance tobogganing into know and trudging up to ignorance again. Cummings was happiest in ignorance, even though he was shy of saying so in his own voice and, for all his sonnets on sensitive love, he had a hankering after the know-nothing, the gross, and the violent. In every future selection from his verse (if only to give his young admirers some perspective) after the obligatory printing of "nobody, not even the rain, has such small hands," there should be printed the Archie-Bunker rant of the newly republished "the boys i mean are not refined," a poem praising the "boys" who "do not give a shit for wit" and "do not give a fart for art":

> the boys i mean are not refined
> they cannot chat of that and this
> they do not give a fart for art
> they kill like you would take a piss
>
> they speak whatever's on their mind
> they do whatever's in their pants
> the boys i mean are not refined
> they shake the mountains when they dance

The admiration for boys who can "shake the mountains when they dance" (and who can hump their girls thirteen times a night) *because* they hate art and wit is a measure of cummings' self-hatred, and the measure of self-hatred is the measure of sentimentality.

Nevertheless, cummings' early volumes done in the twenties— roughly, the first half of this collection—remain a heady experience-in-retrospect, a joke on all New England proper "poyetry," and a preserved exhilaration scampering through Cambridge halls and raising indignant dust.

Another collection, without the finality of cummings', presents the poems of A. R. Ammons written between 1951 and 1971. Bibliographically speaking, the book is confusing, with no information on what volumes the poems originally appeared in, nor with any indication whether poems have been dropped or volumes not included, nor an account of revisions, if any. In short, it is a selected collected poems, with the poems arranged on odd principles (poems composed during a four- or five-year period are grouped together, but not in the sequence in which they appeared at first book publication). In *Briefings* (1971) Ammons brought his difficult form of short poetry to perfection. The poetry he is best able to write is deprived of almost everything other poets have used, notably people and adjectives. (Where would Whitman have been, shorn of his soldiers, sleepers, and shipwrecked women, not to speak of his incandescent palette of adjectives?) Ammons has written some poems about "people," including his mule Silver, and even permits himself an adjective now and then, but rarely one more subjective than an adjective of color or measurement. "Half-dark," "massive," "high," "giant," "distant," "long," "broad," "noticeable," "late," "dry," "diminished," "passable" (implying height of hills), and "quiet" are the crop gleaned from two pages chosen at random (188–189) in the *Collected Poems,* and these "objective" adjectives, Ammons' own, are balanced by only one "subjective" adjective on the same pages ("taxing"— an opinion imputed to a hill trying to be a mountain and finding it hard). Such word-counts are perhaps not very gripping, but I found myself reduced to them in trying to understand what new language Ammons is inventing. (If he never succeeded, it wouldn't matter what he was up to, but since he does bring it off, we need to know how he is working out for us "a new knowledge of reality.") What he does is remarkable both in its sparseness and in its variety. One can't say "richness" because there is no sensual "give" in this poetry—but it does attempt an imitative recreation, no less, of the whole variety of the natural world, if not, regrettably, of what Stevens called its "affluence." But if, as Ammons seems to think, affluence is brought rather by the perceiving and receptive mind, as a quality, rather than inhering in nature itself (nature, who perceives herself singly, we may say, as an acorn here, a brook there, rather than corporately congratulating herself on all her brooks), then a poetry attempting this ascetic unattributiveness must refrain from celebrating the multiplicity of the world in human terms. Why it should be so wrong to let in human gestalt-making is another question; Ammons permits himself entry when the poem is about himself, but he won't have any of those interfering adjectival subjectivities when he's occupied with morning glories or caterpillars or redwoods. This discipline of perfect notation is almost monklike, and, monklike, it takes what comes each day as the day's revelation of, so to speak, the will of God. Ammons wakes asking what the world will today offer him as a lesson and he is scarcely permitted choice: if it is snowing, he has to deduce the mantra in the snow; if it is a night with a masked aurora, it is to the aurora that he must compose that night's address. He is like a guitarist presented every day with a different señorita in the balcony, and commanded, like some latter-day Sheherezade, to think up each day different but appropriate serenades reflecting the lady's different looks.

In one way, given the fertile changingness of the external world, and its numberless inhabitants animal, vegetable, and mineral, this is a very rich discipline. On the other hand, it risks being merely fussy. If one should stop caring just what the weather is doing day after day in Ithaca, all is lost:

> it's snowing now with
>
> the sun shining: squalls with clearings: today is Tues-
> day: yesterday there were 9 hrs and 2 minutes of
> daylight, sunup to sundown: that means light is
>
> broadening: right here at the edge of winter-beginning's
> winter-ending: today will probably be 9 hrs and 3 minutes:
> tomorrow will be different, maybe 9 hrs and 4 minutes.

There is a fair amount of this sort of thing, especially in the rather willed long poem *Tape for the Turn of the Year* (you buy a roll of adding-machine tape and type on it for a couple of weeks until the tape is all typed and then you have finished your poem). There is also a trust that everything you do, like everything the weather

331

does, has its part in the configuration of the whole. Ammons' gas
station tells him his car is ready and he goes to get it:

the total parts came to $7.79, 1 push rod ($1.25), 1
rocker arm ($1.35), 1 rocker retainer ($0.50), 1 set 2
gaskets @ $2.10 ($4.20), and 1 roll electrical tape ($0.49):
the total labor was $10.50: r & r (remove and repair?)

1. (left?) valve cover, r & r both valve covers, replace
rocker arm, push rod, & retainer on #4 cyl intake valve:
all in all I thought I got off easy: one thing interesting

is that Ned's Corners Station is at 909 Hanshaw Road
and I'm 606 Hanshaw Road: that's configuration.

Only if you think it is, is it configuration, and for all Ammons'
jauntiness, he carries this Wordsworthian notion of everything-
adding-up to an extreme. In Wordsworth, it sounds rather saner:

How strange, that all
The terrors, pains, and early miseries,
Regrets, vexations, lassitudes interfused
Within my mind, should e'er have born a part,
And that a needful part, in making up
The calm existence that is mine when I
Am worthy of myself!

Ammons' version of this omnivorousness is offered us in "Hiber-
naculum," one of the several long poems he has recently and self-
consciously written:

In the swim and genesis of the underlying reality things
assume metes and bounds, survive through the wear
of free-being against flux, then break down to swim and

genesis again.

And so he writes his "poem variable as a dying man, willing to try
anything," even catalogues of spare parts. Very often, in his later
poetry, Ammons tries to reassure himself on the value of his poetics
by comparing it to the geological and organic motions of the universe, so molecularly deep and so cosmically all-embracing: we hear
about the genetic code and double helices, cryogenic events and su-
pernovas, colloidal floats and platelets, estuary populations, nuclea-
tions, defoliations, the underground mantle, and so on, through all

the vocabulary, one might say, of *Scientific American*. "*Ecology* is my word," declares Ammons adding "my other word is / *provisional*," and he says elsewhere, half in play and half in earnest:

> I get lost for fun,
> because there's no chance of getting lost: I am seeking the
> mechanisms physical, physiological, epistemological, electrical,
>
> chemical, esthetic, social, religious, by which many, kept
> discrete as many, expresses itself into the
> manageable rafters of salience, lofts to comprehension.

This "Essay on Poetics" is presented with an unusual amount of candor, summing up what we had had glimpses of in "Motion" and "Poetics" and "Zone," and any critic would be glad if one day he understood Ammons as well as Ammons, rather exceptionally among poets, understands himself. "I was thinking last June," he confesses, "so multiple and diverse is the reality of a tree, that I / ought to do a booklength piece on the elm in the backyard here: / wish I had done it now because it could stand for truth, too." In fact, he even begins the tree poem, and in a burst of fancy imagines how he would have to determine the tree's place in space by longitude, latittude, distance from the earth's core, and other methods. Never has there been a poetry so sublimely above the possible appetite of its potential readers. Genial as Ammons' programs are, and impressive as his lava-flows of language become in the long poems, these longer efforts are less likely to win an audience (except those of us captive enough to listen like a three-years' child to anything new and personal being done with words) than the shorter poems.

It is with his short poems, where he does obstinate battle with both multiplicity and abstraction at once, being fair to the weeds and the vines and the grasses and the worms, and at the same time rising to grand speculations on man's nature and the design of life, that Ammons will win a permanent audience. Ammons' conversations with mountains are the friendliest and most colloquial conversations with the inanimate recorded in poetry since Herbert talked to his shooting-star ("Virtu," "Classic," "Reversal," "Schooling," and "Eyesight" belong to this group); another group includes poems rejoicing in the world, like the beautiful "This Bright Day": others retell, over and over, with a satisfying variety in imagery, the climb up to perspective and the slide back down to particularity, that process out of which lyric is built (and these include the splendid

"Two Possibilities," "One More Time," and "High and Low," with
its Emersonian determination and its rueful country debacle):

> A mountain risen
> in me
> I said
> this implacability
> must be met:
> so I climbed
> the peak:
> height shook and
> wind leaned
> I said what
> kind of country is
> this anyhow and
> rubbled
> down the slopes to
> small rock
> and scattered weed.

Then there is another group, not making points at all, just seeing
how things are: these are the ones I like best, and would first an-
thologize, the ones like "Treaties," where Ammons' instinctive
identification with earthly events affords a symbolism which remains natural and, though clear, inconspicuous:

> My great wars close:
> ahead, papers,
> signatures, the glimmering
> in shade of
> leaf and raised wine:
> orchards, orchards,
> vineyards, fields:
> spiralling slow time while
> the medlar
> smarts and glows and
> empty nests
> come out in the open:
> fall rain then stirs
> the black creek and
> the small leaf slips in.

Such poems, though perhaps not Ammons' superfically most ambitious, are the ones that last in the mind, drawing as they do on his

feeling that "if a squash blossom dies, I feel withered as a stained /
zucchini and blame my nature." Ammons has taken into the realm
of nature Donne's "any man's death diminishes me," and so can
write about the lives and deaths in nature as though they were (and
they are) his own. It is a severe poetry, attempting the particularity
of Hopkins with none of what Hopkins' schoolmates called his
"gush," trying for the abstraction of Stevens without Stevens' inhuman remove from the world of fact, aiming at Williams' affection-
ateness toward the quotidian without Williams' romantic drift. Since
Ammons is still in mid-career, we can watch the experiment, we
hope, for a good while yet: if he can succeed (even granting the
absurdity of some of the niches and odds corners of his enterprise),
he will have written the first twentieth-century poetry wholly
purged of the romantic.

As for John Berryman, he appears on the dust jacket of this posthumous volume shorn of three-quarters of his wild beard, his wild
eyes dimmed: not the elegant poet of his earlier pictures, neither
is he the irrepressible Henry, hair flying in the wind, hulking like a
mountain, of the middle photographs. Henry has died in this volume,
pretty much, and the poet died with him, the man waiting, but not
much longer, to die too. A derisive laughter mocks, in *Delusions, etc.*,
all human resources—therapy, hospitals, electroshock:

> She says: *Seek help!* Ha-ha Ha-ha & Christ . . .
>
> I faint for some soft & solid & sudden way out
> as quiet as hemlock in that Attic prose
>
> with comprehending friends attending—
> a certain reluctance but desire here too,
> the sweet cold numbing upward from my burning feet,
> a last & calm request, which will be granted.

Denied this last amenity, Berryman was reduced to an ungainly leap
from a bridge. "Taking cover," he said.
   With the human exhausted, Berryman solicited the divine, and
in this collection he remember all his early fervent reading—in
Hopkins, in Herbert, in Donne—as he writes his "Opus Dei" and
the other religious poems in the volume. They are not good. His
"newly simple heart" and his visions, whatever temporary calm they
gave his soul, gave no new life to his poetry, and the last two poems,
particularly, are intolerable to read, ending as they do "All the black
same I dance my blue head off!" and (after saying that Christ died

to make him happy) "Well, he has! / I am so happy I could scream! / It's *enough!* I can't BEAR ANY MORE. / *Let this be it.* I've *had* it. I can't wait." There are two good poems, "Beethoven Triumphant" and "Henry's Understanding." In the religious poems, Berryman left behind Henry's conspiracies and surreptitiousness, Henry's secret preenings and secret frights and violent self-loathings, his doleful clown-songs, showing him perpetually at a disadvantage. When he became the redeemed child of God, his shamefaced vocabulary drooped useless, and no poet can be expected to invent, all at once and at the end of his life, a convincing new stance, a new style in architecture along with his change of heart. Berryman's suicide threw all finally into question—Henry's sly resourcefulness as much as Berryman's abject faith. In the end, it seems, neither was enough to sustain him, and even though a voice divine the storm allayed, a light propitious shone, this castaway could not avoid another rising of the gulf to overwhelm him.

Eight Poets

On the principle that the best new book by a young poet should be given first place in a group review, I begin with Dave Smith's *Cumberland Station* before going on to other poets, some new, some established, and one—W. H. Auden—who has (to quote his own words about Yeats) "become his admirers."

Smith is not self-explanatory. His opening lines, often obscure, mysteriously referential, flatten out on the page in laconic presence: "He can only drink tea now, screwed and filed"; or "The girl was chosen at random. He pointed / for the mystical brunette behind her." After a while the situations clear up. Smith is not a surrealist; implicit scenarios lie behind these brusque entrances. Smith, judging by his exquisite fitting of lines together, intends his opacity, his length of breath, and his peculiar style, in which full stops scarcely imply the end of anything and sentences which continue for lines and lines nonetheless keep a firm hold on themselves. Smith's first book, *The Fisherman's Whore* (preceded by two small collections), was published in 1974, and a good selection from that volume, as well as a slightly too-defiant essay by Smith on his own verse, can be found in William Heyen's attractive book, *American Poets in 1976*. In the essay, Smith describes both his first volume and this new one:

> Many of my poems root in Poquoson, Virginia, an anonymous fishing village whose name, from the Chiskiac, means "flat land." A peninsula bordered by Back River, the Poquoson River, and the Chesapeake Bay, it lies due south of Yorktown and dates settlement prior to 1631. It is neither quaint nor restored, has changed little except for urban influx in the last decade . . . [A waterman of these marshes] will, in season, set fike nets, clam with a rake in water to his waist, oyster with twelve-foot tongs, crab by baiting

"Recent Poetry: Eight Poets" first appeared in *The Yale Review*, Spring 1977.

337

a pot made of chicken wire, a cube, setting it on the bottom and returning, when the tide turns, to retrieve what he has caught. Pots weigh maybe forty pounds and an average string will exceed eighty pots . . . I am [now] writing away from and out of my swamp poems, beginning to evolve a sequential poem of one family's generational descent. It starts in present time at a funeral, pushes back through "history," and settles up in present time in Poquoson. It's my family, but I'm not confessing.

Smith is at his best writing about America—marshes, oyster scows, "ribbed sealight," night fishing for bluefish, deaths at sea, cemeteries, rotting automobiles, Chicago, cross-country driving, singing as a boy in a church choir, visiting a decaying railroad station:

> Gray brick, ash, hand-bent railings, steps so big
> it takes hours to mount them, polished oak
> pews holding the slim hafts of sun, and one
> splash of the Pittsburgh Post-Gazette . . .
>   In this vaulted hall
> I think of all the dirt poured down
> from shovels and trains and empty pockets.
> I stare into the huge malignant headlamps
> circling the gray walls and catch a stuttered
> glimpse of faces stunned like deer on a track.

Cumberland Station gets better as it goes along; its lapses into imitation (of Hopkins, Thomas, and Lowell—like Berryman's earlier echoes) are forgivable in a second book, by a thirty-four-year-old poet. Smith at his best combines a gift for narrative with a gift for the *mot juste*—talents which rarely go together. He does not yet entirely trust his power of description to carry his feelings, and stops sometimes to make feeling explicit: the title poem ends,

> Grandfather, I wish I had the guts
> to tell you this is a place I hope
> I never have to go through again.

Sentimentality and plain speaking sometimes get confused in this book. But Smith's best landscapes hover over meaning in a way both tantalizing and beautiful. This is a marsh with abandoned houses:

> Today is no different, the waters flood hulks
> of empty houses, leaving beer cans to gleam
> in the indifferent moon. The first stalks of

narcissus break the ground with gold
though March still means tonight to freeze.

I know this place, its small mustering of facts
wind-worn and useless, real and repeated, the same
anywhere. At the end the creek leads to a room,
one placid boat swinging at a stick, pines sieving

air, the cleat ringing like small jewelry.

This reticently elegiac passage gives a clear view of Smith's meditating euphonies and inventive rhythms, strict as classical meter one moment and loose as talk the next. Smith has the unexpectedness of the original poet in closing his description with the ringing boat cleat.

Two theoretical poems help shed light on Smith's intentions. One is a touching American homage to a classic lyric genre, written in obedience to Louise Glück's remark (given as epigraph) that "Everyone should write a spring poem." I quote from the fourth line on:

A car warms
its rusting hulk in a meadow: weeds slog
up its flanks in martial weather. April
or late March is our month. There is a fog
of spunky mildew and sweaty tufts spill
from the damp rump of a back seat. A spring
thrusts one gleaming tip out, a brilliant tooth
uncoiling from Winter's tension, a ring
of insects along, working out the Truth.
Each year this car, melting around that spring,
hears nails trench from boards and every squeak sing.

The last four words are derivative and disappointing, of course: but after all, how many Shakespearean sonnets are written these days? Though there are obvious ironies in the interplay of subject, theme, and form here, Smith is thoroughly traditional in his non-ironic celebration of the way that pun-engendered spring thrusts out one gleaming shoot. But in another set of poems he expresses a critique of the presuppositions of art, and worries over the parts of life generally excluded from lyric—violence, unremarkable lives, obsolete habits of work, drunks, the unemployed. Smith's motives are not political: these are not "proletarian" poems. Rather, his hunger to preserve the excluded is a hunger to perpetuate his own imaginative life, nurtured by these stimuli—to forget them would be to destroy his own canvas. And yet lyric is not propitious to anecdotal, irregular, and crude material. Smith's own difficulties of handling appear in the poem which directly addresses this question, "The Perspective and Limits of Snapshots." The "plot" of the poem is a simple contrast between a photograph of Menchville, Virginia, by Aubrey Bodine in which all is "eloquent peace," and the human realities of Menchville excluded by the photograph, "the county farm and the drunks / pressed against wire screens, sniffing the James," including an oysterman who murdered his wife. The best thing in the poem is the description of the peace of the photograph:

> Two-man oyster scows lie shoulder to shoulder,
> as if you walk them, one land to another,
> no narrow channel hidden in the glossy middle
> like a blurred stroke, current grinning at hulls.
> It is an entirely eloquent peace, with lolling
> ropes and liquid glitter.

Once Smith gets to the murderer, on the other hand, the poem goes soft:

> And if he could he would spit in his hand and tell
> his nameless black cellmate there are many men
> for whom the world is neither oyster nor pearl.

We can say, if we wish, that this is an improbable fiction, that an oysterman-murderer would not be likely to speak in parables of oysters and pearls to his black cellmate; or we can say that Smith is simply substituting his own moral; or that the neatness of the ending is in unhappy conflict with the presumed function of the closing lines —which should contrast the drunkenness and murder with the false peace of the photographer's composition. In spite of such occasional uneasiness of tone, Smith has all the seriousness and power to become a weighty poet.

Ellen Bryant Voigt has mixed success in her first book, *Claiming Kin*. There are good things in almost all of the poems—and bad things, too. She, like Smith, feels her way well into her vowels and consonants; her rhythms, unlike his elastic ones, are rigid and tense, on purpose; and she alternates between a fine clarity and a sporadic want of taste. It is hard to bring off lines like "a piece of love, our mother lode / of tradition, our nigra mammy"; and what reader of poetry can help remembering Williams' "asphodel, that greeny flower" when a young poet writes of "catalpa, that beany tree"? There is in Voigt an interest in the lurid—a man shoots his wife by mistake; a girl is buried alive. It is not clear whether these are to be seen as exceptions or rules. The better poems inhabit a small lyric frame embracing the private self, marriage, and childlessness. There are memorable lines: "Confronting frost, / the trees assume their attitudes of pain"; a woman is "like a hawk adrift in its fine solution of clouds." The most successful single poem, again a poem of American homage to an eternal subgenre, is "Harvest," which retains mystery even in its explicitness:

> The farmer circles the pasture
> checking fences. Deep
> in the broomstraw, the dove withholds
>
> her three notes. The sky
> to the southwest is uniformly
> blue. Years of plowing under
>
> have brought this red clay to its
> green conclusion.
> Down back,
>
> the herd
> clusters to the loading pen.
> Only disease or dogpack
>
> could alter such order. Is that
> what he asks for in the late
> fields, the falling afternoon?

The shapeliness of such a poem avoids both the evil of enumeration-too-long-continued and the evil of banality. When Voigt is banal, she seems to step out of poetry altogether: finding her father asleep, when she visits, she writes in flatfooted sentiment:

> Why isn't he out in the fields, our common passion?
> I want to wake him with kisses,
> I want to reach out and stroke his hand.
> But I turn away, without speech or gesture,
> having for so long withheld my body from him.

These alternations of talent and flaccidity make this a baffling collection. One would like to read more from the Voigt who sees an infant's fist, with its "palm / already mapped and pencilled in," or who describes, in a poem called "Suicides," whales beaching themselves on shore:

Graceful in water, they labor now
toward palmetto and tufted
hillocks, the hot sun bleaching
and drying out. Their fins dig into
something solid, the broad flukes
spade, then anchor in the sand.

Viper Jazz is James Tate's sixth book, and it is a monument to desiccation. Tate's terse sentences were always chilly: now they are, like Matthew Arnold, three parts iced over. Surreal equivalents for life and its emotions march down the page in reportage:

One night Slim Victuals, Estil Loney and
Snörpa Little-Dew were out on a spree—

apricot-juice heads all.
They knocked over a couple of tabularasas.

Snörpa whispered
into the ear of a passing shoplifter:
"You have just made a complete fool of yourself!"

The simple surrealistic appears in Tate's knowledgeable references to hairy cups of coffee, an eyeball with a nipple on it, a doll with fangs, and a creature who "opened his mouth once to let out a dead rat." This sort of thing is the tag end of Surrealism, making an in-joke out of a movement which was, after all, at its inception, full of vitality. Tate's disbelief in art generates a dead-end poetry of the sort seen in the prose-poem called "Same Tits":

It was one of those days. I was walking down the St.
and this poster glassed in a theater billboard caught
my eye. A really gorgeous set of tits. It was noon,
hot as hell outside. So I said what the hell, paid my
$2.50 and went in. Got a seat all by myself right in
the middle. The curtain opens: there's the same poster
by itself in the middle of the stage. I sat there sweating.
Finally decided to get the hell out of there. It was
still noon, hot as hell outside.

A piece which leaves a bad taste in the mouth: representation as representation, tits as swindle, hot as hell, what the hell, get the hell out, hot as hell. It's a point of view—it's even a mood—but does it pay its way on the page, so to speak? The same question rises in the gorge after reading Tate's poem of disbelief in words, called "Who Gets the Bitterroot?" The gimmick here is to substitute for every nominal adjective or noun, common or proper, the plurisignificant blank-die-of-a-word "Bitterroot." Dr. Bitterroot, married to Mrs. Bitterroot, floats down Bitterroot River in his new Bitterroot outboard, and diagnoses the sick wife of a bitterroot farmer:

> Dr. Bitterroot right away
> diagnoses a rotten cancerous bitterroot
> and reached for his bitterroot which he stabbed
> into her bitterroot up the bitterroot canal.

This sort of thing goes on for eleven more lines.

Tate's jazz is better when less viperous. "Man's / undigestible hatred of himself" has grown on Tate until the poems have hardened into forms of predictable repellency. Emily Dickinson's two lovers laid in adjoining tombs—the one who died for Beauty and the one who died for Truth—congeal into Tate's "couple of drifters / on this planet of / some odd billion customers / open all night":

> She was always
> loving and attentive
> but made
> what I considered
> an abnormal number of morbid references,
> so that at times I felt like a fungus.
> Meanwhile, we drank and smoked
> and listened to country music.
> She died in her room
> and I died in mine.

Tate's style is finally too misanthropic to let out more than these wizened sentences. He hoards and counts, deals out stingily, snaps threads. It's a partial truth—of life and art—but only just.

Lawrence Raab's second book, *The Collector of Cold Weather*, mixes two unlikely genres, the paranoid and the disembodied. The paranoid one is trivial: enemies, assassins, guns, plots from Sherlock Holmes:

> The investigators noted:
> 1) The disappearance of the keys,
> 2) The incident of the jumping soap,
> 3) The curious occurrence in the cat's cemetery.

On the other hand, the disembodied fantasies are pleasing in their spectral way: "Snow attempts to circle us with its pale confusions . . . the storm divides before us, closes after us." "Whatever we can discover / remains / hidden by what it shows." A photograph "grows darker / each time the sun touches it." Things drift, disappear, are taken away; people remain enigmatically silent; footsteps pass and recede, and huge snowmen with "blind, smashed faces" appear in public parks. Raab quotes Borges: "The imminence of a revelation that does not take place is, perhaps, the esthetic fact." Raab likes to write sequences leading up to those revelations, but his shorter sequence "Water" seems to me more accomplished than the longer title poem, where the suspense appears contrived. "Water" moves almost imperceptibly:

> Whichever way water
> turns it touches
> itself turning in another direction
>
> Invisible now
> now reflecting whoever
> finds himself looking
> beneath the line of the wind
>
> You remember the rules
>
> Water seeks the level that pleases it
> making a place for itself
> wherever it chooses
>
> calling everything
> it touches its own
> and falling back
> in its own good time.

The symbol, if water is here a symbol, borrows its own fluidity and waywardness for its form until it dies quietly, two poems later, in "a maze of circles." This is mystery without the assassins, and it tastes better on the tongue.

Theodore Weiss's *Fireweeds*, his seventh collection, raises in acute form the question of the viability of "poetic diction." Hopkins is the chief influence on Weiss, everywhere apparent (Weiss published a short essay on Hopkins long ago, and has never lost his affection for Hopkinsian effects); Whitman (a spider's "filaments" and the ocean's "souse"), Crane ("spindrift"), Keats ("a figure urn-engraved"), and Yeats ("a scarecrow on a stick") also are in evidence. Weiss not only imitates particular modern masters, he imitates the whole tradition of poetic language, especially in his long poem "The Storeroom," a sequence about Penelope's waiting for Ulysses. Weiss seems to wish to give Penelope a semi-archaic speech, but the result is a strange pastiche:

> Why any tattered beggar
> might be he. That straggly greybeard, say
> a scarecrow on a stick, and many a day
> skulked about their grounds.
>
> Her glance
> fixed on far distance, on an image graved
> into her memory time's graved the more,
> can she, weeping for her lord, take in
> this man by her, the story he'd be telling?

Some of this diction comes simply from the storehouse of cliché: "Hot tears crash over her," she fears Ulysses "dashed against some savage coast"; an "air . . . springs unbidden from her lips"; we see "the changing moon," something "to highlight . . . her loveliness," "the first warm touch of dawn"; they have "shared . . . the bread of her body," and so on.

These dubious uses of language appear also in poems spoken in Weiss's own twentieth-century voice:

> Yet if a face
> had launched the thousand ships
> that still are sailing,
> Struck a fire
> that has never failed, great art
> it took, breath-stoking words,
> to seal it in.
> Men's arson hearts
> best keep that bonfire's beacon going.

"Whatever flames upon the night, / Man's own resinous heart has fed," the reader obediently echoes. But does Weiss want to re-do Yeats? Weiss's reverence for literature, the literary, the artistic, and the past is so deep that it threatens to overwhelm his own voice. Unable to be free with tradition, he risks being paralyzed by it.

Weiss is most contemporary in the movement of his verse, which resists the conventional in refusing the unit. Most of his poems, though divided into "stanzas," are really one seamless flowing unit, and Weiss is adept in managing the meanders of his form, in following the obscurer reaches of feeling. There is an authenticity to his inlets and coves, his slow terracings, his lapses and turnings. The "incessant, boundless wish for change," as he calls it in one poem, motivates all his writing, and so he needs to be quoted at length. Here he is, like Leopardi, with the infinite:

> Meantime, the mind roams out, its poem,
> grazing in a field at best half known,
> romping with figures so preoccupied
> they hardly tell themselves apart
> from the mist rising out of whitish
> grass.
>   Or maybe lying on a cliff
> that seems miles high, the sky above—
> though resting by you, chin upon your
> rock—one cushiony cloud, looking down
> into a sea, one set of frizzled waves,
> identical warriors in a phalanx, doing
> the same thing over and over again
> that they look standing still.

Weiss praises the state of "not insisting . . . not pressing down upon oneself / as on one's words, hoping to catch them unawares." His poems are meant to disperse and fill a space; less vigorous than Whitman's self-diffusing into air, Weiss's mists re-condense on themselves at the close of his poems, and come to conclusions almost too positive for their nature. If he is enumerating old themes in this collection—he has written before about Ulysses and Caliban, for instance—he is also moving easily in his individual drifts, borrowing stubbornly from certain habits of nature itself, with its gulls "sailing, sailing, never moving," and "that steady drone, almost like the air itself, its sighing."

Elizabeth Bishop's *Geography III* was awarded the National Book Critics' Circle Prize. It is odd that the one translation in the volume, from the Spanish of Octavio Paz, should be the poem most illuminating about Bishop's own practice. Paz is describing Joseph Cornell's boxes, "Hexahedrons of wood and glass, / scarcely bigger than a shoebox, / with room in them for night and all its lights." They contain "marbles, buttons, thimbles, dice, / pins, stamps, and glass beads," are the "hotel of crickets and constellations." Bishop's poems have a deceptively light surface, more often than not, and contain some of the same "trivia" appearing in Cornell. They appear to find stridency the most serious aesthetic sin, and they have a domestic tone. At the same time, as in the creations of Cornell, "the reflector of the inner eye / scatters the spectacle: God all alone above an extinct world." A decisive maker, of an almost Quaker plainness of speech (lightened and softened by humor or tenderness), utters these poems, and within their strict dimensions suggests what one reflective mind has made of the whole human spectacle. The mind is both reclusive and inquiring: in its reclusive phase it would be a seaside Thoreau, living alone in a "crooked box / set up on pilings" on Duxbury Beach:

> I'd like to retire there and do *nothing*,
> or nothing much, forever, in two bare rooms:
> look through binoculars, read boring books,
> old, long, long books, and write down useless notes,
> talk to myself, and, foggy days,
> watch the droplets slipping, heavy with light.

In its inquiring phase, the mind is one of the lively sentient beings in the universe:

> The little dog next door barks in his sleep
> inquiringly, just once.
> Perhaps in his sleep, too, the bird inquires
> once or twice, quavering.
> Questions—if that is what they are—
> answered directly, simply,
> by day itself.

Human questions are not answered so simply, though from time to time an apparition—human, or animal—allays for a moment human restlessness. The three best poems in this volume explore three moments of love: love of a human being, described through Crusoe's delight in Friday; love of natural presence, described through a night appearance of a mild moose; and love of an aesthetic creation, described through the contemplation of a painting. A fourth memorable poem is concerned with a child's discovery, at once, of separateness and connection: waiting in a dentist's office, reading the *National Geographic*, feeling horrified at pictures of savages, hearing her aunt cry out in pain from inside the dentist's office, the child feels vertigo:

But I felt: you are an *I*,
you are an *Elizabeth*,
you are one of *them*.
Why should you be one, too?
I scarcely dared to look
to see what it was I was . . .

Bishop's retention of the naive vision of the child accounts for her utter credibility. It can be seen at its pure best in the opening of her poem, "Crusoe in England," when Crusoe, in old age, remembers his island, with its "fifty-two miserable, small volcanoes":

I used to sit on the edge of the highest one
and count the others standing up,
naked and leaden, with their heads blown off.
I'd think that if they were the size
I thought volcanoes should be, then I had
become a giant;
and if I had become a giant,
I couldn't bear to think what size
the goats and turtles were,
or the gulls, or the over-lapping rollers
—a glittering hexagon of rollers
closing and closing in . . .

My island seemed to be
a sort of cloud-dump. All the hemisphere's
left-over clouds arrived and hung
above the craters—their parched throats
were hot to touch . . .
Was that why it rained so much? . . .
The turtles lumbered by, high-domed,
hissing like teakettles.

The odd combination here of the simple and the violent, the paradoxical confusions of size, the unnamed threats, the unnatural coexistence of rain and the parched throats of craters, the inhuman energy of the sea—all are suggested with the utmost brevity. If this brevity of notation is Bishop's most striking talent (as most discussions of her poetry suggest), it would nevertheless remain relatively meaningless without her sudden dips into emotion (here, Crusoe's):

With my legs dangling down familiarly
over a crater's edge, I told myself
"Pity should begin at home." So the more
pity I felt, the more I felt at home.

348

Most self-pity in poetry is less self-charitable. The expert management of this long poem (almost two hundred lines long) is remarkable. It is the history of a life—or of everything that matters about a
life—with glimpses of terror, of inadequacy, of steadiness, of invention, of intimacy, of bitterness, of exhaustion of emotion, and of
pain. The whole of life's investment and detaching is summed up in
Crusoe's retrospective gaze at his knife, that knife that meant everything to him on his island:

> The knife there on the shelf—
> it reeked of meaning, like a crucifix.
> It lived. How many years did I
> beg it, implore it, not to break?
> I knew each nick and scratch by heart,
> the bluish blade, the broken tip,
> the lines of wood-grain on the handle . . .
> now it won't look at me at all.
> The living soul has dribbled away.
> My eyes rest on it and pass on.

A poet who has written this poem really needs to write nothing
else: it seems to me a perfect reproduction of the self in words. It
contains, in its secure and unfaltering progress, truthful representations of many aspects of Bishop (both the solitary and the affectionate, both the introspective and the observing). It does not shrink
away from interior irrationality ("I'd dream of things / like slitting a
baby's throat, mistaking it / for a baby goat") or from unlovely age
("I'm old. / I'm bored, too, drinking my real tea, surrounded by uninteresting lumber") or from compulsive fear, nightmares of other
islands:

> . . . knowing that I had to live
> on each and every one, eventually,
> for ages, registering their flora,
> their fauna, their geography.

Against the terrors and the boredom, Bishop sets the temporary but
conclusive fact of human attachment: "Friday was nice, and we were
friends." The poem ends with disgust for the meaningless residue
of life once deprived of that intimacy:

> How can anyone want such things?
> —And Friday, my dear Friday, died of measles
> seventeen years ago come March.

It is a classic poem, wonderfully sustained, sparely inclusive, fully considered, sad and complete. It belongs in all the anthologies.

I come finally to the two versions of what Stevens called "The Planet on the Table," by which he meant a volume resuming one human being's world, his point-for-point verbal reconstruction of the larger physical globe. The *Selected Lowell* and the *Collected Auden* are such volumes, and all reservations are in one sense ridiculous in the face of the grand accomplishment in each: any inhabitant of the twentieth century must be glad that both Auden and Lowell were born and have written their poems.

The *Selected Lowell* has been widely reviewed, and Lowell's rearrangement of some poems from his last three books has apparently helped some readers make sense of the sonnets. If this grouping into "sequences" makes the later poetry more available to the public mind, so much the better. Nobody, so far as I know, has approved of the cuts in the poems reprinted from *Near the Ocean*. Lowell has mercifully allowed "The Quaker Graveyard" to stand in full (after reducing it brutally in the British *Selected Poems*). Of course, this volume only provokes (at least in some of us) a cross wish for a *Collected Poems*, or better yet for a *Collected Variorum;* but that is another story. Lowell candidly calls his personal poems "my verse autobiography." It is chiefly as autobiography that the *Selected Poems* coheres; and the burden of experience, real and vicarious, borne by the poems is genuinely oppressive. If there is a spiritual equivalent to being pressed to death by stones, it comes in the reading of Lowell entire, so little is the reader accustomed to living in the full presence of life. To one not used to a perpetual *remembering*—remembering early life, history, books read, pictures seen, places been, scenes lived through, remarks made, relatives known, clothes worn, quotations cited, news, myths, wars, dead languages, and all the rest—living in Lowell's mind seems like living in a many-staged theater, a chamber of talking books, restless ghosts, risen corpses, recurrent dreams, multimedia. And when, to all that detritus of memory, there is added a relentlessly active imagination, irresistibly adding its characterization of events; a pressure and momentum of style; a systematic breaking of form; and an obscurity of complex thought—then, the reader feels driven to the edge of his own resources of response.

And yet there is the other, more delicate, Lowell, who appeared in *Life Studies* and has never since vanished. If the driven Lowell is the Lowell of the verb, the Lowell of the sketches is the Lowell of the adjective. There is scarcely a poem without one of Lowell's memorable vignettes, one of his wonderfully exact representations of a visual scene, or of images of feeling. Feeling and scene are usually indistinguishable, as a matter of fact: for all his learning and his intellectuality, for all his interior "autobiography" even, Lowell is a poet essentially externalized—in data, in description, in scene, in action, in history. The Emersonian metaphysical strain—present in Dickinson, continued in Ammons and Ashbery—runs directly counter to Lowell's rocklike solidity. He is opaque to their transparency, he is mass and weight, while they breathe the thinner air of higher altitudes; he is the pull of gravity, he is concentric and centripetal. It no longer matters much—so completely has he perfected his style—what he writes about: the thing becomes interesting because he writes about it. He has broken the sonnet structure; his sonnets end as often as not in midair. The well-made lyric offends his sense of life. If the length—or shortness, rather—of the sonnet form confines his life-weighted mind to a timed response, its structure must be loosed to allow for at least a minor chaos to reign while the sand slips through the timer. Lowell is now back to publishing free verse; he breaks his molds as he finishes with them, just as in *Life Studies* he broke his earlier formal vessels.

Auden, though a contemporary of Lowell, seems a generation older. Auden was formed exceptionally young, in his twenties in fact; he had done, in essence, everything he was to do before he left England, in his early thirties. His much-discussed changes of ideological reference seem, in retrospect, superficial additions of terminology rather than an evolution of sensibility. Positions in the debate about his worth and his staying power have already hardened, with Jarrell's brilliant essays the most stinging adversary analysis:

> The man who, during the thirties, was one of the five or six best poets in the world has gradually turned into a rhetoric mill grinding away at the bottom of Limbo, into an automaton that keeps making little jokes, little plays on words, little rhetorical engines, as compulsively and unendingly and uneasily as a neurotic washes his hands.

Jarrell's cruelty sprang from cruel disappointment. It is not ever clear why a poet's talents wane (Jarrell drew a parallel with Wordsworth). But Auden's did, perhaps from a misconception of his own gifts. He was by nature more a satirist, a comic poet, and a song writer than a moralist, but moralizing attracted him. His two clergy-men grandfathers may account for some fatal natural bent toward the sermon; the older Auden grew, the more homiletic his verse be-came. It was sprinkled as well with an equally fatal whimsy, deriving from his taste for Lear, Tolkien, and Carroll. "His thoughts," he said of himself in "Profile," "pottered / from verses to sex to God / with-out punctuation." For all his putative engagement with Freud, he felt, finally, only distaste for the Freudian revelation of a mind which could "discard . . . rhythm, punctuation, metaphor, / [and] sink into a drivelling monologue, / too literal to see a joke or / distin-guish a penis from a pencil." In his tireless mustering of defenses (including rhythm, punctuation, and metaphor) against that "drivel-ling monologue" he may have damaged his own insight. The "drivel" emerges in moments of ventriloquism (in Caliban, in Herod), but never *in propria persona*. The guard of irony is usually up in the later poetry, and the originally interesting device of the impersonal fabular voice stiffens into mannerism.

That much having been said, it remains true that any volume of Auden—however late, however marked by archness or fatigue, how-ever mechanical—was superior to most other volumes of poems published beside it. And in this *Collected Poems*, there remain all the beautiful and by now immortal songs, musical pieces, comic turns, and lyric meditations. "Can I learn to suffer," Auden asked in *The Sea and the Mirror* under the mask of Prospero, "without saying something ironic or funny / On suffering?" He never did. He feared "the clutch of eddying Muddle" as he did the drivelling mono-logue. He mourned that "never will his prick belong / To his world of right and wrong," but before that opposition quite hardened, he did "sing agreeably, agreeably, agreeably of love." "His sense of other people's very hazy," he said in his definition of the poet, and his verse shows that lack. If he liked Byron, "master of the airy manner," and found Wordsworth a "bleak old bore," he was only being truthful about his own poetic affinities. His final preference for consciousness as "a parlour / Where words are well-groomed / and reticent" is deplorable, but the terror from which it sprang was real. His clear-eyed sense of disaster did not shrink from prophesy-ing the dissolution he did not escape:

> The mortifying in the bed,
> Powers wasting day by day . . .
> The insulting paralysis,
> Ruined intellect's confusion.

This edition "omits the poems Auden . . . finally discarded" and "prints [the] author's latest text." Edward Mendelson, working under Auden's instructions, felt, understandably enough, "morally obliged to respect the dead man's intentions." The editorial apparatus of this volume—especially the dating of poems, and the lists of omitted poems and variant titles—is extremely useful. I am however made uneasy (though I have no special competence) by Mr. Mendelson's conviction that Auden generally improved in revising, as by his other conviction that "the history of Auden's reputation has consistently followed a pattern in which initial outrage at new developments in manner and subject is supplanted by gradual acceptance and understanding of the merits of Auden's changes." If that means that critics agree that Auden improved with age, I can only say that the judgment is at least not unanimous. Surely the Auden that will last is the prewar Auden—irreverent, vivid, daring, and thoughtful, an adolescent satirist with a child's sense of fairy tale and a lethally adult vocabulary.

Ten Poets

It is hard to say whether what we most ask of our poets is a certain kind of voice or a certain kind of interior attention. By their voices we tell poets apart, but it is by a certain focus of attention that we name them lyric poets at all. Though on first reading a poet, we are struck by the distinctive voice, later, when the voice has become "natural" to us and almost transparent, we feel increasingly that the underlying attentive focusing is the truly constitutive quality of lyric. Disappointment is keenest when that attentiveness is careless or intermittent, but it also arises when the voice is undistinguished or uncertain. Most poets find a single voice and develop it: only the greatest find more than one authentic cadence for themselves. From the young poet one expects an effort at originality, undone usually by inherited language, and the first of this quarter's box of books exhibits just such a deficiency.

It is understandable enough that, after the austere severity of the early modern aesthetic exemplified in Pound and Eliot, poets should long to restore a Dionysian language, and in fact there have been notable efforts in our century along that line. The 1977 Yale Younger Poet, Olga Broumas, wishing to avoid timidity, falls into the pit of a desperately uncertain tone—sensational, full of bluster, pretentious, sentimental, callow. The callowness appears in her schoolgirl catalogue of respect: she wants to say "Great spirits now on earth are sojourning," but the sentiment comes out as self-conscious attitudinizing in a chapel full of niches: "Anne. Sylvia. Virginia. Adrienne, the last, magnificent last."

All art, needless to say, is founded on what is juxtaposed to what, and how the whole is composed. Broumas falls into a jumble of incompatibilities, where juxtaposition is haphazard and composition is that old Romantic cliché, the mount toward climax. In a sex

"Recent Poetry: Ten Poets" first appeared in *The Yale Review*, Autumn 1977.

poem, Broumas' erratic whimsy joins a feminist religion (God is a woman), a Zen tag (the sound of one hand clapping), and a neo-medievalizing inherited from pre-Raphaelite romance. Manita (the beloved) is a Queen, and her lover, the poet, is her female Jester; the Queen's clitoris is a pearl and the two sets of breasts are "four small steeples":

Manita's Love

opens herself to me, my sharp
Jester's tongue, my
cartwheels of pleasure. The Queen's own pearl
at my fingertips, and Manita pealing

my Jester's bells on our four
small steeples, as Sunday dawns
clear in February, and God claps and claps
her one hand.

Stanley Kunitz, the judge of the Yale Younger Poet competition, says in his foreword to *Beginning with O* that this passage contains "an irresistible élan, an exultation—even an ecstasy—of the senses." No doubt that is what Broumas intended, but the ludicrous and shopworn mélange of ingredients actively gets in our way as we read, and the self-conscious tone only makes us embarrassed to be voyeurs at the royal rites of Queen Manita and her Jester. A more literal sex poem from Broumas belongs under the *New Yorker* rubric of sentences we doubt ever got said:

The esplanade of your belly, I said, that
shallow and gleaming spoon.

This naive transcription of feeling into stilted compliment is representative of Broumas' inability, as yet, to find a viable voice.

At the other extreme from Broumas is Robert Creeley, with his minuteness, his scrupulosity, his deliberate refusal of the expansive. A short Creeley poem will say, under its title "Time," nothing but

What happened to her
and what happened to her
and what happened to her?

Creeley's longer poems in these *Selected Poems* give him more room, but he remains so much a follower of Williams, without Williams' rebelliousness, verve, and social breadth, that his verse seems, though intermittently attractive, fatally pinched. He hears "words full / of holes / aching," sees "a face that is no face / but the features of a face, pasted / on a face until that face / is faceless." In Creeley, there is a relentless process of abstraction, of "serial diminishment of progression" with diminishment to the fore. Things are wasted, faded, faint, trembling, wavering, blurred, darkening: the scale is miniature, the dimensions fragile, in this poet of "tender, semi- / articulate flickers" of presence. Creeley, a purist, refuses the puffed-up signs of "intensity"—and his is one way of avoiding bathos; but he purchases composition at the price of momentum and sweep.

Charles Simic, too, is a minimalist of sorts, but he gives houseroom to intensity by his adaptation (in theme and language) of folk motifs. These are not the coy transformations of Sexton (imitated, as Kunitz points out, by Broumas—the heart sinks at the prospect of this new genre), but the real thing, menacing precisely because uninterpreted. Simic's arresting volume, *Return to a Place Lit by a Glass of Milk*, was distinguished by the impeccable finish conferred on its pieces, until they seemed, though full of pent-up feeling, carvings in polished wood. *Charon's Cosmology* represents, I think, a plateau, but contains some of Simic's best-transcribed tableaux of his painful world:

> Distant guard-towers with searchlights
> Following us all
> With malice, regret,
> And also absentmindedly.

Simic's objectivity of statement makes his psychic places vivid with illumination—a deserted street, a grim luncheonette, a death chamber, a penitentiary, a classroom, a maze, Charon's bark. These places are tethered to earth by detail—doubting footsteps, a screen-door screeching, a glass of icewater, a dissected rat, barbed wire, crutches, a bad cough, those "infinite shapes pain assumes." Though he began, he tells us in his *ars poetica* "The Lesson," by thinking he was gaining freedom and discovering a pattern in life which would eventually lead to a happy ending ("given over / entirely / to lyrical evocations of nature"), he realizes now that this was all the practical joke of someone deluding an idiot pupil:

> Unfortunately,
> with time,

> I began to detect in myself
> an inability
> to forget even
> the most trivial detail.
> I hungered more and more
> over the beginnings:
> The haircut of a soldier
> who was urinating
> against our fence;
> shadows of trees on the ceiling.

Now Simic lives in "this classroom / austerely furnished / by my insomnia," writing "at the desk consisting of my two knees."

The poems written out of the unforgettable details seen with a child's clarity, recalled against the amnesia of time, and vainly anatomized for significance, contain Simic's best work. In them, light is both revealing and baffling, and life takes on the appearance of a dumb-show with a lost plot. Simic's forcing of the gates of memory yields him broken treasures that he pores over like an archaeologist. Perception and shattered memory are his substitutes for belief; he is modern to that degree, but nostalgia for some unknown ancient coherence tinges his modernity. As he sorts through his past, he is the Charon of his title poem:

> With only his feeble lantern
> To tell him where he is
> And every time a mountain
> Of fresh corpses to load up
>
> Take them to the other side
> Where there are plenty more
> I'd say by now he must be confused
> As to which side is which
>
> I'd say it doesn't matter

A scavenger in his heap of corpses, Charon goes through the pockets of his dead—"In one a crust of bread in another a sausage." The inedibles—"a mirror or a book"—he throws

> Overboard into the dark river
> Swift cold and deep

The end shows Simic's weakness for climax: his poems tend toward a known shape. If his watchful eye and his candid language were somewhat less the captives of structure, the poems would gain an uncertainty of progress more suited to their blind exploring. The absence of conclusion in a desolate poem about a remembered patch of wall authenticates its perception by its own dismay:

And nothing else, and nowhere
To go back to
And no one else
As far as I know to verify.

This ending, and others resembling it, fit Simic's displaced sensibility better than, say, the ending proclaiming "the small lovely realm / of the possible." Optimism is not his strong suit; a clarity of bleached senses is. Whatever is invoked as a cure, in poetry, needs to be homeopathic with the wounds to which it is applied; sometimes, in Simic, it appears incongruous or antithetically conceived, at least in its function as a rhetorical conclusion.

C. K. Williams is nearly unquotable in a brief review, his long-lined poems in *With Ignorance* being themselves long and relatively unstopped. His endings almost always seem violently sentimental. Some examples:

The voice of God speaking to Moses:
"Now therefore go," He said, "and I will be with thy mouth."
A calf drinking, then lifting her head:
Then she lifts, and it pours, everything, gushes, and we're lost in both waters.
(A sentimental version of "E'l naufragar m'è dolce in questa mare.")
A dream:
And whatever our lives were, our love, this once was enough.
A girl shot by the police:
In the beginning was love, right? No, in the beginning . . . the bullet . . .

Examples could be multiplied: we feel, as we head into the harbor of any given poem, the deadliness of the predictable, and we long for Whitman's urbane letting-us-off-the-hook: "Look for me under your bootsoles." Our disappointment is the more frustrating because Williams has a natural drama of speech that makes him instantly readable. If his endings are stagy, his beginnings hold us captive. More examples:

> I think most people are relieved the first time they actually
>   know someone who goes crazy.
> It doesn't happen the way you hear about it where the person
>   gibbers and sticks to you like an insect:
> mostly there's crying, a lot of silence, sometimes someone
>   will whisper back to their voices.

> When I was about eight, I once stabbed somebody, another kid,
>   a little girl.

> After the argument—argument? battle, war, harrowing; you need
>   shrieks, moans from the pit—
> after that woman and I anyway stop raking each other with
>   the meat-hooks we've become with each other,
> I fit my forehead into the smudge I've already sweated onto
>   the window with a thousand other exhaustions
> and watch an old man having breakfast out of a pile of bags
>   on my front step.

Williams has a musician's ear, a senes of life's scenes, a leaping fantasy-life. He has learned from Whitman and Ginsberg and O'Hara, but his rhythms are more abrupt than theirs:

> These times. The endless wars. The hatreds. The vengefulness.
> Everyone I know getting out of their marriage. Old friends
>   distrustful.

"A whole section of the city I live in has been urban renewed." The man who could write that line can get all of our speech down, if he wants to. Williams is a speech poet, riding on the inflections of American voices, refusing epigram, conclusion, and distillation in favor of narrative, digressions, interpolations, and, above all, a buttonholing assertion of the interest of the whole hectic organism which his poems see as life.

Frank Bidart's best poems in his second volume, *The Book of the Body*, are case-studies, but case-studies motivated not by the projection of the usual dramatic monologue, nor by a covert social history, nor by a sympathy for the grotesque—though they might seem to spring from all of these. Rather, the grotesque becomes in Bidart the figure of the ordinary, the human, the "normal," and casts an eerie oblique cloud over "normalcy" itself. The personages in Bidar's two central poems of this sort are, respectively, an amputee and an anorexic who have—the one by accident, the other by compulsion—been placed outside "Nature." "*I loathed 'Nature,'*" cries the anorexic Ellen West (her story borrowed from Binswanger's account): "I shall *defeat* 'Nature.'" "Nature," Bidart reminds us through Ellen West's tortured perceptions, is loathed even by those of us who won't admit it: a short student carries his body "as if forcing / it to be taller," and a woman who shows her gums when she smiles "often held her / hand up to hide them." Ellen West, though she is dark, big-boned, and fat, determines to become her "ideal," "thin, all profile / and effortless gestures." This unblinking aesthetic is then hopelessly sexualized, as the married Ellen falls in love in the mental hospital with "an elegant, very thin female patient." "Nature" reasserts herself; discharged from the hospital, Ellen eats butter, sugar, chocolate creams, and Easter eggs, writes a letter to her "dearest" in the sanitarium, and poisons herself, unable finally to join the compromised social arrangements we live by. A parallel is drawn with Callas, who starved herself into dramatic credibility and into "pure spirit."

Bidart's amputee attempts a comparable denial of his mutilated body (he is missing an arm, but I expect we are to read that as a displacement upward); he finds that after the initial relief of pretending he was always one-armed and that it is his "normal" state, the whole world "became / cardboard." In a resolution the opposite of Ellen West's, he decides to incorporate the ugly into his consciousness. Thinking of Paris, he recalls

> how Paris is still the city of Louis XVI and
> Robespierre, how blood, amputation, and rubble
> give her dimension, resonance, and grace.

Two comparable cases; two opposing aesthetics.

Bidart's method is not narrative; unlike the fluid dramatic monologues we are used to, his are spliced together, as harrowing bits of speech, an anecdote, a reminiscence, a doctor's journal notes, a letter, an analogy, follow each other in a cinematic progression. These fragments are further fragmented by interpolation, captions, parentheses, blank spaces on the page, idiosyncratic punctuation, quotations, italics, capitals, asterisks, printed matter, lists, and flashes of interior speech. All this violence to the printed page seems to be comparable to cinematic forms of italicizing—the freeze-frame, the speedup, the zoom, the panning, the slow-motion, the shift from color to black-and-white and back, the angle-shot. These are devices to forbid the audience's sinking into conventional expectation of mimetic art: not for more than a few lines at once can we read Bidart without being jolted out of any mimetic illusion. Someone—an author—is "placing" the voices in these poems, accompanying them with his typographical devices as with a weird orchestration, making the voices just slightly inhuman, hitting our ears at a pitch strangely above the level of hearing, jangling one line against another into quarter-tones that abrade the ear:

> When I wake up,
>> I try to convince myself that my arm
> isn't there—
>> to retain my sanity.
>
> Then I try to convince myself it is.

Victimizers of themselves, victims to themselves, the amputee and Ellen West become figures, in their intensity of feeling, from some mannerist hagiographer, like the eunuch Origen or the emaciated anchoritic Magdalen.

Bidart's poetry in propria persona is less severely controlled. The title poem and the long central elegy (partly spoken by his mother) exhibit some unsteadiness, explicable in terms of Bidart's chosen voice—exhibitionistic, disdainful of metaphor, questioning, pleading, qualifying, naked. In these poems he still puts the extreme case with an absoluteness which denies that it is anything other than the universal one. As we stand in Bidart's universe, convention calls up, as responses natural to the event of life, postures as contorted, deformed, and racked as those of the figures in the greenish light of an El Greco.

The two older poets here represented, Robert Graves and Robert Penn Warren, offer a half-century of poems each. Graves, in his *New Collected Poems*, remains unchanged, a poet who found his styles long ago, still moving familiarly in his world of dragons, goddesses, planetary influences, and ogres. He is archaic when it pleases him, and his poems are always construable and rhymed. It is intellectual poetry (for all Graves's preoccupation with love), and structured by its point more than by any gusts of feeling. His more complacent love poems ("She knows, as he knows, / Of a faithful-always / And an always-dear") are less moving than the poems written in abandonment:

> The death of love comes from reiteration:
> A single line sung over and over again.

In both sorts, peaceful and dismayed, Graves finds satisfying, if old-fashioned, last lines:

> It was impossible you could love me less,
> It was impossible I could love you more.

> It was not my fault, love, nor was it your fault.

On the other hand, the love poems, hundreds of them, come to seem almost like finger-exercises in a void, and the appearance of Graves's ironic and satiric tones is felt as a relief. On Ulysses:

> All lands to him were Ithaca: love-tossed
> He loathed the fraud, yet would not bed alone.

And, in a later poem, a comment on the herd of the unimaginative:

> Innumerable zombies
> With glazed eyes shuffle around at their diurnal tasks,
> Keep the machines whirring, drudge idly in stores and bars,
> Bear still-born zombie children, pack them off to school
> For education in science and the dead languages,
> Divert themselves with moribund travesties of living.

Accomplished though he is, Graves is not a compelling poet, whether in voice or attentiveness. His style is generic rather than shaped by each poem, and he believes too strongly that there is one story and one story only. The preordained plot precludes entirely any possibility of the erratic vagary, the unforeseen counterinstance. His poems are finished before they are begun, and proceed imperturbably to their destined point, discursive and magisterial. Confusion, bafflement, and surprise play less of a part in Graves than they do in life. Or perhaps it is truer to say that he is more a man of letters, a man who writes things in any form handy to him, than a poet. This collection is prefaced by a most peculiar flattering essay (by one James McKinley) which runs to portentous sentences like "It was not to be," to tirades ("The nation for which he fought has not seen fit to knight him, obviously preferring Americanized film comedians"), and to bathos mixed with unintended farce:

> He has, frankly, inflicted suffering too. His belief that the Goddess comes to him has led him to emotional involvements with young women which have distressed his wife and children, though their patience has soothed him to serenity in these, his declining days . . . Graves sometimes stands these days on a terrace far above his home, near a sheep shed where he in past days often came to write (and which he has named variously for his incarnate Goddesses).

O fortunatus nimium! But what can Graves have been thinking of to print this trash with his last collection?

Robert Penn Warren's *Selected Poems* are perhaps also best described as those of a man of letters, novelist and critic as well as poet. His collections tend to follow poetic styles rather than to invent them, but within those inherited styles he can work consummately well. Robert Lowell speaks, in a poem dedicated to Warren, of Warren's voice, "haunted not lost, that lives by breaking in berserk with inspiration," and quotes Warren's early poem "Pursuit," which, after successive visions of despair, finds a focus of hope in an unkillable "old lady in black" in a hotel, who

> Admires all the dancers, and tells you how just last fall
> Her husband died in Ohio, and damp mists her glasses;
> She blinks and croaks, like a toad or a Norn, in the horrible light,
> And rattles her crutch, which may put forth a small bloom,
>   perhaps white.

Even this early, Warren had his storyteller's eye, his easy rhythm, and his feel for the horrible and the hopeful. The earlier poems are, like the later ones, alternately folksy and philosophical, swinging like ballads or tautly analytic, embodying a strange cohabitation, it might seem, of Whitman and Marvell, "Who saw, in darkness, how fled / The white eidolon" crossed with "Ages to our construction went, / Dim architecture, hour by hour." Among these influences there appeared, early on, Warren's own individual slant:

> Because he had spoken harshly to his mother,
> The day became astonishingly bright.

The rest of that young poem doesn't live up to its beginning, but the second line has the true surprise of an interior state clarified in language. Warren's essential self, early and late, appears not in the skillfully rhymed or fastidiously analytical poems, but in his long rambles and his short lyrical songs. Among his later poems, I would take as illustration three which seem successful, and slightly flawed, in characteristic ways. The most recent is a poem about the hour of death, in which the last days of an immense oak tree provide the metaphor. The limbs are so heavy that the oak would, left to itself, have split in two long ago; but it has been artificially supported by iron hoops, rods, and cables—all hidden, in summer, by the foliage. But now it is December, and the oak wants,

> In its fullness of years, to describe to you
> What happens on a December night when
>
> It stands alone in a world of snowy whiteness. The moon is full.
> You can hear the stars crackle in their high brightness.
>
> It is ten below zero, and the iron
> Of hoops and reinforcement rods is continuing to contract.
>
> There is the rhythm of a slow throb, like pain. The wind,
> Northwest, is steady, and in the wind, the cables,
>
> In a thin-honed and disinfectant purity, like
> A dentist's drill, sing.

There is a thin-honed purity about the poem up to this point, too. Warren spoils it by becoming overexplicit ("They sing / Of truth, and its beauty"), by repeating, with respect to man, his nice phrase "a thin-honed and disinfectant purity," and by ending with a stage-ominousness, "And no one can predict the consequences." It is a beautiful poem until it starts drawing already evident morals.

The short lyric "Blow, West Wind," on the other hand, remains unmarred and unselfconscious. For its fine simplicity, one would want to put it in school texts, except that the young are not old enough to understand its brief symbols and its cheated bleakness:

> I know, I know—though the evidence
> Is lost, and the last who might speak are dead.
> Blow, west wind, and the evidence, O,
>
> Is lost, and wind shakes the cedar, and O,
> I know how the kestrel hung over Wyoming
> Breast reddened in sunset, and O, the cedar
>
> Shakes, and I know how cold
> Was the sweat on my father's mouth, dead.
> Blow, west wind, blow, shake the cedar, I know

> How once I, a boy, crouching at creekside,
> Watched, in the sunlight, a handful of water,
> Drip, drip, from my hand. The drops—they were bright!
> But you believe nothing, with the evidence lost.

On the whole, though, Warren's best work lies in the poems much too long to quote. The recent elegy for himself and his parents, "I Am Dreaming of a White Christmas," has the gripping realism of vision, as Warren sees, in a dream, his father sitting in his usual Morris chair, but dead; and then his seated mother, dead too; and the cold hearth; and a long-dead Christmas tree; and three presents under the tree; and three chairs: "the little red chair, / For the baby. The next biggest chair / For my little sister, the little red rocker. Then / The biggest, my own, me the eldest. / The chairs are all empty." The poem seems over-long as it follows the dream from Kentucky into New York City and Idaho, but it sticks in the mind for its description of the dead parents. In each of the father's eye-sockets, "which are / Deep and dark as a thumb-gouge," is

> Something that might be taken for
> A mulberry, large and black ripe when, long back, crushed,
> But now, with years, dust-dried. The mulberries,
> Crushed and desiccated, each out of
> Its dark lurking-place, stare out at
> Nothing.
>
> His eyes
> Had been blue.

This kind of descriptiveness, like the song-rhythm of "Blow, West Wind," is a permanent resource of lyric. Warren continues, in these *Selected Poems*, some of the most firmly based and solacing practices of poetry.

John Berryman's posthumous volume, *Henry's Fate*, collects, according to the preface by John Haffenden, "only a fraction of Berryman's unpublished and uncollected work. There are several hundred unpublished Dream Songs, and as many more miscellaneous poems," not to speak of letters, diaries, and so on. "The time is not yet ripe," the preface continues, "for a complete edition . . . it has been thought wisest," and so on. Though Haffenden hints at inferiority of work and considerations of discretion, plain reasons plainly spoken would have been preferable. Since about half of these poems have already been printed in magazines, the volume offers rather thin pickings for those looking for unpublished work. Haffenden's taste, unfortunately, is questionable: he characterizes as "one of the simplest and most moving of [Berryman's] documents" a pitiable "Morning Prayer" of no literary distinction whatever ("Thank you for the great rescues of my life and for the marvellous good luck that has mostly attended me. Enlighten me as to the nature of Christ. Strengthen my gratitude and awe into confident reliance & love of Thee," and so on.) Who would not trade these religiously unexceptional, understandable but pitifully forced phrases for this 1968 Dream Song, in which Eliot's and Hopkins' Sibyl cannot even say "I want to die" or cast oracular leaves:

> Death all endeth, Henry to Sibyl saith.
> Sibyl regurgitates, no word from her.
> Ah, ah, no word from her.
> Flashing existence seems from her to incur
> a bitter silence, vomit, assent to his death
> black as it must occur.

Or, to the morning prayer, must we not prefer, as "simple and moving," this truth about a bad morning:

> With arms outflung the clock announced: Ten-twenty.
> Dozens of demons sprang & preyed on Henry.
> All on a heavy morning.
> The baby was ill, the sky was dark, the I
> was Id, somebody put the sky on like a lid,
> somebody who is not returning.

Henry here depends not on prayer but on feeble, if powerful, drugs:

> Haldol & Serax, phenobarbital,
> Vivactil, by day; by deep night Tuinal
> & Thorazine,
> kept Henry going, like a natural man.
> I'm waiting for them to work, as sometimes they can,
> honey, in the bloodstream.

The charm and vivacity of Berryman's apprehension of the world, even in his last unlivable years, stayed alive in his poems. Berryman was a consummate entertainer, and there is scarcely a song which is not, however horrible its subject matter, entertaining—

"the natural soul," as he says here, "performing, as it will." The most endearing of talkers, he can make even Baudelaire's "hypocrite lecteur" lighthearted:

> Old codger Henry contain within hisself
> Henry young, Henry almost beautiful
> Henry the seducer
> Henry the mad young artist, with *no* interest in pelf
> Whereas now he takes steps to keep both his bank accounts full
> just like: you, Sir!

The alternations of exhaustion and gaiety, self-loathing and affection, witticism and sorrow, flicker like a light-show through these, as through his other songs. "Even in this last *Dream Song*," Lowell wrote in his elegy for Berryman, "to mock your catlike flight / from home and classes." That last song, written "within forty-eight hours of his death" according to Haffenden, imagines the full scenario for the suicide: "unless my wife wouldn't let me out of the house, / unless the cops noticed me crossing the campus / up to the bridge / & clappt me in for observation." This full self-knowledge of the impractical man, sure he cannot plan even his own suicide so that it will come off, exhibits that part of Berryman that was always coldly aware of his escapades. The torture of the contemplative self watching the errant self lies behind the elaborate and successful literary charade of Henry Pussycat, the alter ego enabling the poems, more often than not, to escape the lyric soddenness so evident in the "Morning Prayer." *Sotto voce*, under all the Henry poems, we hear the lyric that would be breathed out by the despairing self if it were to speak straight. The poems about alcoholism and family here are often written directly by the despairing self, and they lack the comic flexibility contributed by Henry, who served Berryman like an arrangement of mirrors to see around corners when a view of his own face in a glass would have undone his language. Oddly enough, for all their affectation of chattiness, the Dream Songs are poems written to be read on the page as well as heard aloud; though their meaning "explodes" (to quote Hopkins) when read with the proper conversational emphasis, their careful shapeliness is visible only on the page. It is to be hoped that the rest of the poetry will appear soon, taste and discretion notwithstanding.

Perhaps only someone who has lived through the full interminableness of winters in upstate New York can feel, as I did, the weight of

A. R. Ammons' *Snow Poems*. Unsentimentally, from the snow-threat at the end of September to the final sleet of May, they chronicle an Ithaca snow-season, often with a fine dry comedy ("today continues the tropical / extravaganza—up to 45"). Ammons is a diarist here, like Thoreau, not wishing to make well-made poems (though he can do those expertly whenever he wants), but rather to write down life as it is at fifty, during a long winter, in a solitary epoch. He runs through all his repertory of styles, from mock-Negro (in one brilliant flash) to Emersonian reflection to Thoreauvian accuracy. Open the book anywhere and there is a ripple of thought, a weather report, a lament, a curious observation of the out-of-doors, and a hard inquiry. The individual poems are named only for their first line: no titular summings-up allowed. The book needs to be lived in for days, reread after the first reading has sorted out its preoccupations and methods, and used as a *livre de chevêt* if its leisurely paths are to be followed in their waywardness. Ammons has developed an annoying tic of turning clichés mechanically around ("being there is the next best / thing to long distance") and a somewhat distracting habit of doodling on the typewriter ("overwhelm whelm helm elm"). All poets do those things in the margins, but they usually leave them behind when the poem reaches the printed page; in accord with some present principle of aesthetic nudity, Ammons has let them remain. His fluency is unstoppable, as always, but here it appears in short lines rather than his recent long ones in *Sphere*. An extremely attractive mind—full of sights, science, quirks, questions, and a million words—appears to unroll itself to us as one would unroll an endless scroll—another "tape for the turn of the year."

Ammons' current of language flows (to mix a metaphor) from his perpetual attempt to draw nectar in a sieve; like Warren, he sees drops trickling through his fingers, but writes of that loss as the only motive for life:

how
grateful we must be that as we reach to take the
much desired in hand it loses shape and color and
drifts apart and must be looked for all over again
so are we shoveled
forward half unwillingly
into the future (where futurity is lost)

The voice reasonable in loss is one Ammons; the eviscerated Ammons, doggedly writing down the weather day after day, is something else, Beckett-like, hard on himself as ice:

who who had
anything else
to be interested
in would be
interested in
the weather

"Sick with a pure / interest in beauty," Ammons lives off the land,
but admits that for anyone hungering for love, "this beauty, though
very / beautiful, is an inconsiderable / feast." Nonetheless, all
Ithacans and ex-Ithacans will recognize that Ammons has delineated
that landscape and that climate for good and all, with an Emersonian
wintriness of voice diluting the ebullience he inherited from Williams. Since the sound of Ammons is deservedly well-known, I
will quote, instead of a more characteristic passage, the opening of
his inspired blackface excursus on being born different from the
American herd. It might be spoken by the bad fairy at the christen-
ing of a doomed genius:

the average person is average
the common people is common
the straight people is straight
you gone be the crooked weird
rare intelligent bird creep type
that what you gone be, honey
    you gone look funny
    when they put you in your
    coffin
    like you something
    unright
    like you ain't
worth dying
like every day when they passes out the
honey
you gone get a little vial of fear and
you gone drink it yes you is

This is allusive poetry for the middle-aged, expecting from its audience a nod of recognition:

you have to feel pretty
good to have a good time:
the aspirant spiral: you remember
the aspirant spiral

Uh huh, we remember the aspirant spiral; we felt pretty good; we had a good time. And so we talk back to Ammons' mumble over the one-way telephone of verse. He has changed the "we" of poetry from the high philosophical mode ("We live in an old chaos of the sun") to the mode of refugees caught together in a bad time. He probably cannot escape what he fears—"the outbreak of destructive clarification" from critics—but more than most poets, he is, though offhand and compressed, a man speaking. "Do you not see," Keats wrote, "how necessary a world of pains and troubles is to school an intelligence and make it a soul?" Ammons has his version:

> to be made of steel!
> so bullets and aches and
> pains and sorrows
> the sorrows of knowing and
> not knowing and witnessing
> bing off you
> that would be so fine
> provided you did not
> remain stiff and
> uneducated.

As poets accompany their discipline of pains and troubles with the discipline of expressive form, an enormous superfluity, it would seem, of ingenuity is required in order to convey the lessons of the Keatsian world-hornbook. How odd it remains that the solitaries who are bedeviled by the possibilities of words remain the chief chroniclers of the emotional history of mankind.

One of the most ingenious poets of our language—or nearly our language—is now given us in a modern version of his Middle English, in the new translation, by Marie Borroff, of *Pearl*. As a model of the fixation of the artist on his medium, *Pearl*—as much about an intelligence becoming a soul as any modern verse—is exemplary. The poem, requiring four a-rhymes and six b-rhymes per stanza, with linking words as well, presents almost insuperable problems to a translator who reproduces, as Borroff does, the original prosody and rhyme scheme. Its mythology—Paradise, the heavenly Jerusalem, the virgins which follow the Lamb whithersoever he goeth—is now almost arcane, but the lyric strength of this poem about the death of a daughter and the father's vision of her in Paradise survives powerfully in Borroff's tour de force:

"O pearl," said I, "in pearls of price,
Are you my pearl come back again,
Lost and lamented with desolate sighs
In darkest night, alone and in vain?
Since you slipped to ground where grasses rise
I wander pensive, oppressed with pain,
And you in the bliss of Paradise,
Beyond all passion and strife and stain,
What fate removed you from earth's domain
And left me hapless and heartsick there?
Since parting was set between us twain
I have been a joyless jeweler."

There is always some element of pastiche and unreality in a translation preserving original form, but Borroff's hand is sure in lilt and cadence, alliteration and rhyme, enough to convey both the father's persistent grief and the decorative splendors of the holy city. It is a gift to the language to have this poem in an accurate and beautiful modern version, set properly, as a jewel should be, in a handsome setting of introduction and afterword, in which Borroff makes the poem technically and thematically accessible to nonmedievalists.

Books Discussed

Ammons, A. R. *Collected Poems.* New York: W. W. Norton, 1972.
————. *The Snow Poems.* New York: W. W. Norton, 1977.
Auden, W. H. *City Without Walls, and Other Poems.* New York: Random House, 1969.
———— *Collected Poems.* New York: Random House, 1976.
Axelrod, Steven Gould. *Robert Lowell: Life and Art.* Princeton: Princeton University Press, 1978.
Berryman, John. *Delusions, etc.* New York: Farrar, Straus & Giroux, 1972.
———— *Henry's Fate & Other Poems, 1967–1972.* New York: Farrar, Straus & Giroux, 1976.
———— *His Toy, His Dream, His Rest: 308 Dream Songs.* New York: Farrar, Straus & Giroux, 1968.
Bidart, Frank. *The Book of the Body.* New York: Farrar, Straus & Giroux, 1977.
Bishop, Elizabeth. *Geography III.* New York: Farrar, Straus & Giroux, 1976.
Borroff, Marie, trans. *Pearl: A New Verse Translation.* New York: W. W. Norton, 1977.
Broumas, Olga. *Beginning with O.* New Haven: Yale University Press, 1977.
Creeley, Robert. *Selected Poems.* New York: Charles Scribner's Sons, 1976.
Cummings, E. E. *Complete Poems, 1913–1962.* New York: Harcourt Brace Jovanovich, 1972.
Eliot, Valerie, ed. *The Waste Land.* A facsimile and transcript of the original drafts including the annotations of Ezra Pound. New York: Harcourt Brace Jovanovich, 1977.
Ginsberg, Allen. *The Fall of America: Poems of These States, 1965–1971.* San Francisco: City Lights, 1972.
———— *Planet News, 1961–1967.* San Francisco: City Lights, 1968.
Glück, Louise. *The House on Marshland.* New York: Ecco Press, 1976.
Graves, Robert. *New Collected Poems.* Garden City, N.Y.: Doubleday, 1977.
Jarrell, Randall. *The Complete Poems.* New York: Farrar, Straus & Giroux, 1969.

————— *The Third Book of Criticism*. New York: Farrar, Straus & Giroux, 1965.

Lowell, Robert. *Day by Day*. New York: Farrar, Straus & Giroux, 1977.

————— *The Dolphin*. New York: Farrar, Straus & Giroux, 1973.

————— *History*. New York: Farrar, Straus & Giroux, 1973.

————— *For Lizzie and Harriet*. New York: Farrar, Straus & Giroux, 1973.

————— *Selected Poems*. New York: Farrar, Straus & Giroux, 1976.

Merrill, James. *Braving the Elements*. New York: Atheneum, 1972.

————— *Divine Comedies*. New York: Atheneum, 1976.

————— *Mirabell: Books of Number*. New York: Atheneum, 1978.

Merwin, W. S. *The Carrier of Ladders*. New York: Atheneum, 1970.

————— *The Miner's Pale Children*. New York: Atheneum, 1970.

Nemerov, Howard. *The Collected Poems*. Chicago: University of Chicago Press, 1977.

O'Hara, Frank. *The Collected Poems*. New York: Alfred A. Knopf, 1971.

Plath, Sylvia. *Crossing the Water*. New York: Harper & Row, 1971.

Raab, Lawrence. *The Collector of Cold Weather*. New York: Ecco Press, 1976.

Randall, Dudley. Publications of the Broadside Press, Detroit.

Rich, Adrienne. *Diving into the Wreck*. New York: W. W. Norton, 1973.

————— *Of Woman Born: Motherhood as Experience and Institution*. New York: W. W. Norton, 1976.

Simic, Charles. *Charon's Cosmology*. New York: George Braziller, 1977.

Smith, Dave. *Cumberland Station*. Champaign: University of Illinois Press, 1977.

Stapleton, Laurence. *Marianne Moore: The Poet's Advance*. Princeton: Princeton University Press, 1978.

Stevens, Holly. *Souvenirs & Prophecies: The Young Wallace Stevens*. New York: Alfred A. Knopf, 1977.

Tate, James. *Viper Jazz*. Middletown, Conn.: Wesleyan University Press, 1972.

Voigt, Ellen Bryant. *Claiming Kin*. Middletown, Conn.: Wesleyan University Press, 1976.

Warren, Robert Penn. *Audubon: A Vision*. New York: Random House, 1969.

————— *Selected Poems, New and Old, 1923–1966*. New York: Random House, 1966.

Weiss, Theodore. *Fireweeds*. New York: Macmillan, 1976.

Williams, C. K. *With Ignorance*. Boston: Houghton Mifflin, 1977.

Wright, Charles. *China Trace*. Middletown, Conn.: Wesleyan University Press, 1977.

————— trans. *La Bufera e altro (The Storm and other poems, 1956)* By Eugenio Montale. Oberlin, Ohio: Field Translation Series 1, 1977.

Details of Copyright